Cyber Law in Italy

Cyber Law in Italy

Third Edition

Giovanni Ziccardi

This book was originally published as a monograph in the International Encyclopaedia of Laws/Cyber Law.

Founding Editor: Roger Blanpain
General Editor: Frank Hendrickx
Volume Editor: Jos Dumortier

Wolters Kluwer

Published by:
Kluwer Law International B.V.
PO Box 316
2400 AH Alphen aan den Rijn
The Netherlands
E-mail: international-sales@wolterskluwer.com
Website: lrus.wolterskluwer.com

Sold and distributed in North, Central and South America by:
Wolters Kluwer Legal & Regulatory U.S.
7201 McKinney Circle
Frederick, MD 21704
United States of America
Email: customer.service@wolterskluwer.com

Sold and distributed in all other countries by:
Air Business Subscriptions
Rockwood House
Haywards Heath
West Sussex
RH16 3DH
United Kingdom
Email: international-customerservice@wolterskluwer.com

ISBN 978-94-035-1872-5

e-Book: ISBN 978-94-035-1894-7
web-PDF: ISBN 978-94-035-1910-4

The Author

Giovanni Ziccardi is a graduate of Modena University and holds a PhD in 'Legal Informatics' from the University of Bologna. A lawyer, he was Founder and Chairman of the 'Italian Cyberspace Law Conference', one of the most important European Conferences concerning cyberspace law. He is the editor-in-chief of the International Scientific Review '*Ciberspazio e Diritto – Rivista Internazionale di Informatica Giuridica*' ('*Cyberspace and Law – Legal Informatics International Review*'). Before teaching law at the University of Milan, Professor Ziccardi spent seven years conducting research at the Research Centre of History of Law, Philosophy and Sociology of Law and Computer Science and Law (CIRSFID) at the University of Bologna. The research was developed under the supervision of Professor Enrico Pattaro, Director of the Centre.

He is admitted to practise before the Italian Courts. He is a full-time professor of 'Legal Informatics', 'Advanced Legal Informatics' and 'Smart Cities, Artificial Intelligence and Digital Transformation Law' at the Faculty of Law of the University of Milan, Italy, Jean Monnet Professor on 'EU Data Governance and Cybersecurity' and the Founder and Director of the post-graduate Courses on *Computer Crimes and Digital Investigation* and on *Coding for Lawyers* and *Legal Tech*. He is the Director of the *Information Society Law Research Center* (ISLC) of the University of Milan and a member of the *Security and Data Protection Committee* and of the *Ethical Committee* of the University.

The Author

Table of Contents

Table of Contents

List of Abbreviations

AGCOM	*Autorità per le Garanzie nelle Comunicazioni* (National Regulatory Agency)
AIPA	*Autorità per l'Informatica nella Pubblica Amministrazione* (Agency for Information Technology in the Public Administration)
ASSINFORM	The Italian Association of Producers of ICT Technologies and Services
BIOS	Basic Input-Output Software
CART	Computer Analysis and Response Team ccTLD County Code Top-Level Domain
CICR	*Comitato Interministeriale per il Credito ed il Risparmio* (Interministerial Committee for Credit and Savings)
CNIPA	*Centro Nazionale per l'Informatica nella Pubblica Amministrazione* (The National Center for Information Technology in Public Administration)
CNS	*Carta Nazionale dei Servizi* (National Services Card)
CONSIP Spa	*Concessionaria servizi informativi pubblici* (Concessionaire of Public Informational Services)
Corecom	*Comitato Regionale per le Comunicazioni*
CRL	*Lista dei Certificati Revocati*
CSL	*Lista dei Certificati Sospesi*
D.P.R.	Decree of the President of the Republic
DBAN	DataBase of Assigned Names
DIT	Department of Innovations and Technology
DNS	Domain Name System
DOI® technology	Digital Object Identifier System
DRS	Dispute Resolving Services
EEC	European Economic Community
EURATOM	European Atomic Energy Community
GATT	General Agreement on Tariffs and Trade

List of Abbreviations

ICT	Information and Communication Technologies
IDS	Intrusion Detection Systems
ISP	Internet Service Provider
ISS	Information Society Services
ISTAT	Italian National Institute of Statistics
IT-NIC	Italian Naming Authority
LAR	Letter of Assumption of Responsibility
LEFT	Legal Electronic Forensics Team
MD5	Message Digest 5
mEDRA	Multilingual European DOI Registration Agency
MHP	Multimedia Home Platform
PCS	Public Connectivity System
PGP	Pretty Good Privacy
PT	Post and Telegraph Administration
RUPA	Unitary Informational Network for the Public Administration
SHA1	Secure Hash Algorithm 1
SIA	*Società Italiana per l'Automazione* (Italian Society for Automatization)
SISDE	The Civilian Intelligence Service
SISMI	The Military Intelligence Service
SMS	Short Message Service
TCP/IP	Transfer Control Protocol/Internet Protocol
TIF	*Testo Unico sull'Intermediazione Finanziaria* (Consolidation on Financial Intermediation)
TRIPS	The Agreement on Trade-Related Aspects of Intellectual Property Rights
TUB	*Testo Unico Bancario* (Consolidation on Banking)
UCB	*Ufficio centrale dei brevetti* (Central Patent Office)
UCC	Universal Copyright Convention
UIC	*Ufficio Italiano Cambi*
UMTS	Universal Mobile Telecommunications System
WCT	WIPO Copyright Treaty
WIPO	Word Intellectual Property Organization
WPPT	WIPO Performances and Phonograms Treaty
WTO	World Trade Organization

Preface

This editorial project, concerning main cyberspace law issues in Italy, was edited, in its first edition, with the contribution of several former (and actual) scholars of CIRSFID research centre of the University of Bologna, and with the overview of Professor Enrico Pattaro.

CIRSFID is one of the main centres of excellence in Italy, and one of the leading centres at international level in the area of computer science and law. The centre is involved in several local, national and European research projects, promotes and organizes undergraduate and graduate university courses (including the only Italian PhD in *Computer Science and Law*), works within national and international bodies and is involved in several publishing initiatives.

Contributors to the First Edition were Dr Fabio Bravo (Part V, Chapters 3 and 4), Dr Claudia Cevenini (Part I, Chapter 5), Dr Giuseppe Corasaniti (Part I, Chapters 1 and 2), Dr Beatrice Cunegatti (Part II, Chapters 1, 3 and 5), Dr Claudio Di Cocco (General Introduction, Chapter IV; Part IV, Chapters 1 and 4), Dr Michele Martoni (Part IV, Chapter 2), Dr Juri Monducci (Part VI), Dr Sergio Niger (General Introduction, Chapter V; Part III, Chapter 7) Dr Enrico Pelino (General Introduction, Chapter 5), Dr Pierluigi Perri (Part VII), Dr Chiara Rabbito (Part II, Chapter 4), Dr Guido Salzano (Part III, Chapter 6; Part V, Chapters 1 and 2), Dr Guido Scorza (Part III, Chapters 1–5), Dr Roberto Sparano (Part I, Chapters 1 and 2) and Dr Samuele Villa (Part IV, Chapter 3).

In a Second, completely renewed Edition, Dr Mara Bolzoni and the staff of the 'Legal Informatics' Course at the Faculty of Law of the University of Milan (Dr Edoardo Artese, Dr Simone Bonavita, Dr Barbara Coccagna, Dr Federico Di Martino, Dr Francesco Di Tano, Dr Giulia Mentasti, Dr Pierluigi Perri, Dr Alessandro Rodolfi, Dr Silvia Scalzaretto, Dr Guglielmo Troiano, Dr Santiago Valori, Dr Valentin Vitkov) helped the author during the draft of the final manuscript, in the update of all chapters and Bibliography and in the check of the final text.

In the Third Edition, updates and changes were drafted personally by Giovanni Ziccardi.

In this Fourth Edition, the research team of the 'Legal Informatics' and 'Advanced Legal Informatics' Courses at the Faculty of Law of the University of Milan helped the author during the draft of the final manuscript with important updates of all Chapters and Bibliography. In particular: Dr Gabriele Suffia wrote Chapter 1 of the Introduction ('General Background of the Country') and Part VII, Chapter 2 ('Application of Substantial Criminal Law in the Area of ICT'), from §1 to §11; Avv. Pietro Boccaccini wrote Chapter 2 ('Telecommunications Infrastructure') of the Introduction except §§11-12, §1 ('The Story and the Evolution of the Italian ICT and Communications Market') of Chapter 3 of the Introduction, Chapter 4 ('E-commerce: Facts and Figures') of the Introduction and Chapter 1 of Part 1 ('Regulation of the ICT Market') except §5 and §6, Chapter 5 ('E-Government and Open Government Initiatives'), §1 and §3; Avv. Giulia Escurolle wrote Part VI, Chapter 1 ('Regulation of Personal Data Processing'); Dr Fernanda Faini wrote Chapter 5 ('E-Government and Open Government Initiatives') of the Introduction except §1, §3 and §9; Prof. Pierluigi Perri wrote Part VII, Chapter 1 ('General Legal Development of Computer Crimes in Italy'), Chapter 3 ('Application of Criminal Procedure Law in the Area of ICT') except §7; Avv. Maurizio Reale wrote §9 ('The Digital Telematic Process') of Chapter 5; Dr Alessandra Salluce wrote Part II ('Protection of Intellectual Property in the ICT Sector'). Dr Andrea Scirpa wrote §14 ('Identity Theft') of Chapter 2, Part VII. Dr Athena Skoufas wrote Part VII, Chapter 2, §15 ('Grooming Online'). Dr Samanta Stanco wrote §13 ('Cyberbullying') of Chapter 2, Part VII. Avv. Gianfranco Valsecchi wrote Part III ('ICT Contracts'). Prof. Giovanni Ziccardi wrote §10 ('The Digital and Connectivity Market in Italy'), §11 ('The Internet of Things Market in Italy') and §12 ('Italy in the Global Connectivity Index of 2018') of Chapter 2 of the Introduction, §2 ('The ICT Market Trends in the Assintel Report 2019') of Chapter 3 of the Introduction, §5 ('The Italian Telecommunications Market in 2018-2019'), §6 ('The AGCOM Report of 2018 and the Future of the Telecommunications Regulation in Italy') of Part I, Chapter 1; §10 ('The Digital and Connectivity Market in Italy'), §11 ('The Internet of Things Market in Italy') and §12 ('Italy in the Global Connectivity Index of 2018') of Chapter 2; §2 ('The ICT Market Trends in the Assintel Report 2019') of Chapter 3; §5 ('ISP Liability in the Social Network and Platform Economy') in Chapter 3, Part V; §12 ('Cyberstalking') of Chapter 2, Part VII; §7 ('The Use of Hacking Tools and Trojan Horses by Law Enforcement in Italy') of Chapter 3, Part VII.

General Introduction

Chapter 1. General Background of the Country

§1. Premise

1. The correct perception (and interpretation) of the legal framework of a country is closely related to its historical and political evolution. Italy, as it is known, boasts a millenary history which, from the beginning, showed great attention to culture and, above all, to the culture of law.

To fully understand the legal institutions and the development of law in Italy, rightly considered 'the cradle of the law', is therefore essential to identify the *two periods* that characterized the historical evolution of the Country. There is a period *before* the unification of Italy, from the noble origins (and influences) of Etruscans, Greeks and Romans to the XIX century, and a period *after* the unification, in which several legal and political events occurred after the troubled process of unification of the State.

§2. Pre-Unitarian History

2. The population of the Italian territory dates back to prehistory: Italy was inhabited at least since the Palaeolithic age, but the information about pre-Roman inhabitants of the peninsula is, in several cases, incomplete. Populations from Indo-European Countries moved to Italy, from Eastern and Central Europe, during centuries and in several waves of immigration. They overlapped with the pre-Indo-European ethnic groups existing in the Italian territory, absorbing them, or establishing a form of peaceful coexistence with resident groups.

Presumably, these migrations began in the Middle Bronze age (i.e., around the middle of the second millennium BC) and lasted until the fourth century BC, with the descent of the Celts in the Po river valley.

Among the ethnic groups of pre-Roman era, the Etruscans deserve special mention: from the eighth century BC, they began to develop a civilization that greatly influenced Rome and the whole Latin world.

Between the eighth and the seventh centuries BC, colonists from Greece began to settle on the coasts of Southern Italy and Sicily Island. During the Greek colonization, the Italian people met a civilization characterized by high artistic and cultural expressions, with different philosophical heritage and values. This fact originated the flowering of philosophers, writers, artists and scientists both of Greek origin and native.[1]

The Greeks were also carriers of political institutions unknown at that time that even prefigured forms of direct democracy.[2]

3. According to Roman mythology, Romulus founded the city of Rome on 21 April 753 BC, on the Palatine Hill. Son of Mars by a Vestal Virgin, Romulus was found abandoned by a she-wolf and suckled, and brought up by a shepherd family. He established the monarchy in the city: up to 509 BC, *seven kings* ruled the city, according to the tradition, with significant contributions to the development of society.[3]

4. The progressive conquest of Italy brought Rome to clash with the other great city of the Western Mediterranean: Carthage. The wars that broke out were of unprecedented ferocity and considerable duration, but finally saw the complete triumph of Rome (in 146 BC). After the conclusion of the wars with Carthage, Rome completed the subjugation of Cisalpine Gauls, defeating both Celts and Gauls that rebelled against Rome during the Second Punic War. The territory of the local population (the Cisalpine Gauls) was reduced to a province around 191 BC. In 177 BC, Istria was also submitted, and two years later the same happened to the Cisalpine Ligurians.

After the hegemony of the whole Western Mediterranean territory, Rome turned its expansionist aims to the detriment of the Hellenistic states of the East, submitting, for over a century, Greece (200 BC–146 BC) and completing the subjugation of Carthage (Third Punic War: 149–146 BC). With the defeat of the enemies against which the Roman reign fought for years on both sides, Rome had become the mistress of the Mediterranean.[4]

---

1. For a complete overview of the Greeks influence in Italy *see, generally*, D. Musti, 'Storia Greca. Linee di sviluppo dall'età micenea all'età romana' (Laterza, Roma-Bari, 1989); C. Bearzot, 'Manuale di storia greca' (Il Mulino, Bologna, 2005); M. Corsaro, L. Gallo, 'Storia greca' (Le Monnier, Firenze, 2010).
2. For an overview of the political aspects of the institutions of ancient Greece, and their influences on Italian primitive forms of government (especially: democracy) *see, generally*, P. Cartledge, 'Il pensiero politico in pratica. Grecia antica (secoli VII a.C.–II d.C.)' (Carocci Editore, Firenze, 2011); S. Gastaldi, 'Introduzione alla storia del pensiero politico antico' (Laterza, Roma–Bari, 2008); D. Musti, 'Demokratìa. Origini di un'idea' (Laterza, Roma–Bari, 1995).
3. For an overview of the Roman mythology concerning the Rome foundation, *see* T. Mommsen, 'Storia di Roma dalle origini alla Repubblica' (Gherardo Casini Editore, Roma, 2001).
4. For an overview of old Roman history, *see* P. Brown, 'Il mondo tardoantico da Marco Aurelio a Maometto' (Einaudi, Torino, 1974); G. Geraci, A. Marcone, 'Storia romana' (Le Monnier, Firenze, 2011); H. H. Scullard, 'Storia del mondo romano' (BUR, Milano, 1992); G. Giannelli, 'Trattato di storia romana' (Patron, Bologna, 1975); S. Mazzarino, 'L'impero romano" (Laterza, Bari-Roma, 1986).

5. According to some historians, the Roman Empire was about to become too large. The complexity of the institutions of the Republic, and the weakness of the Senate, were already evident during the first *Triumvirate*, an informal agreement by which the three most powerful men in Rome (Caesar, Crassus, and Pompey) shared their spheres of influence.

Augustus (63 BC–14 AD) kept 'alive' the old republican institutions, but emptied them of any real power. Although formally the Republic continued to exist, it became a Principality ruled by the Princeps (or Emperor), who was the absolute master of the Empire.[5]

6. The transformation of the Empire lasted four centuries, with periods of so-called military anarchy (from 235 to 284 AD) and different forms of government and the advent of the Christian religion as religion of the Empire. The dialectic between the city (Rome) and the Empire became critical during the centuries, stressed by the 'Barbarian populations' along the borders and the growing importance of the Army inside them. Riots and numerous appointments of usurpers mined the stability of the Empire, which was forced to reduce its dimensions and then slip in two different entities.

7. While the Eastern Roman Empire survived for another millennium, the Western part of the empire collapsed in less than a century (in 476 AD). It is believed that it was due to barbarian invasions, although the success of the barbarians was at least partly facilitated by the internal limits of the Empire. According to some historians, the end of the Western Empire was not a collapse, but a natural transformation.

8. In 568 Lombards invaded the Northern Italy. In a few years, Lombards subdued throughout Northern Italy (except the coastal areas of the Veneto and Liguria), Toscana and much of the Centre-South (which formed the semi-independent duchies of Spoleto and Benevento).

After the final defeat of the Lombards, the Pope regained full autonomy, with the creation of the State of the Church and the legitimacy of temporal power of the Popes through the Declaration of Constantine. Pope Leo III, on Christmas Eve of 800, crowned Charlemagne, king of the Franks, as Emperor of the new *Holy Roman Empire*. After that date, for two centuries Italy was divided between the Carolingians, the Byzantines and the Arabs.

9. In the eleventh century, the Church was involved in an important reform process. This period was characterized by conflicts between the Pope and the Empire. In 1122, Emperor Henry V and Pope Calixtus II concluded the *Concordat of*

---

5. For an overview of economics, political and religious aspects of ancient Rome *see*, *generally*, C. Nicolet, 'Strutture dell'Italia romana (Jouvence, Roma, 1984); F. Jacques, J. Scheid, 'Roma e il suo impero. Istituzioni, economia, religione' (Laterza, Bari–Roma, 2008); F. Rohr Vio, 'Le voci del dissenso. Ottaviano Augusto e i suoi oppositori' (Il Poligrafo, Padova, 2000).

Worms, an agreement that ended, at least temporarily, the controversy on the 'investiture' and that established the prerogative of the Pope and the Emperor in the selection and ordination of bishops. Since that date, the clergy had become part of the feudal hierarchy and political organization.

From the eleventh century, the rebirth of the concept of the 'city' and new urban classes in Northern and Central Italy met to get rid of feudal and imperial authority, and a new political reality born: the *City Council*. Emperor Frederick I, called *Barbarossa*, countered the power of municipalities, which joined the *Lombard League* and defeated Barbarossa at the Battle of Legnano (1176).

10. In 1183, with the *Peace of Constance*, the Emperor Frederick Barbarossa officially recognized political prerogatives to the cities and the autonomy of Municipalities. Many Municipalities, after that event, often came into conflict with one another. In this climate, stronger people in each municipality managed to establish themselves as Lords of the city, and at the end of 1300, in Italy, Lordships took over the old municipal organizations.

In the territories of Southern Italy, the early eleventh century saw the domination of the Byzantines and the Arabs, but soon those Regions were conquered by the Normans, who gave birth to a new kingdom.

11. During the following centuries, both Pope's and Emperor's authorities decline. In the fifteenth century, the entire Italian peninsula was involved in clashes between Italian States (all pursuing an expansionist policy).

Very important was the conflict between the Maritime Republics of Pisa, Genova and Venice, and the wars that involved the Duchy of Milan. In 1454, the *Peace of Lodi* ended the fighting between several major States (the Duchy of Milan, the Republics of Venice and Florence, the Papal States and the Aragonese Kingdom of Naples), ensuring the peninsula a short period of peace.

12. In the first half of the fifteenth century, a long period of wars affected the entire peninsula, originated by the repeated attempts of the stronger States to extend their hegemony.

At the same time, the Italian *Renaissance* was a flowering period of artistic and cultural civilization, born in Florence and, from there, spread throughout Europe by the mid-fourteenth century to the sixteenth century. *Renaissance* aimed to rediscover the ancient classical culture, 'purifying' it from some forms of medieval religiosity.

13. The year 1494 marked the end of a sort of 'political balance' and the beginning of a long period of conflict known as the *Wars of Italy*.[6]

6. For an overview of the modern history of Italy, *see* C. Capra, 'Storia moderna (1492-1848) (Le Monnier, Firenze, 2004); P. Prodi, 'Introduzione allo studio della storia moderna' (Il Mulino, Bologna, 2005).

This date coincides with the end of the Italian freedom: the peninsula felt under the hegemony of several foreign powers (first France, then Spain and then Austria). This subjection will end in 1866, with the victorious outcome of the Third War of Independence.

14. The Spanish hegemony in Italy was ratified by the *Peace of Cateau-Cambrésis*. Spain exercised since then, and until 1714, a direct power on the whole Southern Italy territory and the islands, on the Duchy of Milan and on Southern Tuscany.

The State of the Church, the Grand Duchy of Tuscany, the Republic of Genova and other minor States were forced, in fact, to support the Spanish imperial policy. Only the Republic of Venice was able to retain its independence, but it was not sufficient to preserve it from a slow, but inexorable, decline.

15. In the late eighteenth century appeared, on the Italian political scene, Napoleon Bonaparte. In 1796, he commanded, as a General, the Italian campaign in order to defeat the Kingdom of Sardinia and the Austrians. Wars began on April 9, against Piemonte, and within two weeks Vittorio Amedeo III of Savoia was forced to sign an armistice. On May 15, the French general entered in Milan and was greeted as a liberator.

On 2 December 1804, Napoleon was crowned Emperor of the French. In accordance with the new arrangement, Napoleon also became King of Italy, and the Italian Republic became the Kingdom of Italy.

16. After Napoleon, the history of Italy is inextricably linked to the State's history that united, under its leadership, the Kingdom of Sardinia. With the *Restoration*, which had led to the return of the ancient kings and the sale of Italian Regions to Austria, there was the starting of the development of strong patriotic ideals.

After the Napoleonic wars, national and nationalist forces, supported by the Savoia family, seeing the opportunity to broaden the Kingdom of Sardinia, led to a series of wars of independence against the Austro-Hungarian Empire. In 1848, the King of the House of Savoia, Carlo Alberto, granted the *Statuto Albertino*, one of the most important legal documents (a sort of 'First Constitution', or 'National Statute') of the Italian history.

17. Camillo Benso Conte di Cavour, a politician, patriot and army officer who became Prime Minister of the Kingdom of Savoia in 1852, persuaded Vittorio Emanuele II to participate in the Crimean War on the side of France and England.

After the war, Cavour was able to sit at the table of winners, getting the international support he needed. He agreed with the French a pact that committed them to come to aid Piemonte if Austria had attacked this State. Then, Cavour hastened to strengthen the army and, in 1859, the Austrians sent an ultimatum: if the Piedmontese had not disarmed, they would be attacked. Cavour was expecting this fact, and the French rushed to help.[7]

---

7. Concerning the Cavour politics, *see*, *generally*, L. Cafagna, 'Cavour' (Il Mulino, Bologna, 1999); R. Romeo, 'Cavour e il suo tempo', I-III (Laterza, Roma–Bari, 1969-1984).

18. After some initial successes in Austria, the war turned in favour of Piemonte, which was victorious, thanks to the support of Napoleon III. Just when Piemonte was preparing to occupy the Veneto, however, Napoleon III began negotiations. Peace was signed, and Cavour had to cede Nice and Savoia lands to France.

After the Second War of Independence, a few Duchies (Modena, Parma, Emilia-Romagna and Toscana) joined the Kingdom of Sardinia. The Kingdom of Sardinia, at this point, included the territories of the current regions of Valle d'Aosta, Piemonte, Sardinia, Lombardy, Emilia-Romagna, Liguria and Tuscany. Those of Umbria, Marche and Lazio were submitted to the papal state, in addition to the South.[8]

§3. Unitarian History

19. The Kingdom of Italy (1861–1946) was created after the outcome of the Second War of Independence and after the plebiscite of the other conquered territories.

In 1860, the *Expedition of the Thousand* was organized and led by Giuseppe Garibaldi, an Italian general previously involved in the Uruguayan Civil War. Garibaldi sailed to Sicily with a thousand volunteers, especially from Lombardy, freed from the Austrian Empire. After the liberation of the island, he went up the peninsula and went after new victories in Naples.

Vittorio Emanuele II invaded the Papal States and defeated the papal army, then he rejoined Garibaldi, who gave him the kingdom just conquered.

Plebiscites were held in favour of unification, and on 17 March 1861, it was proclaimed the birth of the Kingdom of Italy.[9] Italy became a nation-state under the reign of King Vittorio Emanuele II.

20. Veneto was still under the Austrian kingdom and Lazio under the Pope influence. The Italian army seemed unable to compete alone against the Austrians, so, in 1866, there was an alliance with Prussia, and war broke out.

The Prussians defeated the Austrians and, signing the peace, Italy annexed the Veneto region. Trento and Trieste remained to Austria, and were annexed to Italy only in 1918. Concerning Lazio, in 20 September 1870 the Italian army entered in Rome and the city became a few months later the capital of the Kingdom. The Pope maintained the possession of Vatican City, but formally only since 1929 Lateran Treaty.

---

8. *See*, *generally*, A.M. Banti, 'Il Risorgimento Italiano' (Laterza, Bari-Roma, 2011); G. Pécout, 'Il lungo Risorgimento. La nascita dell'Italia contemporanea (1770-1922)' (Bruno Mondadori, Milano, 2004); A. Gramsci, 'Il Risorgimento' (Editori Riuniti, Roma, 2000).
9. Concerning the *Expedition of the Thousand*, *see*, *generally*, I. Nievo, 'Diario della spedizione dei Mille' (Mursia, Milano, 2010); D. Mack Smith, 'Garibaldi. Una grande vita in breve' (Laterza, Roma–Bari, 1982).

21. With the first reunion of the Italian Parliament on 18 February 1861, and the subsequent proclamation of March 17, Vittorio Emanuele II became the first King of Italy (1861–1878).[10]

22. The First World War involved Europe and much of the world. Italy entered the war on 24 May 1915, at the side of France and England and against Austria.

In October, 1917, the defeat of Caporetto led to a dramatic retreat of the Italian army, which was unable to stop the Austrians on the line of the Piave river. A year later, it started the counterattack: Austria and Germany collapsed and, in turn, they had to surrender to the French, British and American armies. Losers were forced to sign a humiliating peace agreement, and Italy gained the Trentino, South Tyrol, Trieste and Istria regions: not all the regions that Italy expected from the agreements.

23. Italy had emerged victorious from the First World War, but in very poor economic conditions. The feel of a 'mutilate victory' and general discontent lead to the emerging figure of Benito Mussolini, founder of the Italian Fascist movement and later the *Fascist Party*. In 1922, during a big political crisis of the government, Mussolini organized the *March on Rome*: Fascists marched on the capital without resistance, and King Vittorio Emanuele III appointed Mussolini to form a new government.

Once elected Prime Minister, Mussolini decided to strengthen his power. In the elections of 1924, Mussolini passed a new electoral law that would give the three-fifths of the seats to the list that had collected 40% of the votes. Mussolini got 64.9% of the votes, and the Socialist deputy Giacomo Matteotti challenged the election results. Matteotti was kidnapped and killed, and Mussolini recited a famous speech in which he assumed responsibility for the events taking place. With this speech, Mussolini declared himself as a dictator.

24. In the period 1925–1926, a series of measures against civil liberties in Italy were issued: the political parties were dissolved, the freedom of the press was abolished, unions were suppressed and the right to strike was cancelled.

In 1929, the *Lateran Treaty* was signed. It established the mutual recognition between the Kingdom of Italy and the State of Vatican City.

Mussolini also signed with Adolf Hitler, German Nazi dictator, an alliance which was established by the promulgation, in 1938, of Mussolini's racial laws, that deprived Italian Jews of civil and political rights.

25. During the Second World War, Italy was an ally of Germany but initially stayed out of war. However, Mussolini, in front of the easy victories of the Germans, mistakenly thinking that the war would soon end, decided not to remain

10. Concerning the unification of Italy, *see* A. Di Michele, 'Storia dell'Italia repubblicana (1948–2008)' (Milano, Garzanti, 2008); A. Capone, 'Destra e Sinistra da Cavour a Crispi' (TEA, Milano, 1996); M. Isnenghi, 'I luoghi della memoria. Personaggi e date dell'Italia unita' (Laterza, Bari-Roma, 2010); P. Ginsborg, 'Storia d'Italia dal dopoguerra a oggi' (Einaudi, Torino, 2006); A. Lepre, C. Petraccone, 'Storia d'Italia dall'Unità a oggi' (Il Mulino, Bologna, 2008).

excluded from the opportunity to sit next to Germany at the table of winners. Thus, on 10 June 1940, Italy entered the Second World War as an ally of Germany against France and the United Kingdom.

The results were disastrous, and in 1943, the new Italian Government signed the surrender agreement. Southern Italy was already free, while the Central and North remained under the control of fascists and German troops.

In these Regions the *Resistance* began: several groups of partisans took refuge in the mountainous areas, where they organized attacks against the fascists. Meanwhile, American and British armies were advancing, bringing fascists and Germans to retreat. To commemorate the liberation, 25 April 1945 is designated as a national holiday.

26. After the end of the Second World War in Italy, and after twenty years of fascism and five years of war, the Institutional Referendum of 2 June 1946 established the end of the monarchy and the birth of the Italian Republic. Enrico de Nicola was the first President of the Italian Republic.

The Italians voted for the referendum to decide between *Republic* and *Monarchy*, and 54.3% of voters chose the Republic, decreeing, with a margin of two million votes, the end of the monarchy and the exile of the Savoia royal family. For the first time in Italy, women had the right to vote.

Simultaneously, the delegates were elected to form the *Constituent Assembly*, which would discuss and approve the new Constitution that came into force on 1 January 1948. A constitutional 'democratic republic' replaced Italy's constitutional monarchy in 1946;[11] Italy was a founding member of NATO, of the European Economic Community (EEC), of Council of Europe and of OECD, joined the Economic and Monetary Union in 1999, adheres to the *Schengen Treaty*, is a member of the G7, G8, G20 and participates in the NATO nuclear sharing project.

27. On 14 December 1955, Italy became part of the United Nations by the unanimous vote of the Security Council and of the General Assembly. It was concluded the long history that had engaged the Italian diplomacy for a decade in an effort to gain the entry of the Country in the international body, as well as to share ideals and principles and to determine the end of subjection to the peace treaty and the position of the former enemy.

Italy was also one of the protagonists, together with the other founding Countries of the European Community, in the project to build a Europe without borders and customs barriers. In many cases, Italy has hosted key events for the community history.

Since the autumn of 1941, Altiero Spinelli and Ernesto Rossi – then confined in the island of Ventotene – fixed principles in the *Manifesto for European Federalism*. In 1955, a conference was held in Messina which laid the foundations of the

11. According to Art. 1 of the Italian Constitution, concerning the *Form of State*, 'Italy is a democratic Republic founded on labour. Sovereignty belongs to the people and is exercised by the people in the forms and within the limits of the Constitution'. The English text of the Italian Constitution is taken from *Constitution of the Italian Republic* on the official website of the Italian Senate http://www.senato.it/documenti/repository/istituzione/costituzione_inglese.pdf (31 August 2018).

Treaty of Rome. In 1957 in Rome, representatives of the six founding Countries signed the two Treaties establishing the European Economic Community (EEC) and the European Atomic Energy Community (EURATOM). Both Treaties entered into force in January 1958, after ratification by the respective six Parliaments.[12]

28. The Second World War had done enormous damage, the economic situation was dire and it took a great deal of reconstruction. In Italy, between 1958 and 1963, the process of economic growth that started after 1950 came at the culmination. The development of those years, the second in Europe only to Germany, represented, for Italy, a veritable *economic miracle*. The economic miracle was characterized by a strong industrialization of the Country, and the phenomenon of internal migration led to a depopulation of the countryside and a large process of urbanization.

The year 1968 saw the Italian society radically transformed, as a result of improved living conditions due to the economic boom of the previous years, and the rise of radical movements and of young workers, which brought profound changes to the costume, to the general mentality and particularly to the school and to the empowerment of women. In the Seventies, some of the many political movements, which arose in previous years, degenerated into terrorism activities (*Red Brigades* and neo-fascist groups).

29. In the Eighties and the Nineties, the Sicilian judges Giovanni Falcone and Paolo Borsellino, aided by courageous men of the police forces, managed to stop the activities of many members of mafia gangs. But, on 23 May 1992, Falcone's car was blown up on the highway that connects Palermo to Trapani. On July 19 of the same year, a car bomb exploded under Paolo Borsellino mother's house, while Paolo was there. The judge died with his five bodyguards.

In 1992, the *Mani Pulite* ('Clean Hands') investigation around the growing problem of corruption and tangents led to the involvement and arrest of numerous national and local exponents of Italian parties, and to a rapid decline of the traditional political forces and groups. The 1994 elections meant the end of the so-called *First Republic*, with the disappearance of *Democrazia Cristiana* ('Christian Democratic Party') which, since 1948, had dominated the political scene, and of the *Partito Socialista* ('Italian Socialist Party'), its main ally, as well.

30. From the disaggregation of the old order, arose some new parties like the one created by the entrepreneur Silvio Berlusconi, *Forza Italia*, which became the new party of the Italian centre.

In the modern Italian political framework, there were, in the last years, two alternative governing coalitions: the centre-right, formed by *Forza Italia*, *Alleanza Nazionale* and *Lega Nord*, and the centre-left, formed by PDS, PPI and other minor

12. *See*, *generally*, L. Tosi, 'L'Italia e le organizzazioni internazionali. Diplomazia multilaterale nel Novecento' (CEDAM, Padova, 1999); A. Villani, 'L'Italia e l'Onu negli anni della coesistenza competitiva (1955-1968)' (CEDAM, Padova, 2007); B. Baldi, 'Regioni e federalismo. L'Italia e l'Europa' (Clueb, Bologna, 2006).

forces. The two centre-right and centre-left coalitions alternated in the Government of the Country over the years until today, except short-term technical (or independent) governments.

In 2012 a short-term technical government was established with Professor Mario Monti as Prime Minister, and after new elections two governments were established by the centre-left coalition, with Prime Minister Enrico Letta and, later, Prime Minister Matteo Renzi.

In 2018, new elections saw the mutual victory of three different coalitions and parties, with the government formed by *Movimento 5 Stelle* and *Lega* after three months. This government was described as a 'populist government' by political analysts.

§4. Geography

31. Italy is located in Southern Europe, with a population of 60,483,973 inhabitants in 2017[13] and the capital is Rome (Roma). It is bordered by the Alpine mountains and, from West to East, by France, Switzerland, Austria and Slovenia. The rest of the territory is surrounded by the Ligurian, Tyrrhenian, Ionian and Adriatic seas, and is a peninsula extending into the central Mediterranean Sea, with numerous islands, for a total of 301,340 km^2.

Italy includes the islands of Sardinia (Sardegna) and Sicily (Sicilia); it shares borders with Austria, France, Vatican City, San Marino, Slovenia, and Switzerland.

The independent Countries of San Marino and Vatican City are enclaves within Italian territory. The State of Vatican City was born with the *Lateran Treaty*, concluded between the Holy See and Italy on 11 February 1929 and ratified on 7 June 1929. Its personality as a sovereign body of public international law, distinct from the Holy See, is universally recognized.[14]

§5. Demographic and Cultural Composition

32. The estimated population of Italy amounts to 60.5 million residents, with an incidence of the foreign population of 8.4 percent (5.6 million). Since 2015, our country has entered a phase of demographic decline with almost 100 thousand people less than the previous year (-1.6 per thousand). The distribution that contributes most to the decrease of the population is the Mezzogiorno (-3.9 per thousand).

The growth of the foreign population stops (it shows only an increase of 18 thousand people compared to 2017). A total of 21% of new births have a non-Italian parent, and 14% of new births have both.

13. 1 Jan. 2017 est. For statistics about Italy *see ISTAT*, Italian National Institute of Statistics, Year 2017, http://demo.istat.it/pop2017/index.html (December 2017).

14. *See* G. Della Torre, 'Lezioni di diritto Ecclesiastico' (Giappichelli, Torino, 2008); C. Cardia, 'Principi di Diritto Ecclesiastico' (Giappichelli, Torino, 2002).

Men reached the level of 80.3 years (+0.9 compared to 2014), that of women 84.9 years (+0.4). The gender difference dropped to 4.6 years.[15]

The predominant ethnic group is Italian, and the main religion is Roman Catholicism, although there are also Protestant and Jewish communities and a more recent Muslim immigrant community.

33. Languages spoken are Italian (official), German (parts of the Trentino-Alto Adige Region are predominantly German-speaking), French (there are small French-speaking minorities in the Valle d'Aosta Region) and Slovene (there are Slovene-speaking minorities in the Trieste-Gorizia area).

Italy is divided into twenty Regions and five autonomous Regions, and universal suffrage is granted to all those who fulfil the residency requirements for voting and are 18 years of age and older (except for senatorial elections, where the minimum age required for voting is 25).

Employment rate in July 2018 was 58.7% (+1.2% to July 2017), unemployment rate was 10.4% and inactivity rate was 34.3%.[16]

§6. Political System

34. Italy is a republic, and the legal system is based on civil law. The 1948 Constitution of Italy established a bicameral Parliament ('Parlamento') consisting of a Chamber of Deputies ('Camera dei Deputati') and a Senate ('Senato della Repubblica'); a separate judicial system ('Magistratura'); and an executive branch composed of a Council of Ministers ('Consiglio dei ministri'), headed by the Prime Minister ('Presidente del Consiglio dei Ministri').

Part II of the Constitution outlines the institutions of the Republic and the political system. This part consists of 85 Articles, grouped into six Sections, which define Parliament, President of the Republic, Government, judiciary system, Regions, Provinces, Municipalities and constitutional guarantees.

The Parliament consists of two branches, the Chamber of Deputies (with 630 deputies elected) and the Senate (with 315 senators elected and some senators for life). The normal period of duration of the Chambers ('legislature') is five years.[17]

35. The Parliament plays a *dual role*: it is responsible for the legislative function, and it has the function of direction and political control on the activities of the Government and the Public Administration.

It operates in a joint session only in the cases of election of the President of the Republic (also with the participation, in the election activities, of three delegates for

15. 1 Jan. 2017 est., *see ISTAT*, Italian National Institute of Statistics, Year 2017, http://demo.istat.it/bil2013/index.html (December 2017) and ISTAT Statistics, Year 2018 Report, http://www.istat.it.
16. July 2018 est., *see ISTAT*, Italian National Institute of Statistics, https://www.istat.it/it/archivio/220543 (August 2014) and ISTAT Statistics Year 2018 (http://www.istat.it).
17. *See*, *generally*, 'Istituzioni di diritto pubblico' (Giappichelli, Torino, 2016); V. Onida, 'La Costituzione' (Il Mulino, Bologna, 2017).

each Region), of election of five judges of the Constitutional Court, of a third of the members of the Superior Council of Judges, and in the event of impeachment of the President of the Republic.

An extensive parliamentary reform project has been rejected by the 2016 referendum on 4 December 2016.

36. The President of the Republic ('Presidente della Repubblica') is elected for *seven years* by both Houses of Parliament, sitting in joint session with a small number of Regional delegates. The President nominates the Prime Minister, who then proposes candidates for other ministerial positions (nominees are then formally named by the President). The Council of Ministers must retain the support ('Fiducia') of both Houses.

The President of the Republic is the Head of State and represents the national unity. Any citizen can access to this office, provided he/she is at least 50 years of age.

As for relations with Parliament, the President may dismiss one or both Houses and call an election, and acts to enact laws, after having verified that they do not conflict with the principles of the Constitution.

He/she presides over the Superior Council of Judges, has the command of the armed forces and may grant pardons and commute sentences.

37. The Government consists of the Prime Minister and individual Ministers; together they constitute the Council of Ministers.

The Government shall present its programme to the Parliament, which must be approved by both Houses. The Government must have the support of both Houses.

The Government holds the executive power and can exercise legislative powers in case of necessity and urgency, but its Decrees must be converted into law by the Parliament within 60 days[18] from adoption.

The judiciary system has the judiciary power, is independent from the other branches of Parliament, and the Constitution states that justice is administered in the name of the people and that judges are subject only to the law. Judges are accountable only to the Superior Council of Judges.[19]

18. For a complete overview of the Italian constitutional system *see*, *inter alia*, G. Amato, A. Barbera, 'Manuale di diritto pubblico' (II Mulino, Bologna, 1997); M. Fioravanti, 'Costituzione' (Il Mulino, Bologna, 1999). 'Istituzioni di diritto pubblico' (Giappichelli, Torino, 2016); V. Onida, 'La Costituzione' (Il Mulino, Bologna, 2017).

19. *See*, *generally*, M. Cotta, L. Verzichelli, 'Il sistema politico italiano' (Il Mulino, Bologna, 2011); C. Guarnieri, 'Il sistema politico italiano' (Il Mulino, Bologna, 2006); G. Pasquino, 'Il sistema politico italiano. Autorità, istituzioni, società' (Bononia University Press, Bologna, 2006); N. Bobbio, 'Compromesso e alternanza nel sistema politico italiano' (Donzelli, Roma, 2006).

§7. Political Rights

38. Title IV of the Italian Constitution concerns political and voting rights. All Italian citizens, both men and women, who have attained their majority, are entitled to vote: voting is personal, equal, free and secret. Voting is also an exercise of civic duty.

The law defines the conditions under which Italian citizens residing abroad can effectively exercise their electoral rights, and to this end, a *Constituency of Italians Abroad* exists, which can elect a fixed number of seats in both Houses of the Parliament, as determined by constitutional law. The right to vote cannot be limited, except in cases of incapacity, as a consequence of an irrevocable criminal sentence or in cases of moral unworthiness as established by law.

39. Political rights are regulated by the Italian Constitution in Title IV (Articles 48–54). Article 48 lays down the fundamental principles governing the exercise of the election rights. In addition to determining what should be the four characteristics of the vote ((i) personality, (ii) equality, (iii) freedom, and (iv) secrecy), the article indicates the positive (*citizenship* and *age*) and negative (*moral incapacity* and *unworthiness*) requirements to vote and defines its exercise as a civic duty.

This definition is the result of a compromise between the two theses that were compared in the Constituent Assembly: a part in favour of the introduction of the vote as legally binding, with the consequence that failure to exercise could be punished under criminal law, the other favouring the establishment of the vote exclusively in terms of freedom.

40. The legislation in the past provided some administrative sanctions for those who, without justification, did not exercise their right to vote in general elections, sanctions that were later eliminated. The electorate can also exercise sovereignty on its own, bypassing the mediation of the representative bodies, using institutions like the *petition*, the *popular initiative* and the *referendum.*

Article 50 deals with the petition, defined as the right of each citizen to apply to both Houses of Parliament to request legislative measures or to express needs. In Title IV are also enshrined, in terms of rights, freedom of political association and the right of all citizens (of either sex) to gain access to public offices and elected positions on equal terms.[20]

41. Concerning political parties, all citizens have the right to freely associate in political parties in order to contribute, using democratic methods, to the determination of the national policy.

All citizens may also address petitions to both Houses of Parliament demanding legislative measures, or presenting general requests.

---

20. The English translation of the Italian Constitution, used as a reference here, is taken from the official English version of the Senate of the Republic http://www.senato.it/documenti/repository/istituzione/costituzione_inglese.pdf (31 August 2018).

§8. The Italian Parliament

42. The Parliament consists of the *Chamber of Deputies* and the *Senate*. Entirely consistent with the dualistic form of government provided by the *Statuto Albertino* (under which the model was used to tile a second chamber elected to the House appointed by the King as a function of political counterweight), the bicameral system is more difficult to justify in the context of a form of government that identifies the combination 'Parliament-Government' as the centre of the political system.

The Constituents discussed whether or not to keep the new Parliament and a bicameral structure. The reasons that pushed them to adopt a model of *bicameralism* (to distrust formulas to summon the corporate establishment of the fascist regime) is peculiar and is not reflected in the choices that other European Constituent Assemblies operated in the same period.

43. This model seemed to be the most appropriate way to value the principle of political representation and political opposition.

The choices of the Constituent Assembly, however, have led to the adoption of a model of *equal bicameralism* (equal and undifferentiated) under which both Houses of Parliament exercise the same powers, and parliamentary acts are the result of the necessary agreement of both Houses. The only differences relate to the number of components of each Chamber and to the different electoral system.

In 2016, the extensive project to reform the Parliament aimed to reform the equal bicameralism. The model proposed shaped a Senate based on Regions and Autonomies, with different functions and not equal attribution. The project was rejected by referendum on 4 December 2016.

44. The Parliament functions are legislative and of political control (it controls the executive power). Furthermore, this body can start a special constitutional amendment process in case of commissioning of the impeached President of the Republic for high treason and offences against the Constitution.[21]

45. The Chamber is elected by universal and direct suffrage; the number of representatives is 630, and 12 of them are elected by the constituency of Italians residing abroad. All voters who have reached the age of 25 on election day are eligible.

46. The Senate consists of 315 senators. Senators are elected on a Regional basis, except for 6 assigned to the constituency of Italians residing abroad. Senators are also elected in universal and direct elections, but voters must be older than 25 years. Any voter who has reached the age of 40 on election day is eligible. Members of the Chamber and the Senate are elected for five-year terms, and the term of each House cannot be extended except by law, and only in the event of war.

According to Article 67 of the Constitution, members of Parliament represent the Nation, and they are free from an imperative mandate.

---

21. *See* N. Lupo, L. Gianniti, 'Corso di diritto parlamentare' (Bologna, Il Mulino, 2008). V. Onida, 'La Costituzione' (Il Mulino, Bologna, 2017).

§9. The Lawmaking Process

47. Stages through which the proceedings take place leading to the approval of a law and its entry into force in Italy are: (i) initiative, (ii) discussion and vote, (iii) promulgation and (iv) publication.

The phase of the exercise is carried out by certain entities and individuals who have the power to submit bills and draft laws to the Parliament.

The Constitution recognizes this power, first, to the Government. The legislative initiative lies, in second place, in the members of Parliament, who can pursue either individually or cumulatively, by signing a bill. The initiative is also recognized to the electoral body, the Regional Councils and the *National Council for Economics and Labour.*

48. The second phase of the legislative process takes place inside the Parliament and regards: (i) the examination, (ii) the discussion and (iii) the vote of the bill. The bill is examined by a standing Committee responsible for the topic and, if the proposal affects the jurisdiction of other Committees, the latter are usually called upon to express an opinion.

Once the examination inside the Committee is completed, the text approved may also differ from the original, and there is a discussion on the basis of the report by the Committee. The discussion takes place regarding the general features of the proposal and, then, about individual articles.

Rated all the individual items, the Committee proceeds to a final vote of the full proposal. When the bill has passed these stages in a Chamber, it is transmitted to the other, which proceeds (again) to its examination, discussion and approval.

If the Chamber approves, during the second examination, the same text adopted by the first Chamber, the law is transmitted to the President for the promulgation. If, conversely, the second Chamber makes changes, the proposal goes back to the first Chamber, and this passage from one Chamber to another continues until both are able to approve an identical text.

49. The third and final stage of the legislative process, which affects the production of the regulatory effects of the law, is made within 30 days after the promulgation by the President of the Republic and is called *publication.*

50. Legislative power is exercised jointly by the Chamber and the Senate; the right to initiate the legislation process belongs to the Government, to each Member of Parliament, and to organs and bodies that have this power assigned by a constitutional law.

Electors can also introduce *public initiatives*, consisting of a bill drafted in Articles, and supported by, at least, 50,000 voters.

51. Every bill introduced to one of the Houses of Parliament is first examined by a Committee, as defined by the rules of procedure, and then adopted by the given House article by article first and then with a final vote.

The rules of procedure establish an abbreviated procedure for bills that are declared 'urgent'.

52. Laws are promulgated by the President within a month of adoption by Parliament. However, if a majority in each House declares a bill to be *urgent*, it must be promulgated by the time set in the bill.

Laws have to be published immediately after they are promulgated; they enter into force on the fifteenth day after their publication, unless a law establishes a different time frame.

Before promulgation, the President may ask the Parliament to further deliberate on a law passed. This is done by a 'message to the Chambers', giving the reasons for such a request. However, if the Parliament once again adopts the bill, the law must then be promulgated.

53. When requested by 500,000 voters or by five Regional Councils, a popular *referendum* can be called to decide on a proposal for the total or partial repeal of a law or another act with legal force.

No such referendums can be called for tax or budget laws, amnesties, pardons or for the ratification of international treaties.

The referendum succeeds if a majority of those eligible have participated in the referendum and if the proposal has received a majority of valid votes.

54. Parliament's legislative power cannot be delegated to the Government unless Parliament specifies principles and criteria of guidance for delegation, and the delegation is only for a limited time and well-specified subjects.

The Government cannot issue Decrees with the force of law unless empowered by such a proper delegation.

If necessity or urgency dictates, however, the Government can, as an exception to the rule, issue provisional measures with force of law (*Law Decrees* and *Legislative Decrees*) and submit them on the same day to the Parliament for confirmation. If the Parliament is not in session, it will have to be summoned within five days for the purpose of the confirmation.

Legal decrees lose their effect at the date of issue if they are not confirmed within sixty days from their publication; however, Parliament may regulate temporary rights and obligations arising from decrees that are not confirmed.

§10. The Main Principles of the Italian Constitution

55. In the first part of the Italian Constitution, as in other Constitutions, many principles are explained which aim to establish, from the outset, what are the cornerstones that characterize the Italian constitutional system and the values protected therein.

The text of the Italian Constitution begins with the identification of several fundamental principles (Arts. 1–12). One of the most important issue is the principle of *popular sovereignty*, according to which no organ of Government can independently claim legitimacy in the exercise of the highest functions of the State but must, instead, rely on legitimacy coming from the only 'entity' (the people) that, as the holder of sovereignty, is able to attribute this power to other subjects.

56. A framework is also outlined in which the State's role is summed up in a function that guarantees the full development of individual personality and community values of citizens and, more generally, of all humanity.

Recognized and guaranteed are the 'inalienable human rights', and the liberal principle of equality of all citizens is emphasized too, with 'equal social dignity' and 'equality before the law', without distinction of gender, race, language, religion, political opinion, personal and social conditions.

57. There is also, in the first part of the Constitution, an openness to the values of social pluralism, ensuring the protection of local autonomy, linguistic communities and the various religious denominations.

In the Constitution, in addition to basic rights of freedom (constructed as spheres of autonomy protected by the interference of outsiders) there are also many social rights: the 'inalienable rights' are joined to the 'imperative duties of political solidarity, economic and social' which must be fulfilled.

It is expressed very clearly the favour for the *welfare state*, requiring that it is up to the Republic to remove obstacles to economic and social order that prevent the full development of the human person and the effective participation of all workers in the political, economic and social development of the Country.

58. Italy is a democratic Republic founded on labour; the work activity is the contribution that each citizen gives to the material and cultural progress of society and is the primary social value.

Another distinguishing feature of the first part of the Constitution is the special openness to *internationalism* (with the affirmation of the subordination of Italian law to generally accepted international standards) and the explicit commitment to *peace* (with the principle that Italy, on behalf of peace and justice between Nations, agrees to limitations of sovereignty necessary for this purpose and encourages international organizations).

59. According to the Italian Constitution, sovereignty belongs to the people, who exercise it within the limits of the Constitution.

The Republic recognizes and guarantees inviolable human rights, in terms of both individual rights and the rights of social groups expressing their identity, and it ensures the performance of the unalterable duty to political, economic and social solidarity.[22]

60. All citizens have equal social status and are equal in front of the law, without regard to their sex, race, language, religion, political opinions or personal or social conditions.

It is a duty of the Republic to remove all economic and social obstacles that, by limiting the freedom and equality of citizens, prevent complete individual development and the participation of all workers in the political, economic and social organization of the Country.

---

22. *See, generally*, A. Cassese, 'I diritti umani oggi' (Editori Laterza, Bari–Roma, 2005); S. Rodotà, 'Il diritto di avere diritti' (Editori Laterza, Bari-Roma, 2015).

The Republic recognizes the right of all citizens to work and promotes conditions to fulfil this right. However, according to capability and choice, every citizen also has the duty to undertake an activity or a function that will contribute to the material and moral progress of society.

61. Personal liberty[23] is inviolable. No one can be detained, inspected, searched or otherwise have his (or her) personal liberty restricted, except by a *judicial order* stating the reason for such action, and only in cases and manner provided by law.

As an exception to this rule, under conditions of necessity and urgency strictly defined by law, the police may take provisional measures to detain, inspect or search citizens and their property. These measures must be reported within 48 hours to the judiciary, and, if they are not ratified within another 48 hours, they are considered to be revoked and remain without effect.[24]

Acts of physical and moral violence against persons subject to restrictions of personal liberty are to be punished, and the law establishes the maximum duration of preventive detention.

A personal domicile is inviolable, and no one's domicile may be inspected, searched or seized, save in cases and in the manner laid down by laws conforming to the guarantee of personal liberty.

Verifications and inspections for public health and safety, or for economic and fiscal purposes, are defined by law.

62. According to the Italian Constitution, liberty and secrecy of *correspondence* and other forms of communication (including electronic communications) are inviolable;[25] limitations to these freedoms can only be imposed by judicial decisions that state clearly the reasons for such decisions and are made in accordance with those guarantees defined by law.[26]

All the Italian citizens have the right to freely express thoughts in speech, writing and by other means of communications; the press cannot be controlled by governmental authorities or submitted to censorship.[27]

Governmental interference with the press is permitted only after a judicial order stating the reason for such interference, and only for offences expressly determined by the press law, or for a violation of the obligation to identify the persons responsible for such offences.

In cases of absolute urgency, when immediate judicial decision is impossible, periodicals may be seized by the police, which must then immediately, and in no

23. *See*, *generally*, G. Amato, 'Libertà (Diritto costituzionale)', in Enc. Dir., XXIV, 1974, 172 ss.
24. *See*, *generally*, P. Tonini, 'Lineamenti di diritto processuale penale' (Giuffrè, Milano, 2005).
25. *See*, *generally*, A. Valastro, 'Libertà di comunicazione e nuove tecnologie' (Milano, Giuffrè, 2001); M. Cuniberti, E. Lamarque, B. Tonoletti, G. E. Vigevani, M. P. Viviani Schlein, 'Percorsi di diritto dell'informazione' (Giappichelli, Torino, 2006).
26. *See*, *generally*, V. Zeno-Zencovich, 'La libertà d'espressione' (Il Mulino, Bologna, 2004); P. Barile, 'Libertà di manifestazione del pensiero' in Enc. Dir. XXIV, 1974, 424 ss.
27. *See* Art. 15 of the Italian Constitution.

case later than 24 hours, report the matter to the judiciary. If the measure is not validated by the judiciary within another twenty-four hours, it is considered revoked and has no effect.[28]

Publications, performances and other exhibits offensive to public morality[29] are prohibited, and measures against violations are provided by law.[30]

---

28. *See* Art. 21 of the Italian Constitution. *See*, *generally*, P. Nuvolone, 'II diritto penale della stampa' (CEDAM, Padova, 1971).
29. Concerning the relationship between free speech and new technologies, from an international point of view, *see*, *generally*, G. Ziccardi, 'La Corte Suprema americana e la libertà d'espressione in Internet', in Quaderni Costituzionali, Vol. 1, pp. 123-134 (II Mulino, Bologna, 1998).
30. The English text of the Italian Constitution is taken from 'Constitution of the Italian Republic' on the official website of the Italian Senate http://www.senato.it/documenti/repository/istituzione/costituzione_inglese.pdf (31 August 2018).

Chapter 2. Telecommunications Infrastructure

§1. The Ministry of Economic Development

63. The situation of telecommunications infrastructure in Italy used to be very problematic, but it remarkably improved in the last years.

On the one hand, there were large Government projects that were continually proposed. In the past, they often did not result in a genuine reform of the infrastructure and a real solution to the problems.

Second, the lack of broadband connections and free wireless connections in the main metropolitan areas slowed both public access to the grid and the ability to connect to the Internet economically.

However, encouraging data show that investments in telecommunications infrastructures have been growing consistently[31] (+24% for the fixed network and +15.5% for the mobile network in 2015). In 2018, FWA and fibre lines have increased, respectively, by +23.6% and +95.5%.[32]

64. In Italy, from a political point of view, the development of the telecommunications infrastructure is strictly connected to the activities and the policies of the Government in the last twenty years.

Today, the Ministry of Economic Development[33] is responsible, in Italy, for a wide variety of policies, including:

(i) industrial policy,
(ii) internationalization energy and mineral resources,
(iii) telecommunications, and
(iv) business incentives.

According to Law Decree 16 May 2008, n. 85 ('Urgent Provisions Regarding the Modification of Government Structures'), the functions of the former Ministry of Communications, and its inherent financial, material and human resources, were transferred to the Ministry of Economic Development.[34]

65. The Ministry of Economic Development also takes and publishes technical measures regarding the type, the approval and the utilization of terminal apparatus to be connected, directly or indirectly, to telecommunications networks (granting, afterwards, the relevant *licences*).

---

31. *See* 'L'assetto e le prospettive del settore delle comunicazioni in Italia', Capitolo II, Relazione annuale 2016, AGCOM.
32. *See* Osservatorio Trimestrale sulle comunicazioni n 1/2018 at https://www.agcom.it/documents/10179/3457668/Allegato+7-6-2018/3e3fc87d-f6ab-4979-b162-f86b1d555a72?version=1.0.
33. *See* https://www.mise.gov.it/index.php/en/.
34. Concerning the evolution, in Italy, of this political and legal framework *see*, *generally*, V. Franceschelli, 'Convergenza' (Giuffrè, Milano, 2009); F. Bassan (ed.), 'Diritto delle comunicazioni elettroniche' (Giuffrè, Milano, 2011); R. Bianco, 'Diritto delle comunicazioni di massa' (Laterza, Bari–Roma, 2007).

The office carries out approvals for telecommunications apparatus; grants licences, authorizations and permissions adopting the relevant provisions; determines technical regulations considering both users' interests and services quality levels; and arranges plans for the grant and allocation of radio frequencies which conform with the aforementioned licences, authorizations and permissions.[35]

Regarding the management of telecommunications infrastructure, the latter is entrusted to private operators by means of *frequency allocation* with an auction conducted by public and AGCOM Department of Telecommunications[36] (the Italian Telecommunications Authority).

66. Fixed telephony is managed by many telephone operators (the most important are Telecom Italia, Tiscali, Fastweb and Vodafone). The mobile phone network, at present, is divided among three players owning the frequencies: TIM, Vodafone Italy and Wind Tre.

In turn, these handlers sublease the network to many other operators (including Fastweb, Postemobile, Tiscali, etc.).

67. The Ministry of Economic Development is keeping a Register of the companies authorized to offer services of electronic communication (i.e., sale of telephone traffic, Internet Service Providers, internet points and Wi-Fi providers).[37]

§2. The Department of Communications and the Italian Digital Agenda

68. The Department for Communications carries out its duties and functions through central and peripheral organs.

Its expertise ranges from amateur radio issues to the issuance of stamps, including the policies for the expansion of broadband.

The Department for Communications has essential functions of promotion, development and regulation of the communications sector, alongside dealing with issues of securities as well as of planning, control and supervisory (with consequent disciplinary powers).

69. Through its Directorates, the Department for Communications deals with the discipline in the electronic communications sector and the issues of concessions, licences and permits.

It draws the *National Plan of Allocation of Frequencies*, conducts the verification of universal service obligations in the areas of communications, deals with issues relating to radio and television, drafts the regulation of the postal sector and postal stamps.

---

35. *See also* 'Spectrum Management and Policy Issues in the EU and Italian framework', AGCOM, 7 October 2011.
36. *See* http://www.agcom.it/.
37. The Register may be accessed at the link http://www.sviluppoeconomico.gov.it/index.php/it/component/content/article?id=68306.

Very important functions are, also, the business relationships with the universal service provider (Italian Post Office), the allocation of rights of use for frequencies and numbers and the control of radio frequency emission and interference.

Moreover, other sectors of pertinence include information technology, network security, studies and scientific research in the areas of communications and information technology (ICT), standardization (including aspects relating to numbering, accreditation, certification and standardization in ICT, and the definition of quality standards in the ICT services), market control, monitoring compliance with industry regulations and application of sanctions.[38]

70. The Ministry of Economic Development drafted, also, the *Digital Agenda*, to explain the Italian strategy for achieving several political (and technological) objectives.

The Italian Digital Agenda (adopted with the Law Decree 179/2011) was created following the signature by all European Union Member States of the Digital Agenda, presented by the European Commission in 2010.

Each State has committed to incorporate it into its legal system, introducing several principles, including that of a 'digital single market', based on the Internet and on interoperable software, able to communicate with each other and to use data without compatibility problems.

71. On 9 February 2012, the objectives of the *Italian Digital Program* were established to provide a regulatory architecture for the telecommunications sector and to promote its development and modernization.

Among the objectives to be pursued (as defined in the so-called *Control Room*), there are the creation of an infrastructure, the development of e-commerce and e-government, the attention to open data, research and innovation.[39]

72. Contributing to this institutional framework is the AGCOM, Independent Administrative Authority, which carries out its supervisory, regulatory and dispute resolution functions in the telecommunications sector, with powers of inspection and regulatory sanctions.

73. Among its tasks, there are the implementation of *deregulation* in the telecommunications sector, the rationalization of resources, the antitrust enforcement in the telecommunications and the verification of any dominant position, as well as the supervision on quality and methods of distribution services, including advertising.

74. Moreover, with the '*Decreto Sviluppo*' (Law Decree 83/2012), the *Agenzia per l'Italia Digitale* (AgID, Agency for Digital Italy) was created to take place of DigitPA, the Italian National Center for the Digitalization of the Public Administration.

Its task is to verify that the plans and guidelines of the Digital Agenda are respected.

---

38. *See* https://www.mise.gov.it/index.php/en/.
39. Decree Law 5/2014.

75. AgID also issued the 'Piano Triennale per l'informatica nella Pubblica Amministrazione' (Three Year Plan for IT in the PA).

The Three-Year Plan is a strategic and economic policy document through which the Strategic Model of the evolution of the Public Administration information system is declined.

76. Provided by AgID by-laws and 2016 Stability Law (Law 208/2015), the Plan was created to effectively guide the digital transformation of the Public Administration and becomes a point of reference for central and local administrations in the development of their IT systems.

It defines the guidelines of the operational strategy for the development of public information technology; establishes the fundamental architectural principles, the rules of usability and interoperability; specifies the logic for classifying ICT expenses; and clarifies the model for digital development.

§3. Connectivity in Italy: An Introduction

77. In addition to digital TV, decoders and optic fibre, which play an important part in the current development in Italy, other technologies are emerging through the years, such as Wi-Fi and Wi-Max, which can help satisfy the needs of broadband connectivity in the Country.

Today, wireless technologies can help to rapidly reach areas that have no broadband service.

The former Ministry of Communications, according to the Ministerial Decree of 4 October 2005, planned (several years ago) to work to extend Wi-Fi access areas.

On the other side, as regards Wi-Max, experimentation ended on 31 December 2006, and, on the basis of the results, public consultation procedures and the subsequent procedures for the allotment of frequencies were defined.

78. An old agreement between the former Ministry of Communications and a private company (*Infratel Italia* Spa) concerned the establishment of regulations for the implementation of specifically created and integrated infrastructure, taking concrete action to reduce the digital divide that exists in the Country, and setting outlines for intervention procedures to be implemented either directly or through subsidiary or affiliated public companies, other specially created consortiums and project financing.

79. *Infratel* company is responsible for planning all interventions aimed at creating and integrating the telecommunications infrastructure needed in target areas.

The interventions range from laying cables to setting up advanced wireless systems, guaranteeing managerial expertise to get the infrastructure up and running (optic fibres, wireless equipment) and high-quality service to safeguard public investment and ensure network functionality, accessibility and interoperability.

80. Furthermore, *Infratel* is able to coordinate with other institutions, in particular regulatory authorities and the Regions, to ensure that connectivity and infrastructure access is offered to Public Administration offices, telecommunication operators and providers on equal and non-*discriminatory* conditions.

More specifically, one of Infratel's goals is to reach the second objective of the European digital agenda which must be implemented by 2020, namely to bring at least 30 Mbps connectivity to all Europeans, ensuring that at least 50% of European households subscribe to Internet connections of over 100 Mbps.

The idea is increasing the competitiveness and innovation of the country, providing jobs and opportunities for young people, preventing the delocalization of economic activities or migratory phenomena and attracting investments and developing exports.

The path taken by Italy to fulfil this objective is described in the National Broadband Plan, approved by the European Commission with decision C (2012) 9833 of 18 December 2012.

81. On 3 March 2015, the Italian Council of Ministers approved the new Italian ultra-broadband strategy that has the ambitious goal of maximizing coverage over 100 Mbps, while still ensuring to all citizenship at least 30 Mbps.

The priority is to guarantee a 100 Mbps coverage to offices and public buildings (schools and hospitals, in particular), for areas of major economic interest and demographic concentration, for industrial areas, for the main tourist locations and logistic hubs.

In any event, Infratel does not directly provide connections to users, but to telecommunications companies and Internet providers, which are then able to utilize infrastructures on equal terms, and which will be responsible for selling access services to clients.

§4. Connectivity Data in Italy (From 2011 to 2017) and Digital Divide

82. Already in 2011, data showed an increase in Internet connections within Italian families.

Compared to 2010, the share of households having a personal computer grew (from 57.6% to 58.8%), as well as those with access to the Internet (from 52.4% to 54.5%) and a broadband connection (by 43.4% to 45.8%).

This positive trend has been confirmed, since, in 2017, compared to 2016, the percentage of households having access to the Internet at home has increased from 69.2% to 71.7%. As a result, families with a broadband connection increased from 67.4% to 69.5%.[40]

In particular, families with at least a minor were in 2011 the most 'wired': a total of 84.4% owned a personal computer (in 2013: 87.8%), 78.9% had Internet access and 68% used this for a broadband connection.

40. *See* the ISTAT (*Italian National Institute of Statistics*), annual and sectorial reports for 2017, www.istat.it.

Such percentage continued to grow over time: indeed, in 2017, 9 of 10 families with at least a minor had a broadband connection.

83. However, in Italy, inequalities at a territorial level still persist regarding ICT usage. Indeed, in 2011, in the North, about 60% of households owned a personal computer, and about 57% had Internet access at home, while in the South of Italy the percentages were, respectively, around 53% and 48%.

In 2017 there is still a strong imbalance in the use of the Web between regions, as well as in metropolitan, urban rather than extra-urban contexts.

The families of the Centre-North having Internet access are more than 56%, while approximately 49% have a broadband connection, compared with values respectively equal to 48.6% and 37.5% in the South. However, the gap between the North and the South of Italy is reduced compared to 2016 (from 11.4% to 9.5%).

The regions that registered the highest increases are Campania (from 54.6% to 59.6%) and Sicily (from 53.5% to 58.4%).[41]

84. Broadband Internet coverage in Italy is not uniform: in metropolitan areas, this service may be available with connection speeds from fixed network up to 20 Mbit/s (except for some places, where pilot projects of the new generation network at 100 Mbps are carried out), while in remote rural areas these services drop dramatically.

This is due to the fact that providing such places with broadband connections is too burdensome for operators who would not get short-term returns on their investment.[42]

85. It is noteworthy that the use of Internet is also characterized by a strong social gap. Indeed, if it has reached levels close to saturation among graduates (91.6%) and managers, entrepreneurs and professionals (93.8%), this share decreases to 63.9% among those in possession of a middle school degree and 77.6% between workers and apprentices.[43]

86. Gender differences have gradually mitigated: if, in 2005, women using the Internet were little more than a quarter (26.9%), in 2011 they were almost the half (46.7%), while men quota moved from 37.1% to 56.6%.[44] In 2017, about 69.5% of men and 61.3% of women surfed the Internet.[45]

Today, devices to connect to the Internet have multiplied, thanks to the evolution of technologies. In Italy in 2016, 78.3% of regular Internet users aged 15 and over

41. *See* the ISTAT (*Italian National Institute of Statistics*), annual and sectorial reports for 2017, www.istat.it.
42. *See* the ISTAT (*Italian National Institute of Statistics*), annual and sectorial reports for 2017, www.istat.it.
43. *See* the ISTAT (*Italian National Institute of Statistics*), annual and sectorial reports for 2017, www.istat.it.
44. *See* the ISTAT (*Italian National Institute of Statistics*), annual and sectorial reports for 2017, www.istat.it.
45. *See* the ISTAT (*Italian National Institute of Statistics*), annual and sectorial reports for 2017, www.istat.it.

used a smartphone to access the Net, 49.6% a PC, 31.1% a laptop or a netbook, 28.8% a tablet and 5.8% other mobile devices such as e-book and smartwatch.[46]

87. In 2011, 26.3% of the individuals aged 14 and over surfed the Web during shopping activities online; by 2017, Internet users buying online were 53.0%; among those who did not make purchases in the last 3 months, 43.2% have sought information on goods or services and/or sold goods online.

Among the top ranking of goods and services purchased via the Web there used to be *travel* and *accommodation* for vacation, while in the last years online purchases mostly concerned clothes and household articles.[47]

88. It is interesting to note how data related to digital skilled have not changed dramatically over the years.

Indeed, data from 2016 show that only 28.3% of Internet users had high digital skills, while the majority had basic skills (35.1%) or low (33.3%).

There was still a niche of Internet users with no digital competence (3.3%).

In this respect, age is a relevant aspect to consider: young people aged 16-24 had almost advanced levels in 40% of cases.

Another discriminating factor is the degree of education (47.6% of graduates using the Internet reportedly had high digital skills).[48]

89. Internet users demonstrated to have more advanced digital skills related to communication (64.9%) and information (64.6%) compared to those related to problem-solving (50.6%) and to have the ability to manipulate/convey digital content (49.2%). Only a minority had a level of high competence for all domains.[49]

90. In 2016, 85.8% of Internet users used the Web to access cultural contents; 68.9% watched online video contents from sharing services (e.g., YouTube), more than half (55.2%) consulted newspapers and online magazines and 49.9% listened to music (e.g., web radio and music instreaming).

28% of Italians used the Internet to watch television in streaming or on demand. Most of the users of online cultural contents, with the exception of reading newspapers or magazines, are between 15 and 24 years old.[50]

91. The Web is also an important tool for social interaction.

---

46. *See* Internet@Italia2018. Domanda e offerta di servizi online e scenari di digitalizzazione, ISTAT (Italian National Institute of Statistics) and Fondazione Ugo Bordoni.
47. *See* the ISTAT (*Italian National Institute of Statistics*), annual and sectorial reports for 2017, www.istat.it.
48. *See* the ISTAT (*Italian National Institute of Statistics*), annual and sectorial reports for 2017, www.istat.it.
49. *See* the ISTAT (*Italian National Institute of Statistics*), annual and sectorial reports for 2017, www.istat.it.
50. *See* the ISTAT (*Italian National Institute of Statistics*), annual and sectorial reports for 2017, www.istat.it.

More than half of the internauts (57.8%) used it to create a user profile, send messages or other on Facebook or Twitter; over 80% of people aged 15 to 24 regularly used a social network.

If just over 50% of Internet users sent messages on chat rooms, blogs, forums online discussion, as much as 64.9% used instant messaging services to communicate.

The use of these fast communication services on the Internet showed an increase by 5 percentage points compared to 2015.[51]

92. Rapid technological innovations and increased connectivity have helped to spread forms of 'sharing economy', which allows the exchange and share not only of goods but also of skills, money and physical spaces.

In 2017 in Italy, there were about 6 million Internet users aged 16-74 who have used the Internet to find accommodation by directly contacting a private person via websites/apps like AIRBNB or Homeaway.[52]

This practice is more popular among people aged 20-44 (over 22%), among residents in the north-east (23.3% against 11.5% in the South), in the central municipalities of the metropolitan area (22.7%) and among executives, entrepreneurs, professionals, managers, employees (about 30%).

The use of these platforms to travel was less popular: only 3.6% have used a transport service by contacting a private person directly via websites or apps.

Regarding the sharing of cultural content, 55.4% of people aged 6 and over have consulted a wiki to get information on any subject, while almost a third (30.2%) has published on the Web some content of their own creation (such as texts, photographs, music, video and software), but the share is close to 50% among young people aged 20 to 24.

93. In 2011, about 94.3% of enterprises with ten persons employed had an Internet connection.

About 88.3% of companies were connected to the Internet via fixed or mobile broadband, but 73.3% of businesses connected to the Internet still used speeds up to 10 Mbit/s; in terms of diffusion of the mobile broadband usage, only 8.4% of the persons employed were provided by the enterprises with devices for a mobile broadband connection to the Internet.

An increase over time can be noticed; since 2017, 95.7% (94.2% in 2016) of companies with at least 10 employees used fixed or mobile broadband connections. 93.6% were connected in fixed broadband. The mobile broadband connection grew from 63.8% in 2016 to 70.9%.[53]

---

51. *See* the ISTAT (*Italian National Institute of Statistics*), annual and sectorial reports for 2016, www.istat.it.
52. *See* the ISTAT (*Italian National Institute of Statistics*), annual and sectorial reports for 2017, www.istat.it.
53. *See* the ISTAT (*Italian National Institute of Statistics*), annual and sectorial reports for 2017, www.istat.it.

94. In 2011, 62.6% of businesses had a website, but only 35% of these sites provided a service of high interaction with the user.[54]

Instead, in 2017, 72.1% of companies had their own website, but only 15.0% (13.8% in 2016) allowed site visitors to make online orders or reservations; this percentage rises up to one of four of the largest companies and reaches 82.6% among the accommodation services companies.

It is interesting to note that the number of companies using at least one social media is still growing (44.0%, 39.2% in 2016), as well as the percentage of those using at least two of them (17.5%, 15.6% in 2016).

95. The Regional distribution of the digital divide for fixed network in Italy has three components:

(i) percentage of resident population not covered by ADSL via fixed network;
(ii) percentage of population covered by nodes capable of issuing only speeds below 2 Mbit/s ('lite' ADSL); and
(iii) percentage of the population covered by broadband only nominally because, in fact, they are unable to access the services for problems due to the physical distance of the user from the network node.

Regions with the biggest digital divide are Molise, Basilicata, Puglia and Calabria, followed by Sicilia and Valle d'Aosta.

As it has emerged in recent years, the phenomenon does heavily affect not only the Regions of the South but also some of the large Regions of the North (Piemonte, Veneto and also, partially, Lombardia) characterized by mountain ranges and vast plainlands where the low population density makes it difficult to reach out to all users and provide them with efficient communication services.

To the contrary, at the top of the list, with less than 10% of the population suffering from digital divide, are most of the large Regions of the South that have high population densities or where the location of the land and the urban characteristics are particularly favourable (as in the case of Puglia).[55]

96. Also, the components of the digital divide vary widely from place to place: large populations that do not have ADSL are found not only in Molise but also in Umbria, Veneto and Friuli Venezia Giulia.

In Calabria and Basilicata, instead, most of the population suffering from digital divide has access to speeds of less than 2 Mbit/s, since the ADSL coverage is the so-called lite version which was the initial response to the problem of digital divide in remote areas.

---

54. *See* the ISTAT (*Italian National Institute of Statistics*), annual and sectoral reports for 2011 and 2012, www.istat.it. *See also,* the Digital Agenda Italy e-Gov Report of 2010 drafted by the Department for Digitization of Public Administration and Technological Innovation, at the address http://www.digitpa.gov.it/.
55. *See* the ISTAT (*Italian National Institute of Statistics*), annual and sectorial reports for 2017, www.istat.it.

97. Today, however, the 'lite' version is no longer an adequate response to current needs in terms of Internet connection.

The population that cannot access the service due to 'long line' reasons is a very small proportion at national level, but the figures are high for some territories like Marche, Sardegna and Puglia, where it represents the main reason for the digital divide.

98. Some territories (especially the Regions, but also, in some cases, the Provinces) have started broadband infrastructure projects in areas where there is a large digital divide.

Not all these projects appear to have been completed yet, and in some cases, they have led to the implementation of (fixed or mobile network) technologies providing speeds that are below the minimum 2 Mbit/s (which is, now, considered to be the *entry level* for broadband connections).

Even though it is not possible to obtain precise data on the impact of public infrastructure projects on reducing the digital divide, in examining the data it must be kept in consideration the fact that, in some cases, the digital divide percentage would probably be even greater if these actions had not been taken.

99. In analysing the extent of the digital divide, account must be kept also of radio coverage that could help reduce the digital divide at least for the proportion of population that is not reached by the fixed network.

At present, the technologies used to provide broadband services via radio are Wi-Max, UMTS and HSDPA. These services are provided by mobile operators.

100. The overall digital divide drops to 8–9% of the population. Regions with the largest digital divide are Molise and Basilicata, while the comparison with the digital divide for the fixed network shows that radio connections now provide coverage for most of the population of Umbria and Calabria, where the digital divide drops to below 20%.

101. The Alpine range and the Po Valley, with the exception of the larger towns, present a digital divide that is much greater than the Italian average, while in the Centre-South the areas at a greater disadvantage are located on the Apennines.[56]

§5. Public Connectivity in Italy and Connectivity of the Public Administration

102. With respect to an increase in Internet use of about 17% over the period 2011-2016 (from 57.3% to 73.7%), the percentage of users of the PA sites has remained almost constant.

The only activity that shows an increase is the sending of completed forms to the PA (which grew by about 5 points and reached 13.1%).

---

56. *See* the Digital Agenda Italy e-Gov Report of 2010 drafted by the Department for Digitization of Public Administration and Technological Innovation, at the address http://www.digitpa.gov.it/.

However, the number of users looking for information and downloading modules remains stable, settling in 2016 respectively at 21.8% and 18.3%.[57]

103. On average, in the Municipalities in Italy there are 84 personal computers per 100 employees; also in the areas where the ratio is lower, there is at the least one personal computer for every two employees.[58]

Just over 40% of Italian Municipalities are endowed with an intranet; only in two Regions does the deployment of the intranet exceed 80% of the Municipalities: notably the Autonomous Province of Bolzano, and Veneto.

However, in Piemonte and Valle d'Aosta, the percentage is below the Italian average, probably because of the presence in these territories of very small (<5000 inhabitants) and medium-small (between 5000 and 10000 inhabitants) Municipalities.

104. In Italy, almost 57% of Municipalities are distributing digital signatures to their employees; the deployment of digital signatures is highest in Toscana, in the Autonomous Province of Bolzano and in Emilia-Romagna, with proportions that are above 80%.

However, digital signature is available to less than 40% of the employees of the Municipalities of Abruzzo, Molise, Calabria and Sicilia.

105. About 92% of Italian Municipalities are endowed with an *electronic document registration system*, which means that this instrument has almost entirely replaced the old paper registers.

The most advanced Region is Umbria, where the electronic document registration system is available in all Municipalities; in the Autonomous Province of Trento and Sicilia this system is available in 80% of the Municipalities.[59]

106. All Italian Municipalities are endowed with a traditional or broadband connection to the Internet.

Internet connections are available to 71% of employees, albeit with high variability between different territories; indeed, while several Regions do not exceed the figure of 80% of municipal employees being connected, there are some where the percentage is even lower than 50%.

The availability of connectivity in Public Administrations is very diverse. In general, Public Administrations – especially local ones – have an average undersized situation, which does not meet the criteria defined by the public system of connectivity.[60]

---

57. *See* Internet@Italia 2018. Domanda e offerta di servizi online e scenari di digitalizzazione, ISTAT (Italian National Institute of Statistics) and Fondazione Ugo Bordoni.
58. *See* the Digital Agenda Italy e-Gov Report of 2010 drafted by the Department for Digitization of Public Administration and Technological Innovation, at the address http://www.digitpa.gov.it/.
59. *See* the Digital Agenda Italy e-Gov Report of 2010 drafted by the Department for Digitization of Public Administration and Technological Innovation, at the address http://www.digitpa.gov.it/.
60. Piano Triennale per l'informatica nella Pubblica Amministrazione 2017-2019, Agenzia per l'Italia Digitale.

107. Almost 75% of Municipalities have broadband Internet connections at a speed greater than 2 Mbit/s.

Deployment is above 90% in the Municipalities of Emilia-Romagna and Puglia and almost 100% in the Autonomous Province of Bolzano. Valle d'Aosta is the only Region where the percentage is below 60%.

108. The VoIP technology is not yet very common in Italy: only 15% of Municipalities have stated that they use this technology. Emilia-Romagna is the Region with the highest percentage, followed by Sicilia, Toscana, Umbria and Valle d'Aosta.

Well below 10% of Municipalities in Abruzzo, Molise and Basilicata use VoIP technology.

109. From a general point of view, being part of the *Public Connectivity System* (SPC) through the ICAR (*Interoperability and Regional Cooperation on Applications*), guarantees interaction between the Central and local Public Administration and all the bodies connected to the Internet, as well as the networks of other bodies, is endowed with a high level of security, confidentiality of the information and protection; it also guarantees that the data held by each Public Administration is autonomous.

110. As provided by law, AgID has the task of carrying out a census of the PA data centres in order to propose a rationalization plan, i.e. rules aimed at consolidating the digital infrastructures of the Public Administration, in order to obtain higher levels of efficiency, safety and speed in the provision of services to citizens and businesses.

In the period 1 June 2013–31 July 2013, AgID carried out an initial census on 990 data centres of the Public Administration, noticing a strong fragmentation of the resources and frequent situations of technological inadequacy.

A total of 20% of the infrastructures considered did not have disaster recovery or business continuity mechanisms, 12% of the CAP infrastructures and 50% of the infrastructures of the LAPs considered had access controls considered insufficient, 94% of the data centres for the CAPs and 84% for PALs were created and used by a single administration, with duplication of costs and resources.[61]

111. Concerning the Web activities of the Public Administration, the central administrations with the highest number of *hits* are the Ministry of the Economy and Finance, the Ministry for Education, Universities and Research (for the schools), the Ministry of Justice (also for Justices of the Peace), the Ministry for Agricultural, Food and Forestry Policies followed by the Guardia di Finanza and the National Institute for Social Security (INPS).

All the administrations that have entered into an agreement for being part of the SPC requested transport services; half of them also requested security services,

61. Piano Triennale per l'informatica nella Pubblica Amministrazione 2017-2019, Agenzia per l'Italia Digitale.

while request for VoIP services was the lowest and, above all, interoperability services were requested only by about a dozen central administrations.

112. The connection of Local PA (PAL) to the *Public Connectivity System* includes the bodies that signed a contract with accredited suppliers while it excludes those with a connection through Regional networks or Regional Community Networks, with which many bodies are connected, thanks to the initiatives of the Regions.

To these bodies, a limited number of accesses to the SPC concentrated in the Regional hub is provided.

113. Veneto is the Region which has the largest number of local administrations that have autonomously joined the SPC (78), followed by Sicilia (63) and Lombardia (56).

The smallest number of direct agreements refers to the local administrations of Molise, Valle d'Aosta and Emilia-Romagna.

It is worthwhile recalling that these data do not reflect the deployment of SPC at the local level because bodies are connected to the Regional networks and to the community networks set up by the Regions that comply with the SPC/ICAR model.

114. The Public Cooperation System (SPCoop) is the enabling infrastructure for integration of the information held by the administrations connected by the SPC.

The integration of the processes and data of the administrations, that cooperate on applications, occurs through the architectural interface instruments used by the different systems and organizations to present and share their data and services.

Through the deployment of the SPCoop a single infrastructure is therefore obtained which is based on shared standards that enable citizens and companies to have an integrated view of the services of the central and local Public Administrations irrespective of the delivery channel.

115. A fundamental step for joining the Public Cooperation System is the qualification of the applicant's domain gateway, a component through which access is provided to the application domain of the Administration, in order to use its services and that acts as gateway to the data and services available in the domain; it is also the exit gateway from the domain to access external services.

In particular, a domain gateway traces the boundary of responsibility of an administrative body and contains all the applications that it manages.

In the Central Public Administrations there are 39 qualified domain gateways.

116. Almost all Regions have a domain gateway. In 13 cases, the gateway operates and is qualified in accordance with SPCoop specifications, whereas in 3 Regions qualification procedures are under way.

It must also be pointed out that also the Regions which do not have a domain gateway take part in the ICAR project which defines the basic aspects of the infrastructure according to the SPC model, also for the aspects related to cooperation on applications.[62]

§6. Post Offices Connectivity

117. There is, currently, a very interesting project in Italy concerning broadband installed in 1,000 post offices pursuant to a memorandum of understanding signed by the former Ministry of Communications together with other private companies (Poste Italiane, Infratel and Sviluppo Italia). Among these, 150 were equipped with optical fibres by means of an agreement with Telecom Italia, and the remaining 850 linked by wireless mode.

The *Italian Post Office Certified Mail* offers a service, through which citizens can communicate with the Public Administration and send and receive documents of public importance.

Documents may be obtained, petitions may be sent and practices may be conducted by connecting to the Internet, without the need to go to public offices.

Basic services for citizens are free and for professionals (e.g., lawyers) are provided for fixed rates.

118. There are other telematic services very useful to the citizen as, for example, the so-called Input Voltage (through which the citizen can see in real time the physical location of any parcel or letter connecting to the website of the post office) and the ability to do different tasks (such as *complaints*) online.

A recent project was started to equip the Italian Post Office workstations of free Wi-Fi hot spot.

Initially, 22 post offices were equipped with Wi-Fi network where people could access from their laptop or smartphone by completing a short form of access. Now, the service has been expanded and more post offices are provided with a Wi-Fi connection available to the public (<*www.posteitaliane.it*>).

§7. The Wi-Fi Decree

119. The former Minister for Communications issued a Decree, in 2005 (Ministerial Decree of 4 October 2005) with a programme to extend Wi-Fi to the whole territory of the Country.

The Decree aimed to create the conditions for companies to invest and allowed for programme interventions; from a technical point of view, Wi-Fi works on frequencies from the 2.4 GHz to the 5 GHz range, in accordance with the Italian National Frequency Allotment Plan.

---

62. *See* the Digital Agenda Italy e-Gov Report of 2010 drafted by the Department for Digitization of Public Administration and Technological Innovation, at the address http://www.digitpa.gov.it/.

120. The Decree enabled the connection of access points belonging to the same and different providers, in accordance with interconnections rules; however, network security against non-authorized access and services for the pursuit of justice must be guaranteed.

Different providers were able to make roaming agreements, similar to those of mobile telephone services providers.

121. On 26 July 2005, it was also issued the so-called *Pisanu Decree* (Law Decree n. 144/2005), presented as antiterrorism legislation and providing stringent regulations on the use of the network.

The Decree established that anyone wishing to open an 'Internet point', but not limited to (any private club or public house in which are made available equipment and terminals used for communications, including data transmission), should ask for the *licence* to the commissioner, in addition to write a communication to the Ministry.

122. In addition, the project envisaged a rigorous process of *identifying* the user along with other stringent requirements: the operator must take delivery of an identity document, photocopy and transcript of records of the data received. What is more, the tenant had to store and maintain data on the date and time of the connection (log files) and the type of service used.

123. In 2012, the Decree was not extended, then it is considered to be repealed.

However, for operators of 'Internet point' some formalities are still necessary if they want to accomplish a Wi-Fi area. For example, they have to fill a request to the Ministry as a Wireless Internet Service Provider and request a frequency too.

124. In addition to this, in 2013 Article 10 of the so-called *Decreto del Fare* (Decree n 69/2013 converted into Law 98/2013) provided that all obligations have fallen for business, shops and restaurant owners offering Wi-Fi to the public.

Liberalization is envisaged 'when the offer of Internet access does not constitute the predominant commercial activity of the service operator'.

Therefore, not only any operator, shop, hotel, restaurant, but also any Public Administration, can liberally set up a hot spot, connect it to the Internet and offer such service to the public, without having to track users, their connections, provide accounts and passwords or ask for permissions.

§8. The Development of Connectivity in the South of Italy

125. The Government's commitment for the last ten years to spread new technologies in the South of Italy is proceeding.

126. To bridge the gap between different parts of Italy, various solutions were proposed. In 2009, a plan of Minister Romani (Deputy Minister for Economic Development) provided the possibility of extending broadband to 20 megabits to 96% of the population and the remainder to 2 megabits.

However, an investment of EUR 800 million was necessary and the Government stopped the plan, not being considered a priority at that time.

On 3 March 2015, the Council of Ministers approved the 'Italian strategy for the Ultra-broadband' with the aim of filling the country's digital delay both on the infrastructural and on the services level, in line with the objectives of the European Digital Agenda. In May 2015, *Infratel* Italia launched a consultation to update the map of the availability of Ultra-Broadband connectivity. Italy has thus been divided into two distinct clusters: areas on which operators have expressed an interest in investing directly and areas on which it is considered necessary to finance interventions with public funds.

As part of this strategy, the Government promoted the development of ultra-broadband through the simplification of the regulatory framework, the creation of new drivers for development, the use of tax incentives and the reduction of installation costs.

127. Another solution lies in the fibre optic technology. After Sicily, additional kilometres of fibre optic network enabled Campania, Puglia and Calabria to improve significantly in the telecommunications field, reducing their infrastructural gap with other areas of the Country.

Currently, Campania has a fibre optic network coverage of 41% of its municipalities. It is therefore second in the ranking: better only did Calabria, with its 57% coverage of optical fibre network. Puglia and Sicily are also doing very well (35% and 33% respectively). In third place, one can find Tuscany, with a 36% coverage.

128. The Wi-Max may be another less 'invasive' way, but in addition to a delay in its development than the European average (the few frequencies dedicated to this technology were, until recently, preserve of the Ministry of Defence), the antennas are located so far from useful areas.

§9. The National Broadband Ultra-Wide Band Plan

129. The Ministry of Economic Development announced recently the continuation of the *National Broadband Plan*, which is being implemented through its in-house company *Infratel Italia* for the executive design and creation of fibre optic infrastructure for broadband networks.

The total amount for the work exceeds EUR 69 million and is part of a measure involving an investment of over EUR 95 million for the provision of broadband services, through the construction of a 2,000-km fibre optic network covering over 400 municipal and sub-municipal areas, mainly in high-density rural areas and industrial estates – benefitting over 358,000 citizens.

130. There are several ongoing projects in which the State seeks to commit to spread and develop broadband in the Country, all linked to NGN (*New Generation Networks*) and the *Digital Italy Plan* founded in 2010.

In these projects are included:

(i) the Italian and European Digital Agenda;
(ii) the ISBUL Research Programme ('Infrastructure and Services in Broadband and Ultra-Wide'), a project that consists of three levels (technological, economic and legal) and has for its object the search of ways and means to develop broadband in the Country;
(iii) the NRP (National Reform Programme), a project played at State and Regional level and with the support of telecom operators and that contains two more projects: (i) bridging the digital divide and (ii) establishing, by 2020, ultra-fast networks and fixed-line, for least 50% of the population, both on the mobile network (in the most densely populated areas).

131. From a legal point of view, Law Decree n. 112/2008 was one of the first norms enacted to *simplify*, for operators, procedures for carrying out works on the electronic infrastructure such as the installation of fibre optic networks, UMTS, buildings and public facilities.

It also disciplined urgent provisions for economic development, simplification, competitiveness and the stabilization of public finance and tax equalization.

Law n. 69/2009, then, contained simplifications, at the operational level, for the siting of new facilities and infrastructure.

Law 18 June 2009, n. 69, finally, had provisions for economic development, simplification, competitiveness and the so-called civil trial and the 'electronic justice'.

132. On 3 March 2015, Italian Government has approved the *Italian Strategy for Ultra-Wide Band* with the goal of reducing the existing infrastructural gap with the creation of conditions favourable for the integrated development of fixed and mobile telecommunications infrastructures. This strategy has in the European Digital Agenda its framework (<http://bandaultralarga.italia.it/piano-bul/strategia/>).

133. The targets of the Italian Strategy for Ultra-Wide Band are:

(i) coverage with speeds of at least 100 Mbps for 85% of Italian citizens;
(ii) coverage with speeds of at least 30 Mbps for the rest of the population;
(iii) coverage with speeds of at least 100 Mbps for public buildings (schools, hospitals, etc.), for area of major interest from an economical perspective, for area with greater concentration of population, for industrial areas and for the most important logistic and touristic areas.

134. The *Italian Strategy for Ultra-Wide Band* is in line with the new targets 20125 of the European Commission set out in the Communication COM(2016)-587 'Connectivity for a Competitive Digital Single Market – Towards a European Gigabit Society' of 14 September 2016.

§10. The Digital and Connectivity Market in Italy

135. In these last two years, the market has started to grow again.

After a 2.3% increase in 2017, to EUR 68,722 million, the Italian digital market promises to grow again: 2.3% in 2018, 2.8% in 2019 and 3.1% in 2020.
These latest projections discount the continuation of national innovation stimulus plans and from now to 2020 indicate a compound average annual growth rate of the entire market of 2.7%.[63]

136. The expected progression (in constant conditions) combines two dynamics:

(i) contained for the area of the ICT most settled (2017-2020 to +0.9%) and
(ii) very lively for the most innovative, that of the Digital Enablers (+16.5%), with the IoT, the Cloud, Cybersecurity, Mobile Business and similar technologies.[64]

137. The ICT Services sector, which reached EUR 11,057 million in 2017, promises sustained growth (2017-2020 of 5.3%), thanks to the boost of development, system integration and consulting services (linked to the adoption of new tools and solutions), and the strong dynamics of cloud services (2017-2020 to +20.3%).[65]

138. Always on equal terms, the expected progress from the software and ICT solutions segment is even more sustained (2017-2020 of +7.3%) and is attributable primarily to the IoT, big data and social network application products, to middleware and the IT management & governance, information management and security components.[66]

139. The digital content and advertising (2018-2020 of 7.7%), driven by entertainment content, are among the drivers of the growth of the digital market.[67]

140. The devices and systems (2017-2020 of 2.2%) should be affected by the growth of IaaS services and a transversal slowdown to personal computers, printers and tablets, contrasted however by the performance of the components associated

---

63. *See* Anitec Assinform Report about the digital market in Italy in 2018 (http://www.assinform.it/sala_stampa/dati-di-mercato-ict/anitecassinform/dati-di-sintesi-rapporto-anitec-assinform-il-mercato-digitale-in-italia-2018.kl).
64. *See* Anitec Assinform Report about the digital market in Italy in 2018 (http://www.assinform.it/sala_stampa/dati-di-mercato-ict/anitecassinform/dati-di-sintesi-rapporto-anitec-assinform-il-mercato-digitale-in-italia-2018.kl).
65. *See* Anitec Assinform Report about the digital market in Italy in 2018 (http://www.assinform.it/sala_stampa/dati-di-mercato-ict/anitecassinform/dati-di-sintesi-rapporto-anitec-assinform-il-mercato-digitale-in-italia-2018.kl).
66. *See* Anitec Assinform Report about the digital market in Italy in 2018 (http://www.assinform.it/sala_stampa/dati-di-mercato-ict/anitecassinform/dati-di-sintesi-rapporto-anitec-assinform-il-mercato-digitale-in-italia-2018.kl).
67. *See* Anitec Assinform Report about the digital market in Italy in 2018 (http://www.assinform.it/sala_stampa/dati-di-mercato-ict/anitecassinform/dati-di-sintesi-rapporto-anitec-assinform-il-mercato-digitale-in-italia-2018.kl).

with the new digital paradigms, high band servers, storage and networking equipment, mobile devices (+8.3%) and wearable devices (wearable, +29%).[68]

141. In the network services (2017-2020 of -2.2%), both the mobile network, especially the voice component, and the fixed network are slowing down, slowed down by the decline in voice services.

However, connectivity and data transmission services linked to the cloud and mobile applications are growing.[69]

142. All sectors, except for the Public Administration, recorded an increase in digital demand in 2017, expected to accelerate from now until 2020.[70]

143. Still in constant conditions, the average annual growth rate 2017-2020 of business demand will be 4.3% (against +0.6% of consumer demand) with peaks of 6.5% in utilities and around 6% in supply chains that integrate industry, distribution and services, thanks to projects guided above all by IoT, wearable, AI / cognitive and big data.

They will follow with over 5% banks and insurance / finance and transport, with priority focus on mobility, AI / cognitive and security (in insurance also IoT and big data).

Changes in the environment should slow down investments in the telco / media area, which will nevertheless maintain appreciable dynamics (2017-2020 at +2.3%) with a focus on cloud, security and big data.

In the public sphere, in the absence of further stimuli, dynamism is expected only for healthcare (2017-2020 at +3.1%), while the digital demand for central and local Public Administration is estimated in trouble (2017-2020 flat and -0.4% respectively), despite the cloud, security and big data push.[71]

144. Banks and telco / media are the sectors most oriented to digital transformation in a strategic key, through the redesign of processes.

---

68. *See* Anitec Assinform Report about the digital market in Italy in 2018 (http://www.assinform.it/sala_stampa/dati-di-mercato-ict/anitecassinform/dati-di-sintesi-rapporto-anitec-assinform-il-mercato-digitale-in-italia-2018.kl).
69. *See* Anitec Assinform Report about the digital market in Italy in 2018 (http://www.assinform.it/sala_stampa/dati-di-mercato-ict/anitecassinform/dati-di-sintesi-rapporto-anitec-assinform-il-mercato-digitale-in-italia-2018.kl).
70. *See* Anitec Assinform Report about the digital market in Italy in 2018 (http://www.assinform.it/sala_stampa/dati-di-mercato-ict/anitecassinform/dati-di-sintesi-rapporto-anitec-assinform-il-mercato-digitale-in-italia-2018.kl).
71. *See* Anitec Assinform Report about the digital market in Italy in 2018 (http://www.assinform.it/sala_stampa/dati-di-mercato-ict/anitecassinform/dati-di-sintesi-rapporto-anitec-assinform-il-mercato-digitale-in-italia-2018.kl).

Follow on the same line insurance, industry and energy and utility. The same applies to distribution, services, logistics and transport, but only for larger companies. In contrast, the Public Administration, while having a systemic plan, is slowed down by financial, regulatory and cultural constraints.[72]

145. Concerning the connectivity and broadband market in Italy, in April 2018 the real estate units reached by the ultra-wide band were 52.4% against the target of 71% at the end of 2018. The highest coverage is in Lombardy, even for 100 Mbps with 18.8%.

The latest surveys envisage a 2020 scenario with an increase in white areas (unattractive to operators) up to 8.2% of real estate units, an overall coverage of 24% for the ultra-wide band at one Gb and 38% for the ultra-wide band at 30 Mbps.[73]

146. To give equal opportunities to the different areas of the country, public support for infrastructure investments in white and grey areas (with only one operator present) should include stimulating demand for value-added services on ultra-fast connectivity.

This area now includes the Business Plan 4.0, the Italia Wi-Fi project and the testing of services in 5G. The 5G take-off is expected around 2022, with significant coverage starting in 2023.[74]

147. Also, Digital Public Administration projects have started but are not yet in line with expectations.

The progress of the various projects of the Digital Public Administration is very heterogeneous.

SPID, the Public Digital Identity System, in March 2018, involved over 4,000 central and local Administrations, but with no more than 2.3 million digital identities issued;

Concerning PagoPA (the public payment system), in March 2018 there were 16,000 subscriptions, but with too few transactions (just over 7 million, against a target of 50 million for 2018 and 150 million for 2020).

Concerning the diffusion of open data, the objective has already been reached in terms of the Administrations involved.

---

72. *See* Anitec Assinform Report about the digital market in Italy in 2018 (http://www.assinform.it/sala_stampa/dati-di-mercato-ict/anitecassinform/dati-di-sintesi-rapporto-anitec-assinform-il-mercato-digitale-in-italia-2018.kl).
73. *See* Anitec Assinform Report about the digital market in Italy in 2018 (http://www.assinform.it/sala_stampa/dati-di-mercato-ict/anitecassinform/dati-di-sintesi-rapporto-anitec-assinform-il-mercato-digitale-in-italia-2018.kl).
74. *See* Anitec Assinform Report about the digital market in Italy in 2018 (http://www.assinform.it/sala_stampa/dati-di-mercato-ict/anitecassinform/dati-di-sintesi-rapporto-anitec-assinform-il-mercato-digitale-in-italia-2018.kl).

The Electronic Health Record, again in March 2018, was already operational in 17 Regions (of 20 by 2020). A total of 25% of the clients had activated the service (2020 target of 70%) for coverage on the total number of reports issued of 43%.[75]

148. The latest AGCOM surveys[76] (June 2018, with detailed procedures, based on 360 thousand census sections) say that 5.6 percent of the population in Italy has no ADSL coverage (since it could be halved if we include fixed wireless access coverage, of which, however, not there are official maps), to which you can add a 2.37 percent of people that is covered but does not reach 2 Megabits.

Coverage from 30 Megabits up (Vdsl2-fibre up to cabinets or fibre in homes) is 60.6 percent. Other disclosed data are more generous because they are based on aggregate-approximate methodology.

The ultra-wide broadband (500 gigabit) covers 10.4 percent of the population. The figures drop if we consider the coverage on civic numbers: 92 per cent ADSL, 577 per cent on VDSL, 29.3 per cent in Evdsl, 4.5 per cent on Ftth.

149. In 2017, the Authority for Communications Guarantees adopted the first Italian system for mapping access networks (fixed and mobile) to the Internet, namely the Broadbandmap.[77]

Based on the provisions of Law no. 9/2014 (the so-called Save Italy decree), the AGCOM has made available to all an interactive map that can be consulted from either a fixed or mobile location via a smartphone or tablet, to gather extremely detailed information on the existing infrastructures and on the services available on the entire national territory.

150. The BroadbandMap is a simple, intuitive and interactive tool that enables each user to independently analyse at any time the development status of the network access offer relative to their residential address as well as perform comparative evaluations on the various technologies and speeds available.

The portal provides statistically processed data on coverage (in copper, fibre optic, wireless technology, on 2G, 3G and 4G cellular networks) and on the speed of networks (copper and optical fibre) as well as on the number of internet subscriptions (national, regional, provincial and municipal).

§11. The Internet of Things Market in Italy

151. The Italian Internet of Things market continues to grow rapidly even in 2018, reaching the value of EUR 5 billion, with an increase of 35% compared to

75. *See* Anitec Assinform Report about the digital market in Italy in 2018 (http://www.assinform.it/sala_stampa/dati-di-mercato-ict/anitecassinform/dati-di-sintesi-rapporto-anitec-assinform-il-mercato-digitale-in-italia-2018.kl).
76. *See* https://www.agcom.it.
77. *See* https://www.agcom.it/mappatura-delle-reti-di-accesso-ad-internet.

2017, driven both by applications that exploit the 'traditional' cellular connectivity (EUR 2.8 billion, +27%) and from those that use other communication technologies (EUR 2.2 billion, +47%).[78]

The growth of the Italian market is in line with that of the other Western Countries, where it fluctuates between +25% and +40%, driven above all by services enabled by connected objects that now cover 36% of the market, equal to EUR 1.8 billion of and up to 44% over the previous year.

152. The Smart Metering and Smart Asset Management solutions for utilities are confirmed as the main segment of the Internet of Things, with 28% of the market and a value of EUR 1.4 billion (+45%), mainly due to obligations regulations that led to the installation in 2018 of four million connected gas meters and 5.2 million of second-generation smart electricity meters.

The second most developed area is the Smart Cars, which are worth just over a billion and represent 21% of the market (+37%), with 14 million connected vehicles, a third of the car fleet circulating in Italy.

Connected vehicles are in 69% of cases equipped with GPS / GPRS boxes for locating and recording driving parameters for insurance purposes, but growth is mainly driven by natively connected cars (31%): 70% of vehicles registered in 2018 it is equipped with a SIM or Bluetooth connection system since production.[79]

153. Followed by applications for the Smart Building (EUR 600 million, +15%), mainly for video surveillance and management of energy consumption within the building, IoT solutions for logistics are used for the management of company fleets and for satellite burglar alarms (465 million, +29%) and Smart City solutions (395 million, +24%).

Then comes Smart Home (380 million), the area with the highest growth, equal to +52%, Smart Asset Management applications (270 million, 25%), the Smart Factory (250 million, +40%) and smart agriculture (EUR 100 million, 2% of the market).[80]

---

78. These are the main results of the Research of the Internet of Things Observatory of the School of Management of the Politecnico di Milano, presented this morning in Milan at the conference 'Happy Birthday Internet (of Things)'. https://www.osservatori.net/it_it/osservatori/internet-of-things. A summary is at the address https://www.corrierecomunicazioni.it/digital-economy/iot-in-italia-il-mercato-vola-a-5-miliardi-di-euro-35/.
79. These are the main results of the Research of the Internet of Things Observatory of the School of Management of the Politecnico di Milano, presented this morning in Milan at the conference 'Happy Birthday Internet (of Things)'. https://www.osservatori.net/it_it/osservatori/internet-of-things. A summary is at the address https://www.corrierecomunicazioni.it/digital-economy/iot-in-italia-il-mercato-vola-a-5-miliardi-di-euro-35/.
80. These are the main results of the Research of the Internet of Things Observatory of the School of Management of the Politecnico di Milano, presented this morning in Milan at the conference 'Happy Birthday Internet (of Things)'. https://www.osservatori.net/it_it/osservatori/internet-of-things. A summary is at the address https://www.corrierecomunicazioni.it/digital-economy/iot-in-italia-il-mercato-vola-a-5-miliardi-di-euro-35/.

154. The IoT solutions offer is very dynamic and in continuous development also, thanks to start-ups. A total of 665 new innovative companies are active internationally, of which 540 are financed by institutional investors, for a total of 13.5 billion dollars in funding collected in the 2016-18 three-year period and an average investment of 43 million dollars in 2018 (+67% compared to 2017, +114% compared to 2016).[81]

155. As mentioned, the segments that record the most significant growth are the Smart Home (+52%), driven by the speaker for the connected home, and the Industrial IoT (+40%), thanks also to the incentives provided by the National Industry 4.0 Plan.

Smart Asset Management applications are growing by 25% in contexts other than utilities, mainly for monitoring gambling machines used for gambling, elevators and vending machines.

The Smart City also recorded a good growth rate (+24%) with consolidated applications such as security, public transport, lighting and new waste collection projects, parking management and monitoring of environmental parameters.[82]

156. According to the observatory forecasts, the growth of the Italian IoT market will continue also in 2019, concentrated mainly in the Smart Metering, Smart Car, Smart Home and Industrial IoT segments.

In the coming months, another 4 million smart meters will be installed, along with 5.8 million second-generation electricity meters.

Furthermore, starting from the end of 2020, also the newly installed heat meters must be remotely manageable and from 2027 the obligation will concern all the meters in use.[83]

157. There will also be significant growth in Smart Cars, with entry into force in March 2018 for new approvals of the obligation linked to eCall (automatic alert to activate rescue services in the event of an accident) and for the offer new services enabled by connectivity, such as preventive maintenance based on component monitoring and the integration of smart speakers in cars, which will allow users to interact with their vehicle via voice.

---

81. These are the main results of the Research of the Internet of Things Observatory of the School of Management of the Politecnico di Milano, presented this morning in Milan at the conference 'Happy Birthday Internet (of Things)'. https://www.osservatori.net/it_it/osservatori/internet-of-things. A summary is at the address https://www.corrierecomunicazioni.it/digital-economy/iot-in-italia-il-mercato-vola-a-5-miliardi-di-euro-35/.
82. These are the main results of the Research of the Internet of Things Observatory of the School of Management of the Politecnico di Milano, presented this morning in Milan at the conference 'Happy Birthday Internet (of Things)'. https://www.osservatori.net/it_it/osservatori/internet-of-things. A summary is at the address https://www.corrierecomunicazioni.it/digital-economy/iot-in-italia-il-mercato-vola-a-5-miliardi-di-euro-35/.
83. These are the main results of the Research of the Internet of Things Observatory of the School of Management of the Politecnico di Milano, presented this morning in Milan at the conference 'Happy Birthday Internet (of Things)'. https://www.osservatori.net/it_it/osservatori/internet-of-things. A summary is at the address https://www.corrierecomunicazioni.it/digital-economy/iot-in-italia-il-mercato-vola-a-5-miliardi-di-euro-35/.

On the independent driving front, we are still in the experimental phase: Modena and Turin are among the first cities that, during 2018, allowed companies to start testing these solutions in Italy as well.[84]

158. Voice assistants will also be the main driver of the growth of Smart Home solutions, with large investments in marketing promoted by the arrival on the Ott market and with the driving effect on the sale of other smart items for the home.

Finally, the Industrial IoT will benefit from the incentives for training, super-amortization and hyper-amortization provided for in the latest Budget law, with attention shifted from large companies to SMEs, which have so far made less use of tax advantages.

In 2019 there is also expected to be an evolution of projects initiated by large companies, especially in terms of the use of the data collected, which are still little used compared to their potential.[85]

159. The most common applications are mainly related to factory management (Smart Factory, 62% of cases) for real-time production control and preventive or predictive maintenance, followed by those supporting logistics (Smart Logistics, 27%), focused on the traceability of assets within the warehouse and along the supply chain, and by the Smart Lifecycle (11%), for the optimization of the process of developing new models and updating products.

More than half of the projects (58%) are still in the pilot or preliminary analysis phase.

One of the main directions of development of the Industrial IoT is the analysis and management of the collected data, but only 33% of the sample has already started to do so (and whoever does it is always satisfied with the benefits).[86]

160. The main factors that drive companies to start Industrial IoT projects are the possibility of obtaining efficiency (75%) and effectiveness (58%) benefits, but there are still many companies that indicate the lack of skills as barriers to adoption (59%) and the ability to understand a priori the value of the solutions offered (51%).

84. These are the main results of the Research of the Internet of Things Observatory of the School of Management of the Politecnico di Milano, presented this morning in Milan at the conference 'Happy Birthday Internet (of Things)'. https://www.osservatori.net/it_it/osservatori/internet-of-things. A summary is at the address https://www.corrierecomunicazioni.it/digital-economy/iot-in-italia-il-mercato-vola-a-5-miliardi-di-euro-35/.
85. These are the main results of the Research of the Internet of Things Observatory of the School of Management of the Politecnico di Milano, presented this morning in Milan at the conference 'Happy Birthday Internet (of Things)'. https://www.osservatori.net/it_it/osservatori/internet-of-things. A summary is at the address https://www.corrierecomunicazioni.it/digital-economy/iot-in-italia-il-mercato-vola-a-5-miliardi-di-euro-35/.
86. These are the main results of the Research of the Internet of Things Observatory of the School of Management of the Politecnico di Milano, presented this morning in Milan at the conference 'Happy Birthday Internet (of Things)'. https://www.osservatori.net/it_it/osservatori/internet-of-things. A summary is at the address https://www.corrierecomunicazioni.it/digital-economy/iot-in-italia-il-mercato-vola-a-5-miliardi-di-euro-35/.

Despite this, only 39% of companies intend to develop IoT skills in the future through the hiring of specialized staff or appropriate training programmes aimed at employees already present in the company.[87]

161. Moving on to the topic of Smart City, over one Italian municipality in three (36%) has launched at least one project in the last three years (2016-2018), down 15% compared to the three-year period 2014-2016. A total of 80% of the projects stop at the testing phase, but at the same time, the willingness to adopt more innovative solutions that bring tangible benefits to the communities emerges.

This is revealed by the survey conducted by the Observatory on 112 Italian municipalities with more than 15,000 inhabitants.[88]

162. The lack of skills is the first barrier to launching Smart City projects, indicated by 65% of the sample, followed by a lack of economic resources (62%).

Municipalities have little knowledge of technological innovations and are not aware of how to exploit them in the supply of valuable services: 60% do not know of the existence of LPT IoT networks, suitable for their characteristics to support applications for Smart City. The third most frequent barrier is the difficulty of coordination between the different actors involved within a Smart City project (27%).[89]

§12. Italy in the Global Connectivity Index of 2018

163. Italy ranked 28th in GCI 2018. Fibre optic supply is relatively lagging behind for Italy and computer household experienced a drop of 1 point this year.[90]

Italy has one of the highest mobile usage per capita ratios in the world, but Italy's powerful 4G networks are hindered by their lack of coverage.

There are signs of improvement as the Country's biggest operators expand their LTE footprints, brings expanded 4G coverage, increase smartphone penetration rate, faster broadband download speed and improved Mbb affordability.

87. These are the main results of the Research of the Internet of Things Observatory of the School of Management of the Politecnico di Milano, presented this morning in Milan at the conference 'Happy Birthday Internet (of Things)'. https://www.osservatori.net/it_it/osservatori/internet-of-things. A summary is at the address https://www.corrierecomunicazioni.it/digital-economy/iot-in-italia-il-mercato-vola-a-5-miliardi-di-euro-35/.
88. These are the main results of the Research of the Internet of Things Observatory of the School of Management of the Politecnico di Milano, presented this morning in Milan at the conference 'Happy Birthday Internet (of Things)'. https://www.osservatori.net/it_it/osservatori/internet-of-things. A summary is at the address https://www.corrierecomunicazioni.it/digital-economy/iot-in-italia-il-mercato-vola-a-5-miliardi-di-euro-35/.
89. These are the main results of the Research of the Internet of Things Observatory of the School of Management of the Politecnico di Milano, presented this morning in Milan at the conference 'Happy Birthday Internet (of Things)'. https://www.osservatori.net/it_it/osservatori/internet-of-things. A summary is at the address https://www.corrierecomunicazioni.it/digital-economy/iot-in-italia-il-mercato-vola-a-5-miliardi-di-euro-35/.
90. *See* https://www.huawei.com/minisite/gci/en/country-profile-it.html.

More investment is required to serve the growing subscriber base, which is especially important given that the Government would enclose more people in rural areas in the digital plan.

Italy has also showed increased in its investment in cloud computing over the year.

164. Concerning opportunities, the Report states that Italy Government approved its three-year digital transformation plan, coordinating some EUR 4.6 billion in e-government actions whereby the goal is to make Public Administrations more efficient and place the citizen at the centre.

The plan defines the reference model for public sector ICT, and a strategy for digital transformation where it should result in significant ICT cost savings, as well as investments in innovation and development.

Public services will be made available for citizens and businesses accessible in an easy manner, via a mobile first approach, with reliable, scalable and fault-tolerant architectures, based on clearly defined APIs.[91]

165. The plan supports the different central and local government departments in making the best and most data-driven decisions, thanks to the adoption of big data and machine learning techniques.

It will coordinate the different Government and stakeholders to manage existing and future digital programmes in an integrated manner with an agile methodology and an open data approach and at the same time identify new digital and technology transformation initiatives.[92]

166. However, Italy needs to address its severe digital skills gap.

Digital skills are nowadays needed in every sector, but the fact is that only half of the Italian population possess digital skills at an adequate level.

This can be an important barrier to the Country's economic development. Italy has also a low percentage of population with a STEM (science, technology, engineering and mathematics) degree, which hinders the nation to be an advanced high technology economy.[93]

---

91. *See* https://www.huawei.com/minisite/gci/en/country-profile-it.html.
92. *See* https://www.huawei.com/minisite/gci/en/country-profile-it.html.
93. *See* https://www.huawei.com/minisite/gci/en/country-profile-it.html.

Chapter 3. The Information and Communications Technology Market

§1. The Story and the Evolution of the Italian ICT and Communications Market

167. The evolution of the ICT market in Italy has been affected, in the last fifteen years, both by *internal* factors (the regulatory framework, the preferences of users and consumers and the information policy adopted by the Government) and by *external* factors (especially the global economic crisis).[94]

Data concerning market trends are usually made public by the *industry associations*, which are monitoring the economic performance of all sectors, which constitute the multifaceted field of national ICT.

168. From a general and preliminary point of view, after a heavy negative performance in the years 2009 and 2010, and after the global economic crisis in 2011, the Italian ICT market registered, in 2011, an overall decline of 3.6% over the previous year, with the strongest contraction (–4.1%) recorded by the Information Technology sector itself and, in 2013, an overall decline of 4.4% over the previous year.[95]

169. From an international (and comparative) point of view, only Spain registered a market decrease of –5.3%, compared with an EU average of +0.5%. In France, market trends were positive (+0.3%), in Germany too (+2.3%) and in the UK there was, instead, a light negative trend of –0.7%.[96]

170. The big consultancy company SIRMI issued an interesting analysis of the Italian digital technology market for the first quarter of 2011, with provisions for 2012 too.[97]

In this study, the market maintained a negative trend (–2.5%) in comparison with the same period of the former year, owing to the persisting economic critical situation; no sign of recovery was expected, in this study, for the full year, and also for 2012.

---

94. For an overview of the typical Italian ICT market framework *see*, *generally*, A. Sterlacchini, 'ICT, mercato del lavoro, produttività' (Carocci, Roma, 2005).
95. *See* the ISTAT (Italian National Institute of Statistics), annual and sectoral reports for 2011, 2012 and 2013, on the Internet at the address http://www.istat.it. *See also*, Digital Technology Italian Market Trends on the Internet at the address http://emi-group.com/news/2011_06_14_digital-technology.php, and the ASSINFORM reports on the Internet at the address http://www.areeriservate.assinform.it/Site_in_English/I_Dati_In_Inglese/Anteprima/ and ISTAT Statistics for the Year 2013 http://www.istat.it.
96. *See* the ISTAT (Italian National Institute of Statistics), annual and sectoral reports for 2011 and 2012, on the Internet at the address http://www.istat.it and ISTAT Statistics for the Year 2013 http://www.istat.it.
97. *See* http://www.sirmi.it.

According to SIRMI, in the first quarter of 2011, ICT market trend in Italy was negative due to the critical economic and financial moment and the consequent reduction of propulsion to expense by families and enterprises.

ICT market registered a total end user contraction of –2.5%, and all IT market sectors decreased, with the exception of software, that showed a flat trend. Services was the category with the strongest decrease, especially management services (–2.8%) and development services (–5.9%).

171. The first quarter of 2011 closed with a total decrease of –2.3% in terms of end user expenses; in particular, the TLC fixed maintained a strong negative trend (–4.1%).

172. Finally, according to ASSINFORM[98] ('Italian Association of Information & Communication Technology') reports and studies, in 2013 information technology in Italy recorded a setback and a negative growth rate was recorded (–4.4%).[99]

ASSINFORM data confirmed the major uncertainty faced by the IT sector in Italy: the national economic scenario was not providing the necessary driving force for the IT sector to overcome the difficulties faced due to the global crisis.

Alongside a positive growth by software (+0.4%), in the last five years there was a loss in hardware (–2.1%), in IT services (–1.5%), in TLC (–4.2%), in TLC Services (–3.8%) and in equipment (–5.9%).

The main problem was a big delay in the digitalization process in Italy compared to other EU Countries, with major differences among Regions.[100]

173. Software segment, digital contents and advertising and cloud computing services were the *only* IT segment in Italy showing a positive growth in the last ten years.

The innovative segment of telecommunication services, which accounted for 30% of the total, supported demand for new information technologies, as, finally, *cloud computing*, which was worth EUR 130 million.

Results in the telecommunications sector were still affected by delays in investment in new infrastructures and, above all, by dropping prices due to an increasingly fierce competition among operators.

A 4.2% drop was recorded by the TLC market in the first quarter of 2011 compared to the same period in 2010.[101]

174. The situation in the IT market was different.

An interest in renewing ICT equipment and in new services was observed, but the interrelation with GDP was problematic.

---

98. *See* http://www.assinform.it.
99. *See* the ASSINFORM reports on the Internet at the address http://www.areeriservate.assinform.it/Site_in_English/I_Dati_In_Inglese/Anteprima/.
100. *See* the ASSINFORM reports on the Internet at the address http://www.areeriservate.assinform.it/Site_in_English/I_Dati_In_Inglese/Anteprima/.
101. *See* the ASSINFORM reports on the Internet at the address http://www.areeriservate.assinform.it/Site_in_English/I_Dati_In_Inglese/Anteprima/.

In fact, GDP at national level increased by 1% in the first quarter, below the European average and below the average in Countries with which Italy usually competes (i.e., Germany, +4.9%).

In the first quarter of 2011, gross fixed investment in Italy did not increase by more than 1.5%. This has had impacts on the IT market, which dropped by 1.3% in the first quarter. However, the trend started to improve, compared to the 2.9% drop in the first quarter of 2010 versus the first quarter in 2009.

Different results were recorded by the various segments: hardware, –2.1% (–2.3% in 2010/2009), software, +0.4% (–1.5% in 2010/2009), IT services, –1.5% (–3.8% in 2010/2009) and technical support –2.9% (–4.9% in 2010/2009).[102]

175. As far as the following years' forecasts are concerned, uncertainties at national and international level suggested two different scenarios:

(i) a pessimistic scenario, in which the situation would not change and the ICT market in Italy would continue to drop by about –4.5%.

Probably, the biggest decrease will be recorded by telecommunications (–5.8%), while a smaller drop could be expected in IT (–0.8%);

(ii) if we assume that the national economy will improve, and therefore the propensity to invest in innovation will increase, the ICT market should show a –0.1% growth rate in the next years, resulting from –0.6% in telecommunications and +1.3% in IT.[103]

176. Despite these negative predictions in the past, according to ASSINFORM, the Italian Digital Market in the last four years has restarted.

In 2016 it grew by 1.8%, exceeding EUR 66 billion and strengthening a recovery started at the end of 2015 after years of decline.

The projections for the next few years forecast a further improvement in growth rates.

It is the effect of a profound change in demand in all the main sectors, from finance to industry, to distribution to utilities.

177. Demand of the so-called Digital Enablers (IoT, Cybersecurity, Cloud, Big Data, Web and Mobile Services, 4.0 Industry) has been increasing in Italy.

These are the most innovative components, because they allow to do new things in terms of digital transformation. For this reason, the market associated with the main Digital Enablers is growing at double-digit rates.

This is because Digital Transformation is becoming a priority for Italian companies and the Public Administration, even if, in the case of companies, they have very different commitments depending on the sectors they belong to and their size.

---

102. *See* the ASSINFORM reports on the Internet at the address http://www.areeriservate.assinform.it/Site_in_English/I_Dati_In_Inglese/Anteprima/.

103. *See* the ASSINFORM reports and forecasts on the Internet at the address http://www.areeriservate.assinform.it/Site_in_English/I_Dati_In_Inglese/Anteprima/.

178. The investments attributable to the traditional ICT perimeter show a very low growth rate, substantially flat in 2016 and probably slightly higher between 2017 and 2019.

It should, however, be underlined that – compared to the previous years – the ICT market was characterized by a variegated recovery, which involved many hardware and software components (mainly Personal Computer, laptops and servers and traditional application platforms) with positive effects on the demand for professional services, primarily System Integration and Consulting.

More generally, technological investments are fuelled by the ferment of initiatives and projects in which the digital sector drives a redesign of processes across the entire company.

This is evidenced by the above-mentioned growing trend of the market associated with Digital Enablers.

This lays the foundations for a structural and continuous growth of the digital market.

179. The adoption of cloud architectures and the growing mobility of business users is determining an increase in the demand for connectivity and data transmission; the launch of initiatives related to big data, social networks and IoT leads to an increase in the demand for services for the implementation and management of new applications; the growing need for protection to companies and their technological assets and business leads to growth in investments in cybersecurity.

180. The growth of the software and ICT solutions market is particularly relevant in contexts in which big data, IoT and mobile business solutions are adopted, characterized by numerous areas of application depending on the business activities considered and the sectors to which the companies belong.

181. Differently, the situation related to cloud services is more negative: the affirmation of the SaaS (Software as a Service) model entails, in fact, a gradual reduction in the spending for the purchase of licences of cloud services, even if, at the moment, this is limited only to some specific areas.

182. Finally, the devices and systems sector (home & office devices, enterprise & specialized systems, personal & mobile devices, ICT infrastructures) appears to be eroded by the affirmation of cloud systems, although it seems clear that cloud architectures will replace only in few cases the total physical infrastructures of companies.

The impacts on the devices and systems market deriving from the adoption of other paradigms are attributable to the increase in demand for appliances and engineered systems (big data), control systems and connectivity services (IoT), mobile devices and transmission networks (mobile business), next-generation firewall, firewall router, access point (security).

183. Forecasts for the next three years confirm a progressively improving trend: between 2017 and 2018, the increase is expected to significantly exceed 2% (+2.3% in 2017 and +2.6% in 2018) and in 2019 it should reach 3%.[104]

§2. The ICT Market Trends in the Assintel Report 2019

184. The traditional (yearly) Assintel Report (a national association of ICT and Internet companies) is one of the most interesting marketing studies in Italy concerning new technologies.

According to this study, the past twelve months were those in which the threshold of EUR 30 billion was finally reached and even exceeded, albeit slightly, with an overall +0.7% compared to the market value of last year.

The best performances refer to software (up 4.7% compared to 2017) and IT services (which registered a +1.4%); while a slight drop is recorded, partly predictably, as regards both hardware and telecommunications services (which lost 1.4% and 2.2% respectively in 2018).[105]

185. The big players in the ICT market were above all large companies with over 250 employees (almost half of which are related to these) and operate in the world of industry (23%) and finance (21%).[106]

186. Not even the geographical distribution of investments drawn in the Report is surprising: Lazio, Lombardia and Piemonte have been, and will also be, the Italian big spenders for the near future, followed only at a distance by Regions such as Emilia Romagna.[107]

187. The gap between northern and southern Italy, if it exists, is however linked to the nature of the businesses and the economic context in which they operate.[108]

188. If the perspective is widened to a national dimension, moreover, just 8% of Italian companies have already achieved all the objectives of digitization, and almost a fifth has not yet defined any strategy.

---

104. 'Il digitale in Italia 2017', ASSINFORM at http://www.rapportoassinform.it/il-digitale-in-italia-2017/il-digitale-in-italia-2017.kl.

105. *See* the ICT Market Assintel Report 2019 at the address https://www.assintel.it/osservatori-2/assintel-report/assintel-report-2019/and a summary at the address https://www.insidemarketing.it/mercato-ict-in-italia-assintel-2019/.

106. *See* the ICT Market Assintel Report 2019 at the address https://www.assintel.it/osservatori-2/assintel-report/assintel-report-2019/and a summary at the address https://www.insidemarketing.it/mercato-ict-in-italia-assintel-2019/.

107. *See* the ICT Market Assintel Report 2019 at the address https://www.assintel.it/osservatori-2/assintel-report/assintel-report-2019/and a summary at the address https://www.insidemarketing.it/mercato-ict-in-italia-assintel-2019/.

108. *See* the ICT Market Assintel Report 2019 at the address https://www.assintel.it/osservatori-2/assintel-report/assintel-report-2019/and a summary at the address https://www.insidemarketing.it/mercato-ict-in-italia-assintel-2019/.

The obstacles that prevent the ICT market in Italy from performing better are soft and linked to the corporate culture, rather than to economic questions.

According to Assintel, in fact, first of all there is a lack of digital skills (a response valid for 33% of the questions made to the market operators) and a real interest in the theme of digital innovation (27%), and only in the second place there is the fact that the economic-financial resources are limited (24%).[109]

189. The trends and forecasts for 2019 regarding the ICT market in Italy, among other things, appear to be positive.

Over the next twelve months, investments should increase, recording an overall growth of at least 1.6%.[110]

190. Once again, the IT market should be the driving force behind growth.

It is self-evident, according to the Report, that the big issues and the big areas of development will be cloud, big data analytics, technologies related to cybersecurity or AI and augmented reality.[111]

191. According to Assintel, those who invested in innovation technologies during 2019 are focusing primarily on automating or optimizing IT processes and on reducing and controlling costs, as well as improving service quality and time.

Regardless of the nature of the business and its size – and, that is, regardless of whether they are large companies or small- and medium-sized companies – the ICT market in Italy is already driven today, and will be even more so in the near future, by subjects that in the digital transformation *see* above all the opportunity to improve the relationship with customers (between the macro-objectives of 45% of the Assintel sample) or the levels of internal automation (42%) and that of differentiating themselves from competitors (26%).[112]

192. In 2019 the change in ICT spending will be substantial, especially for small enterprises and microenterprises (for subjects like these, in fact, an increase of over 78% compared to previous surveys is expected), just to underline how digital transformation represents a driver growth today everything except negligible.[113]

---

109. *See* the ICT Market Assintel Report 2019 at the address https://www.assintel.it/osservatori-2/assintel-report/assintel-report-2019/and a summary at the address https://www.insidemarketing.it/mercato-ict-in-italia-assintel-2019/.
110. *See* the ICT Market Assintel Report 2019 at the address https://www.assintel.it/osservatori-2/assintel-report/assintel-report-2019/and a summary at the address https://www.insidemarketing.it/mercato-ict-in-italia-assintel-2019/.
111. *See* the ICT Market Assintel Report 2019 at the address https://www.assintel.it/osservatori-2/assintel-report/assintel-report-2019/and a summary at the address https://www.insidemarketing.it/mercato-ict-in-italia-assintel-2019/.
112. *See* the ICT Market Assintel Report 2019 at the address https://www.assintel.it/osservatori-2/assintel-report/assintel-report-2019/and a summary at the address https://www.insidemarketing.it/mercato-ict-in-italia-assintel-2019/.
113. *See* the ICT Market Assintel Report 2019 at the address https://www.assintel.it/osservatori-2/assintel-report/assintel-report-2019/and a summary at the address https://www.insidemarketing.it/mercato-ict-in-italia-assintel-2019/.

Chapter 4. E-commerce: Facts and Figures

§1. The E-Commerce Evolution in Italy

193. In recent years, the evolution of electronic commerce in Italy has always been conditioned by different factors: a strong regulatory delay, a diffusion of technology that has suffered the economic crisis (apart from the widespread of mobile phones) and the delay in the interest, by large international operators for the Italian market.[114]

In 2010 (a key-year for our historical overview), the e-commerce in Italy grew by 43%, surpassing EUR 14 billion.

The increase was probably due to a physiological growth and a greater dissemination of the Internet, including the entry of new global players such as Groupon and Amazon.

The dominance of the major international players soon became clear: they imposed themselves on the market as the first destination for the purchases of many consumers.

However, it is important to note also a significant growth of national players moving in the e-commerce environment.

Through the years, the most important e-commerce sectors have confirmed to be the *tourism* and *leisure*, generating 70% of the total e-commerce revenues. In particular tourism, one of the most mature sectors, shows a growth of around 9%.

The publishing sector continues to grow, albeit slowly, thanks to digital and on-demand services such as Spotify, Netflix and Infinity, which have achieved a good share of users.[115]

194. Recently, the existence of a direct and positive relationship between digitization, internationalization and exportation in Italian SMEs has been demonstrated.[116]

The percentage of small digitized companies maintaining external relations is four times higher than the percentage of non-digitized companies, while the percentage of digitized medium-sized enterprises that have external relations grows more than 50% compared to non-digitized ones.

It is clear that, through e-commerce means, SMEs have the opportunity to expand their business.

However, an effective online export strategy requires a careful analysis of the e-commerce characteristics of each Country, often very different from those of the Italian context.

The online communities are increasingly central to marketing companies, together with social media like Facebook and Twitter, with the integration of tools on their sites for evaluation and/or propagation.

---

114. *See* the study by Casaleggio & Associati concerning e-commerce in Italy E-commerce in Italia 2018, https://www.casaleggio.it/e-commerce/.
115. ISTAT, ICT 2017, https://www.istat.it.
116. *See* the study by Casaleggio & Associati concerning e-commerce in Italy E-commerce in Italia 2018, https://www.casaleggio.it/e-commerce/.

195. The model of 'impulse buying' tied to special offers, such as restricted stock or discounted prices for a defined time, has spread also in Italy and is now offered by many players in e-commerce for services too.

Finally, in the last ten years, there was an initial spread of mobile e-commerce applications and info-commerce associated with the physical location of the potential buyer.

196. According to Istat,[117] in January 2017, compared to the same period of 2016, retail sales fell by 1.2% both in large retail outlets and in small shops, while e-commerce recorded an increase of 2.4%. EUR 595 *per capita* have been spent during the last year.

Two Italians of three (67%) have visited an online store while more than half (53%) have purchased a product or a service online.

These data indicate a good suitability of the Italian consumer to buy online; greater frequency and spending could be boosted by an expansion of online services, an expansion that, in Italy, remains limited if compared to other European Countries.

197. In recent times, there was in Italy the creation of groups for sales to increase the number of companies that put their products on the Internet: Amazon first, once landed in the domestic market, has opened the way for initiatives online in a consortium, allowing the creation of websites, such as <iloveitalianshoes.it>, <profumerie.it>, or grouping the offerings of individual merchants by categories.

The B2C e-commerce market in Italy generated a turnover of EUR 35.1 billion in 2017, growing by 11% overall compared to 2016.

E-commerce revenues show positive results in all sectors and overall growth is in line with that of the previous year.

The value of e-commerce in Italy in 2017 was estimated at EUR 35.1 billion, with an increase of 11% over 2016.[118]

198. The demographic profile of buyers in Italy is very similar to that of the Internet users in the Country: biased towards young people and consumers with a high income.

In this context, Millenials (born in the period 1980-2000) are the stronger influencer of the overall purchasing behaviour.

However, the entry into the market of the Z Gen (born in the period 2001-2015) will introduce new patterns, not clearly visible yet.[119]

The features differ in individual sectors: women buy more in tourism and fashion sectors, men in consumer electronics and games/video games.

The differences are geographical too: shoppers in the South buy more consumer electronics, and those of the Northern part of Italy are more interested in tourism.

---

117. *See* ISTAT, ICT 2017, Coldiretti at https://www.coldiretti.it/economia/consumi-595-euro-anno-spesi-e-commerce.
118. *See* the study by Casaleggio & Associati concerning e-commerce in Italy E-commerce in Italia 2018, https://www.casaleggio.it/e-commerce/.
119. *See* the study by Casaleggio & Associati concerning e-commerce in Italy E-commerce in Italia 2018, https://www.casaleggio.it/e-commerce/.

199. The credit card is the most widespread method of payment, used in 46% of online purchases (43% in 2017).

The trend in the growth of payments with digital wallets continues, used in 35% of transactions (27% in 2017).

Payment on delivery and bank transfers are both used in 18% of cases (both at 13% in 2017).

Mobile payments remain stable at 1%, while other methods of payment (3% in 2017) are growing at 13%.

Among the credit card management systems (VPOS), Paypal is used by 91% of business owners, normally with other systems.[120]

200. Concerning the shipping services, unlike other European Countries, the national postal service is not the main choice and it is used only by 25% of the Italian e-commerce companies.

Leader of the market in Italy is Bartolini, followed by DHL.[121]

To be able to meet all the needs of customers, operators use most shipping systems together in 60% of cases.

201. The Italian e-commerce companies tend to send their e-mail communications to customers through internal systems (55%).[122]

Systems also used are ContactLab (22%), MailUp (20%), MailChimp (7%), MagNews (4%) and eC-messenger (2%).

202. Software platforms are built largely ad hoc (84%) by external companies or web-agencies.[123]

Among the platforms mentioned are used Net Magento (12%), osCommerce (12%), IBM Websphere (2%) and OpenCart (1%).

In several cases, the platforms used are integrated with each other.

203. The mobile is a channel that is seeing the greatest growth in e-commerce, due to the high penetration of mobile devices in the Italian population and the removal of limits on the Wi-Fi imposed earlier by the *Pisanu Law*.[124]

There has been a rapid increase in mobile traffic over the years, and it keeps growing. Indeed, a growth of 10% of mobile traffic was registered in 2017.

---

120. *See* the study by Casaleggio & Associati concerning e-commerce in Italy E-commerce in Italia 2018, https://www.casaleggio.it/e-commerce/.
121. *See* the study by Casaleggio & Associati concerning e-commerce in Italy E-commerce in Italia 2018, https://www.casaleggio.it/e-commerce/.
122. *See* the study by Casaleggio & Associati concerning e-commerce in Italy E-commerce in Italia 2018, https://www.casaleggio.it/e-commerce/.
123. *See* the study by Casaleggio & Associati concerning e-commerce in Italy E-commerce in Italia 2018, https://www.casaleggio.it/e-commerce/.
124. *See* the study by Casaleggio & Associati concerning e-commerce in Italy E-commerce in Italia 2018, https://www.casaleggio.it/e-commerce/.

204. A total of 67% of Italians choose to buy from an online store rather than from another based on advantageous shipping options, while 72% say they make a single purchase for more products to take advantage, when available, of 'free shipping'.

Indeed, this proves to be an important variable for those who buy on the Web. Among Italian consumers, the desire for a premium service with quick delivery is also growing (33%).[125]

205. The future (and success) of e-commerce market in Italy will be probably influenced, in the next years, by several important factors.

Among these, the digitization of the Public Administration and the widespread use of certified e-mail (PEC) would save EUR 7.5 billion.

§2. The Complex Legal Framework of E-Commerce in Italy

206. Regarding the general characteristics and the *status* of electronic commerce in Italy, the widespread diffusion of Internet and computer technologies, the dematerialization of documents and the establishment of new practices for creating and sharing contents have led to a dangerous instability of the legal certainty based on the paperwork, and have led the Legislator to make a strenuous work of tuning of the legal framework in order to give legal certainty to telematic relationships, to protect consumers and to increase users confidence and trust during online transactions.

In this context, it is correct to define, generally, e-commerce as a particular form of economic activity, relative to goods and services, which takes place on the Internet (or through computer networks).[126]

It consists, essentially, in carrying out electronically commercial activities and transactions and includes various activities such as electronic marketing of goods and services, the online distribution of digital contents, the conduct of electronic financial transactions and stock exchange, the electronic public procurement and other procedures.[127]

---

125. *See* the study by Casaleggio & Associati concerning e-commerce in Italy E-commerce in Italia 2018, https://www.casaleggio.it/e-commerce/.

126. For an introduction to the evolution of the e-commerce legal framework in Italy *see* M. Morelli, 'Il commercio elettronico: dall'immagine al profitto' (Franco Angeli, Milano, 2006); C. Parolini, 'E-Business. Una introduzione' (EGEA, Milano, 2003).

127. For a complete overview of the legal framework of electronic commerce in Italy *see*: C. Rossello, G. Finocchiaro, E. Tosi, 'Commercio elettronico, documento informatico e firma digitale (Giappichelli, Torino, 2003); F. Bravo, 'Contrattazione telematica e contrattazione cibernetica' (Giuffrè, Milano, 2007); L. Manna, 'La disciplina del commercio elettronico' (CEDAM, Padova, 2005); F. Delfini, 'Il commercio elettronico' (CEDAM, Padova, 2004); U. Draetta, 'Internet e commercio elettronico. Nel diritto internazionale dei privati' (Giuffrè, Milano, 2005); C. Rossello, 'Commercio elettronico. La governance di internet tra diritto statuale, autodisciplina, soft law e lex mercatoria' (Giuffrè, Milano, 2006); G. De Cristofaro, A. Zaccaria, 'Commentario breve al diritto dei consumatori' (CEDAM, Padova, 2010); E. Tosi, 'Contratti informatici, telematici e virtuali' (Giuffrè, Milano, 2010); R. Clarizia, 'Contratti e commercio elettronico', in M. Durante and U. Pagallo

207. With reference to the legal status of the subjects involved, also in Italy it has become common to distinguish between different types of electronic commerce, and in particular:

(i) *business to business* (B2B) e-commerce, to identify the online activity of entrepreneurs or professionals with other entrepreneurs or professionals;
(ii) *business-to-consumer* (B2C) e-commerce, with reference to the activity between professionals/entrepreneurs and consumers;
(iii) *consumer to consumer* (C2C) e-commerce, with regard to trade in goods and services between individuals;
(iv) *business to Public Administration* (B2Pa) e-commerce, which includes the economic relationship between a professional and a Public Administration; and
(v) *citizen to government* (C2G) e-commerce, when the economic relationship is between a citizen and a Public Administration.

208. Another categorization is based on different kinds of goods falling under the contractual relationship, and includes *direct electronic commerce*, where all elements of the transaction, including the delivery of the goods, should be made electronically (i.e., buying online a software or an e-book) and *indirect electronic commerce*, when, after electronic contractual negotiations and the online agreement, the physical delivery of the goods through traditional distribution channels follows (this is the so-called offline phase).

209. Electronic commerce has been the subject of a first regulation wave at European level with Directive 2000/31/EC of the European Parliament and Council of 8 June 2000, 'on certain legal aspects of information society services, in particular, electronic commerce, in the Internal Market' (Directive on electronic commerce).

This regulation, issued on the outcome of a long (and intense) debate, aims to contribute to the smooth functioning of the internal market through the free movement of information society services and the establishment of a clear, and simple, legal framework.[128]

The Directive has the purpose of ensuring a high level of community legal integration in order to establish a real area without internal borders for information society services.

(ed.), 'Manuale di informatica giuridica e diritto delle nuove tecnologie' (UTET, Torino, 2012); F. Sarzana di Sant'Ippolito, 'I contratti di internet e del commercio elettronico' (Giuffrè, Milano, 2001).

128. Concerning the e-commerce Italian legal framework, *see* L. Manna, 'La disciplina del commercio elettronico' (CEDAM, Padova, 2005); U. Draetta, 'Internet e commercio elettronico. Nel diritto internazionale dei privati' (Giuffrè, Milano, 2005); C. Rossello, 'Commercio elettronico. La governance di internet tra diritto statuale, autodisciplina, soft law e lex mercatoria' (Giuffrè, Milano, 2006); G. De Cristofaro and A. Zaccaria, 'Commentario breve al diritto dei consumatori' (CEDAM, Padova, 2010).

In order to ensure legal certainty and consumer confidence, the Directive must lay down a clear and general framework to cover certain legal aspects of electronic commerce in the internal market.

The Directive coordinates, to the extent necessary for the achievement of the objective, national provisions on information society services relating to the internal market, the establishment of service providers, commercial communications, electronic contracts, the liability of intermediaries, codes of conduct, out-of-court dispute settlements, court actions and cooperation between Member States.

210. Following the Directive dispositions, the e-commerce sector in Italy is subject to certain legal constraints that must be diligently observed.

Concerning economic activity in general, Internet services must respect the same rules drafted for the same activities performed in a 'traditional' manner.

Therefore, it is necessary that all the *subjective conditions* (and assumptions of legitimacy) comply with the rules concerning the product or service offered.

211. From a legal point of view, it is essential the possession, by the party concerned, of all the requirements that the law establishes to perform the activity.

Consider, for example, a person seeking to conduct Internet business in Italy for which *registration* is required.

The fact that the same activity is performed 'on the Internet' does not exclude the obligation, by the interested party, with respect to the enrolment in the relevant register.

The *enrolment* could be also mandatory (i.e., enrolment in a *Chamber of Commerce*, in the case of an asset held for sale of products), and the fact that the service is offered only on the Internet is not relevant.

212. The Italian legal system has implemented the mentioned European Union Directive 2000/31/EC on e-commerce with legislative decree no. 70 of 9 April 2003, whose main objective was to ensure the proper functioning of the market through the promotion of the free movement of information society services.

This Decree regulates any service normally provided against remuneration, at a distance (and hence without the presence of simultaneous parties), by electronic means and with the individual request of a recipient of services.

One of the assumptions of the *free movement* of information society services (and one of the most important principles of the Italian framework on electronic commerce) is the freedom of the activity. It means the *non-subordination* of the starting of the exercise of a supplier of services to prior *authorization* or other measures with an equivalent effect that could restrict the entrepreneur freedom.

213. In terms of application of the Italian rules, we must distinguish between three different *status*:

(i) the *recipient* of the service, meaning the person who, for professional aims or otherwise, uses an information society service, in particular to research or make available information;

(ii) the *consumer*, or any person acting for purposes not related to the commercial, business or profession;
(iii) the *provider*, or the natural or legal person providing a service in the information society.

214. The subjects that are involved into the operation determine the application of the legislation, especially in services related to the B2B and B2C (excluding the C2C) for a provider established in the Italian territory (Article 3, paragraph 1 of the Italian Legislative Decree), i.e. by a person who actually carries out an economic activity in Italy through a permanent establishment for an indefinite period (Article 2, paragraph 1, lett. C of the Italian Legislative Decree).

The fundamental principle of *Country of Origin* (or 'internal market clause') contained in Article 3, paragraph 1, of the Italian Legislative Decree, was already contained in the point 19 of the Directive, where it was clarified that 'the place at which a service provider is established should be determined in conformity with the case-law of the Court of Justice according to which the concept of establishment involves the actual pursuit of an economic activity through a fixed establishment for an indefinite period; this requirement is also fulfilled where a company is constituted for a given period; the *place of establishment* of a company providing services via an Internet website is not the place at which the technology supporting its website is located or the place at which its website is accessible but the place where it pursues its economic activity; in cases where a provider has several places of establishment it is important to determine from which place of establishment the service concerned is provided; in cases where it is difficult to determine from which of several places of establishment a given service is provided, this is the place where the provider has the centre of his activities relating to this particular service.'

215. Any provider of services in the information society must offer adequate guarantees as to its identity and seriousness, fulfilling specific requirements for information.

Just with the aim of avoiding risks to the frequent difficulty of ascertaining the precise identity and assess the seriousness of the provider and the content of legal relations related to the contract, and to increase confidence in electronic commerce by recipients of services (more so when it comes to consumer), legislative decree no. 70/2003 provides for three different orders of *information obligations*:

(i) the obligation to provide certain general information,
(ii) the information requirements on commercial communications and
(iii) the obligation to provide information directly to the conclusion of the contract.

They integrate a minimum core, guaranteeing an adequate level of *transparency*, to which may be added, depending on the specific subject matter of the contract, further obligations under special laws.

216. Interesting are also the provisions dictated by legislative decree no. 206 of 6 September 2005, amending the Italian Consumers Code ('*Codice del Consumo*'), drafted with the ambitious aim of operating an important rationalization and systematization of the legal framework on consumer protection, and already massively modified.

Since this *corpus* sets standards for professionals entering into *distance contracts*, especially disclosure obligations, the interpreter has the task of obtaining the overall content of the information provided to consumers through a unified reading and interpretation of the provisions contained in the Consumers Code and legislative decree no. 70/2003.

217. The legal framework just outlined should be completed with a plurality of sources and especially the Italian Civil Code norms on obligations and contracts, legislative decree no. 196 of 30 June 2003, about data protection and privacy (the provisions of which will not be applied while in contrast with the EU Regulation 2016/679 – General Data Protection Regulation), and many other rules governing specific aspects of this subject.

Among many other sources, it is worth mentioning the rules contained in the Digital Administration Code (legislative decree no. 82, of 7 March 2005) that collects and organizes, into a single set of rules, the main provisions relating to the electronic signatures and legal significance, the conditions of validity and probative value of electronic documents and procedures for transmission of data.

218. From a practical point of view, the contract of electronic commerce is the instrument through which negotiation takes place on trade in goods and services over the Internet or computer networks.

In relation to the *medium* that allows the completion of the contractual agreement, the Italian doctrine tends to distinguish between *atypical virtual contracts* (or contracts in a broader sense), when the contract is concluded by using electronic mail or other similar devices based on the Internet for the transmission of the message contained in the contract negotiation, and *traditional virtual contracts* (or contracts in a strict sense) to designate those contracts concluded via the Web, just by pressing the virtual negotiation instrument proposed ('point and click').

219. This last type of contract ('point and click'), targeting the provisions of legislative decree no. 70/2003 (which, by contrast, *does not a*pply to contracts concluded by e-mail exchange), is characterized by the absence of negotiations between the parties and in establishing a unilateral offer to the general public.

It is correct to speak, in this regard, about contracts 'without agreement', because the system leads to the formation of a bond by filling out a form or by the mere push of a button and ends up the customization of the negotiations to provide a consensus.

220. In both types, the Legislator has refrained from regulating the *time* of the contract, and merely establish the substantial equivalence between computerized contracts and agreements entered into traditional forms, referring to the previous norm dictated by Title II of Book IV of the Civil Code, and to special laws.

Article 13 of legislative decree no. 70/2003 states, in fact, in the first paragraph that 'The rules on the conclusion of contracts also apply to cases where the recipient of a good or a service places his order by computer.'

The regulatory provision at issue was the subject of a lively debate, particularly with respect to issues of coordination of principles for the conclusion of the contract contained in Articles 1326 et seq. of the Italian Civil Code.

One of the most debated issues was related to the legal order made by the customer, and the receipt of the order submitted by the provider, according to provisions of legislative decree no. 70/2003, in order to identify the *time* and *place* of the conclusion of the contract electronically.

221. However, given that, pursuant to the Italian Civil Code (Article 1326, paragraph 1), the contract is deemed concluded at the time and place where those who made the proposal has knowledge of the other party's acceptance, thoroughly questioned if the two statements should be qualified as an *offer* and as an *acceptance*.

222. According to the main doctrine, the offer via the Web for products and services can be classified as a *general invitation to offer*, so the order made by the recipient would have the value of a contract proposal that would follow the acceptance of the lender in the form of a receipt of order.

For another part of the doctrine, the supply of products and services should be qualified as an offering to the public, pursuant to Article 1336 of the Civil Code and following Articles, so the order would have the value of formal acceptance.

In the latter case, the obligation laid down in the second paragraph of Article 13 of the Decree, containing a summary of general and special conditions applicable to the contract, the information on the characteristics of the goods or service and detailed indication of price, means of payment, the withdrawal, delivery costs and applicable taxes, is a mere *accessory* that does not affect the completion of the contract, but is merely a confirmation of receipt of order.

223. Finally, the Legislator took care to remedy the concrete practical impossibility of identifying the *exact moment* at which the order, or the receipt of the order, reaches the recipient's address, through a *presumption of knowledge* that coincides with the moment, easily ascertainable, in which they will be registered on the server of the provider of the recipient (Article 13, paragraph 3 of the Decree).

224. Great importance is given, in the Italian legal framework, to the way in which, materially, the activity is carried out:

(i) *offline*, with actual delivery of the goods being purchased (it is called *indirect electronic commerce*); or
(ii) in the *network*, with direct supply of the goods or services directly to the virtual location of the purchaser (it is called *direct electronic commerce*).

The indirect electronic commerce was seen as a technological form of traditional sales, and was then treated, from a fiscal point of view, as a 'distance sales tax'.

225. Another interesting norm, in the Italian e-commerce legal framework, is legislative decree no. 114 of 31 March 1998 ('Reforming the Law on Electronic Commerce') and, especially, Article 18 of the Decree, providing that e-commerce definition includes 'mail order, television or other communication systems', so including all cases of retail sales through a website.

The Italian discipline states that retail activity by mail order, or through television, or other communication systems, is subject to a prior notice to the Municipality, in which is communicated the operator's residence. Activities can be initiated after 30 days from the receipt of the notice.

It is forbidden to send products to the consumer unless a specific request is made, but it is possible to send product samples, or free gifts, at no cost or liability for the consumer.

In those cases where sales transactions are done through television, the broadcaster must ensure, before putting them 'on air', that the holder of the activity is meeting the requirements of the Decree for the whole year of sale.

During the transmission, the name, the business name and address of the seller, the number of entry in the register of enterprises and the number of VAT must be given. Supervisors are allowed to a free access to the room designated as the location of the seller.

226. Particular attention should be dedicated, also, to the 'common' rules governing the contracts needed to perform new e-commerce activities and the legal implications that follow.

Article 15, Paragraph 2, of Law n. 59, of 15 March 1997 gave legal force to all intents and purposes, documents, deeds, data, contract sizes, from private and Public Administration, using computers, transmitted by electronic means and written with the formalities prescribed by Presidential Decree n. 444 of 28 December 2000 (repeal of the regulation applying the same law, Presidential Decree 10 November 1997, n. 513, referred to as *Rules*), containing the criteria and procedures for treating, storage and transmission of electronic documents.

227. From a general legal point of view, and not strictly connected to the e-commerce rules, Article 1326 of the Italian Civil Code provides that the contract is concluded when those who made the proposal have knowledge of the other party acceptance.

Offer and acceptance shall have effect from the moment they are known by the relevant receiver (Article 1334 of the Civil Code). The Italian system provides for a rebuttable presumption of knowledge (and therefore effectiveness) of acceptance which, according to Article 1335, occurs when the acceptance arrives at the address (e-mail) of the addressee, unless proof can be given by the addressee that he was unable to take knowledge of it, without his fault.

Contracts can also be entered directly from the computer. In these cases, the customer fills out the model proposed by the seller. The conclusion of the contract takes place at the moment when the recipient has communicated to the seller the conclusion. Article 1328 of the Civil Code provides for the revocability of the proposed contract until the contract is not concluded, and acceptance may be revoked only if the withdrawal reaches the offeror before he has knowledge of acceptance.

In other terms, while the proposal can be easily revoked by the offeror until the contract is not concluded, the buyer must make sure that the withdrawal reaches the offeror before he is aware of acceptance.

In the silence of the law, doctrine and jurisprudence believe that a contract is concluded at the place where the proposer is at the time in which notice of acceptance is given, or at the registered office where the company has its headquarters.

It is appropriate that companies expressly state where their premises are located ('the State') for the purposes of applicable law.

228. Other minor changes happened through the years in terms of legislation regulating the e-commerce environment. One of these is the '*Decreto sblocca Italia*', Decree Law 133/2014 (subsequently converted into law). It provides for the adoption of an extraordinary plan to promote 'Made in Italy' products abroad, and it also includes 'measures to support the use of e-commerce tools by SMEs'. However, this piece of legislation did not establish clearly the contents and financial resources of the plan.

Another (limited) intervention of the Italian legislator concerning e-commerce is the so-called *Legge di stabilità* (Stability Law, 2015). This law includes some measures for the implementation of the Italian Digital Agenda, for example in the field of justice and health, but very little is envisaged with reference to the e-commerce sector.

The most significant novelty has perhaps been the reduction of VAT on e-books to 4%, as advocated by the operators of the sector, thus avoiding unfair disparities with respect to the VAT regime on paper publishing.[129]

229. The Italian Parliament recently introduced distributed ledger technologies (DLTs) into the Italian legal system.[130]

Law Decree No. 135/2018 – which was passed into law on February 7 2018 by the Italian Parliament – provides a precise definition of DLTs as 'technologies and IT protocols using a shared, distributed, replicable and simultaneously accessible ledger, decentralized and encrypted, which enable the registration, validation, updating and storage of data, whether encrypted or not, which cannot be modified or forged'.

The new legislation provides that the storing of an electronic document by means of DLTs shall have the legal effect of an electronic time stamp, pursuant to Article 41 of EU Regulation No. 910/2014 (on electronic identification and trust services for electronic transactions in the internal market) and hence can be used as evidence in legal proceedings.

129. E-commerce: scenario di riferimento e quadro normativo – Proposte, indicazioni e priorità per uno sviluppo sostenibile, NETCOMM, https://www.consorzionetcomm.it/dati-e-ricerche/e-commerce-scenario-di-riferimento-e-quadro-normativo-proposte-indicazioni-e-priorita-per-uno-sviluppo-sostenibile_paper.kl.

130. *See* the summary description of this legislative reform in F. Maruffi, *Distributed Ledger Technologies and Smart Contracts in Italy*, http://blockchain.bakermckenzie.com/2019/02/28/distributed-ledger-technologies-and-smart-contracts-in-italy/.

In addition, Law Decree No. 135/2018 introduces the smart contract, which is defined as 'a computer program based on DLTs which execution is legally binding upon two or more parties with reference to the effects previously agreed by the same parties'.

According to the new legislation, smart contracts shall satisfy the requirement that a contract be in writing upon electronic identification of the relevant parties. But that will be done in accordance with a procedure which has yet to be issued by the Agency for Digital Italy ('AgID').

Chapter 5. E-Government and Open Government Initiatives

§1. The E-Government in Italy and the Digital Administration Code: Digital and Open Administration

230. The legislation on digital administration finds an indirect constitutional source in Article 97, paragraph 1, of the Italian Constitution: digitalization is a tool to guarantee the good performance of the Public Administration.

231. In this regard, the regulatory reference point consists of the Digital Administration Code (hereinafter also 'CAD'), legislative decree no. 82/2005, subject to repeated modifications and additions over the years, some of which are particularly incisive, such as legislative decree no. 159/2006, legislative decree no. 235/2010 and legislative decree no. 179/2016, followed by the so-called corrective decree, legislative decree no. 217/2017.

232. The Code regulates the most significant aspects of digital administration, such as the rights of citizens and businesses, which constitute digital citizenship, the related obligations of the administration and the tools capable of giving life to digitalization: digital identity, IT documents, electronic signatures, digital domicile, management and conservation of documents, data, online services, development, acquisition and reuse of IT systems and public connectivity system.

In this regard, the scope of these rules is particularly wide, since the provisions of the Code concerning the IT document, electronic signatures and transmission of IT documents also apply to relations between individuals and not only between Public Administrations or between individuals and administrations.

233. Alongside the Code, there are a number of additional provisions, some of which are transversal (Law no. 241/1990 on the administrative procedure and the right of access to documents; Presidential Decree no. 445/2000 which deals with the IT protocol and the management of document flows; legislative decree no. 196/2003 on the protection of personal data, profoundly amended by legislative decree no. 101/2018 for the purposes of the adjustment to the Regulation (EU) 2016/679; and legislative decree no. 33/2013, as amended by legislative decree no. 97/2016, on the transparency of Public Administrations, on the right of simple civic access and on the right of generalized civic access), others more sectorial, for example the legislation dedicated to certified e-mail, such as Presidential Decree no. 68/2005.

The secondary standardization and the technical rules, fundamental acts for the implementation of the legislative provisions, are also particularly relevant in this area.[131]

131. For an overview of e-government and law in Italy, *see*, *inter alia*: G. Cassano, C. Giurdanella (ed.), 'Il Codice della Pubblica Amministrazione digitale' (Giuffrè, Milano, 2005); E. Belisario, 'La nuova Pubblica Amministrazione Digitale. Guida al Codice dell'Amministrazione Digitale dopo la Legge n. 69/2009' (Maggioli, Santarcangelo di Romagna, 2009); L. De Pietro (ed.), 'Dieci lezioni per capire ed attuare l'e-government' (Marsilio Editori, Venezia, 2011); M. Iaselli (ed.), 'La nuova Pubblica Amministrazione. I principi dell'agenda digitale' (Aracne, Roma, 2014); M. Di Francesco

234. In the regulatory evolution of the Digital Administration Code, in line with the International and European reference context, an evolution towards open government emerges: administration as well as being digital, must be open, based on the principles of transparency, participation and collaboration.

In particular, from this point of view, the CAD is integrated by the legislation on transparency and, in particular, by legislative decree no. 33/2013, as amended by legislative decree no. 97/2016: transparency contributes to the creation of an open administration, at the service of the citizen (Article 1).[132]

235. In Italy, strategies have been undertaken aimed at shaping the digital Public Administration, following the impulse of the international and European reference context.

236. At the European level, the 'Digital Agenda for Europe' and its action plan are relevant.

The 'Digital Agenda for Europe' is one of the seven 'flagship' initiatives identified in the wider 'Europe 2020' Strategy, which aims to achieve a smart, sustainable and inclusive growth.

237. The Digital Agenda for Europe, in the creation of a European digital single market, gives a key role to information technology and is aimed at making the most of technological potential to foster innovation, economic growth, competitiveness and progress.

238. The related action plans are linked to the 'Digital Agenda for Europe': the current EU eGovernment Action Plan 2016-2020 aims to accelerate the digital transformation of the Public Administration.

To this end, the Plan provides, as strategic priorities, to modernize the Public Administration with digital technologies, facilitate cross-border mobility with interoperable public services and encourage digital interaction between administrations and citizens/companies for quality public services.

The Plan includes, among the basic principles, digital by default, openness and transparency, inclusiveness and accessibility, interoperability and security.

239. The Italian strategies dedicated to digital administration have taken shape earlier in the action plans for e-government and, more recently, in the Italian Digital

---

Torregrossa, 'La pubblica amministrazione nella società digitale' (Editoriale scientifica, Napoli, 2017); F. Faini, 'L'amministrazione digitale e aperta', in F. Faini – S. Pietropaoli, 'Scienza giuridica e tecnologie informatiche' (Giappichelli, Torino, 2017, pp. 149-194); E. Guarnaccia – M. Mancarella, 'Il Codice dell'amministrazione digitale 2018. Alla luce del d.lgs. 13 dicembre 2017, n. 217, in vigore dal 27 gennaio 2018' (Dike giuridica, Roma, 2018).

132. On open government *see*, *inter alia*: E. Carloni (ed.), 'L'amministrazione aperta. Regole strumenti e limiti dell'open government' (Maggioli, Santarcangelo di Romagna, 2014); F. Di Donato, 'Lo stato trasparente. Linked open data e cittadinanza attiva' (Edizioni ETS, Pisa, 2010); F. Faini, 'La strada maestra dell'open government: presupposti, obiettivi, strumenti' (Ciberspazio e diritto, fasc. 2, 2013, pp. 213-238).

Agenda, in strategies for high-speed broadband and Digital Growth 2014-2020 and in the Three-Year Plan 2017-2019 for ICT in the Public Administration.

240. The Italian Digital Agenda is foreseen in Article 47 of Decree Law no. 5/2012, converted with amendments into Law no. 35/2012 with the aim of modernizing relations between Public Administrations, citizens and businesses through coordinated actions aimed at encouraging the development of demand and supply of innovative digital services, enhancing the offer of connectivity broadband, encouraging citizens and businesses to use digital services and promoting the growth of adequate industrial capacity to support the development of innovative products and services.

241. To pursue the objectives of the Italian Digital Agenda, the Council Presidency, together with the Ministry of Economic Development, the Agency for Digital Italy (hereinafter also 'AgID') and the Agency for Cohesion, adopted in 2015 the 'Italian Strategy for high-speed broadband' and the 'Strategy for Digital Growth 2014-2020'. AgID monitors the main digital transformation projects of the Strategy for Digital Growth.[133]

242. The 'Three-Year Plan 2017-2019 for ICT in the Public Administration',[134] provided for in Article 14-*bis* of legislative decree no. 82/2005, introduced by legislative decree no. 179/2016 and amended by legislative decree no. 217/2017, drawn up by the Agency for Digital Italy, was approved on May 31st, 2017 by the President of the Council of Ministers.

The Plan contains the identification of the objectives and the main interventions for the development and management of the information systems of the Public Administrations: it is configured as the operational and technical declination of the 'Strategy for Digital Growth 2014-2020', aimed at guiding the digital transformation of the Public Administration and becoming the reference for administrations in the development of their information systems.[135]

243. In synergy with the strategies for digital administration, European and national strategies dedicated to open government are relevant.

244. In the field of open government, a significant impulse comes from international policies and strategies. In this regard, key dates are 21 January 2009, the date of the Memorandum on Transparency and Open Government, and 8 December 2009, the date of the Open Government Directive: with these acts, the President of the United States Barack Obama has prescribed the principles of open philosophy,

---

133. The site dedicated to monitoring the main digital transformation projects is https://avanzamentodigitale.italia.it/it.
134. The site dedicated to the three-year plan for information technology in Public Administration 2017-2019 is https://pianotriennale-ict.italia.it.
135. *See* F. Sciacchitano, 'Disciplina e utilizzo degli Open Data in Italia' (in 'Rivista di diritto dei media', fasc. 1, 2018, p. 300).

transparency, participation and collaboration, pillars of the open government model and has identified open data as a strategic instrument for the participation of citizens and businesses.

245. The European path in this regard opened in 2009, thanks to the Open Declaration on European Public Services promoted by a set of citizens and associations, which proposed the principles of transparency, participation and empowerment, founding pillars of open government.

The contents of the document have been adopted by the 2009 Malmö Declaration, which set among its objectives the development of user-centric services, the involvement of civil society and stakeholders, the increase in the availability of information and public data for their reuse, the transparency of administrative processes and the promotion of active participation.

246. The European eGovernment Action Plan 2011-2015, adopted in 2010, reflects the priorities of the 2009 Malmö Declaration and the current EU eGovernment Action Plan 2016-2020 gives centrality to principles of transparency and openness, declined in the possibility of access, control and correction of their data by users and in the involvement of stakeholders in the design and provision of services.

247. At national level, the Italian government has joined the international initiative Open Government Partnership (OGP), promoted in 2011 and aimed at encouraging transparency and openness of governments through accountability and active participation of citizens, associations and businesses, in order to create active citizenship and more effective, open and responsible governments.

248. In 2012 Italy set up its first Action Plan 2012-2014; subsequently, the second National Action Plan 2014-2016 and the third Action Plan 2016-2018 were approved: to elaborate the third plan, the Government set up, on 6 June 2016, the Open Government Forum, made up of representatives of the civil society, the university world, businesses and consumer protection associations, to ensure a broad and participated debate on the topics of open government.

In 2018, the work of drafting the fourth National Action Plan for Open Government 2019-2021 began.[136]

249. The strategic model for the evolution of the Public Administration information system, which emerges from the ‘Strategy for Digital Growth 2014-2020’ and the ‘Three-Year Plan 2017-2019 for ICT in the Public Administration’, constitutes the reference framework on which to make the planned projects, platforms and programmes operational.

The Strategic Model was designed to overcome the ‘silos’ approach, historically adopted by the Public Administration, and to favour the creation of a real information system for the Public Administration.

---

136. The site dedicated to strategies and plans related to Italian open government is http://open.gov.it.

250. To this end, the Strategic Model relies on:

(i) tools for the generation and dissemination of digital services, which define common rules, facilitate the design and implementation of digital services, define guidelines and development kits and create communities of participation and cooperation;
(ii) ecosystems, i.e. the sectors or policy areas in which the action is carried out by Public Administrations, such as health, school and justice;
(iii) interoperability model, which defines the mechanisms that facilitate and guarantee the correct interaction between the actors of the system, favouring the transparent sharing of data, information, platforms and services;
(iv) intangible infrastructures, composed of enabling platforms, i.e. infrastructural services and application solutions capable of providing the country with some key assets to enable the development of innovative digital services, such as SPID, PagoPA, FatturaPA and ANPR, and PA Data, i.e. databases of national interest, open data and controlled vocabularies. In this context, the Data & Analytics Framework is a centralized environment that acquires and makes public data of interest more usable, allowing the development of data applications;
(v) physical infrastructures, that is the hardware assets necessary for the realization of the Plan: this includes the rationalization of the data centres, the systematic adoption of the cloud paradigm and the development of connectivity;
(vi) security, which includes the activities for the regulation of cybersecurity in the PA and the CERT-PA as an operational tool to support the adoption of the correct levels of security in the Public Administration.

251. Finally, the Strategic Model deals with the management of change as a component that is transversal to the others in order to meet the need for coordination, management and monitoring of the activities necessary for the development of the three-year plan.

252. The 'Strategy for Digital Growth 2014-2020' and the 'Three-Year Plan 2017-2019 for ICT in the Public Administration' provide for the rationalization of ICT assets, the consolidation of data centres and the development of cloud computing.

253. Specifically, it is necessary to rationalize data centres, in order to reduce management costs and to standardize and increase the quality of services offered by Public Administrations.

In this regard, AgID, pursuant to Decree Law no. 179/2012, converted with amendments into Law no. 221/2012 has the task of carrying out a census of the data centres of Public Administration in order to propose a rationalization plan.

In particular, an evolutionary path towards an efficient and flexible use of ICT technologies by the administrations is necessary, in order to guarantee high management savings and greater reactivity in providing services that are more suited to the needs of citizens and businesses.

This path involves the study and definition of the strategic evolutionary model of Public Administration cloud to be implemented following the rationalization of data centres and plans to identify a set of existing physical infrastructures owned by the Public Administration that will be elected to National Strategic Poles.

254. Lastly, among the actions are planned those aimed at increasing the connectivity to the Internet by the Public Administration in conjunction with the 'Italian Strategy for high-speed broadband', rationalizing expenses for connectivity and increasing the spread of wireless connectivity in public places and in the offices accessible to the public, also in order to facilitate access to services by citizens.

§2. Digital Citizenship

255. The Italian legislation deals with digital citizenship, i.e. the configuration of citizens' rights towards institutions, made possible by new technologies.

In particular, the Digital Administration Code, legislative decree no. 82/2005, provides for digital rights in respect of Public Administrations in the first provisions (Article 3 and following), confirming the centrality that must be reserved for users in the public action.

256. The Digital Administration Code, legislative decree no. 82/2005, provides in Article 3 the right to use technologies in relations between citizens and public subjects, a right which necessarily also implies the right of access to the Internet.

257. Specifically, anyone has the right to use, in an accessible and effective way, the solutions and tools provided by the CAD in relations with public entities, also for the purposes of exercising access rights and participation in the administrative procedure.

This right is the foundation of digital citizenship and concerns every phase of the relationship between institutions and the community. The provision, in case of violation, is provided with the relative judicial protection before the administrative judge.

258. The right of access to the Internet is also declined from the cultural point of view in Article 8 of legislative decree no. 82/2005, on the 'Digital literacy of citizens', which obliges Public Administrations to promote initiatives aimed at encouraging the dissemination of digital culture among citizens, in order to foster the development of skills and the use of digital services.

In this regard, the need arises to contrast the digital divide, a declension of inequality, the overcoming of which is necessary to affirm the rights and the development of the person.

259. The CAD also provides a series of rights 'derived' from the right to use the technologies, some relating to the procedure and communications and others that find their matrix even in the model of open government, such as the right to simple and integrated online services and the right to democratic electronic participation (e-democracy).

260. Digital rights must be read together with the related obligations placed on administrations, which translate into implementing the tools provided by the CAD, necessary to guarantee digital citizenship and to be able to implement relations between citizens and Public Administration using ICTs.

§3. Relationship Between Citizens and Public Administration

261. In the relationship between private individuals (citizens, associations and businesses) and administrations, the IT document, electronic signatures and digital domicile are regulated by the Digital Administration Code, legislative decree no. 82/2005, as arising from the modifications and additions made necessary also by the normative evolution at European level.

262. In particular with legislative decree no. 179/2016, the need arose to adapt the provisions to Regulation (EU) no. 910/2014 of 23 July 2014 on electronic identification and trust services for electronic transactions in the internal market (eIDAS regulation – electronic IDentification Authentication and Signature).

263. The rules confer full centrality on the IT document, widely defined as the electronic document that contains the IT representation of acts, facts or legally relevant data (Article 1, paragraph 1, letter p), legislative decree no. 82/2005).

As evidence of the prevalence of bytes on paper, the definition of an analogue document is derived in negative and consists in the 'non-computer' representation of documents, facts or legally relevant data (Article 1, paragraph 1, letter p-*bis*), legislative decree no. 82/2005).

264. The IT document, even without subscription, has its own legal value, but the electronic signature plays a fundamental role because it is an instrument for identification and imputation of the IT document and, therefore, of the statements contained therein with the related legal consequences.

265. The Italian legal system, in legislative decree no. 82/2005, outlines a system of multilevel subscriptions, a gradual system of electronic signatures, capable of attributing different legal and probative value to the document to which they are attached, in accordance with the different capacity to guarantee technical security and reliability about the identity of the subjects and the integrity of the data.

There are four types of electronic signature: simple, advanced, qualified and digital.

The first three signatures (simple, advanced and qualified) are foreseen and defined by the eIDAS regulation, which the CAD refers to.

266. The digital signature is provided specifically by our legal system, and the definition is therefore contained in the CAD (Article 1, paragraph 1, letter s): this is a particular type of qualified signature based on a cryptographic key system, a public one and a private one, related to each other, which allows the owner of electronic signature through the private key and a third party through the public key, respectively, to make manifest and verify the origin and integrity of an IT document or of a set of IT documents.

267. The digital domicile is an electronic address elected at a certified e-mail (PEC) or a qualified certified electronic delivery service, as defined by the eIDAS regulation (Article 1, paragraph 1, letter n-*ter*), legislative decree no. 82/2005).

268. Public actors, professionals required to register in lists and subject required to sign up in the register of companies have the obligation to have a digital address registered in the lists of addresses provided (IPA and INI-PEC).

Citizens have the right to elect their digital domicile to be registered in the specific list of addresses envisaged (Article 6-*quater*); in this regard the CAD has provided that by decree of the President of the Council of Ministers or the Minister delegated, the date will be established from which communications between public subjects and those who have not provided to elect a digital address will take place exclusively in electronic form.

269. Certified e-mail (PEC) is a communication system able to certify the sending and delivery of an e-mail message and to supply receipts that can be opposed to third parties (Article 1, paragraph 1, letter v-*bis*), legislative decree no. 82/2005; in the same sense Article 1, Presidential Decree no. 68/2005).

270. If you want to make a parallel with the traditional paper documents, the PEC corresponds to the registered mail with acknowledgement of receipt, while the e-mail corresponds to the ordinary mail.

271. In the case of PEC, the guarantee is provided, in addition to the technological aspect, by the presence of a third party offering the service, i.e. the certified e-mail manager, who meets certain professional requirements, guarantees the process and is subject to supervision and responsibility in carrying out their activities.

272. Electronic communications transmitted to a digital domicile produce, at the time of dispatch and receipt, the same legal effects as communications by registered mail with return receipt and are equivalent to the notification by means of post unless otherwise provided by law.

These communications are intended sent by the sender if sent to its operator and are intended to be delivered if made available to the recipient's digital home, subject to proof that the non-delivery is due to fact not attributable to the recipient.

The date and time of transmission and reception of the IT document are opposable to third parties if they are applied in accordance with the guidelines (Article 6, legislative decree no. 82/2005).

273. Communications via digital domiciles are carried out at the addresses included in the lists provided for by legislative decree no. 82/2005, in order to facilitate communications and make it possible to find digital domiciles easily and securely.

274. The public lists are three and cover the types of subjects involved in communications: the national index of digital domiciles of companies and professionals (INI-PEC) (Article 6-*bis*),[137] the index of digital domiciles of Public Administrations and public service operators (IPA) (Article 6-*ter*)[138] and the national index of digital domiciles of natural persons and other private law entities, not required to register in professional registers or in the business register (Article 6-*quater*).

The digital domiciles contained in this last list will be transferred from the AgID to the ANPR, National Register of the Resident Population, referred to in Article 62, at the time of its completion.[139]

275. The online consultation of the lists is allowed to anyone without the need for authentication.

In the absence of prior authorization of the holder of the address, the use of digital domiciles for purposes other than the sending of communications having legal value or in any case related to the achievement of institutional purposes of public entities is prohibited.

276. On 8 January 2019, there are more than 1,490,000 PEC addresses of professionals, covering more than 1,735 orders and professional colleges, and almost 4,500,000 PEC addresses of companies (firms and individual enterprises).

On 2 February 2019, there are 22,798 accredited IPA entities and the PEC addresses present on the IPA are 123,356.

On 28 January 2019, the Municipalities entered in ANPR are 1,633 and the population present in ANPR is 18,804,164.

§4. Data of the Public Administration: Open Data and Big Data

277. The data form the 'mine' of public information assets and the attention of the legislation focuses on the possibility of using them in analysis, services and solutions capable of generating cultural, economic and social growth.

278. legislative decree no. 82/2005 in Article 50 provides for the principle of availability of public data: the data of Public Administrations must be formed, collected, stored, made available and accessible with information technologies that allow use and reuse, under the conditions set by the law, by other Public Administrations and individuals.

---

137. The site is https://www.inipec.gov.it.
138. The site is https://www.indicepa.gov.it.
139. The site is https://www.anpr.interno.it.

The limits to the knowability of the data required by the laws and regulations, the rules on the protection of personal data and the compliance with European legislation on the reuse of public sector information are maintained.

279. In recent years, Italian legislation has explicitly promoted open data, under the stimulus of the international scene and of the European Union, which has dedicated directives and strategies to the exploitation and reuse of information in the public sector.

The data made available with the technical and legal characteristics necessary to be freely used, reused and redistributed by anyone, at any time and anywhere, are open data; the open data are a strategic tool for implementing the open government model.

280. legislative decree no. 82/2005, in Articles 52, 53 and 68, modified and integrated over the years, provides for the definition of open data in the legal, technological and economic dimensions that characterize them and for general provisions for the purpose of rationalizing the process of enhancing the national public information assets.

281. Specifically, Public Administrations are required to publish the catalogue of data and metadata, as well as the related databases in their possession and the regulations governing the exercise of the faculty of electronic access and the reuse of such data and metadata, without prejudice to data in the Tax Registry.

282. The favour towards open data is evident in the significant 'open data by default' principle: the data and documents published by the administrations in any way, without the express adoption of a standard licence for reuse, are intended to be released as open data, except for cases where the publication concerns personal data.

283. In this regard is also important legislative decree no. 36/2006, approved in implementation of Directive 2003/98/EC and amended by legislative decree no. 102/2015, which implemented Directive 2013/37/EU, which strengthened the institutions' obligations regarding open data, providing that administrations ensure that documents are reusable for commercial or non-commercial purposes in the manner envisaged.

284. As regards spatial information, Directive 2007/2/EC, which establishes an Infrastructure for spatial information in the European Community (INSPIRE), was implemented in Italy with legislative decree no. 32/2010.

285. In 2011, the Italian government launched the national open data portal, which constitutes the national catalogue of metadata relating to data released in an open format by Italian Public Administrations and has been updated over the years.[140]

The Portal is promoted by the Italian Government and managed by AgID with the support of FormezPA.

Furthermore, thematic portals,[141] territorial portals (Regions, Municipalities, etc.)[142] and portals belonging to Italian user projects regarding open data have been created.[143]

With regard to open data, the 'Three-Year Plan 2017-2019 for ICT in the Public Administration' sets objectives such as the definition and approval of the dynamic dataset basket and constant monitoring.

On 21 January 2019, the datasets published in the dati.gov.it portal were 23,601 and the administrations that publish data in open format were 403.

286. Big data are huge volumes of data, coming from different sources and analysed by means of algorithms, data mining techniques, big data analytics software, machine learning applications and specific technologies.

With legislative decree no. 217/2017, the CAD was modified by providing interesting provisions regarding big data in the public sphere.

287. Pursuant to Article 50, paragraph 2-*bis*, legislative decree no. 82/2005, introduced by legislative decree no. 217/2017, the Public Administrations, in the context of their institutional functions, proceed to the analysis of their data also in combination with those held by other public entities, without prejudice to the limits established by the law, and are required to carry out this activity according to the methods identified by AgID in the guidelines.

288. In this regard, the Data & Analytics Framework (DAF) is particularly significant, as envisaged by Article 50-*ter* of legislative decree no. 82/2005, introduced by legislative decree no. 217/2017, and already identified as a strategic project by the 'Three-Year Plan 2017-2019 for ICT in the Public Administration'.

289. The Presidency of the Council of Ministers is required to promote the design, development and testing of the DAF, aimed at promoting the knowledge and the use of information assets held, for institutional purposes, by Public Administrations, as well as the sharing of data between subjects who have the right to access

---

140. The site is https://www.dati.gov.it; the national repertoire of territorial data is http://geodati.gov.it/geoportale.

141. Among these we mention SoldiPubblici (http://soldipubblici.gov.it), OpenDemanio (https://dati.agenziademanio.it), OpenCantieri (http://opencantieri.mit.gov.it).

142. Regions have been particularly active in terms of open data. *See*, *for example*, http://www.dati.piemonte.it; https://dati.trentino.it; http://dati.toscana.it; https://www.dati.lombardia.it; https://dati.lazio.it.

143. Among these we mention http://www.monithon.it (independent initiative of civic monitoring of projects financed by European policies) and https://www.confiscatibene.it (portal for transparency and promotion of the reuse of confiscated assets to organized crime).

them for the purpose of simplifying the administrative obligations of citizens and businesses, in compliance with the regulations in force; the methods of implementation are established with Decree of the President of the Council of Ministers.

290. The DAF is based on a big data platform and is part of the activities aimed at enhancing the national public information assets, focusing on quality and standardization of data and facilitating the development and dissemination of open data and API economy.

§5. Digital Identity and Online Services

291. The Digital Administration Code, the 'Strategy for Digital Growth 2014-2020' and the 'Three-Year Plan 2017-2019 for ICT in the Public Administration' show attention to digital identity and online services and regulate to this end the Public Digital Identity System (SPID), the access tools to online services and 'Italia Login', that is the 'home' of the citizen.

292. These instruments, together with the others related to the administrative procedure, implement the first digital principle, which permeates the legislation, in particular following the reforms of legislative decree no. 179/2016 and no. 217/2017, approved on the basis of the delegated Law no. 124/2015 which contains that principle.

293. Digital identity is normally defined as the computerized representation of the correspondence between a user and his identifying attributes, verified through the datasets collected and recorded in digital form according to the modalities envisaged (Article 1, paragraph 1, lett. u-*quater*), legislative decree no. 82/2005).

294. In order to facilitate the dissemination of online services and facilitate access to them, the Public Digital Identity System of citizens and businesses (SPID) is established.

SPID is constituted as an open set of public and private subjects that, after accreditation by AgID, according to modalities defined by decree, identify users to allow them access to online services (Article 64, legislative decree no. 2005).

295. SPID is configured as a login system that allows citizens and businesses to access with a single digital identity to all online services of Public Administrations and member undertakings.

296. The SPID identity consists of credentials with different characteristics based on the level of security required for access and is issued, at the request of the party concerned, by the Identity Provider, a legal entity accredited by AgID. There are nine Identity Providers (Aruba, InfoCert, Poste, Sielte, TIM, SpidItalia, Lepida, Namirial and Intesa).

In December 2017, 4,000 Public Administrations allowed access to online services also through SPID. On 22 January 2019, 3,340,479 digital identities were issued.[144]

297. Access to online services provided by Public Administrations requiring IT identification is via SPID. Access can also take place with an Electronic Identity Card (CIE) and the National Service Card (CNS).

In this regard, however, by decree of the Prime Minister or the Minister for simplification and Public Administration, the date will be established from which public entities will use only digital identities for the purpose of identifying users of their online services.

The electronic CIE and CNS cards are governed by Article 66, legislative decree no. 82/2005.

298. The Electronic Identity Card (CIE) is the identity document with elements for the physical identification of the holder issued on an IT support by the municipal administrations with the main purpose of proving the identity of the owner (Article 1, paragraph 1, letter c), legislative decree no. 82/2005).

299. The National Service Card (CNS) is the document issued on an IT support to allow access by telematic means to the services provided by Public Administrations (Article 1, paragraph 1, letter d), legislative decree no. 82/2005).

300. The SPID system and the electronic cards allow access to online services:

> In this regard, in order to achieve effective digitalization of public administrations, 'Italia Login' is expected to be created, a single access point and a single platform, oriented and centered on the user, who wants to act as a real 'online home' for citizens aimed at overcoming current complexities and differences.

Public entities are required to make their services available online through the telematic access point activated at the Presidency of the Council of Ministers (Article 64-*bis*, legislative decree no. 82/2005, introduced by legislative decree no. 179/2016).

'Italia Login' is the frame of reference for the new way to relate between Public Administration and individuals, through a unique place, able to put the citizen at the centre and to simplify access to online services.

301. As regards the presentation of requests and declarations by electronic means to public subjects, alternative methods are envisaged with the use of various digital tools provided by the CAD: digital or qualified or advanced signature; identification via SPID or electronic cards CNS and CIE; use of the digital domicile provided that the relevant access credentials have been issued upon identification of the

144. The reference site is https://www.spid.gov.it.

holder and this is attested by the operator; signing and presentation together with a copy of the identity document (Article 65, legislative decree no. 82/2005 and Article 38, Presidential Decree no. 445/2000).

§6. Electronic Payments and Electronic Invoicing

302. Public entities are obliged to accept payments due for any reason, through the technological platform made available by AgID, through electronic payment systems (Article 5, legislative decree no. 82/2005).

303. PagoPA ('PayPA') platform, an electronic payment management system for the Public administration, was created to give citizens and businesses the opportunity to make any electronic payment to public entities, being able to choose the service provider, the tools and the channel of payment.

304. On 5 January 2018, the Public Administrations and the managers of public services that formally joined PagoPA were 17,187: among these, those that have completed the activation procedure and are operative were 13,890. On 31 October 2018, private entities (banks, post offices, payment institutions) providing payment services were 412.

305. Starting from 31 March 2015, electronic invoicing towards all national and local Public Administrations has become compulsory and, starting from 1 January 2019, electronic invoicing has also become compulsory even among private individuals, excluding those exempted.

§7. Cyberspace Protection and Cybersecurity

306. In terms of security, the Digital Administration Code, legislative decree no. 82/2005 devotes a specific provision, Article 51: by means of guidelines, the appropriate technical solutions to guarantee the protection, availability, accessibility, integrity and confidentiality of data and the operational continuity of the systems and infrastructures are identified.

AgID (the Italian Agency for the Digital Strategies) implements, as far as it is responsible for and in conjunction with the other relevant authorities, the National Strategic Framework for Cyberspace Security and the National Plan for Cyberspace Protection and ICT Security.

307. In this regard, with Decree of the President of the Council of Ministers of 17 February 2017, the 'Directive on cybernetic protection and national cybersecurity' was approved and on 31 March 2017 the 'National Plan for Cyberspace Protection and ICT Security' was adopted, which is in continuity with the previous one (two-year period 2014-2015) and set out the guidelines for a concrete implementation of the 'National Strategic Framework for Cyberspace Security', approved in December 2013.[145]

308. In the 'Strategy for Digital Growth 2014-2020', the Digital Security Project for Public Administration was created to increase the level of security of information and digital communications to allow new levels of services for citizens and businesses.

The aim is to protect the privacy, integrity and continuity of Public Administration services, a crucial infrastructure for the country.

309. This project also includes the CERT-PA, i.e. the Computer Emergency Response Public Administration Team, which operates within AgID and is responsible for supporting administrations in preventing and responding to cybersecurity incidents.

As of 31 December 2018, 60 Public Administrations are served by CERT-PA and the reports received by CERT-PA are 2620.[146]

310. The Digital Security project involves all Public Administrations, as well as all those actors in the private sector that provide solutions and services to the Public Administration, and is monitored by the Steering Committee for the Cybersecurity of the Council Presidency.

311. The 'Three-Year Plan 2017-2019 for ICT in the Public Administration' provides, in the field of security, the strengthening of the role of CERT-PA, in order to structure the security plans of Public Administrations, to monitor with regular checks on the implementation plans, and emphasizes the rationalization of ICT resources as a priority method to increase the level of security by reducing the 'surface' exposed to cyberattacks.

§8. Digital Health and Other Digital Ecosystems

312. Digital ecosystems are, in Italy, the sectors, or areas, of intervention in which the actions of Public Administrations are carried out, from health to agriculture, from school to cultural heritage, as provided for by the Italian 'Three-Year Plan 2017-2019 for ICT in the Public Administration'.

313. The 'Health Card' and the 'Electronic Health Record' (FSE) play a central role in the health ecosystem in Italy.

314. The 'Health Card' is the personal document issued to all Italian citizens entitled to benefits provided by the National Health Service (SSN), which enables

145. The site dedicated to national security is http://www.sicurezzanazionale.gov.it/sisr.nsf/index.html.
146. The dedicated website is https://www.cert-pa.it.

access to health services provided by the SSN throughout the national territory and is a health insurance card for the purpose of recognizing healthcare in EU countries, as well as serving as a tax code.

The 'Health Card – National Service Card' (TS-CNS), equipped with microchips, in addition to the health services normally used with the TS, once activated also allows access to CNS services offered online by the Public Administration, in security and in respect of privacy.[147]

315. The 'Electronic Health Record' (FSE) is the tool through which citizens can track, consult and share their health history with health professionals.

The FSE infrastructure manages all the health and social-health digital data and documents generated by present and past clinical events concerning the patient.

316. The FSE, as described in Decree of the President of the Council of Ministers n. 178/2015, containing the Regulation on FSE, contains the patient's medical history represented by a set of data and documents.

Among these, some are mandatory and are part of the so-called minimum nucleus, and others are, instead, supplementary and optional documents that depend on the choices made by the regional institutions and on the level of maturation of the process of digitization of individual documents produced by hospitals.

317. Particularly important is the 'Patient Summary', which can be considered as the 'health identity card' of the patient.

Inside it are contained, in addition to the identification data, all the clinical information describing the status of the patient as the relevant problems, diagnoses, allergies, pharmacological therapies for any chronic diseases and all the essential indications to guarantee patient care.

318. On 7 January 2019, there are 17 active Regions, 13 Regions with electronic health records implemented and operational and 11 Regions which, having successfully passed the interoperability tests with the central FSE platform, are members of the interoperability on the national infrastructure; the percentage of citizens who have activated the FSE out of the total number of SNN assisted is 20%.[148]

319. A further relevant profile is the introduction of the digital prescription in substitution of the paper recipe, which provides for the complete computerization of the entire life cycle of the traditional medical prescription.

It is a process of dematerialization of paper pharmaceutical prescriptions, replacing them with equivalent digital documents, throughout the national territory.

320. Also important is the dematerialization of medical reports and medical records, which aims to create a flow of digital documents with full legal value that will lead to the replacement of all paper equivalents, with the aim of improving services to citizens.

---

147. The reference site is https://sistemats1.sanita.finanze.it/portale.
148. The reference site is https://www.fascicolosanitario.gov.it.

321. Other solutions foreseen by the 'Three-Year Plan 2017-2019 for ICT in the Public Administration', which will make accessible computerized health services, are the Single Reservation Center (CUP) and the 'Telemedicina' (Tele-medicine) project.

322. The Single Reservation Center (CUP), the centralized computerized system for the unified reservation of services, was created to facilitate access to assistance and reduce waiting times.

323. The 'Telemedicina' project was created to offer services that improve the usability of treatment, diagnosis services and remote medical advice, in addition to the constant monitoring of vital parameters.

324. Next to health, the 'Three-Year Plan 2017-2019 for ICT in the Public Administration' identifies another twelve digital ecosystems: (i) welfare; (ii) public finance; (iii) school; (iv) higher education and research; (v) defence, security and legal aid; (vi) law; (vii) infrastructures and logistics – mobility; (viii) development and sustainability; (ix) cultural heritage and tourism; (x) communications; (xi) agriculture; (xii) Italy in Europe and the world.

Each ecosystem identifies a thematic sector with homogeneous characteristics.

For each ecosystem, AgID recommends the establishment of a working group, which deals with the management and technological development of the ecosystem itself.

325. In the 'Three-Year Plan 2017-2019 for ICT in the Public Administration', the Digital Justice ecosystem revolves around:

- (i) telematic civil process;
- (ii) telematic tributary process;
- (iii) telematic criminal trial;
- (iv) telematic administrative process; and
- (v) constitution, considering the extent and heterogeneity of the users, of the access points, technological-organizational structures that provide access to the portal to the authorized subjects outside the Ecosystem of Justice telematic services.

326. With regard to the digital school ecosystem, the initiatives are contained in the National Digital School Plan, foreseen by Law no. 107/2015, adopted by Ministerial Decree no. 851 of 27 October 2015, a multi-annual document of the Ministry of Education, University and Research for the promotion of innovation and digitalization of the Italian school.

The Plan identifies a series of different actions, such as digital environments for teaching, the electronic register, the administrative digitalization of the school, the students' skills, the training of staff, the digital animators in schools.[149]

149. *See* the website http://www.istruzione.it/scuola_digitale.

§9. THE DIGITAL TELEMATIC PROCESS

327. It is possible to trace the origin of the telematic process, from a strictly regulatory point of view to the provisions of Law n. 59/1997 which, with Article 15, attributes to IT documents, to the deeds and data of the Public Administration, formed on computer media or transmitted electronically, value and relevance to all legal purposes; with the following d.p.r. n. 513/1997 is then introduced in the Italian system the legislation concerning the digital signature.

328. The first real legislative intervention of the Legislator is however of 13 February 2001 with the d.p.r. n. 123 from whose reading it is possible to deduce how, with the use of the information technology in the process, is tried to facilitate the saving of material and personal energies and the functionality of the entire procedural system, all in an attempt to make work easier not only for Public Administration personnel but also, and above all, for lawyers and for all citizens.

329. The telematic civil trial had to pass an experimental phase initially set for September 2004, then postponed to September 2005 and, finally, carried out in 2006.

330. The Courts of Genoa and Milan were the first to move from the theoretical phase to the practical phase of using telematics and this happened during the year 2006.
In particular, on 11 December 2006, the experimentation was concluded and the Court of Milan could thus benefit from the activation of the telematic injunction where, initially, around 300 lawyers, 30 magistrates and 15 Chancellors were involved, while, as of 30 May 2007, there were about 1,300 electronic injunction decrees managed with an average of 15/20 daily deposits.

331. The use of the telematic process, as well as being, as we shall see, mandatory as of 30 June 2014, for the filing of some types of deeds, offers a series of opportunities that undoubtedly contribute to facilitating the development of the legal profession.

332. The digital signature device is very important in the Italian system and has a dual function:

(i) it allows online interaction with the websites that require the user to identify themselves in a certain manner and in compliance with the regulations in force so that the same can be recognized by the 'Justice system' as a qualified subject to the use of the telematic process;
(ii) it permits to digitally sign the documents drawn up in the form of an electronic document with the same legal value as the handwritten signature affixed to the analogical (paper) document, ensuring the electronic document, after its signature, integrity (guaranteeing the identity of the person who signed the document) and non-modifiability (guaranteeing that the document has not been modified after its subscription).

333. PEC (certified electronic mail) is the tool, for the user, to legally deposit and receive the deeds of the process and, following the d.m. 21 February 2011 n. 44, has become the official means of communication in the PCT.

It is a tool similar to e-mail but, unlike this, the messages sent have the same value as a registered letter with return receipt, given that after sending a PEC message to the sender two receipts will be returned, the one of acceptance and that of delivery.

The first one (acceptance receipt) comes from the server of the software house with which the sender has activated the PEC service, while the second one (delivery receipt) attests that the message has been delivered in the PEC box of the recipient.

By law, the message is understood to be known and known to the recipient as soon as it is delivered in his PEC and this even in the absence of reading or actual knowledge, and it is always from that moment (delivery) that any terms to be observed run to avoid forfeiture procedural.

334. The PDA (access point to the Justice system), following the technical rules dictated by Ministerial Decree 21 February 2011 n. 44, may be private (made available by private individuals authorized by the Ministry of Justice) or public (through the Portal of Telematic Services of the Justice domain).

The PDA (public or private) has the function of identifying and recognizing with absolute certainty those who want to access online justice by checking their identity and role (lawyer or qualified practitioner, magistrate, expert witness, etc.) through the site authentication certificate.

335. The 'deed editor' is the tool with which the lawyers, after having prepared their deeds in the form of digital native computer documents (transformed into the PDF format obtained without scanning) and the documents to be deposited (the latter also scanned from the paper) make the actual electronic deposit, giving rise to a 'telematic envelope' (file act.enc) created according to the PCT rules and technical specifications in force and sent, always in compliance with the aforementioned rules, through the PEC.

336. The Italian Legislator, for the first time, dares a definition of the electronic document with Article 3 of the law of 23 December 1993 n. 547 which introduces, in the Penal Code, Article 491-*bis*: 'If any of the falsehoods provided for in this chapter concerns a public or private computer document, the provisions of the chapter itself concerning public deeds and private deeds are applied. To this end, an electronic document is any computerized medium containing data or information having evidential value or programmes specifically designed to process them.'

337. Having made this necessary premise, and wanting to reconstruct the normative evolution of the telematic process, it is possible to affirm that the Legislator sets the 'first stone' of what, in the following years, would later become its technical-legal structure, with Article 15 paragraph 2 of Law 15 March 1997 n. 59, dedicating for the first time a rule to the use of technology and IT tools: 'The deeds, data and documents formed by the Public Administration and by individuals with IT or electronic tools and even the contracts stipulated in the same forms, are valid and relevant to all effects of the Law.'

338. Since that distant 1997, there have been numerous rules in the regulation of the electronic process; we have already mentioned the d.p.r. 13 February 2001 n. 123, with which was issued the Regulation laying down the rules on the use of IT and telematic tools in the civil process, in the administrative process and the process before the jurisdictional sections of the Court of Accounts which, in Article 1, defined the general picture.

339. Another fundamental rule is legislative decree 7th March 2005 n. 82, better known as the Digital Administration Code, which incorporates, expands and clarifies some of the concepts contained in the d.p.r. 13 February 2001 n. 123 and which, to date, constitutes the real 'vertebral column' and the regulatory reference point for the entire digitalization sector of the Public Administration.

The last change to the Digital Administration Code was made by legislative decree no. 179/2016, with which the Legislator has tried to standardize the content of European Regulation eIDAS n. 910/2014, entered into force on 1 July 2016.

340. More specific, from the point of view of content, for the electronic civil process, the technical rules of July 2008, those of February 2011 (d.m. n. 44/11); the technical specifications of 18 July 2011; the changes made to the d.m. n. 44/11 from the d.m. n. 209/12; the legislative decree 179/12, the law 221/12 which provided for the civil trial, starting from 30 June 2014; the new technical specifications of April 2014 for the deposit of some documents and documents instead of the traditional paper deposit recalled and wanted by Article 34 of the d.m. n. 44/11 which, therefore, replaced those of 18 July 2011 and the legislative decree no. 90/14 (converted with law n. 114/14); the legislative decree no. 132 of 12 September 2014 (urgent de-jurisdictionalization measures and other interventions for the definition of the backlog in civil proceedings) which, with the fourth paragraph of Article 18, modified Article 16-*bis* of legislative decree 18 October 2012 n. 179, for which, starting from 31 March 2015, the obligatory electronic filing is extended to all the documents (including the introductory ones) relating to the forced expropriation proceedings (Articles 518, 543 and 557 of the Italian Code of Civil Procedure); and, most recently, the dl n. 83/15, converted with Law n. 132/15 which led, in January 2016, to the modification of the technical specifications with the introduction of Article 19-*ter* containing provisions relating to the manner in which to carry out the certificate of conformity to be included in a separate electronic document.

341. Before the publication and entry into force of legislative decree no. 179/12, the filing of deeds and documents in electronic form was permitted and had legal value only if the judicial office in which the deposit was sought had obtained a specific Decree of the Ministry of Justice, issued by them pursuant to and for the effects of Article 35 of the legislative decree no. 44/11.

This decree, in fact, allowed the professional to electronically deposit his own deed or document in compliance with the c.p.c. without the need to also deposit the document or the paper document.

342. With Article 16-*bis* of legislative decree no. 179/12, the obligatory electronic filing of the documents and documents '[...] by the defenders of the previously constituted parties [...] in the same way is filed for the filing of the documents and documents by the persons appointed or delegated by the judicial authority. The parties shall, in the manner set out in this paragraph, deposit the documents and documents originating from the persons appointed by them'.

343. The same article also provided for the obligatory electronic filing also for the injunction procedure.

344. From 30 June 2014, therefore, in all the Courts, the rule would have been that of the electronic filing of documents and documents in the following proceedings:

(i) civil proceedings, disputes, voluntary jurisdiction;
(ii) executive processes;
(iii) insolvency proceedings;
(iv) injunction procedure.

345. For insolvency proceedings, the same law always required the mandatory filing of documents and documents electronically only 'by the trustee, the judicial commissioner, the liquidator, the liquidator and the extraordinary commissioner', not also, therefore, for the defender.

346. There is no doubt that Article 16-*bis* of legislative decree 179/12 represented a real revolution for the civil trial since, for the first time, the Legislator placed a real regulatory prohibition for the deposit of certain acts and documents with the traditional form, the paper form.

347. The problem is to clearly understand for which documents and deeds the lawyer has obligatorily to proceed with their electronic filing.
From the careful reading of the article in question, it was deduced that the obligation of the electronic filing would have concerned only and exclusively documents deposited by the previously constituted parts, maintaining therefore the possibility of depositing the paper not only for the party that had to start and to establish the judgment with a writ of summons or appeal but also for the party that, in a judgment already incardinated, had to be formed on behalf of its client.

348. Article. 16-*bis* also states that '... the parties shall, with the methods referred to in this paragraph, deposit the documents and documents originating from the persons appointed by them'.

This meant that it would have been the lawyer's obligation to electronically file not only the documents of his production but also those, for example, of the technical consultants who, appointed by his client during the procedure with the task of supporting the consultant appointed by the judge, would have delivered to the professional, in the form of an electronic document, their elaborate, so that the latter then proceeded to deposit it electronically.

349. Legislative decree no. 179/12 introduced significant innovations also in the field of telecommunications communications (tickets), in both civil and criminal proceedings.

Previously, the matter was regulated by Article 51 of legislative decree no. 112/2008, amended by the law of 22 February 2010 n. 24 and by Article 35 of legislative decree no. 44/2011 and 136 c.p.c. as amended by law n. 183/11 effective from 1 February 2012.

350. With paragraph 4 of legislative decree no. 179/12 in the civil proceedings was confirmed and reiterated, as an official and primary means for communicating to the defenders of the chancellery tickets, that of the certified electronic mail.

351. With paragraph 6 of the aforementioned decree it was stated that notifications and communications to the subjects for whom the law provided for the obligation to provide themselves with a certified e-mail address and that they had not established or communicated the aforementioned address, would have been performed exclusively by filing in the Registry and the same procedures would have been adopted in the event of non-delivery of the certified e-mail message for reasons attributable to the recipient.

352. On 24 June 2014, the legislative decree was published in Official Journal. n. 90, 'Urgent measures for simplification and administrative transparency and for the efficiency of judicial offices'.

The rules contained in Title IV brought significant changes to the rules of the electronic civil process, also remodelling the obligatory electronic filing of some documents which, in the absence of such a decree, would enter into force on 30 June 2014.

353. The following terms were thus established in the Courts:

(i) from 30 June 2014, the obligation of electronic filing of: (a) appeals for injunctions; (b) proceedings indicated by Article 16-*bis*, paragraph 4, of legislative decree no. 179/2012 (procedural documents and documents on the part of the defenders of the previously constituted parties) registered to the role from 30 June 2014. The obligation of electronic filing therefore concerned procedural documents and documents by the defenders of the previously constituted parties (e.g., writ of summons and appearance of constitution and reply remained excluded from the obligation of electronic filing, for which the obligation was related to the filing of pleadings pursuant to Article 183 of the Italian Civil Code);

(ii) from 31 December 2014, the obligation to electronically file the documents relating to the proceedings already pending on 30 June 2014 and indicated by Article 16-*bis*, paragraph 4, legislative decree no. 179/2012.

(iii) from 30 June 2015, the obligation to electronically file in the Courts of Appeal the procedural documents and documents by the lawyers of the parties previously established, proceeding, similarly, for the filing of the documents and deeds by the appointed subjects or delegated by the judicial authority. The parties, then, had to deposit, with telematic methods, the documents coming from the subjects appointed by them.

354. In Article. 52 of the legislative decree it is also established that 'the defender, the technical consultant, the delegated professional, the curator and the judicial commissioner' could have extracted by electronic means, analogical or computerized copies of the deeds and provisions and attest 'the conformity of the copies extracted to the corresponding deeds in the electronic file with total exemption of payment of copying rights'.

355. The last regulatory change of 2014 (entered into force on 11 December 2014) for the online process occurred with the publication of legislative decree no. 132 of 12 September 2014 and the relative conversion took place with the law of 10 November 2014 n. 162.

This change involved the procedures of forced expropriation (securities, real estate and third-party attachment) not only from a procedural standpoint but also with reference to the electronic filing obligation.

356. For the forced expropriation proceedings, which began on December 11th 2014, until March 30th 2015, the lawyer could have filed the related registration notes in paper form, and this was shown by coordinating among them Article 16-*bis*, paragraph 2, of legislative decree no. 179/12 and Article 18 of legislative decree no. 132/14.

357. Consequently, for the procedures started from 11 December 2014, since the bailiff no longer lodges the attachment deed in the Registry but as the defender has to fulfil this deposit, until 30 March 2015, the registration in the role in the Forced expropriation proceedings could be carried out in the traditional (paper) manner and only for subsequent deposits it was obligatory to proceed electronically, while, as of 31 March 2015, as required by Article 18, paragraph 4, of the legislative decree no. 132/14, the obligation of the defender was established at the electronic deposit of the note of registration in the role.

358. Finally, the d.l. n. 83/2015, published in the Official Journal on 27 June 2015, containing 'Urgent measures in bankruptcy, civil and procedural civil matters and the organization and functioning of the judicial administration' contained innovative provisions on the subject of electronic data processing and telematic administrative process, then also confirmed by the law of conversion 132/15:

(i) the introduction of an extended system of optional electronic filing of documents, released from the limits of Article 35 d.m. n. 44 of 2011;
(ii) the extension of the power of authenticity conferred on lawyers, with the extension of this power when the electronic filing had also concerned computer copies (scans) of procedural documents of part or court orders held by the defender in analogical original form or in a copy of the original;
(iii) the simplification and rationalization of the procedures for certifying the conformity of IT copies, releasing them from those provided by d.p.c.m. 13 November 2014 and, in particular, from the need to indicate the footprint of the file containing the computer copy (also by image) obtained, in January 2016, with the introduction, in the technical specifications, of Article 19-*ter* containing provisions relating to the manner in which the certificate of compliance was to be executed to be included in a separate electronic document.

359. In summary, the obligatory electronic filing was introduced by the Legislator with legislative decree no. 179/12 which, as already mentioned, provided with Article 16-*bis*, as of 30 June 2014, the electronic filing of certain deeds, such as endoprocessual ones, as well as the filing of the appeal by injunction.

360. Therefore, it passed from the right to electronic filing to the electronic filing obligation; Article 44, paragraph 1, of legislative decree no. 90/2014 then remodulated this obligation by providing, for endoprocessual acts, the compulsory electronic filing only for those relating to the proceedings registered to the role from 30 June 2014 while, for the documents relating to proceedings entered before 30 June, the mandatory was deferred to 31 December 2014.

361. To date the obligation of electronic filing is arranged for: (i) appeal by injunction; (ii) endoprocessual acts (Court and Court of Appeal); (iii) enforceable property, real estate and third-party proceedings.

Part I. Regulation of the ICT Market

Chapter 1. Regulatory Framework of the Telecommunications Sector

§1. A Brief History of Telecommunications Services in Italy

362. Initially, telecommunications services in Italy were only State-exclusive services, run by administrative bodies or by public service concessionaires.

Many concessionaires were established by the Italian public holding IRI, the company founded in 1933 and used by the Government for the State intervention activity in the industry and economics sectors.

A lot of subsidiaries in the telecommunications field were controlled by the STET company, a holding controlled by IRI.[150]

363. In 1992, Law n. 58/92 provided that the management of all telecommunications services was to be assigned to a *concessionary*.

364. In 1994, the Italian Government created the company *Telecom Italia* by merging all concessionaires, aiming to foster industrial efficiency.

365. In 1995, then, it established *Telecom Italia Mobile*, a company aiming to develop the mobile telephony market.

Moreover, *Omnitel Pronto Italia*, a competitor to *Telecom Italia*, entered into the telecommunications market.

366. As a matter of fact, starting from 1995, in accordance with the European Union competition policies, the sector started to face a progressive *liberalization*, and State monopoly on telecommunications services was progressively abandoned.

367. The necessity to guide the transformation of the market and the need for regulation and intervention in many specific matters, such as, conflicts and relations

150. For an overview of the Italian legal framework *see*, *generally*: V. Franceschelli, 'La convergenza nelle telecomunicazioni e il diritto d'autore nella società dell'informazione' (Giuffrè, Milano, 2009); F. Bassan (ed.), 'Diritto delle comunicazioni elettroniche' (Giuffré, Milano, 2010); S. Sica, V. Zeno-Zencovich, 'Manuale di diritto dell'informazione e della comunicazione' (CEDAM, Padova, 2012); P. Carretti, 'Diritto dell'informazione e della comunicazione' (Il Mulino, Bologna, 2010).

between competitors, suppliers and consumers, were faced by creating the national regulatory agency AGCOM ('Autorità per le Garanzie nelle Comunicazioni'), established by Law n. 249/1997.

§2. Liberalization of the Telecommunications Market in Italy

368. legislative decree no. 103/1995 implemented in Italy the European Union Directive n. 90/388/CEE on the *competition* in the markets for the telecommunication services.

369. The liberalization process developed gradually in the following five years.
In such period, several European Directives were implemented, and many regulatory rules were enacted by AGCOM to respect the general legal framework designed by the European Union institutions.

370. Such processes took into account the 'universal service' requirement of the European Union Legislation, as well as the safeguards of State and public interests.
One example of the latter is the so-called golden share regulation, i.e. the Italian Government's power attributed by law to *block* an acquisition of *Telecom Italia*.

371. Some key moments of the liberalization process were the assignment of radio and telecommunication services to concessionaires in 1992, the merger of concessionaires into *Telecom Italia* in 1994, the liberalization of telecommunication services and the entry of a new mobile operator in 1995, the liberalization of satellite service, the voice telephony market and the creation of the national regulatory agency AGCOM in 1997, the entry of other new mobile operators between 1999 and 2000.

372. The market was made more vital by the regulatory activity of AGCOM aimed to foster the use of the telecommunication networks physically owned by *Telecom Italia* by other competitors (the so-called unbundling).

373. A very important moment in the process of liberalization was the enactment of legislative decree no. 259/03 ('Code of Electronic Communications').
In particular, Section 3 of the Code formally recognizes the *freedom* to use means of electronic communications, as well as the freedom to supply electronic communications services in competition regime.
Section 25 of the Code defines a *general authorization* regime, according to which activity in conformity with the general authorization is *free* upon notice to the Ministry of Communications.

374. Such process was strengthened by the enactment of legislative decree 70/03 on the e-commerce and the liability of service providers, implementing the European Union Directive 2000/31/CE.

375. During the years, new players entered the market.

Some of them chose to instal and manage their own networks,[151] others participated in auctions of spectrum dedicated to mobile telephony and some did not survive.[152]

Other operators chose to use Telecom Italia infrastructures.

376. Currently, in Italy the sector faces also the so-called *convergence phenomenon.*

Technological changes allow contents to be digitalized and to flow through networks and different electronic devices.

So, there is convergence between former one-to-many broadcasting networks and telecommunications networks.

377. The broadcasting sector, and mainly the television sector, is intersectioning the telecommunications one: telecommunications networks are capable to broadcast, thanks to connectivity bandwidth increase, and television networks are capable to transmit using radio waves, digital television and Internet.

Such networks are also experimenting new forms of interactivity with users.

378. The same AGCOM authority has powers, also, in the broadcasting and audiovisual services.

The laws design complex relationships between AGCOM and the Ministry of Economic Development.[153] The legislative *corpus* is very complex and implements several European Directives.[154]

§3. The Italian Legislation

379. Many Italian telecommunication laws implement European Union Directives, conforming the Italian legal framework to the law and policies of the European Union.

For instance, legislative decree no. 55/93 and Presidential Decree n. 318/97 implemented the *Open Network Provision* Directive n. 90/387; legislative decree no. 89/94 and Presidential Decree n. 318/97 implemented Directive n. 92/44, amended by Directive n. 97/51 on leased lines; voice telephony Directives n. 95/62 and n. 98/10 were implemented with Presidential Decree n. 318/97 and AGCOM resolution n. 101/99; Presidential Decree n. 318/97 and AGCOM decisions n. 657/00 and n. 467/00 implemented Directive n. 97/13 on licensing; Ministerial Decree

151. This was a strategic choice of *Fastweb*, for instance.
152. The case of the *Blu* telecommunications company may be mentioned. The company started as a mobile operator, but retired from the market after it had capital shortage while participating in an auction for UMTS frequencies and sold its assets to the other players on the mobile market.
153. The former Ministry of Communications became part of the Ministry of Economic Development.
154. Currently, the fundamental law is Legislative Decree n. 177/2005, amended by Legislative Decree n. 44/2010, which implements Directive n. 2007/65/EC. Some other fundamental laws to be mentioned are the law that started the digitalization of the Italian television system, Law n. 249/97, and the law that granted AGCOM the power to enact AGCOM rules 435/2001/CONS on the terrestrial digital television.

of 23 April 1998 and AGCOM decisions of 29 July 1999, 3/CIR and 4/CIR in 1999 implemented Directive n. 97/33 as modified by 98/61 on interconnection, number portability and carrier preselection.

380. Currently, the central national telecommunications law is legislative decree no. 259/2003 ('Code of Electronic Communications'), enacted in order to implement the so-called telecom package of 2002.[155]

381. However, the discipline is going to change in order to comply with Directive 2009/140/CE, amending Directives 2002/21/EC, 2002/20/EC, and 2002/19/EC.[156]

Some provisions of the Universal Services are also modified by Directive 2009/136/EC.[157]

§4. The Italian Telecommunications Authority

382. AGCOM, the Italian Telecommunications Authority, was established by Law n. 249/97.

It is a key autonomous and Independent Administrative Authority, with regulatory and sanctionary powers, as well as powers of supervision and control.

383. The Authority has a very wide range of competences, both in the sector of telecommunications and in the sector of audiovisual services. Such competences and powers derive from different laws,[158] regulating different sectors.[159]

384. Some important regulatory powers of the Authority involve spectrum planning and allocation, together with the Ministry of Economic Development, keeping the register of communications operators ('Registro degli Operatori di Comunicazione'),[160] numbering, as well as number planning and management, quality of service monitoring, price interventions, access to telecommunications infrastructures and interconnections.

---

155. *See* Directive 2002/21/EC (so-called Framework Directive), Directive 2002/20/EC (so-called Authorization Directive), Directive 2002/19/EC (so-called Access Directive) and Directive 2002/22/EC (so-called Universal Service Directive).
156. According to s. 5 of the Directive, the new measures are to be applied from 26th May 2011. The Italian Government is proceeding to enact shortly a Legislative Decree in order to implement both Directive 2009/140/CE and Directive 2009/136/CE.
157. Directive 2009/136/EC is modifying also the processing of personal data rules.
158. For instance, s. 10 of Law n. 177/2005, as amended by Law n. 44/2010, provides that the Authority has competences concerning matters of the provision of audiovisual media services and that AGCOM ensures the respect of the fundamental rights of the individuals in the communications sector.
159. The Authority has powers and competences both in the field of telecommunications and in the field of broadcasting, press, television and publishing, involving the use of both spectrum and networks and the activities themselves.
160. The operators obliged to enrol in the register are listed in s. 1 para. 6 lett. n. 5 of Law n. 249/1997 and resolution of AGCOM n. 608/10/CONS.

385. It is controversial whether the Authority has the power to regulate in the field of copyright and intellectual property infringements on the Internet, given that there is no clear rule of the law in such sense.
One of the key powers of the Authority is to signalize to the Parliament situations which would suggest the Parliament to create new laws.

386. AGCOM's structure is composed of a Council and two Commissions: the Commission for Infrastructures and Networks and the Commission for Services and Products.

387. The *Council* is composed of the *President* and all *Commissioners.*
Each Commission is composed of four Commissioners and the AGCOM's President.

388. The procedure to appoint the President of the Authority and the Commissioners aims to individuate *independent* members.
Four Commissioners are nominated by the Senate of the Republic, and other four are nominated by the Chamber of Deputies.

389. The President of AGCOM is appointed by Decree of the President of the Republic, on the basis of a proposal of the Prime Minister, in agreement with the Minister of Communications, after hearings in front of parliamentary commissions.

390. The Commissaries are elected by the Senate and the Chamber of Deputies and are appointed by Decree of the President of the Republic.

391. AGCOM's maximum number of employees is limited by law to 260 persons.

392. Each year the Authority is required to present a *report* on its annual activity and programmes.
Such report is a valuable source of information about the development of the telecommunications and media sector in Italy.

§5. The Italian Telecommunications Market in 2018-2019

393. According to the AGCOM 2018 report, revenues from the telecommunications sector in Italy go beyond the EUR 32 billion threshold. And it rises to 54 billion, over 3% of the national GDP, if media and postal services are included, the other two items that make up the communications market.[161]

394. The 'fixed' segment is the one that is recording the highest performance: the positive sign returns in infrastructure investments (+1.6%), equal to 7 billion,

161. *See* M. Fiordalisi, a comment to Relazione AGCOM 2018, https://www.corrierecomunicazioni.it/telco/126111/.

thanks to the recovery trend of investments on the fixed network that compensates for the physiological decrease of those on the mobile network after the leaps forward of past years.[162]

395. The growth of the telecommunications segment is due to the acceleration recorded in the spread of broadband and ultra-broadband access from fixed networks (+3.8%), able to positively offset the overall reduction recorded for mobile network services (–1.9%).

A similar positive trend concerns the total expenditure on services by companies and families (+1.7%).

And with regard to traffic volumes, in the face of the continuing retreat of traditional traffic (telephony), broadband subscribers on the fixed network increase by about one million and double ultra-broadband accesses (from 2.3 to 4.5 million).[163]

396. The increase in bandwidth and data traffic (+30%) is due to the growing demand for online video content on the fixed network.

The consumption of data by users has grown even more (approximately +48%) in mobile telephony.

And remarkable dynamism is observed in the fixed wireless access (FWA) services segment, whose revenues show a growth close to 30%, with a number of users exceeding one million.

On the fixed network market, the geographical expansion of the 'wholesale only' Open Fibre operator continues in the areas subject to public financing, while in mobile telephony we have seen the launch of the first commercial offers by the operator iliad.[164]

397. The improvement in performance in terms of coverage of NGA networks is clear and brought Italy, in just one year, from 23rd place in 2016 to 13th in 2017 in the ranking of Member States (Desi).[165]

398. The level of competition on the infrastructures is growing, thanks to the entry into the market of new subjects, to the investment synergies by the traditional operators for the development of the FTTH and FTTC fibre and to the trend of the FWA accesses.

The total number of NGA wholesale services increased by 80% in one year and the coverage in 2017 reached 87% of families, thus attesting Italy above the EU average (80%).

---

162. *See* M. Fiordalisi, a comment to Relazione AGCOM 2018, https://www.corrierecomunicazioni.it/telco/126111/.
163. *See* M. Fiordalisi, a comment to Relazione AGCOM 2018, https://www.corrierecomunicazioni.it/telco/126111/.
164. *See* M. Fiordalisi, a comment to Relazione AGCOM 2018, https://www.corrierecomunicazioni.it/telco/126111/.
165. *See* M. Fiordalisi, a comment to Relazione AGCOM 2018, https://www.corrierecomunicazioni.it/telco/126111/.

As regards rural areas, the NGA coverage data are positive in relative terms (+23% compared to 2016), but still insufficient in absolute terms, since the coverage of 39% is below the EU average (47%).[166]

§6. The AGCOM Report of 2018 and the Future of the Telecommunications Regulation in Italy

399. The year 2018 has been an important year for AGCOM: in addition to some significant events that have characterized its activity, in March 2018, a twenty-year-long cycle of history ended.

Europe pushes for the strengthening of the digital single market and the competitiveness of European companies. After roaming and interventions in the field of net neutrality, the actions to ensure universal coverage of 100 megs to all citizens remain a priority and go further: push ultra-fast connectivity to pave the way for the Giga Society in 2025, with the objectives 5G and the development of access infrastructures.[167]

400. In the past, some significant events have characterized the Italian road in this direction. The path traced by the 2018 budget law for the release of the 700 MHz band from radio and television uses and the allocation of frequencies to 5G services and applications.

The AGCOM Report highlights the steps taken in this regard in this year, starting from the publication of the results of our survey on 5G, the start of experimentation projects on the territory, the evaluation of network development projects on frequencies 3.4–3.6 GHz, the regulation for the allocation of the 700 MHz, 3.6-3.8 GHz and 26 GHz frequencies.

In terms of the consequences of the liberation of the 700 MHz band, the adoption of the new national plan for frequency allocation for the television sector and the start of work for the determination of the new generation digital terrestrial networks.[168]

401. During 2018, the issue of the unbundling of the Telecom Italia fixed access network was again strongly proposed. The Authority, already engaged in strengthening the equivalence model and in improving the quality and performance of wholesale services, is evaluating the request for legal separation received from the company.

It was also the year of the termination of Vivendi's prohibited position established following the achievement of the double connection held in Telecom Italia and Mediaset.

---

166. *See* M. Fiordalisi, a comment to Relazione AGCOM 2018, https://www.corrierecomunicazioni.it/telco/126111/.

167. *See* the AGCOM 2018 Report at the address https://www.agcom.it/documents/10179/3572789/Relazione+annuale+2018/24dc1cc0-27a7-4ddd-9db2-cf3fc03f91d2.

168. *See* the AGCOM 2018 Report at the address https://www.agcom.it/documents/10179/3572789/Relazione+annuale+2018/24dc1cc0-27a7-4ddd-9db2-cf3fc03f91d2.

The year of the approval of the new public service contract RAI (the Italian state television) that will see us engaged in the control of the obligations and the year of the implementation of the reform in the field of cinema and audiovisual that has seen us engaged in the elaboration and adoption of the new framework of rules.[169]

402. In the postal sector, the last segment of monopoly has disappeared, with the liberalization and the subsequent regulation of the market for the management and delivery of judicial documents. At the same time, the Authority has launched important reflections on the logistics and parcel management market and related fast delivery services, which are undergoing a profound transformation due to the increase in e-commerce and the new OTT business models.[170]

403. The year 2018 was also characterized by the novelties and the complexity of consumer protection issues and guarantee of the principles underlying the media.

In addition to the issues of transparency and correctness that were involved in the issue of invoicing and monthly renewal of telecommunications service fees, there have been numerous and complex responses to the changes brought about by the increasing use of the Internet on rights guarantees.

In this case, the intervention tools must be weighed against a regulatory framework that is not suited to the timing and complexity of the interventions in a system structured as a global network.

In fact, AGCOM carried out regulation activities in a legislative vacuum, which is increasingly risky if we consider phenomena such as Russiagate and Cambridge Analytica, on the subject of the Web and the use of online content, often with courage or foresight.[171]

404. Starting from the developments of the regulation on the protection of online copyright, the Observatory on guarantees for minors and fundamental personal rights on the Internet, the guidelines on the fight against racism, the damage to personal dignity, to cyberbullying on the media including the Web, up to the most recent establishment of the Technical Table for the guarantee of pluralism and the correctness of information on digital platforms.

Always in the wake of the development of exchanges and consumption through the Internet and the transformation of business models, AGCOM launched the fact-finding survey on the use of big data and in particular on the multiple aspects of correlation with our skills, such as protection of digital consumers, advertising in the communications system, information pluralism and the right to be informed.[172]

---

169. *See* the AGCOM 2018 Report at the address https://www.agcom.it/documents/10179/3572789/Relazione+annuale+2018/24dc1cc0-27a7-4ddd-9db2-cf3fc03f91d2.
170. *See* the AGCOM 2018 Report at the address https://www.agcom.it/documents/10179/3572789/Relazione+annuale+2018/24dc1cc0-27a7-4ddd-9db2-cf3fc03f91d2.
171. *See* the AGCOM 2018 Report at the address https://www.agcom.it/documents/10179/3572789/Relazione+annuale+2018/24dc1cc0-27a7-4ddd-9db2-cf3fc03f91d2.
172. *See* the AGCOM 2018 Report at the address https://www.agcom.it/documents/10179/3572789/Relazione+annuale+2018/24dc1cc0-27a7-4ddd-9db2-cf3fc03f91d2.

Chapter 2. Regulation of Competition in the ICT Market

§1. Competition in Italy

405. In Italy, a specific legislation on competition occurred much later than in the United States of America and the rest of Europe.

In fact, only in 1990 was enacted Law n. 287, of 10 October 1990, providing 'Rules for the protection of competition and the market'.

The process to achieve the enactment of this provision was very difficult: the first proposal dates back to 1955.

Today, competition in Italy is regulated by the European Union Law (especially the EC Treaty), by the Italian Constitution (especially Articles from 41 to 47) and by some rules of the Italian Civil Code.

406. The legislative reform of 1990 has, however, introduced a complex regulatory environment, implementing the constitutional provision protecting and guaranteeing the right to economic initiative and regulating three specific cases: (i) collusive market, (ii) the possible abuse of dominant position and (iii) concentrations of businesses.

407. The Italian Civil Code devotes several articles to *unfair competition* from the perspective of private law.

In carrying out its activities, the entrepreneur acts to the attainment of profit, but this should not be achieved with resources that could damage other entrepreneurs and consumers.

Such conduct, detrimental from the point of view of private law, as mentioned above, generates hypotheses involving damages.[173]

408. At a European Union level, there is a very broad discipline, dating back to the formation of the European Economic Community and the Treaty of Rome.

The Italian Act of 1990 explicitly arises in a context of *subsidiarity* with respect to what is already covered in the Treaty of Rome.

The principle adopted by the Legislator is the one of 'inverted subsidiarity', whereby the internal rules apply only to the extent that community rules are inapplicable.

However, the Italian legislation and the European Union Legislation operate on different levels: the national legislation, obviously, wants to regulate the domestic sphere, while the community is aimed at a harmonization of the markets that are part of the community. It is clear that, acting on their own legislation, some Countries, maybe even indirectly, can benefit the domestic production but, at the same time, can alter the European market.

Very often there have been problems of interpretation of conflicts of competence at national and European Union level in terms of competition.

---

173. *See* F. Ghezzi, P Magnani, 'Banche e concorrenza' (EGEA, Milano, 1999).

In 2017, the annual law for the market and the competition (law 4 August 2017, n. 124, annual law for the market and the competition) entered into force on 29 August 2017 to prospect a uniform regulation of the sector.

409. To summarize, it could be argued that the legislation applicable in Italy in terms of competition has several aims, not merely to avoid creating a monopolistic situation to the detriment of the market, but has its basis in the affirmation of the right of each person to *compete* on the market and, second, the power of the State to *intervene* to limit competition or abuse of dominant position, for the creation or the permanence of a competitive market structure.

§2. The Italian Competition Authority

410. The Legislator, to better ensure the effectiveness of the 1990 Law and its applications, has decided to support the judiciary (ordinary and administrative) system with an organization specifically dedicated, constituting the *Guarantor Authority for Competition and the Free Market* ('AGCM', or 'Antitrust').

Title III of Law n. 287/1990 (Articles 21 to 24) regulates the powers of knowledge and advisory of this body.

411. As a general overview, the Italian Competition Authority ('Autorità Garante della Concorrenza e del Mercato' (AGCM)), better known as the *Antitrust Authority*, was established in Italy in 1990.

It is an independent body, meaning that the decisions are based on the law, and it is impossible for the Government, or for any political party, to interfere.

Having as aim the citizens' welfare, the Authority enforces those rules which prohibit anticompetitive agreements among undertakings, abuse of dominant position, as well as any possible mergers which may create or strengthen dominant positions detrimental to competition.

As of 2007, the Antitrust has been in charge of protecting consumers from any unfair commercial practices among undertakings, as well as from all misleading advertising.

In order to guarantee fair market competition, it also intervenes against all comparative advertising which may bring discredit on competitors' products or cause confusion among consumers.

As of 2004, the Italian Competition Authority has also been in charge of enforcing laws against conflicts of interest for holders of public office.

412. The Italian Competition Authority was established by Law n. 287 of 10 October 1990 (The Competition and Fair Trading Act'), which introduced antitrust law to Italy for the first time.

Subsequent laws endowed it with additional powers, the most important of which concern the repression of unfair commercial practices, misleading and unlawful comparative advertising and the application of conflict of interests' laws to government-office holders.

Being an independent Authority, it has the status of a public agency whose decisions are taken on the basis of the Act without any possibility of interference by the Government.

413. The Antitrust Authority's independence is reinforced by the appointment procedures and prerequisites of its Chairman and three members.

They remain in office for a seven-year non-renewable term and are jointly appointed by the Presidents of the Chamber of Deputies and Senate.

The prerequisites for the Chairman include a reputation for independence and service in other high-level institutional positions.

The members must also manifest the values of independence and are selected from among the magistrates of the State Council, the Court of Auditors and the Court of Appeals, full university professors of economics or jurisprudence and outstanding personalities from the economic sector with impeccable reputations of professionalism.

414. The Antitrust Authority is financed by annual allocations through a special chapter of the Ministry of Economic Development's budget.

The Financial Law of 2006 introduced partial self-financing starting on 1 January 2006 in a form commensurate with covering the costs incurred for monitoring merger operations.

The Antitrust Authority determines contributions on an annual basis and has full control over the management of these funds for its own operations.

Law Decree n. 207/2008, last of all, granted the Authority additional self-financing through the fines paid as a consequence of unfair commercial practices.

§3. The Italian Antitrust Law

415. The Authority's financial statements have to be approved by April 30 of the following year and are subject to auditing by the Court of Auditors.

The primary task attributed to the Antitrust Authority – its reason for being – is the implementation of Law n. 287 of 1990 (the Italian antitrust law).

Parliament introduced the national antitrust legislation to enact Article 41 of the Constitution, which protects and guarantees the right of free enterprise, and in order to bring Italy's legislation into line with European Community Law.

416. The law's main objectives are: (i) to ensure the basic preconditions for freedom of enterprise by providing economic operators with equal opportunities for market access and competition; (ii) to protect consumers by promoting price containment and quality improvement for products derived from the free play of competition.

417. Another task of the Antitrust Authority is to apply the laws contained in legislative decree no. 145/2007 (enactment of Directive 2005/29/EC) on misleading and unlawful comparative advertising, and in Title III, Section II of legislative decree no. 206 of 2005 (the 'Code of Consumption'), as modified by legislative decree no. 146/2007 in regards to unfair commercial practices.

418. Lastly, to the Authority was given the responsibility of controlling for conflicts of interest in order to ensure that public government-office holders dedicate themselves exclusively to the public interest during the performance of their duties and refrain from deeds or collegial deliberations that manifest conflicts of interest.

It is also required to submit reports to Parliament and the Government and to provide them with consultancy services.

419. The tasks of this Authority gradually increased over time, extending well beyond the provision of Law n. 287/1990, thereby expanding its skills to any situation that could compromise the orderly market.

420. In 2004, the powers were extended to the monitoring of conflict of interests of the holders of the offices of government: thus, the holders of government office, while exercising their functions, must dedicate exclusively to the care of public interests and should refrain from engaging in actions, and participating in collegial decisions, when there is a conflict of interest, identifying a number of situations of incompatibility.

This norm seeks to avoid unpleasant situations that occur especially in public procurement.

421. In 2007, powers were extended to the protection of consumers and, since 2012, including microbusinesses.

In such cases, the task is always to protect those most vulnerable from unfair trade practices and misleading advertising companies.

To ensure that, the Authority operates fairly well against comparative advertising, which discredits the products of competitors or which can confuse consumers.

Since 2012 the Authority has been entrusted with the power to exercise administrative protection against unfair terms in contracts with consumers.

422. The Authority's activities come to report to the Government, Parliament, the Regions and local authorities the legal and administrative measures already in force, or in training, introducing restrictions on competition.

From 2010 onwards, in fact, the Authority, in its annual Report to the Presidency of the Council, indicates all laws which impede competition and must therefore be eliminated or reformed.

The Government presents to the Chambers a bill, the law's annual competition, which is incorporated in the Authority's directions, possibly indicating the areas in which it decided not to follow its remarks.

423. The Competition Authority also has a *searchable database* where it is possible to review the measures and the opinions expressed, thus allowing both consumers and entrepreneurs to well understand the rules to be observed and how not to run into unlawful, or at least incorrect, conduct.

To this end, in fact, the Competition Authority has activated a service of complaints and reports of incorrect situations.

In this way, the activity of AGCM is very important to adjust at all levels the correct compliance with the rules of the market.

424. In these years, in Italy, the first step to be taken would be to bring to completion the reforms started with the annual law for the market and the competition (law 4 August 2017, n. 124, annual law for the market and the competition), which entered into force on 29 August 2017.

The approval of this law, albeit with some criticalities, represents a step forward in the process of dissemination of the pro-competitive principles within our system.

However, there must be delays in the state of implementation which negatively affect the liberalization processes.

First of all, the postponement to 1 July 2020 of the definitive relevant liberalization of the electricity and gas markets.

The transition from the regime of greater protection to the free market concludes the liberalization process started in the mid-1990s of the last century and will allow consumers to identify and select the offers that best meet their needs, which, in the medium term, may allow reductions annual expenditure not negligible even with respect to the current system of regulated tariffs.

§4. Types of Antitrust Decisions

425. The many powers extended over time have resulted in a variety of very heterogeneous activities of the AGCM.

Without claiming to be exhaustive, it is important to mention some significant interventions, which can explain how this Authority seeks to remedy misconduct in the market.

426. Activity was carried out under very tight protection of consumers and small firms.

There are hundreds of AGCM interventions among these measures, in some field of electronic commerce too, either in the event of services rendered in a misleading or unclear manner.

Very important was also the Authority's intervention designed to lead to greater market liberalization. There have been numerous cases of AGCM designed to prevent collusion in the field of airlines or to punish some opaque conducts carried out by banks and insurance companies.

The Antitrust Authority has sought also to extend its action (although so far with little success) to the professionals.

427. In the national environment, the function of Antitrust aimed at liberalizing the market is essential.

In Italy, for a historical matter, many companies that provide *basic services* (i.e., electricity, gas, telecommunications) are in situations of near monopoly or, at least, in a dominant position.

Examples are the actions of ENEL in the field of electricity, of Eni in the gas commerce, of RAI in broadcasting and the Italian Poste SpA for postal services and banking.

428. One area often subject to the intervention of the AGCM regards *communications*.

The once State-run phone company *Telecom Italia* SpA has been often punished for abuse of dominant position. Other phone companies have been sanctioned too, especially for misconduct in a competitive environment, deceptive advertising and proposals of promotions omitting many important details of the offer.

429. In conclusion, the Competition Authority in Italy has gradually come to act on all aspects of the market and competition at a national level, though, to be fair, the *extensive powers* of the independent Italian Authority have often been criticized.

§5. The AGCM 2018 Report and the Status of Antitrust and ICT in Italy

430. In the annual Report of AGCM (2018), the new sectors related to the development of digital technologies appear to be, today, those that show the greatest growth prospects and, at the same time, those in which development is accompanied by non-negligible critical issues, on which it is necessary to intervene promptly.[174]

431. Among the most critical issues, there are those linked to the development of hi-tech markets, which have become global in a short time: this implies that those who wish to operate there must have ever greater capital and more advanced technologies (such as those that allow the rapid processing of so-called big data).

However, these elements risk becoming insurmountable barriers to entry for new entrants.[175]

432. In particular, the presence of the global markets of the c.d. Big Tech (Amazon, Google, Facebook and Apple) and, to a lesser extent, the c.d. FinTech (non-bank operators active in brokerage through digital platforms), if not properly supervised, risks leading to the excessive consolidation of already existing dominant positions.

The crystallization of market structures, in turn, significantly reduces or nullifies the possibilities of access for new operators in the various (and increasingly numerous) markets in which these subjects operate, as is demonstrated, finally, also by the

---

174. *See* the 2018 AGCM Report at the address https://www.agcm.it/dotcmsdoc/relazioni-annuali/relazioneannuale2018/Relazione_annuale_2019.pdf.

175. *See* the 2018 AGCM Report at the address https://www.agcm.it/dotcmsdoc/relazioni-annuali/relazioneannuale2018/Relazione_annuale_2019.pdf.

recent sanction imposed by the European Commission to Google for its anticompetitive behaviour in the smartphone operating system market.[176]

433. The social problems connected to the rapid diffusion of new digital technologies in the production processes are no less relevant.

According to estimates elaborated by the OECD over the next 15 years, 14% of traditional and serial jobs will be replaced by automated processes, while it is expected that a substantial part of the current tasks (between 30% and 40%) will have to change radically.[177]

434. The European Union has already started a programme to develop and spread artificial intelligence (AI) within its economy, with the aim of regulating all the most critical aspects.

In order to anticipate developments and application developments of the AI, it is necessary to create a context capable of attracting investments in research and development and to facilitate access to the most advanced technologies by all potential users, in particular small and medium enterprises active in traditional sectors, which remain the least digitized.

At the same time, it is necessary to prepare the society as a whole, both by offering highly specialized courses able to adequately train a part of the future workforce and by preparing forms of social protection for workers in occupations most at risk of transformation or extinction.[178]

435. It is necessary to foster the development of a widespread climate of trust that can incentivize both businesses and individual citizens to use AI.

With this in mind, the Commission has set itself the goal of creating a digital single market, also through the presentation of some legislative proposals such as the regulation on the free circulation of non-personal data, the proposed regulation on e-privacy and that for a law on computer security, which will help strengthen citizens' trust in online markets.[179]

436. In fact, a digital single market needs certain, common and shared rules: the existence of non-homogeneous or even conflicting regulations is one of the main barriers to investment aimed at developing innovations.

Furthermore, the excessive differentiation of regulations imposes significant adjustment costs on companies that operate in several markets, with consequent increases in the price of goods and services offered.[180]

---

176. *See* the 2018 AGCM Report at the address https://www.agcm.it/dotcmsdoc/relazioni-annuali/relazioneannuale2018/Relazione_annuale_2019.pdf.
177. *See* the 2018 AGCM Report at the address https://www.agcm.it/dotcmsdoc/relazioni-annuali/relazioneannuale2018/Relazione_annuale_2019.pdf.
178. *See* the 2018 AGCM Report at the address https://www.agcm.it/dotcmsdoc/relazioni-annuali/relazioneannuale2018/Relazione_annuale_2019.pdf.
179. *See* the 2018 AGCM Report at the address https://www.agcm.it/dotcmsdoc/relazioni-annuali/relazioneannuale2018/Relazione_annuale_2019.pdf.
180. *See* the 2018 AGCM Report at the address https://www.agcm.it/dotcmsdoc/relazioni-annuali/relazioneannuale2018/Relazione_annuale_2019.pdf.

437. More generally, the removal of unnecessary and non-proportionate regulatory barriers allows increasing the level of market competitiveness through the creation of a single competitive arena that facilitates the comparison between companies.[181]

438. This is the direction taken, for example, by Regulation (EU) 2018/302 containing measures aimed at preventing unjustified geographical blocks (c.d. geoblocking).

The aim is to promote intra-community trade (in particular, but not exclusively, through digital tools) by eliminating any artificial segmentation of the internal market based on the nationality, residence or place of establishment of the customers.

These segmentations of the markets, in fact, allow companies to maintain artificially differentiated prices for the same products, based on the place where they are purchased, as the European Commission itself has also recently noted, sanctioning anticompetitive agreements that limited cross-border sales in the case Guess.[182]

439. The Regulation applies to cross-border transactions involving the offer, both online and offline, of tangible movable assets and / or services by a 'professional' established within the EU or in a third country in favour of a 'Customer' EU citizen or resident or established within the EU. The Regulation is, of course, directly applicable in each Member State.[183]

440. Finally, it is worth emphasizing that the large-scale use of tools capable of using AI in business-to-consumer transactions must be in compliance with consumer protection legislation; in particular, it appears essential to increase the transparency of this type of transaction for the benefit of consumers, who should receive clear information on the use, characteristics and properties of products capable of using AI.

Only in this way is it possible to allow the person to control the technology and not vice versa.[184]

441. For such an ambitious project, the cooperation of all Member States is needed: in this way, in fact, it will be possible to avoid the fragmentation of the single market and stimulate the emergence of start-ups for the AI.

Furthermore, collaboration between states will make it possible to share good practices, identify synergies and align actions to maximize the impact of investment in AI, in order to make the EU an actor capable of competing globally.[185]

---

181. *See* the 2018 AGCM Report at the address https://www.agcm.it/dotcmsdoc/relazioni-annuali/relazioneannuale2018/Relazione_annuale_2019.pdf.
182. *See* the 2018 AGCM Report at the address https://www.agcm.it/dotcmsdoc/relazioni-annuali/relazioneannuale2018/Relazione_annuale_2019.pdf.
183. *See* the 2018 AGCM Report at the address https://www.agcm.it/dotcmsdoc/relazioni-annuali/relazioneannuale2018/Relazione_annuale_2019.pdf.
184. *See* the 2018 AGCM Report at the address https://www.agcm.it/dotcmsdoc/relazioni-annuali/relazioneannuale2018/Relazione_annuale_2019.pdf.
185. *See* the 2018 AGCM Report at the address https://www.agcm.it/dotcmsdoc/relazioni-annuali/relazioneannuale2018/Relazione_annuale_2019.pdf.

Chapter 3. Regulation of Cryptography and Other Dual-Use Goods

§1. Export Control Regime in Italy and Cryptography: An Introduction

442. In this strategic topic, the European Union Legislation (especially Regulation (EU) N. 1232/11 of the European Parliament and of the Council of 16 November 2011, amending Council Regulation (EC) n. 428/2009, setting up a community regime for the control of exports, transfer, brokering and transit of dual-use items, and Council Regulation (EC) n. 428/2009 of 5 May 2009, setting up a community regime for the control of exports, transfer, brokering and transit of dual-use items) was implemented in Italy with a Ministerial Memorandum n. 53261 of 29 February 2012, concerning the *New Union General Export Authorisations*, with a legislative decree no. 96/2003, with a legislative decree of 4 August 2003 (concerning the *National General Authorisation*) and with a legislative decree of 14 May 2009, n. 64 (laying down the penalties applicable to infringements of the provisions of Regulation (EC) n. 428/2009).

443. The legal framework concerning cryptography, in Italy, is at a very early stage: from a general point of view, there are *no prohibitions* concerning the import of cryptography technologies into Italy.

On 15 March 1997, the Italian Parliament passed Law n. 59/97, and Article 15(2) of the law established a framework for electronically signed documents using digital signatures.

For the first time in Italy, the digital signature system involved asymmetric encryption, and the technical standards concerning the encryption keys were implemented under a separate law.

These systems are controlled, in Italy, by certificate authorities to be licensed by the Government.[186]

444. From a general point of view, Italy controls exports of cryptography pursuant to the *Wassenaar Arrangement* and the EU Dual-Use Regulation.

In December 1998, Italy subscribed to the more restrictive Wassenaar Dual-Use Control List.

The Ministry of Foreign Trade controls exports of cryptographic products, and it is advised on export licences by the Defence Ministry, Foreign Ministry, Interior Ministry, the military intelligence service (SISMI) and the civilian intelligence service (SISDE).

Authority to control cryptographic exports is contained in Article 2 of Italian Law n. 89 of 24 February 1997.[187]

---

186. *See* www2.epic.org/reports/crypto1999.html#_Toc450793167.
187. *See* www2.epic.org/reports/crypto1999.html#_Toc450793167.

445. Law n. 185 of 9 July 1990, concerning 'New regulations governing export control, import and transit of military goods', together with the related implementing regulation (DPCM n. 93 of 14 January 2005, which replaced the previous paragraph 448 of the Law 25 September 1999), is currently the basic regulatory measure in the field of transfer of assets classified as *strategic weapon materials* in Italy.

446. Undergone some changes to Law n. 148 of 17 June 2003, necessary to give practical implementation to the *Framework Agreement*, signed at Farnborough on 27 July 2000, between France, Germany, Spain, Sweden, Britain and Italy on the restructuring and the activities of European defence industry, the legislation, despite the limitations of inevitable compromises, identifies procedures, methods of control and target areas, to ensure that the marketing activities in the area of transfers of weapon materials are solely intended to provide responses to natural and indispensable *defence needs* that animate any Country.

447. To achieve that goal, it introduced a substantial change in the way of regulating the matter, in the past allowed to the exclusive sphere of discretionary administrative department, namely the involvement in decision-making explicitly clear at the highest levels of political apparatus, even if such intervention is now partially reduced, due to some changes in the meantime that led, in fact, the main body of political reference, the Committee of Ministers CISD, to no longer operate.

448. For all these materials, largely due to the *three categories* of common gunpowder weapons (considering that both the sporting and hunting weapons, replicas of ancient weapons and muzzle-loading models prior to 1980, to consider common weapons are already under said Law n. 110/75), the non-automatic handguns gun (whatever their configurability as weapons of war or not) and type of explosives for the civil industry, the law, especially in view of their marketing also to private persons, states non-applicability of the general control rules provided for supplies of weapons and materials (Article 28, paragraph 4) and establish a *simplified authorization procedure*, designed solely to aspects of public security, the responsibility of the police, to Article 31 of TULPS, it replaces any other authorization and in particular the Ministry of Foreign Affairs provided for the materials considered weapons under the law.

449. It should finally be noted that all the materials in question, even if excluded from the scope of the Act, may, in exceptional cases, be subject to *general prohibition* of export to certain Countries pursuant to Article 15, paragraphs 7 and 8.

450. The regulation of exports of strategic goods to be configured as dual-use results, conversely, more diverse than that of military goods, being characterized by multiple sources of primary and secondary legislation, the community to national level.

451. Currently, the main regulatory reference is the primary source of EC Regulation n. 428/2009 of 5 May 2009, which replaced the previous Regulation n. 1334/2000 of 22 June 2000.

Since community legislation only provides general guidelines and leaves the Member States discretionary margins about the choice of application methods, in Italy the discipline was integrated with legislative decree 96 of 9 April 2003 about the requirement for National General authorization and the Ministerial Decree of 4 August 2003.

452. legislative decree no. 96/03 implements certain provisions of the Regulations, and Joint Action Council n. 2000/401/CFSP of 22 June 2000, on the control of technical assistance related to certain military, sets the basic elements of the administrative procedure related to the issuing of *permits*.

453. At the national level, Ministerial Decree n. 313 of 14 July 1990, laying down the final regulation applicable to systems of import and export of goods introduces further export restrictions, for reasons of public security or human rights.

454. Finally, in terms of specific control measures, the full implementation of the provisions of Article 12 of legislative decree no. 96/03 is pending, and Ministerial Decree n. 599 of 18 November 1993 for the control of the export and transit of high technology products is still partially applicable (never formally repealed).

455. Concerning materials used for the *violation of human rights*, there are some norms that put under control of the community the transfers of some types of materials used to cause offence and injury to persons on the basis of the recent European Union regulation n. 1236/2005 of 27 June 2005, entered into force on 30 July 2006.

456. Law n. 185/90 is inspired by some principles that form the foundation of the constitutional structure of the Italian State, relying in the first place, even if indirectly, on the principle that *peace* among Nations is a primary objective to be pursued in international coexistence, and which Italy intends to fully comply.

This Law explicitly states the general principle of conformity to the provisions of Article 11 of the Italian Constitution that rejects war as a means of solving international conflicts, even when it is called directly, according to the same Article 11 of the Constitution.

457. The intervention and direct control in an area of such high importance for the export, import and transit of armament materials, including the assignment of the relevant production licences, can only be made on the basis of specific authorization of the State.

In other words, it affirmed the principle that State's prime task is to direct, through their own choices, not arbitrary but bounded by areas that are already established, the policy of the arms trade, thus subordinating the general principle of freedom in trade with foreign Countries.

458. Consequently, it follows that State's prime task is to identify, where appropriate, against certain countries' (belonging, for example, to alliances involving Italy) lanes of the most streamlined procedures and to deny, vice versa, where under certain circumstances, the opportunity to work towards others.

§2. The Rules Governing Exports of Dual Material

459. The control of exports of dual technology and materials, unlike conventional armaments, makes almost exclusive reference to community legislation and international agreements (in particular: the guidelines of the various non-proliferation regimes) which, although not formally included in specific provision in the context of national laws, are the necessary precondition and the natural reference check.

In practice, the EU Regulation in the sector has operated a process of gradual and continuous replacement of the national legislation: today we can say that substantially all of the provisions of primary source material are drafted only to make effective regulations and decisions of the European Union.

460. In Italy, Law n. 222 of 27 February 1992, which constituted the first comprehensive regulation of the sector, as well as legislative decree no. 89 of 24 February 1997, fully implemented the first community legislation (Regulation EC n. 3381 of 19 December 1994).

461. In Italy the export and transit of dual-use technologies should be in accordance with the principles underlying the *National Foreign Policy*, in harmony with the fundamental interests of State-security, ensuring non-proliferation of technologies and products of military interest, develop active development cooperation in civilian areas between Italy and the Countries not participating in multilateral export control regimes, to be compatible with international agreements and conventions to which Italy participates with the principles of the UN Charter, to be compatible with the guidelines of international bodies by which Italy would be obliged.

462. The principles mentioned above are now mentioned in EU Regulation n. 1334/2000 which, in this respect, merely states that an effective common system of export controls is necessary to ensure compliance with international and European Union Member States' commitments and responsibilities, in particular, on non-proliferation.

463. In terms of principle of legality, the limits of State intervention are still those established in Decree of the Ministry of Foreign Trade n. 313 on 14 July 1990.

Article 1 states that 'the import and export of goods are free, unless exceptions and limitations placed specifically in relation to international and EU commitments or requirements of national interest, with measures of the Minister of Foreign Trade, in consultation with the Minister of Finance. These measures are published in the Official Gazette of the Italian Republic. The sale of goods identified in the measures referred to in paragraph 1, by persons resident in Italy, may be subject to control even when the movement of goods takes place outside the customs territory or territories outside the customs and similar, with the exception of goods purchased and resold in the same country. They may also be subject to authorization of indirect goods such transits that give rise to entry in warehouses and customs warehouses and subsequent shipment abroad by residents in Italy.'

§3. The Italian Ministry Rules Concerning Dual-Use Goods

464. According to the Italian Ministry For Economic Development Rules, dual goods and technologies are considered those that can be used not only in civil applications but also in the production, development and use of military assets; they differ from the armament materials as they are not specifically designed for military use (*see* Regulations).

An effective export control system for dual-use products is needed to ensure compliance with the international commitments and responsibilities taken by the States, which have adhered to export control regimes, particularly in the field of non-proliferation.

The existence of a common system of norms and policies harmonized in export controls in all the Member States of the Union represents a prerequisite for there to be a free circulation of dual-use products within the European Union.[188]

465. The export of dual goods and technologies is governed by a variety of standards, criteria and application procedures that meet national and international security needs, as follows: Reg. (CE) 428/09 and subsequently modified by the Reg. (EU) 2268/2017, which establishes a community regime for the control of exports of dual-use products and technologies included in the All. THE.

In Italy, the provisions of Reg. 428/09 have been implemented with legislative decree no. 221 of 15 December 2017. The list in Annex I on the Ministry website represents the sum of the choices made by the following international control regimes: WASSENAR ARRANGEMENT (high technology sector) and MTCR Group (missile products sector); NSG Group (nuclear sector) and Australia Group (biological chemical sector).[189]

466. According to these rules, authorizations may take the form of: (i) individual specific authorizations: they are issued on the advice of the Advisory Committee, issued from time to time, and concern operations that cannot benefit from procedures that are in any case facilitated. The provision is issued on the basis of a specific order or contract (Article 10 of legislative decree 221/2017); (ii) National General Authorization – AGN: the export of dual-use goods can take place with AGN limited to the countries of destination which are indicated in the decree of the Ministry of Productive Activities of 04/08/2003 – Antarctica (Italian Base), Argentina, South Korea, Turkey – valid in all Member States of the European Union and for all dual-use items specified in the categories listed in Annex I of Reg. (EC) 428/2009, amended with Reg. (EU) 1232/2011, with the exception (a) of the provisions of Annex II octies of the same Reg. (EU) 1232/2011, (b) of the goods / countries included in the new AGEU (*see* Annex II, da *bis* a *septies*, Reg. (EU) 1232/11).[190]

---

188. *See*, on the Ministry website, https://www.mise.gov.it/index.php/it/commercio-internazionale/import-export/dual-use.
189. *See*, on the Ministry website, https://www.mise.gov.it/index.php/it/commercio-internazionale/import-export/dual-use.
190. *See*, on the Ministry website, https://www.mise.gov.it/index.php/it/commercio-internazionale/import-export/dual-use.

467. The AGN cannot be used if the exporter is informed by the Ministry that the products being exported are or may be, in whole or in part, destined for any of the uses referred to in Article 4 – paragraphs 1, 2 and 3 – of Reg. (CE) 428/2009 and subsequent amendments or if the Company is aware that the same products are intended for the aforementioned uses.

From the date of issue of the Authorization, the Company is registered in the specific Register required by Article 13, paragraph 3, of legislative decree 221/2017.[191]

468. The authorization may be denied, cancelled, revoked, suspended or modified in accordance with the provisions of Article 14 of legislative decree 221/2017.

It is necessary to send, even if negative, a six-monthly report – January and July – to communicate all the exports made, as per circular letter 79932/12 of the Gd. Avv. Teti.[192]

469. General authorizations of the European Union: the authorizations are valid in all the Member States of the European Union, to certain countries of destination, to the conditions and requirements of use listed in the attachments from II *bis* to II *septies*, as established by Article 1, paragraph 3, of Reg. (EU) 1232/2011, which modifies Article 9, paragraph 1 of Reg. (CE) 428/2009, and for the following products: all dual-use items specified in the categories set out in Annex II, da *bis* a *septies*, of Reg. (EU) 1232/2011, except as provided in Annex II octies of the same Reg. (EU) 1232/2011.[193]

470. These authorizations can be used with a notification (in the 30 days prior to the first export to be made) to the competent authority that issues a letter of receipt of the notification (as per circular letter 79932/12 of the D.G. Avv. Teti).

Authorizations may be denied, cancelled, revoked, suspended in accordance with the provisions of Article 14 of legislative decree 221/2017.

From the date of issue of the letter of receipt of the notification of the Authorization, the Company is registered in the specific Register provided by Article 12, paragraph 2, of legislative decree 221/2017.

It is necessary to send, even if negative, a six-monthly report – January and July – to communicate all the exports made with each type of AGEU, as per circular 79931/12 of the GD Avv. Teti.[194]

471. The AGEUs automatically cancel all the Community General Authorizations issued to exporters before the entry into force of EU Reg. 1232/11.[195]

---

191. *See*, on the Ministry website, https://www.mise.gov.it/index.php/it/commercio-internazionale/import-export/dual-use.
192. *See*, on the Ministry website, https://www.mise.gov.it/index.php/it/commercio-internazionale/import-export/dual-use.
193. *See*, on the Ministry website, https://www.mise.gov.it/index.php/it/commercio-internazionale/import-export/dual-use.
194. *See*, on the Ministry website, https://www.mise.gov.it/index.php/it/commercio-internazionale/import-export/dual-use.
195. *See*, on the Ministry website, https://www.mise.gov.it/index.php/it/commercio-internazionale/import-export/dual-use.

472. Individual global authorizations: the export of dual-use goods listed in the All. I of Reg. (CE) 428/09 can take place with individual global authorization, issued to a single exporter, for all types or categories of dual-use goods and for one or more countries of specific destinations, which have adhered to the Regimes international and issued after consulting the Advisory Committee, valid for no more than three years and with the possibility of extension (Article 11, paragraph 1 of legislative decree 221/2017).[196]

473. Promotion of respect for human rights – Reg. (EU) 125/2019: one of the top priorities of EU external relations is the promotion of respect for human rights, which is also one of the main objectives of the common foreign and security policy (CFSP). The fight against torture and other cruel, inhuman or degrading treatment or punishment, although numerous international instruments prohibit this kind of serious violations of human dignity, is still necessary today.[197]

To this end, EU Regulation n. 1236/05 of the Council, which established a specific regime for the trade of certain devices and products that could be used precisely for torture or inhuman treatment. This regulation was recently repealed and replaced by Regulation (EU) 2019/125 of the European Parliament and of the Council of 16 January 2019.

196. *See*, on the Ministry website, https://www.mise.gov.it/index.php/it/commercio-internazionale/import-export/dual-use.

197. *See*, on the Ministry website, https://www.mise.gov.it/index.php/it/commercio-internazionale/import-export/dual-use.

Chapter 4. Legal Status of Standardization

474. Italy is a country that, over time, has achieved a growing awareness on the issues related to the 'standardization'.

And, in fact, organizations increased awareness of the importance of equipping their production facilities of internationally recognized methodologies, and to rethink internal processes to core business (planning, organization, management) for continuous improvement.

This is reflected also in the special attention that the Legislator has given to the matter of the spread of standards relating to management systems.

475. The 'Code of public contracts for works, services and supplies', described in European Directives 2004/17/EC and 2004/18/EC, introduced some incentives for organizations in possession of ISO 9001.

Italian legislative decree no. 163 of 2006 ('Procurement Code') has made a number of changes in the rules for awarding works, services and supplies to the Public Administration.

Article 75 contains a provision that recognizes businesses in possession of the *Certification of Quality* Management a 50% decrease in the amount of the sureties to guarantee supply.

476. Article 30 of Law Decree n. 112 of 25 June 2008 containing 'Urgent provisions for economic development, simplification, competitiveness, the stabilization of public finance and tax equalization' in subsection 1 states that 'for companies subject to *environmental certification* or issued by an accredited certifying entity in accordance with international and European standards, periodic inspections carried out by certification bodies replace administrative controls or additional administrative verification, including for the purpose of renewal or updating of authorizations for activity. The verification of the competent administrative bodies has as the object, in this case, only the timeliness and completeness of the certification'.

This measure, while remaining de facto unapplied in default of appropriate decrees, has undoubtedly provided a guideline to address well-defined policy.

477. The principle, though controversial, legal decision was made by the Italian Constitutional Court in judgment n. 322, of 4 December 2009 (on appeal from the Emilia-Romagna Region), stating that: '[...] Such certification must be capable of ensuring, simultaneously, to businesses, regardless of their geographical location, the ability to obtain, without having to be subjected to unnecessary and heavy duplication of controls, with consequent advantages in terms of efficiency, credibility and effectiveness; to all users of the products or services provided by those companies, ensuring proper compliance of the above to the minimum quality standards set by internal technical, European and international trade, carried out by third entities independent, being specially appointed [...].'

478. Later, Law n. 180, of 11 November 2011, concerning 'Regulations for the protection of freedom of enterprise', introduced, for the first time into the Italian legal framework, the 'statute of companies'.

Article 11, 'Replacement Certification and verification procedure', in paragraph 1 states that 'The certification relating to products, processes and systems to companies issued by standards bodies authorized to do so and by professional companies or replacement of qualified professionals are verified by the Government and competent authorities, subject to the criminal profiles.'

479. The government Monti, with the enactment of the so-called Simplifications Decree provided for a 'rationalization', through reduction or elimination of controls on businesses, taking account of the possession of a certificate of quality management system ISO, or other appropriate certification issued, compared with harmonized standards, by a body certification accredited by an accrediting agency designated by a Member State of the Union pursuant to Regulation 2008/765/CE, or a signatory of international agreements of mutual recognition (IAF MLA).

480. Such Decree also scheduled the issue of certain regulations by the end of 2012.

The objective is the replacement of the environmental licensing process, allowing the companies self-certification on documents held by UNI EN ISO 14000 or EMAS, 'with reference to the assets of the same certifications, and for interventions in ecologically equipped areas'.

481. In the banking sector, the regulations of the Payment Services Providers (PSPs) are required to be established by legislative decree no. 11 of 2010, to ensure that instruments of payment granted to customers be submitted to appropriate security profiles from both the technical and organizational point of view.

The compliance of the whole process is detailed in Section IV of the Bank of Italy 'Obligations of the provider payment services in relation to the provision of services and issuance of payment instruments'. In terms of security, it 'shall be inserted references to ISO27001 for the use of independent assessment'.

For example, the Assessor may be an external auditor, a Finance Authority (Monitoring/ Supervision) or an accredited ISO 27001 Certification.

482. In October 2011, the Italian *Privacy Authority* has issued an opinion (on request by DigitPA) relative to a framework of guidelines on *disaster recovery* in the Public Administration.

The Authority for the protection of personal data introduces, in this opinion, the structure that the document should have: 'The technical solutions necessary to ensure the preservation of data and computer applications in Public Administration are not the only object of the measure at issue, which has a wider scope. The outline of guidelines addresses a broad spectrum inside the theme of continuity, beginning with its objectives within the Public Administration (chapter 1), the changes introduced by recent changes to the Digital Administration Code and in particular legislative decree 30 December 2010, n. 235 (Ch. 2), from a wide range of standards and international best practices reference for the implementation of business continuity, starting from the British Standard BS 25999 and BS 25777, up to the standards ISO 22399, ISO 22301, ISO 24762, ISO 27031 and ISO 27002 and ITIL guidelines and NFPA (Ch. 3).'

483. Certified Italian companies are very well placed internationally.

As regards to the certification for excellence, CD 'Quality' (ISO 9001) Italy boasts 138,892 well-certified companies, thus occupying the second place, after China (297,037) and ahead of the Russian Federation (62,265); it is worth adding that, in Europe, the Nations closer to the results of our Country are Spain with 59,854 and Germany with 50,583 certifications. Italy is also third on the list relating to the growth trend with a score of 8,826.

484. Even in the environmental sector, Italian organizations are particularly virtuous: with 17,064 certified ISO 14001, our Country won the fourth place and left, briefly, the lowest rung of the podium in Spain (18,347), but leaving behind the United Kingdom. Excellent also the trend of growth with 2,522 certificates (3rd place).

485. With regard to a particular requirement for the application of ISO 9001:2008 for the mass production and spare parts in the automotive industry (ISO / TS 16949:2009), Italy with 1,118 certifications occupies the 8th place in the world rankings but, at European level, is 2nd only to Germany (3,178) and precedes France (1,033).

486. Systems management for information security (ISO / IEC 27001) are enjoying great international success (as under high-tech processes), and Italy is 8th with 374 certificates and a decent growth trend to increase with the spread of cloud computing services.

487. The food safety management system standard ISO 22000 is statistically the sector with the highest growth rate worldwide (18,630 certificates issued in 138 different Countries), but Italy holds only the 15th place (226 certificates).

488. As for the quality management system used by the organizations responsible for the design and manufacture of medical devices and organizations which design and deliver services related to them (ISO 13485), Italy totals 1,881 certificates (3rd place overall) recording the best growth compared to 2009 (70%).

489. In view of the above data, it can be said that Italy plays a major role in the field of 'Standardization', placing among the first Countries in the world in terms of absolute certification.

This result is enhanced by the fact that the number of companies is much smaller than that of Nations like China, USA, Brazil, India and the United Kingdom.

490. The credit for this should be definitely identified in the Italian legislation: it has prescribed *mandatory* for participation in the construction industry (ISO 9001), has shown a willingness to focus on bureaucratic simplifications to achieve certification and to ensure measures security technology to regulate the operation of payment systems in banking and business continuity in Government.

491. Among those not mentioned in the ISO Survey, it is expected, then, that the standards relating to Management Systems Health and Safety at Work (OHSAS 18001) and those related to corporate social and ethical aspects (SA 8000) will collect in our Country increasing attention from organizations.

This, on the one hand, is to address the many serious accidents involving every year a large number of workers, and partly to demonstrate to the competent authorities the adoption of organizational models pursuant to legislative decree no. 231/2001.

In this context, it is also very likely that, in future, there will be the requirement of the integration of management systems (BS PAS 99) to generate significant additional benefits due to simplifications and auditing activities with a general reduction of costs.

492. In addition, the culture of standardization in Italy has been consolidated through the creation of the authority *Accredia*, in December 2009, which now holds an important position in the system of national certification, especially in the training of professionals who provide auditing and inspection.

Accredia provides adequate assurance of both businesses and consumers about the quality of products and services that are certified.

493. The combination of regulatory intervention, the endemic culture of Made in Italy (to guarantee the quality of our services / products) and the benefits of profitability that the 'Standardization' provides to organizations make Italy a country definitely cutting edge with a good growth rate in the short to medium term.

Chapter 5. Legal Status of Out-of-Court Dispute Settlement in the ICT Sector

§1. Introduction

494. The Italian legal system provides, under certain assumptions (principally for reasons of *procedural economy*), the reliance on private parties of the right to decide for themselves and personally, or to delegate to third parties the resolution of disputes concerning them.

495. By way of introduction, the main instruments to replace the Italian civil courts are so categorized: (i) transaction, (ii) arbitration, (iii) conciliation, (iv) mediation and (v) alternative dispute resolution.

496. *Transaction* is the agreement whereby the parties, through mutual concessions, resolve a started dispute or prevent a dispute that may arise between them.

With these concessions (also different from the subject of litigation) can be started, amended or terminated between the parties (according to Article 1965 of the Italian Civil Code).

497. *Arbitration* is the process by which the parties rely on the resolution of the dispute to third parties not belonging to the judiciary, which will supersede the civil law Court.

The relevant final decision has the value of a judgment from the date of its signature.

The filing of the award, however, at the Registry of the Court is required solely for the purpose of the declaration of enforceability that shall be made by Court order.

498. *Conciliation* is the agreement reached between the parties, on free enterprise or through specific organs or public offices (between which we can include the Justice of the Peace and the conciliation commission established at the Provincial Directorate of Labour).

It is, in any case, a means that replace the jurisdiction, as intervening prior to the introduction of the case.

Taking place in a non-contentious framework, these procedures need to be distinguished from settlements that are, instead, tempted by the Civil Court pending the litigation, according to Article 185 of the Italian Civil Procedural Code.

499. *Mediation*, recently introduced in Italy by legislative decree no. 28 of 4 March 2010, is an activity performed by an independent and impartial body that aims to assist two or more parties in the resolution of a dispute arising between them, with the scope of reaching an amicable solution of the dispute before it continues to judicial authorities.

500. Alternative Dispute Resolution (ADR) is, more generally, any method or technique, however foreign to the jurisdiction, to be used to provide a solution to legal disputes relating to available rights.

In particular, there are increasingly popular companies specializing in civil or commercial dispute resolution in private, fostering mediation between the parties and the eventual achievement of a final contract agreement.

Recently, particular forms of ADR conducted through the use of the Internet, called *Online Dispute Resolution*, have encountered an increasing use with particular reference to electronic commerce and domain names issues.

501. Besides these, the Italian legal system provides for additional and specific procedures related to its various sectors, clearly deserving separate and extrajudicial methods of dispute resolution: for example, attempts of conciliation in front of the Co.Re.Com (Regional Committee for Communications) to resolve disputes between users and providers of electronic communications services, as well as the proceedings in front of the Italian Privacy Authority in relation to violations of regulations on protection of personal data.

§2. Arbitration in the Civil Procedure Code

502. Preliminarily, it should be noted that the institution of *arbitration*, governed by Articles 806 and following of the Italian Code of Civil Procedure and profoundly changed, especially in the years 1983 and 1994, was last revised by Decree n. 40 of 2 February 2006.

The Legislator has provided, in particular, that the new provisions concerning arbitration shall apply to agreements concluded after the entry into force of the reform (i.e., after 2 March 2006).

503. The Italian Civil Code provides legal different figures related to arbitration with regard to function and achievement (and, at the same time, different in terms of structure).

504. First, we must introduce the institution of *arbitration*, disciplined by Article 1349 of the Civil Code for the case where, during the conclusion of a contract, the parties have referred to a *third party* for the determination of the issue covered by the contract or for the completion of an element of the negotiation.

The third party, called the arbitrator, must proceed in that capacity in *equity*.

It is not, in any case, a judgment because, instead of solving a dispute not yet arisen, it is merely thought to solve a conflict at the time of the contract.

505. Free, or informal, arbitration, is a procedure under Article 808-*ter* of the Code of Civil Procedure, the function of which is to resolve a dispute already in place.

It has, therefore, the function of judgment, although it does not necessarily possess all the structural characteristics.

This institute represents the settlement of a dispute that in its formative moment of judgment has certain characteristics and the actual content of which is determined by the arbitrator (or arbitrators).

Third impartial parties are entrusted the task of composing, with a judgment after trial, a dispute by an act of negotiation, sometimes adopting the form of a transaction.

The only remedies available against any informal arbitration are those related to the substantive law as grounds for cancellation of the contract: i.e. the breach of the limits of the mandate, altered perception or misrepresentation of fact submitted to the arbitrators (excluding error of judgment).

506. The arbitration is governed by Articles 806 and following of the Procedural Code and has the function and structure of a judgment.

It consists of a true judgment based on law or equity that the person relying on one or more arbitrators concludes through a transaction (agreement or arbitration clause).

Although this is a private judgment, the final arbitration award has the effect similar to the one of a Court (judgment).

To achieve this, it becomes necessary an act of the Court that, after checking the form of the award filed, gives to it the above-mentioned effect.[198]

§3. Mediation

507. Mediation, as provided by Decree 28/2010, has the function of merging parties to an amicable agreement to resolve a dispute. In the Italian legal framework, both the voluntary mediation and the mandatory mediation are contemplated.

508. The mediator is defined as the person or persons who, individually or collectively, have the power to make judgments or decisions binding on the recipients of the service itself (Article 1).

Mediation, by express legislative provision, takes place at a *body of mediation*, which can be either public or private, provided with written authorization and in a special register kept by the Ministry of Justice.

According to Article 2 of the Decree, anyone can go to mediation for the settlement of a dispute relating to civil and commercial available rights.

509. Voluntary mediation was introduced into the legal system on 20 March 2010, in relation to all civil and commercial disputes relating available rights.

It should regard the rights which individuals have an objective availability, intended as a functionality ability on the right (e.g., the sale of goods) and subjective understanding as the absence of conditions that can modify the rights (e.g., the interdiction).

198. *See* G. Verde, 'Lineamenti di diritto dell'arbitrato' (Giappichelli, Torino, 2006); C. Mandrioli, 'Diritto Processuale Civile' (Giappichelli, Torino, 2011); R. Sammartano, 'Il diritto dell'arbitrato' (CEDAM, Padova, 2005).

Even before 20 March 2010, parties of the mediation process could entrust the resolution of disputes as an alternative means to ordinary courts. However, it is only through legislative decree 28/2010 that a growing relevance and role are attributed to mediation.

Thanks to this legislation, in fact, for the attorney is mandatory to inform the client of the possibility of recurring to the mediation process.

510. The mandatory mediation entered into force on 20 March 2011, too, and is different because it *must* be activated, by law, by the parties before filing a civil claim.

More correctly, it must be considered as a condition of admissibility (and not for proposing the application) of the judgment.

The issues in which it is expected to operate are the following: in rem rights, divisions and inheritances, family agreements, loans, leasing of businesses, compensation for damage caused by vehicles and boats, medical liability and defamation with the means of press or other means of advertising, contracts of insurance, banking and financial services.

However, during the mediation process, it is possible to ask ordinary courts urgent decrees if there is a need for the protection of fundamental rights. On the other way, mediation is excluded as admissibility requirement for proceedings like injunction proceedings and the relative opposition, validation of licence or eviction, incidental or opposition proceedings in the enforcement of cognition, proceedings in private and civil action pursued in the criminal trial.

511. The delegate mediation (or 'solicited by the Court'), as provided by Article 5, paragraph 2 of the Decree, happens every time the judge, in Court of Appeal proceedings, having assessed the nature of the case, the state of education and the conduct of the parties, invite the parties at any time, by order, to proceed to mediation.

This invitation, however, must be addressed prior to the final hearing, i.e. before the discussion of the case.

If the parties adhere to the call, the Court fixes the next hearing after the expiry of four months (according to Article 6) and, when the mediation has not been experienced, it assigns the term to the parties of fifteen days to submit demand for mediation.

512. The process, as regulated by Article 8 of the Decree, is not subject to particular formalities.

Once the application for mediation is filed, the person in charge of the mediation shall appoint a mediator and set the first meeting between the parties within fifteen days from the filing.

The latter and the first meeting shall be communicated to the other party by any appropriate means to ensure the reception.

The procedure, then, as mentioned, takes place informally at the address of choice, or at the place specified in the Rules of Procedure.

513. Once started the process, its final phase, however, can have two possible outcomes.

If amicable settlement is reached, the mediator shall write the minutes, which are then attached to the text of the agreement, signed by the parties.

If, however, the agreement is not reached, the mediator may make a proposal for settlement (this is the aforementioned mediation proposals), which becomes mandatory only if the parties request it by mutual agreement.

The proposal must then be communicated to them in written form.

The parties, then, will send to the mediator, in writing and within seven days, the eventual acceptance or rejection of the proposal.

In case of failure to respond within seven days, the proposal has to be rejected.

514. Assuming that the amicable settlement is reached, or that the parties accept the mediator's proposal, the minutes are formed, which must be signed by the parties and by the mediator, and the mediator must also certify the signatures of the parties or their inability to subscribe.

If, by this agreement, the parties conclude a contract or commit any act for which the Civil Code requires the transcription (according to Article 2643 of the Italian Civil Code), to proceed to the transcript of the signing of the minutes is necessary the certification by an authorized public official.

If, however, no agreement is reached, Article 11 provides that the mediator forms minutes with details of the proposal. The minutes then must be signed by the parties and the mediator, who also certifies the authenticity of the signature of the parties or their inability to subscribe. In the same minutes, the mediator acknowledges the lack of participation of any party to the mediation process.[199]

§4. Conciliation

515. Conciliation is usually an instrument of dispute resolution where a third party, usually different from the judge and with no decision-making powers, helps the parties in mutual communication and negotiation. In this case, the primary purpose is leading them to a satisfactory agreement.

The main distinction to highlight, in the wide range of existing conciliatory examples, is the one between *judicial conciliation* and *conciliation court*. The first one occurs in proceedings taking place before the State judge, while the second one is related to processes that take place before a person external to the Italian judicial system.

516. The conciliation in the Court is expressly referred to, first, by Article 185 of the Code of Civil Procedure, which provides, for determination by the investigating judge, a special hearing for the personal appearance of the parties and the attempt at conciliation, following a joint request of the parties, or ex officio according to Article 117 of the Code of Civil Procedure.

A further example of conciliation, always framed in the context of legal proceedings, is regulated by Article 198 of the Code of Civil Procedure. In particular, when

199. *See* T. Fragomeni, 'Mediazione e Conciliazione' (La Tribuna, Piacenza, 2010).

it is necessary to examine documents and accounting records, the judge may give a commission to an expert, also entrusting the task of reconciling the parties.

The next article also provides that, if the reconciliation is successful, the judge will draw up minutes of settlement, signed by the parties and the consultant and then added to the file in the office.

Additionally, a similar effort can be done by a technical consultant ex Article 696-*bis* of the same Code. In particular, it is expected that the consultant tries, whenever possible, the reconciliation of the parties and, if there is the agreement, provides to prepare appropriate minutes.

Finally, a last attempt of conciliation is inserted in the process of separation of spouses: Article 708 of the Code of Civil Procedure provides that the President of the Court, after having heard the spouses, first separately and then jointly, tries the reconciliation.

§5. Other Procedures of Conciliation

517. In the Italian legal system, in addition to the procedures outlined above, there are other conciliation procedures under which the parties rely on to resolve a dispute out of Court.

Many of those, in particular, regard *consumers* (i.e., individuals who buy or use goods or services for purposes not related to business and professional activity) and are included in the *Italian Code of Consumption* (enacted with legislative decree no. 206 of 6 September 2005).

518. Concerning the relationship between ADR procedures and the Italian Chambers of Commerce system, Law n. 580 of 29 December 1993, provides the opportunity, for the Chambers of Commerce, to promote the establishment of *conciliation commissions* for the amicable resolution of disputes between businesses and between businesses and consumers.

In such cases, it does not arise any legal relationship between the parties and the mediator, the latter being a mere employee of the institution.

In particular, the *Code of Consumption* provides that consumers associations and users can activate, before going to Court, the conciliation process in question, which must be defined in any case *within 60 days.*

If an agreement is reached, then the judge will approve the conciliation.

519. Alternatively, the same *Code of Consumption* provides for the establishment of an appropriate *list of organisms of consumers*, which will be addressed by consumers groups and users, to promote out-of-Court procedures regarding consumers' issues.

520. With Resolution 173/07/CONS, the Italian Authority for Communications (AGCOM) has approved, on 19 April 2007, a Regulation concerning the procedures for resolution of disputes between *electronic communications operators* and *users*.

Those who wish to sue for an asserted violation of a right are required to promote a preliminary attempt of conciliation before *Co.Re.Com* (Regional Committee for Communications) of the Region of origin.

521. The *joint mediation* is, also, a means of dispute resolution that takes place with a comparison between consumer and company, through their representatives, defined *conciliators*, who are known as the *Conciliation Commission*.

These subjects, when is decided to try to resolve the dispute, operate directly without the intervention of a third party, trying to find the resolution of the dispute to submit, then, to the attention of interested parties.

The only necessity in order to be able to rely on this procedure is the membership to an association of consumers, which gives the mandate to reconcile.

Among the most important Italian companies that use the joint mediation system, there are companies such as *Enel*, *Telecom*, *Tim* and other telecommunications operators.

522. Following an agreement between the most representative consumer associations and *Ania* (the National Association of Insurance Companies), it was introduced a special procedure that allows voluntary conciliation to resolve disputes relating to *liability insurance* for up to EUR 15,000.00.

Under this procedure, in the first place, the consumer will exhibit damages in his case, through a complaint. The company, within 30 days, must propose a solution.

If the insured is not satisfied with the response from the company, he/she may contact an association of consumers asking to participate in this procedure.

The case will, then, be examined by a commission of conciliation made by the representative of the consumer and of the insurance company, which will decide within 30 days.

The decision of the Board will occur, then, within 60 days after the first report of the problem.

523. Legislative decree no. 179 of 8 October 2007 has set up a room of conciliation and arbitration in *Consob* for resolving disputes between *investors* and *financial intermediaries*.

The Consob is the Italian competent authority for ensuring: (i) transparency and correct behaviour by securities market participants; (ii) disclosure of complete and accurate information to the investing public by listed companies; (iii) accuracy of the facts represented in the prospectuses related to offerings of transferable securities to the investing public; (iv) compliance with regulations by auditors entered in the Special Register. It conducts investigations with respect to potential infringements of insider dealing and market manipulation law.

The conciliation procedure can also be initiated personally by investors presenting to the Chamber a written application for conciliation and arbitration.

Such application, however, may not be submitted if the same case is already under investigation by another body, or if no complaint has been made to the intermediary, or more than 90 days have elapsed from the presentation without that the intermediary in turn expressed its determinations to the investor.

The process, however, must be concluded within a maximum period of 60 days from the date of submission of the application for conciliation.

§6. Other Means of Dispute Resolution

524. Very peculiar, in Italy, are those dispute resolution proceedings that are conducted before the *Italian Authority for Data Protection* (Garante per la Protezione dei dati Personali).

Only with respect to violations of the rules contained in the *Code for the Protection of Personal Data*, or *Privacy Code* (enacted with legislative decree no. 196 of 30 June 2003), there are *three* different types of procedures that individuals can propose in front of the *Privacy Authority* to safeguard their rights.

525. First, it is possible, within the meaning of Article 141, paragraph 1, lett. B of the *Privacy Code*, to ask (also informally) the Authority to intervene (if necessary) and control the application of the regulations governing the protection of personal data.

This message/report may be submitted on plain paper and does not have to follow specific formalities.

526. Second, the *complaint* to the *Privacy Authority* is, however, an act by which the *Authority* is, first, informed about a violation of the regulations governing the protection of personal data.

It can be proposed when there is an issue concerning the protection of rights and is aimed to promote a decision of the Authority on any matter within its jurisdiction.

The complaint is usually followed by a preliminary enquiry and an administrative proceeding during which various measures can be adopted.

527. *Recourse* to the Authority, then, is an act presented solely to enforce rights under Article 7 of the *Privacy Code*, and only when the response of the owner (or manager, if appointed) for the processing of personal data ('Titolare') to the instance is not received within the time specified, or is not satisfactory, or the expiry of the deadline would expose him/her to an imminent and irreparable harm.

528. Last but not least, in Italy, there are very interesting Alternative Disputes Resolution systems regarding Internet *domain names*.

Disputes between owners of domain names and third parties, relating to the registration and use of domain names, can be managed using the same procedures for ADR that can be activated in front of one of the service companies approved by ICANN.

The amicable dispute resolution procedures are carried out by the bodies trustees, according to *rules* (policies) predetermined by ICANN itself, depending on the specific matter under investigation, and directly accessible through the website of the institution.

Part II. Protection of Intellectual Property in the ICT Sector

Chapter 1. Application of Copyright in the Area of ICT

§1. The Normative Sources

529. The main Italian Copyright Law is Law n. 633/1941.

The text of such law was amended several times in order to comply both with International Treaties ratified by Italy and with the European Union Law.

530. Italy ratified many copyright-related International Treaties.

For instance, Law n. 923/1956 ratified the Universal Copyright Convention signed in Geneva on 6 September 1952; Law n. 866/1973 implemented the Convention of Rome of 21 October 1961, related to the protection of interpreters and performer artists, producers of phonograms and radio-diffusion organizations; Law n. 399/1978 ratified the Berne Convention for the Protection of Literary and Artistic Works; Law n. 747/1994 ratified the TRIPS Agreement, part of the Uruguay Round multilateral commercial negotiations.

531. Following the WCT (WIPO Copyright Treaty) and the WPPT (WIPO Performances and Phonograms Treaty) signed in Geneva on 20 December 1996, the European Union enacted Directive 2001/29/CE.

In Italy, such Directive was implemented by legislative decree no. 68/2003. In particular, section 13 of the Italian Copyright Law was amended, in order to *extend* the exclusive right of reproduction and to include in it also temporary reproduction of copyrighted works, as well as a very extended exclusive right to communicate them to the public.

Finally, the new discipline allows and protects the use of technological protection measures (TPM) on copyrighted works, as well as the possibility to include digital copyright information in the body of the work (watermarking).

532. Directive 91/250/EEC regarding the legal protection of computer programs and Directive 96/6/EC regarding the legal protection of databases were implemented by inserting specific provisions into the Italian Copyright Law, respectively by legislative decree no. 518/1992 and by legislative decree no. 169/1999.

In a similar way, specific provisions in the main Italian copyright law were inserted by legislative decree no. 685/94 in order to implement Directive 92/100/

EEC on lending and rental rights, as well as on other copyright-related rights, such as the fixation of performances or broadcasts and cases of limited limitations to the exclusive rights contemplated in the Directive.

533. Directive 93/98/EEC harmonizing the term of protection of copyright and certain related rights were implemented by legislative decree no. 154/97 and then repealed by Directive 2006/116/EC1.

In 2011, Directive 2011/77/UE was published, further amending Directive 2006/116/EC. In particular, it furtherly extends the term of protection for performers and sound recordings.

534. Law n. 2/2008 should also be mentioned. It added part 1-*bis* to section 70 of Law n. 633/41 and introduced the possibility to publish freely on the Internet low resolution or degraded quality images and music.

Such possibility is subject to strict conditions, i.e. publishing must be for free, aimed at a didactical or scientific use and only if such use is a non-profit one.

The law designs a procedure, involving the Government and parliamentary commissions, in order to define the limits to didactical or scientific use of music and images.

535. The essential copyright laws mentioned above determine a quite complex network of exclusive rights.

For what enforcement is concerned, the key law is currently Law n. 140/2006.

Moreover, the new norms provide alternative criteria to calculate damages or other compensations or penalties.

Similar judicial remedies are present also in the Italian legislative decree no. 30/2005 (the Intellectual Property Code) and may be concurrent in case the alleged violation does not only concern works protected by copyright but also concern other types of intellectual property like trademarks.

536. It should be noticed that the telecommunication networks copyright enforcement and intellectual property enforcement norms are to be interpreted keeping in mind also the norms of legislative decree no. 70/2003, implementing Directive 2000/31/EC (the so-called Directive on Electronic Commerce), EU General Data Protection Regulation n. 679/2016 (the so-called GDPR) and the provisions of the Italian Personal Data Protection (or Privacy) Code.

§2. Works Protected

537. Intellectual works having a creative character and appertaining to literature, music, the graphic arts, architecture, the theatre and cinematography, whatever their mode or form of expression, shall be protected according to Law n. 633 of 1941.

Computer programs shall further be protected as literary works, pursuant to the Berne Convention for the Protection of Literary and Artistic Works, which was ratified and enforced by Law n. 399 of 20 June 1978.

538. In particular, in the Italian legal framework, the following works are protected: (i) literary, dramatic, scientific, didactic and religious works, whether in written or oral form; (ii) musical works and compositions, with or without words, dramatic-musical works and musical variations which constitute original works; (iii) choreographic works and pantomimes, the acting form of which is fixed in writing or otherwise; (iv) works of sculpture, painting, drawing, engraving and similar graphic arts, including scenic art, even when such works are applied to an industrial product if their artistic value is distinct from the industrial character of the product with which they are associated; (v) architectural plans and works; (vi) works of cinematographic art, whether in silent or sound form; (vii) works of photographic art and those expressed with processes analogous to photograph; (viii) computer programs, whatever may be the form of their expression, provided they are an original work as resulting from the author's intellectual creation; (ix) databases meant as collections of works, data or other independent materials which are systematically or methodically arranged and can be individually accessed by electronic or other means; and (x) works of industrial designs which themselves have a creative and artistic value.

539. The protection provided by the Italian law does not apply to *ideas* and principles underlying any program component, including those underlying the interfaces thereof.

Program also means preparatory materials used for developing the said program. The copyright protection for databases shall not extend to their contents and shall be without prejudice to any rights subsisting in said contents.

540. Collective works formed by the assembling of works, or part of works, and possessing the character of a self-contained creation resulting from selection and coordinator for a specific literary, scientific, didactic, religious, political or artistic purpose, such as encyclopaedias, dictionaries, anthologies, magazines and newspapers, are protected as original works, independently of and without prejudice to any copyright subsisting in the constituent works or parts thereof.

541. Without prejudice to the rights subsisting in the original work, elaborations of a creative character of any such work, such as translations into another language, transformations into any other literary or artistic form, modifications and additions constituting a substantial recasting of the original work, adaptations, reductions, abridgements and variations which do not constitute an original work, are also protected.

542. The provisions of Law n. 633/41 do not apply to the texts of official acts of the State or of Public Administrations, whether Italian or foreign.

§3. Subjects of the Right

543. Copyright, in Italy, shall be acquired by the creation of a work resulting from an intellectual effort.

In the case of a collective work, the person who organizes and directs its creation shall be deemed to be the author.

Within the limits of his contribution, the person who has elaborated a work shall be deemed to be the author of such elaboration.

544. The person who, in the customary manner, is indicated as an author, or is announced as such in the course of the recitation, performance or broadcasting of a work shall, in the absence of proof to the contrary, be deemed to be the author of the work.

Any pseudonym, professional name, initials or customary sign, well known as being equivalent to a true name, shall be deemed to have the same value as such true name.

545. Any person who has performed, or in any manner published, an anonymous or pseudonymous work, shall be entitled to assert the rights of the author reveals his identity.

546. If the work has been created by the indistinguishable and inseparable contributions of two or more persons, the copyright shall belong to all the co-authors in the common.

In the absence of proof of a written agreement to the contrary, the undivided portions shall be presumed to be of *equal value*.

The provisions which regulate property owned in common shall be applicable.

Moreover, defence of the moral right may, at any time, be exercised individually by any co-author and the work, if unpublished, may not be published, nor may it be modified or utilized in a form differing from that of first publication, without the agreement of all the co-authors.

However, in the case of unjustified refusal by one or more co-authors, publication, modification or new utilization of the work may be authorized by the judicial authority upon such conditions and terms as that authority may order.

547. Copyright in works created and published under the name, on the account, and at the expense of the State, the Provinces and Communes shall belong to them.

In the absence of agreement to the contrary with the authors of the works published, a like right shall also belong to private legal entities of a non-profit character, as well as to Academies and other public cultural organizations, in respect of collections of their proceedings and their publications.

§4. Protection of the Economic Utilization of the Work

548. The author shall have the exclusive right to *publish* his work.

He shall, in addition, have the exclusive right to the *economic utilization* of the work in any form or manner, whether original or derivative, within the limits fixed by the Italian Copyright Law, and especially as regards the exercise of the exclusive rights.

The first form of exercise of the right of utilization shall be considered to be the *first publication.*

549. In the absence of any contrary stipulation, if a computer program was created by an employee in the performance of his tasks, or upon instructions given by the employer, the latter shall have the exclusive right to the economic utilization of the program thus created. In the absence of any contrary stipulation, if a work of industrial design is created by an employee in the performance of his tasks, or upon instruction given by the employer, the latter shall have the exclusive right to the economic utilization of the work of design thus created.

550. The exclusive right of reproduction has for its object the multiplication of copies of the work by any means, such as handcopying, printing, lithography, engraving, photography, phonography, cinematography and any other process of reproduction.

551. The exclusive right to transcribe has for its object the use of means suitable for transforming an oral work into a written work or into a work reproduced by one of the methods indicated in the text of the Law.

552. The exclusive right of public performance or recitation has for its object the performance or recitation however effected, and with or without payment, of a musical, dramatic or cinematographic work, of any other work suitable for public exhibition, and of oral works.

553. The performance or recitation of a work within the normal family circle, or within a college, school or institute of retreat or treatment, provided it is not given with gainful intent, shall not be deemed to be public performance or recitation. Acting in public museums, archives and libraries for the exclusive purpose of cultural promotion and enhancement of the works themselves identified on the basis of memoranda of understanding between the S.I.A.E. (Italian Society of Authors and Publishers) and the Ministry of Cultural Heritage and Activities and Tourism shall not be deemed to be public.

554. The exclusive right of diffusion has for its object the use of any means of diffusion over a distance, such as telegraphy, telephony, radio or television broadcasting and other analogous means.

555. The exclusive right of *distribution* has for its object the right to commercialize, to circulate or, at all events, to make available to the public, whatever means and for whatever purpose, the work or the copies thereof, and shall include, in addition, the exclusive right to introduce, into the territory of the Countries of the European Union, for purposes of distribution, copies of the work made in Countries not members of the European Union.

556. The delivery, free of charge, of copies of the work for advertising purposes or for teaching or scientific research purposes, when carried out and allowed by the person entitled thereto, shall not be deemed to be a form of exercise of the exclusive right of distribution.

557. The exclusive right of *translation* has for its object the translation of the work into another language or dialect.

The exclusive right of *elaboration* includes all forms of modification, elaboration and transformation of the work specified in the text of the Copyright Law.

The author shall, in addition, have the exclusive right of publishing his works in a collection.

Finally, he shall have the exclusive right of introducing any modification into the work.

558. The exclusive right of *lease* has for its object the granting of the use of the original works, of copies thereof or of supporting materials, protected by copyright, for a limited period of time and for the purpose of achieving economic or commercial benefits, whether directly or indirectly.

The exclusive right of *loan* has for its object the granting of the use of the original works, of copies thereof or of supporting materials, protected by copyright, made by institutions open to the public, for a limited period of time and for purposes other than those as per the previous point.

The author, even when granting the right of lease to a producer of phonograms or cinematographic or audiovisual works or of sequences of motion pictures, shall retain the right to obtain fair remuneration for the lease contract made by the said producer with third parties.

Any contrary stipulation shall be void.

559. The exclusive rights specified in the preceding points are independent of one another.

The exercise of any one of them shall not exclude the exercise of the other rights.

They shall pertain to the work in its entirety and to each of its parts.

§5. Moral Right of the Author

560. Independently of the exclusive rights of economic utilization of the work referred to in the provisions of the preceding paragraphs, and even after the transfer of such rights, the author shall retain the right to claim authorship of the work and to object to any distortion, mutilation or any other modification of, and other derogatory action in relation to, the said work, which would be prejudicial to his honour or reputation.

561. However, in the case of works of architecture, the author may not oppose modifications found necessary in the course of construction.

He may not, moreover, oppose other modifications which may be necessary in any such completed work.

However, if the work is recognized by the competent State authority as having an important artistic character, the author shall be entrusted with the study and execution of such modifications.

562. The author of an anonymous or pseudonymous work shall at all times have the right to reveal his identity and to have his position as author recognized by judicial procedure.

Notwithstanding any prior agreement to the contrary, persons who have derived title from an author who has revealed his identity shall be required to indicate the name of the author in publications, reproductions, transcriptions, performances, recitations and diffusions or in any other form of manifestation or announcement to the public.

563. The rights indicated in the preceding points shall be inalienable.

However, if the author was aware of, and accepted, modifications in his work, he shall not be entitled to intervene to prevent the performance thereof or to demand its suppression.

564. After the death of the author, rights may be asserted, without limitation of time, by his spouse and children and, in the absence thereof, by his parents and other direct ascendants and descendants, by his brothers and sisters and their descendants.

If the public interest should so require, such action may also be taken by the premier ('Presidente del Consiglio') after hearing the competent syndical association.

565. The right of publishing unpublished works shall belong to the heirs of the author or the legatees of the particular works unless the author has expressly forbidden publication or has entrusted it to other persons.

When the author has fixed a period of time to precede publication, unpublished works shall not be published before the expiration thereof.

When the persons indicated are two or more in number, and there is disagreement between them, the matter shall be decided by a judicial authority after hearing the representative of the public interest.

The wishes of the deceased person, when expressed in writing, shall in all cases be respected.

§6. Duration of Rights of Economic Utilization of a Work

566. The rights of economic utilization of a work shall continue for the life of the author and until the termination of the seventieth calendar year after his death.

567. In the case of works indicated in Article 10 of the Law, and of dramatico-musical and choreographic works and pantomimes, the duration of the rights of economic utilization belonging to each collaborator shall be determined in relation to the life of the last surviving co-author.

In the case of collective works, the duration of the rights of economic utilization belonging to each collaborator shall be determined in relation to the respective lives of such collaborators.

The duration of rights of economic utilization of the work as a whole shall be seventy years from the date of first publication, whatever the form in which publication was effected, except in the case of magazines, newspapers and other periodical works to which the provisions of Article 30 of the Copyright Law shall apply.

568. In the case of anonymous or pseudonymous works other than those specified in the second paragraph of Article 8, the duration of the rights of economic utilization shall be seventy years from the date of first publication, whatever may be the form in which publication was effected.

If, before the expiration of the said term, the author has revealed his identity, or his identity has been revealed by the persons indicated in Article 23 or by the persons authorized by the author, and in the manner established by the following Article, the term specified in Article 25 shall then apply.

569. The duration of the rights of economic utilization of computer programs shall be computed, in each case, as of the 1st of January of the year following that in which the event occurred.

570. In order to acquire the benefits or normal duration of the rights of economic utilization, the revelation of identity must be made by means of declaration to the Office of Literary, Scientific and Artistic Property ('Ufficio della proprietà letteraria, scientifica ed artistica') of the Office of the Chairman of the Council of Ministers in accordance with the provisions established by the Regulations.

The declaration of revelation shall be published in the form required by said provisions and shall, as regards third parties who have acquired rights in the work in its anonymous or pseudonymous condition, have effects as from the date of its deposit.

571. The duration of the rights of economic utilization belonging, within the terms of Article 11, to the State, the Provinces, the Communes, the Academies, or public cultural organizations, or private legal entities of a non-profit character, shall be twenty years from first publication was effected.

In the case of communications and memoranda published by Academies and other public cultural organizations, such term shall be reduced to two years, after which the author shall wholly reacquire the right to the unrestricted disposal of his writings.

572. When parts or volumes of a given work are published separately and at different times, the duration of the rights of economic utilization, when fixed in years, shall run from the year of publication of each part or volume. The author shall enjoy the benefit of fractions of years.

In the case of collective periodical work, such as a magazine or newspaper, the time is calculated from the end of the year of publication of the individual parts or numbers.

573. In the case of works published for the first time after the death of the author, the duration of the rights of economic utilization shall be seventy years from first publication, irrespective of the place and form of such publication, provided publication occurs within twenty years from the death of the author.

574. The rights of economic utilization of a cinematographic work shall continue for fifty years from the first public showing, provided this takes place not later than five years from the end of the calendar year in which the work was produced. If this period of five years is exceeded, protection shall continue for seventy years from the year following that in which the work was produced.

575. The rights of economic utilization of a photographic work shall continue for fifty years from the year in which the work was produced.

§7. Special Provisions Governing the Right of Economic Utilization of Certain Categories of Works

576. In the absence of a special agreement between collaborators in respect of operas, operettas, melologues, musical compositions with words and dance and ballet music, the following provisions shall apply.

577. The author of the musical part shall be entitled to exercise the rights of economic utilization; however, the rights flowing from the common ownership of the parties are not affected.

The profits derived from economic utilization shall be shared in proportion to the values of the respective literary and musical contributions.

578. In the operas, the value of the musical part shall be regarded as being three quarters of the total value of the work.

In operettas, in melologues, in musical compositions with words, in dance and ballet music, the value of the two contributions shall be considered equal.

Subject to the provisions of the following points, each collaborator shall be entitled to use his own work separately and independently.

579. The author of the literary part may dispose thereof for the purpose of its union with some other musical work, only in the following cases: (i) if, after the final text of the manuscript of the literary contribution has been sent to the composer, he does not set it to music within five years in the case of a libretto for an opera or operetta, or within one year in the case of any other literary work to be set to music; (ii) if, after having been set to music and considered by the parties as being ready for performance, the work is not performed within the periods specified in the preceding subsection, except as longer periods may be granted for performance in accordance with Articles 139 and 141; (iii) if, after a first performance, the work ceases to be performed for a period of ten years in the case of an opera, an oratorio, a symphonic poem or an operetta, or for a period of two years in the case of any other composition.

The composer, in the cases specified in points (ii) and (iii), may make use of the music in other ways.

580. In the case specified in point (i) of the preceding Article, the author of the literary part shall reacquire the right of unrestricted disposal thereof, without prejudice to any ultimate action for damages that he may take against the composer.

In the cases specified in points (ii) and (iii), and without prejudice to any action for damages referred to in the preceding paragraph, the community rights as such shall be maintained in respect of the work which has already been set to music, but the work itself may not be performed without the consent of both collaborators.

581. In the case of choreographic works or pantomimes, and in the case of other works consisting of music with words, dancing or mimicry, such as musical reviews and similar works, in which the musical part does not constitute the principal function or value, the exercise of the rights of economic utilization shall, in the absence of agreement to the contrary, belong to the author of the choreographic or pantomimic part, and in the case of musical revues to the author of the literary part.

582. In the case of a collective work, the rights of economic utilization shall, in the absence of agreement to the contrary, belong to the publisher of the work, without prejudice to any right deriving from the application of Article 7.

The right to utilize their own contributions separately shall be reserved to the individual collaborators in collective works, provided they observe any subsisting agreements or, in the absence of agreements, the rules set out below.

583. If, without prior agreement, an article is sent to a magazine or newspaper by a person outside the editorial staff, for the purpose of reproduction, the author shall reacquire the right to dispose of it unrestrictedly if he does not receive notice of acceptance within one month from notification of such acceptance.

In the case of an article furnished by a member of the editorial staff, the director of the magazine or newspaper may defer reproduction beyond the periods indicated in the preceding paragraph.

However, once the period of six months from the delivery of the manuscript has expired, the author shall be entitled to utilize the article for reproduction in a volume, or in a separate form in the case of newspaper, and also in any other periodical in the case of a magazine.

584. In the absence of agreement to the contrary, the collaborator, in a collective work other than a magazine or newspaper, shall be entitled to have his name appear in a customary manner in the reproduction of his work.

In the absence of agreement to the contrary, such a right shall not belong to the editorial staff of the newspaper.

585. The director of a newspaper shall, in the absence of agreement to the contrary, be entitled to introduce into an article submitted for reproduction such modifications of form as are required by the nature and objects of the newspaper.

In articles to be reproduced without indication of the name of the author, this right shall extend to the omission or reduction of parts of the said article.

586. The author of an article or other work reproduced in a collective work shall be entitled to reproduce it in a separate form, or to include it in a volume, provided he indicates the collective work from which it has been taken and the date of publication.

In the case of articles appearing in magazines or newspapers, the author shall, in the absence of agreement to the contrary, also have the right to reproduce them in other magazines or newspapers.

587. The publisher or director of magazine or newspaper shall not be compelled to preserve or to return the manuscripts of unreproduced articles which have been sent to him without his request.

588. The author of the subject, the author of the scenario, the composer of the music and the artistic director shall be considered as co-authors of a cinematographic work.

589. The exercise of the rights of economic utilization of a cinematographic work shall belong to the person who has organized the production of the said work.

The person who is indicated in the cinematographic film as the producer shall be deemed to be the producer of the cinematographic work.

590. The exercise of the rights of economic utilization belonging to the producer shall have as its object the cinematographic exploitation of the work produced.

In the absence of agreement to the contrary, the producer shall not make or show elaborations, transformations or translations of the produced work without the consent of the authors indicated in Article 44.

The authors of music, of musical compositions and of the words which accompany music shall be entitled to collect directly from persons publicly showing the work a separate payment in respect of such showing.

In the absence of agreement between the parties, the payment shall be fixed according to the provisions of the Regulations.

591. The authors of the subject and of the scenario and the artistic director, in cases where they are not remunerated upon the basis of a percentage of the receipts derived from public showing of the cinematographic work, shall, in the absence of agreement to the contrary, be entitled to receive an additional payment when the receipts have attained a level to be fixed by contract with the producer.

The form and amount of such payment shall be fixed by agreement between the categories of persons interested.

592. The producer shall have the right to make such modifications in works utilized in a cinematographic work as are necessary for their cinematographic adaption.

In the absence of agreement between the producer and one or more of the authors referred to in Article 44 of the Law, the question of whether modifications effected or to be effected in a cinematographic work are necessary shall be decided by the Chairman of the Council of Ministers in accordance with the rules contained in the Regulations.

The findings of the College shall be final.

593. The authors of a cinematographic work shall be entitled to have their names, together with an indication of their professional functions and their contributions, mentioned in the showing of a cinematographic work.

594. The authors of the literary or musical parts of a cinematographic work may reproduce them or utilize them separately in any manner, provided no damage is thereby occasioned to the rights of utilization, the exercise of which belongs to the producer.

595. If the producer fails to complete the cinematographic work within a period of three years from the delivery of the literary or musical parts or does not show the completed work within three years from its completion, the authors of the said parts shall be entitled to dispose unrestrictedly of the work itself.

596. By reason of the nature and purpose of broadcasting as a service reserved to the State, which carries on such service either directly or by means of concession, the exclusive right of broadcasting, either directly or by any intermediate means, shall be regulated by the following special provisions.

597. Under the conditions and within the limits indicated in this and the following points, the organization which carries on the broadcasting service shall be entitled to broadcast intellectual works from theatres, concert halls or any other public place.

Proprietors, impresarios and all persons involved in the performance shall be required to permit such installations and technical tests as may be necessary in preparation for the broadcast.

The consent of the author shall be required for the broadcasting of new works and for the first performance in any given season of works which are not new.

A theatrical work which has been publicly performed in three different theatres or other public places shall not be deemed to be new.

598. Where the season for theatrical performances or concerts is not less than two months, the right of the organization indicated in the preceding point may be exercised once a week in respect of theatrical performances, and once for every five concerts or fractional part thereof.

The duration of a theatrical or concert season shall be understood to be the season specified in notices or programmes published before the commencement of the season.

599. The task of ascertaining whether broadcasts comply with proper technical standards shall be the exclusive duty of the State organizations responsible for the supervision of broadcasting and having the powers conferred by Article 2 of Royal Decree Law of 14 June 1923, No. 1352, and of Article 2 of Royal Decree Law of 3 February 1936, No. 654, converted into the law of 4 June 1936, No. 1552.
The name of the author and the title of the work shall be broadcast at the same time as the work itself.

600. Without prejudice to the rights of the author in connection with the broadcasting of his work, the organization carrying on the broadcasting service is authorized to record the said work upon a record or metal tape or by some analogous process, for the purpose of its deferred road cast, when this is necessitated by considerations of time or technology, provided that after its use, the said recording is destroyed or rendered unusable.

601. The author of a work broadcast in accordance with the preceding points shall be entitled to obtain from the organization carrying on the broadcasting service the payment of remuneration, the amount of which in the case of disagreement between the parties shall be settled by a judicial authority.
Application may only be made to the judicial authority after an effort of conciliation made in the manner and form established by the Regulations.

602. The amount of remuneration shall be based upon the number of transmissions.
The Regulations shall determine the criteria for establishing the number and manner of deferred or repeated transmissions.

603. The author shall be entitled to equitable remuneration for the performance in public establishments of broadcast works by means of sound radio receivers equipped with loudspeakers, the amount being determined periodically by agreement between the Società Italiana Autori ed Editori (S.I.A.E.) and the representatives of the competent syndical association.

604. The broadcasting of intellectual works from the premises of the organization carrying on the broadcasting service shall be subject to the consent of the author, in accordance with the provisions contained in the third Chapter of this part; the provisions of the foregoing Articles, except those of Article 55, shall not be applicable to such broadcasting.

605. The broadcasting organization may, by order of the Chairman of the Council of Ministers, make special broadcasts of cultural and artistic propaganda intended for other countries, subject to payment made in accordance with the Regulations.

606. The author shall have the exclusive right, within the meaning of the provisions of Section I of Chapter III: (1) to adapt and record the work upon phonograph records, cinematographic films, metal tapes or any analogous material or mechanical contrivance for reproducing sounds or voices; (2) to reproduce, to distribute, to lease, to lend, as well as to authorize lease and loan of copies of the work adapted or recorded as above; (3) to perform in public and to broadcast the work by means of the record or other mechanical contrivance indicated above.

The assignment of the right of reproduction or the right of commercial circulation shall not, in the absence of agreement to the contrary, include assignment of the right of public performance or broadcasting.

607. Copies of a phonograph record or any like contrivance for reproducing sounds or voices in which an intellectual work has been recorded shall not be commercially distributed unless they bear, in an indelible manner, the following indications: (1) the title of the work reproduced; (2) the name of the author; (3) the name of the performing artist. Orchestral or choral groups shall be indicated by their customary name; (4) the date of production.

608. The record or like Contrivance must be made or utilized in such a manner that the moral right of the author is respected within the terms of the Law.

Modifications of a work necessitated by the technical requirement of recording shall be considered lawful.

609. Any concession permitting a national establishment which issues phonograph records to utilize the matrices of the State Record Library (Discoteca di Stato) for the purpose of making records to be distributed for sale, whether in Italy or abroad, within the terms of Article 5 of the law of 2 February 1939, No. 467, containing provisions for the reorganization of the State Record Library, shall, insofar as the works recorded are protected works, be subject to the payment of royalties in accordance with the provisions of the Regulations.

§8. Special Provisions on Computer Programs

610. The exclusive rights conferred by this law regarding computer programs shall include the right to perform or authorize: (a) reproduction, whether permanently or temporarily, partially or totally, of the computer program by whatever means or in whatever form. Insofar as such operations as the loading, the visualization, execution, transmission or storage of computer programs require reproduction, they shall be performed subject to authorization by the person entitled to the aforesaid rights; (b) translation, adaptation, transformation and any other modification of the computer program, as well as reproduction of the work resulting therefrom, without prejudice to the rights of the person who modifies the said program; (c) any form of distribution to the public, including lease, either of the original computer program or of copies thereof. With the first sale of a copy of the program performed within the European Economic community by the person entitled to the said rights, or with the latter's consent, there shall cease to exist the right of distribution of the aforesaid copy within the Countries of the ECC, except for the right to supervise any further lease of the program or of a copy thereof.

611. In the absence of any contrary stipulation, the authorization by the copyright holder shall not apply to the activities as per subheadings (a) and (b) of Article 64 *bis*, whenever such activities are necessary for the program to be used, in conformity with its purposes, by the person who legally purchased it, including for the correction of errors.

Whoever is entitled to use a copy of the computer program may not be prevented by contract to make a backup copy of the selfsame program where this is necessary for its use.

Whoever is entitled to use a copy of the computer program may, without being authorized by the copyright holder, evaluate, study or test the operation of such program in order to identify ideas and principles underlying each component of the selfsame program, provided he carries out such acts in the course of operations of loading, visualization, execution, transmission or storage of the program which he is entitled to perform. Any contractual agreements infringing the provisions of this paragraph shall be void.

612. No authorization by the copyright holder shall be required if the reproduction of the program code and translation of its form as per subheadings (a) and (b) of Article 64 *bis*, carried out to modify the code form, are necessary to obtain the information allowing a program developed autonomously to be interfaced with other types of programs, provided that: (a) the aforesaid activities are carried out by the licensee or by another entitled to use a copy of the program or, on behalf of the latter, by a person authorized to do so; (b) the persons as per subheading (a) cannot already access, easily and rapidly, the information required to allow interfacing; (c) the aforesaid activities concern exclusively those components of the original program which are necessary to allow interfacing.

613. The provisions as per paragraph 1 shall preclude that the information obtained through their implementation: (a) be used for purposes other than the interfacing of a program developed autonomously; (b) be communicated to third parties, without prejudice to the need to allow interfacing of the program developed autonomously; (c) be used for developing, producing or commercializing a computer program which is basically similar, as to the form of its expression, to the aforesaid one, or for any further activities infringing copyright.

Any contractual agreements infringing those points shall be void.

Pursuant to the Berne Convention for the protection of Literary and Artistic Works, ratified and enforced by Law no. 399 of 20 June 1978, the provisions of this article may not be construed so as to let their application be unduly prejudicial to the lawful interests of the copyright holder, or in conflict with the customary utilization of the program.

§9. Free Utilizations

614. Articles of current interest of an economic, political or religious character, published in magazines or newspapers, may be freely reproduced in other magazines or newspapers, or may be broadcast, unless such reproduction is expressly reserved, provided an indication is given of the magazine or newspaper from which they are taken, the date and the number of the said magazine or newspaper and, in the case of a signed article, the name of the author.

615. Discourses upon matters of political or administrative interest delivered in public assemblies or in any other public manner may be freely reproduced in magazines or newspapers, as well as broadcast, provided an indication of the source is given, together with the name of the author and the date and place in which the discourse was delivered.

Works or portions of works may be reproduced for use in judicial or administrative proceedings, provided an indication is given of the source or the name of the author.

616. The reproduction of single works or portions of works for the personal use of readers, when made by hand or by a means of reproduction unsuitable for circulating or diffusing the work in public, shall be free.

The photo-copying of works existing in libraries, when made for personal use or the services of the library, shall be free.

The circulating of such copies in public and, in general, any use thereof in competition with the rights of economic utilization belonging to the author shall be forbidden.

617. Loans granted by libraries and record libraries pertaining to the State or to public authorities, exclusively for purposes of cultural promotion and personal study, shall not require authorization by the person entitled to the relevant right, to whom no remuneration shall be due, and shall exclusively concern: (a) printed copies of the works, except for music scores; (b) phonograms and videograms containing cinematographic or individual works or sequences of motion picture, with or without soundtrack, provided at least eighteen months have elapsed since the first act of exercise of the right of distribution.

618. The abridgement, quotation or reproduction of fragments or parts of a work for the purpose of criticism or discussion, or for instructional purposes, shall be free within the limits justified for such purposes, provided such acts do not constitute competition with the economic utilization of the work.

In anthologies for scholastic use, reproduction shall not exceed the extent specified in the Regulations, which Regulations shall also fix the manner for determining equitable remuneration in respect of such reproduction.

The abridgement, quotation or reproduction must always be accompanied by a mention of the title of the work and the names of the author, the publisher and, in the case of a translation, the translator, provided such indications appear upon the basic work.

619. Musical groups and bands of the armed forces of the State may perform musical pieces or portions of musical works in public without payment of any fees in respect of copyright, provided the performance is not for profit.

§10. JUDICIAL PROTECTION AND SANCTIONS

620. Any person having reason to fear the infringement of a right of economic utilization belonging to him according to this Law, or who seeks to prevent continuation or repetition of infringement which has already occurred, may institute judicial proceedings to ensure that his right be recognized and the infringement forbidden.

The action shall be regulated by the rules of this Section and by the provisions of the Code of Civil Procedure.

621. Any person who is entitled to exercise the rights of public performance of a work suitable for such performance, including a cinematographic work or a work of musical composition may, in accordance with the provisions of the Regulations, request the Prefect of the province to prohibit any performance for which written proof of his consent is not shown.

The Prefect shall, upon request and on the basis of the notices any documents submitted to him, authorize or forbid the performance, subject to the right of the interested party to have recourse to the judicial authority for final decision.

622. Any person injured by the exercise of a right of economic utilization belonging to him may institute legal proceedings for the removal or destruction of the material constituting the infringement or for payment for damages.

623. The removal or destruction referred to in the foregoing Article may be effected only as regards specimens or copies illegally reproduced or disseminated and contrivances employed for reproduction or dissemination which, by their nature, are not capable of use for the reproduction or dissemination of other matter.

If a part of the specimen copy or contrivance in question is capable of use for the reproduction or dissemination of other matter, the interested party may, at his expense, request the separation, in his interest, of such part.

If the specimen, copy or contrivance of which the removal or destruction is requested has special artistic or scientific value, the judge, ex officio, may order its deposit in a public museum.

The injured party may, at any time, ask that the specimens, copies and contrivances liable to destruction be delivered to him and their appraised value applied to the reparation due him.

The provisions for destruction and delivery shall not apply to infringing specimens or copies acquired in good faith for personal use.

624. Removal or destruction shall not be demanded in the last year of the term for which the right endures. Seizure of the work or the product may be ordered at any time up to the end of the said term. If the damages arising from the infringement of the right have been paid, seizure may be authorized even at a date prior to that indicated above.

625. For the purposes of the proceedings referred to in the previous Articles, the judicial authority may order an inventory a report, an expert appraisal or the seizure of all matter constituting an infringement of the right of utilization.

Seizure may not be affected in the case of works resulting from the collaboration of two or more persons, except in case of special gravity or when the infringement is imputable to all the co-authors.

The judicial authority may also, in especially grave cases, order the seizure of profits due to the author of the disputed work or product.

The provisions of this Section shall also apply to any person circulating, in whatever manner, or detaining, for commercial purposes, unauthorized copies of computer programs and any contrivance intended exclusively for allowing or facilitating the unauthorized removal or the operational disconnection of protection devices for computer programs.

626. The measures provided for by the preceding Article shall be authorized, upon request of the interested party, by an order of the Pretore of the district where they are to be carried out, whatever may be the value involved; provided that when litigation is pending between the parties before a court of two or more judges, the measure in question shall be authorized by an order of the Pretore or when the suit is pending before a collegiate court, by the investigating judge.

In case of urgency, the measures may also be authorized by the Pretore of the district in which they are to be carried out.

The same order may require the claimant to deposit suitable security.

Except in the case where delay would involve danger, the judicial authority, before ruling upon the request, shall summon to Chambers for a summary hearing, the party against whom the measure would be executed and the party making the request.

The order shall, before its execution or simultaneously therewith, be notified to the party against whom it is to be executed. Execution shall be effected by a judicial official and, where necessary, with the assistance of one or more experts named in the said decision.

In the case of public performances, the limitations of days and hours specified by the Code of Civil Procedure for measures of such nature shall not apply to the execution of orders hereunder.

627. Unless otherwise decreed in the order of seizure for the purposes of penal justice, the measures referred to in the preceding Articles shall, without need for pronouncement by the judicial authority, be of no effect if, within eight days following their execution, action has been taken before the competent judge to confirm the measures in relation to the person against whom they were taken.

628. If the actions for which provision is made in this and the following Section are instituted by one of the official legal entities referred to in Articles 180 to 184, the following rules shall be observed: (1) the officers of the above-mentioned entities may, without special authorization and upon proof of their status as such, institute the actions mentioned above in the interests of the owner of the rights; (2) such legal entities shall be relieved of the obligation of furnishing security for carrying out acts in respect of which security is prescribed or authorized; (3) such legal entities may avail themselves of the procedure for securing an injunction under the conditions specified in Articles 3 and 12 of the Royal Decree of 7 August 1936 No. 1531, according to the provisions of the Regulations which designate the State and public officials authorized to deliver the attestations and to receive the declaration specified in the articles indicated above.

629. The author of a work which is the object of the right of utilization may, after the assignment of such right, intervene at any time, in order to protect his interests, in proceedings instituted by the assignee.

630. The judge may, at the instance of the interested party or ex officio, and at the expense of the unsuccessful party, order the operative portion of the judgment to be published, more than once if necessary, in one or more newspapers.

631. The rights of economic utilization recognized by this Law may also be judicially enforced by any person legitimately entitled to such rights.

632. In proceedings concerning the exercise of the moral right, the provisions contained in the preceding Section shall be applicable, insofar as the nature of this right permits subject to the application of the provisions of the following Articles.

633. Actions in defence of the rights bearing upon the authorship of the work shall give rise to the sanction of removal and destruction only when the injury cannot be remedied by means of the addition or suppression of indications on the work which will refer to its authorship or by other means of publicity.

634. Actions in defence of the rights bearing upon the integrity of the work shall give rise to removal or destruction of the deformed, mutilated or otherwise modified copy of the work only when it is not possible to re-establish the said copy in its original form at the expense of the party interested in avoiding removal or destruction.

635. Without prejudice to the provisions of Article 171-*bis*, any person shall be punishable by a fine of from ITL 100,000 (EUR 51) to ITL 4,000,000 liras (EUR 2,051) who, without having the right, and for any purpose and in any form: (a) reproduces, transcribes, recites in public, disseminates, sells or offers for sale, or otherwise commercially distributes the work of another person, or reveals the contents of such work before it is made public, or introduces or circulates within the State copies produced abroad contrary to Italian law; (a-*bis*) makes available to the public, by placing it in a system of telematic networks, by means of connections of any kind, a protected intellectual work or part of it; (b) performs or recites in public or diffuses, with or without variations or additions, the work of another person suitable for public performance, or a musical composition. Performance includes the public showing of a cinematographic work, the performance in public of musical compositions included in cinematographic works, and broadcasting by means of a loudspeaker operated in public; (c) commits the acts indicated in the preceding clauses by means of any of the forms of elaboration referred to in this Law; (d) reproduces copies or gives performances in excess of the number which he had the right to reproduce or perform; (e) repealed (f) in violation of Article 79, retransmits by wire or by broadcasting, or records upon phonograph records or other like contrivances radiophonic transmissions or retransmissions, or sells phonograph records or other contrivances which have been unlawfully made.

The penalty shall be imprisonment up to one year or a fine of not less than ITL 1,000,000 (EUR 516) if the acts referred to above are committed in relation to a work of another person which is not intended for public disclosure, or by usurpation of the authorship of the work, or with deformation, mutilation or other modification of the work and such acts constitute an offence against the honour or reputation of the author.

636. Whoever unlawfully duplicates computer programs for purposes of gain, or imports, distributes, sells, detains for commercial purposes or leases the said programs, for the selfsame purposes and being aware or having reason to be aware of the fact that such copies were not authorized, shall be punished by imprisonment for between three months and three years and by a fine of between ITL 5,000,000 (EUR 2,582) and 30,000,000 (EUR 15,493). The same punishment shall be not less than imprisonment for 2 years and a fine of ITL 30,000,000 (EUR 15,493) if the offence is serious or if the program which was unlawfully duplicated, imported, distributed, sold, detained for commercial purposes or leased had been previously distributed, sold or leased on media bearing the mark of the Italian Authors' and Publishers' Association pursuant to this law and to the relevant Regulations as per Royal Decree no. 1369 of 18 May 1942.

Conviction for any of the offences as per paragraph 1 shall entail publication of the judgment in one or more newspapers and in one or more specialized magazines.

637. Imprisonment for between six months and three years and a fine of between ITL 5,000,000 (EUR 2,582) and 30,000,000 (EUR 15,493) shall be imposed, if the act is committed for non-personal use, on any person who, for purposes of gain: (a) unlawfully duplicates or reproduces, for purposes of gain and by whatever means, works intended for cinematographic or television distribution, records, tapes or like media as well as any other media containing phonograms or videograms of cinematographic or audiovisual works or sequences of motion pictures; (b) though not participating in the duplication or reproduction, offers for sale, leases or, at all events, grants the use of, for purposes of gain, performs a public showing of or broadcasts by television the duplications or reproductions as per subheading (a); (c) sells or leases videotapes, music tapes or any other media containing phonograms or videograms of cinematographic or audiovisual works or sequences of motion pictures which do not bear the mark of the Italian Authors' and Publishers' Association (S.I.A.E.) pursuant to this law and to the relevant Regulations; (d) holds for sale or distribution, markets, sells, rents, transfers under whatever title, publicly shows, broadcasts by any means video cassettes, audiocassettes, any carrier containing phonograms or videograms of musical works, cinematographic or audiovisual works or sequences of moving images or any other carrier which do not bear the SIAE mark or bear a counterfeited or altered mark, in all cases where the SIAE mark is compulsory according to this law; (e) without a prior consent of the lawful distributor, retransmits or broadcasts, by whatever means, an encrypted service received by means of devices or parts of devices capable to decode the conditioned-access transmissions; (f) introduces onto the territory of the State, holds for sale or distribution, sells, rents, transfers under whatever title, promotes for commercial purposes, sets up special devices or decoding elements which allow to have access to an encrypted service without paying the due subscription fee; (f-*bis*) manufactures, imports, distributes, sells, rents, transfers under whatever title, advertises for sale or rental, holds for commercial purposes devices, products or components or provides services whose main purpose or commercial use is to circumvent any effective technological measures under art. 102-*quarter*, or which are primarily designed, manufactured, adapted or performed for the purpose of enabling or facilitating the circumvention of said measures. These technological measures shall comprise the measures that are applied or that remain after certain measures are removed by rightholders voluntarily or by virtue of agreements with the beneficiaries of exceptions, or in compliance with an injunction by an administrative or judicial authority; (h) unlawfully removes or alters the electronic rights-management information under art. 102-quinquies, or distributes, imports for distribution, broadcasts, communicates or makes available to the public protected works or other subject matters whose electronic information has been removed or altered.

638. Moreover, any person who: (a) unlawfully reproduces, duplicates, broadcasts, sells or markets, transfers under whatever title or imports more than fifty copies or carriers of works protected by copyright and neighbouring rights; (a-*bis*) in violation of Article 16, for business purposes, communicates to the public by introducing it into a system of computer networks, by means of concessions of any kind, an intellectual work protected by copyright, or part of it; (b) for business purposes, effects the reproduction, distribution, sale or marketing, import of works protected by copyright and neighbouring rights, thus making himself guilty of the offences under paragraph 1; (c) promotes and organizes the unlawful activities under paragraph 1 shall be liable to imprisonment for a one-up-to-four-year period and to a fine between EUR 2,582 and EUR 15,493.

Conviction for any of the offences as per paragraphs 1 and 2 shall entail publication of the judgment in one or more newspapers and in one or more specialized magazines.

639. Except where the act amounts to a more serious offence, imprisonment for up to one year or a penalty of between EUR 5,000 and EUR 30,000 shall be imposed on any person who, without being authorized to do so and for purposes of gain: (a) leases or, at all events, grants the use, for whatever purpose, of original specimens or of copies or of the media, obtained lawfully, of copyright works; (b) records the artistic performances as per Article 80 on audio, video or audiovisual media.

640. The penalties specified in the preceding Articles shall apply in all instances where the acts in question do not constitute a more serious offence within the meaning of the Penal Code or other laws.

641. In penal proceedings under this Section injured party, as a civil complainant, may at any time request the penal judge to apply the measures and sanctions specified in Articles 159 and 160.

§11. Official Legal Entities Constituted for the Protection and Exercise of the Rights of Authors

642. The right to act as an intermediary in any manner whether by direct or indirect intervention, mediation, agency or representation, or by assignment of the exercise of the rights of performance, recitation, broadcasting and mechanical and cinematographic reproduction of protected works shall be reserved exclusively to the S.I.A.E.

643. Its activities shall be exercised to effect: (1) the granting of licences and authorizations for the economic utilization of protected works, for the account of and in the interests of the persons entitled to the rights; (2) the collection of the proceeds arising from the said licences and authorizations; (3) the distribution of the said proceeds among the persons entitled thereto.

644. The SIAE shall, moreover, carry on its activities, in accordance with the provisions established by the Regulations, in those foreign countries in which it possesses organized representation.

The said exclusivity of powers shall not prejudice the right of the author or his successors in title to exercise directly the rights recognized in their favour by this Law.

645. In the distribution of the proceeds referred to under clause (3) of the second paragraph, a portion shall be reserved to the author in all cases. The limits and the methods of distribution shall be determined by the Regulations.

If, however, the rights of economic utilization of the work are capable of giving rise to the collection of funds abroad on behalf of Italian citizens domiciled or resident within the Republic and the owners of these rights do not for any reason effect the collection of such funds, then, after the lapse of one year from the date when liability for payment arose, the S.I.A.E. shall be empowered to exercise the rights for the account and in the interests of the author or his successors in title.

646. The funds mentioned in the preceding paragraph, which are collected by S.I.A.E., shall, after deduction of the expenses of collection, be held at the disposal of claimants for a period of three years. If this period elapses without such funds being claimed, they shall be paid to the National Federation of Professional Artists (Confederazione Nazionale professionisti ed artisti) to assist categories of authors, writers and musicians.

647. In addition to the functions indicated in the foregoing Article and those imposed upon it by this Law and other provisions, the S.I.A.E. may, pursuant to its statutes, exercise other activities connected with the protection of intellectual works. The S.I.A.E. may undertake, for the account of the State or of public or private institutions, the services of ascertaining and collecting taxes, contributions and fees.

648. The S.I.A.E., in order to prevent and ascertain infringements to this Law, and each one within the tasks conferred by law are entrusted with supervising: (a) the reproduction and duplication, by any means, on audiovisual and phonographic carriers, and any other carrier, as well as with supervising premises where the use in public by air or by cable takes place and the broadcasting activity made by any means; (b) the public show in cinemas of the works and recordings protected by copyright and neighbouring rights; (c) the distribution, sale, rental, broadcasting and utilization in any form of the carriers under point (a); (d) public or private reproduction centres, which use in their own premises or make available to third parties, even for free, photocopiers, xeroxcopiers or analogous reproduction system; (d-*bis*) on the manufacturing, import and distribution of the devices and of the media under art. 71-septies.

649. Within the tasks it is entrusted with by law, S.I.A.E. shall coordinate, pursuant to paragraph 1, with the Authority for telecommunications.

650. For implementing the tasks under paragraph 1, the Authority for telecommunications may assign inspecting functions to its officers and may act in coordination with S.I.A.E.'s inspectors. The placing of Italian non-musical dramatic works with theatrical companies and enterprises shall be subject to the preliminary authorization of the Office of the Chairman of the Council of Ministers, in accordance with the provisions of the Regulations.

The author and his successors' *causa mortis* shall not be required to obtain such authorization.

However, translators of foreign works shall be subject to such requirement.

The placing of such works shall be subject to the supervision of the Office of the Chairman of the Council of Ministers in accordance with the provisions of the Regulations.

651. Any person who places Italian non-musical dramatic works in foreign countries shall make declaration thereof within three days to the Italian Society for Theatrical Exchanges (Ente italiano per gli scambi teatrali), and the Society shall transmit monthly to the Office of the Chairman of the Council of Ministers a list of the declarations received, together with any observations and proposals.

The Italian Society for Theatrical Exchanges shall also exercise such other functions as its statutes may require.

The provisions of Article 182 shall apply to the Italian Society for Theatrical Exchanges.

§12. Field of Application of the Law

652. Subject to the provisions of Article 189, this Law shall apply to all works of Italian authors, wherever first published.

It shall likewise apply to the works a foreign author domiciled in Italy which are first published in Italy.

Apart from the conditions of protection indicated in the preceding paragraph, this Law may likewise be applied to the works of foreign authors when the conditions indicated in the following Articles are fulfilled.

653. The international conventions for the protection of intellectual works shall govern the field of application of this Law to works of foreign authors.

If the convention contains a general stipulation of reciprocity or equality of treatment, such stipulation shall be interpreted according to the rules of actual equivalence of the two protections as provided in the following Articles.

654. In the absence of international agreements, works of foreign authors which do not comply with the conditions specified in the second paragraph of Article 185 shall, within the limits of actual equivalence, enjoy the protection granted by this Law, provided that the State of which they are citizens grants to the works of Italian authors protection which is effectively equivalent.

If the foreigner is a stateless person or if his nationality is uncertain, the rule of the preceding paragraph shall operate with reference to the State in which the work is first published.

655. Actual equivalence, in accordance with the following rules, shall be certified and regulated by Presidential Decree.

The duration of protection of a foreign work shall in no case exceed that enjoyed by the work in the State of which the foreign author is a citizen.

If the law of the said State includes a period of compulsory licensing during the term of protection, the foreign work shall be submitted to an equivalent rule in Italy.

If the law of the said State makes protection subject to compliance with formalities, declarations of reservation, or the deposit of copies of the work, or any other formality, the foreign work shall, in Italy, be subject to equivalent formalities, as determined by Presidential Decree.

The Presidential Decree may, moreover, subject the protection of the foreign work to the fulfilment of other special formalities or conditions.

656. The provisions of Article 185 shall apply to cinematographic works, to phonograph records or like contrivances, to the rights of performing actors or artists, to photographs and to engineering works, if such works or products are created in Italy or may be considered national works according to this Law or any other special law.

In the absence of the conditions indicated above, the provision of Articles 186, 187 and 188 shall be applicable to the said works, rights or products.

§13. PERMANENT CONSULTATIVE COUNCIL ON COPYRIGHT

657. A Permanent Consultative Council on Copyright shall be established under the direction of the Office of the Chairman of the Council of Ministers.

The Council shall proceed to the study of matters bearing upon copyright or connected therewith and shall furnish information upon questions relating to such matters, when so requested by the Office of the Chairman of the Council of Ministers, or when special provisions so require.

658. The Council shall consist of: (a) a Chairman designated by the Office of the Chairman of the Council of Ministers; (b) one Vice-Chairman each from the Corporations of the Professions and Arts of Spectacles, and of Stationery and Printing; (c) one representative each of the Ministers of Foreign Affairs, of Grace and Justice, of Finance, and of Corporations and two representatives of the Minister of Public Instruction; (d) the general director for entertainment of the Ministry of Tourism and Entertainment and the heads of the information department and of the department for literary, artistic and scientific property at the Office of the Chairman of the Council of Ministers; (e) the Presidents of the Confederations of Professionals, of Artists, and of Industrialists and three representatives of each of the Confederations above indicated, especially competent in the matter of copyright, as well as a representative of the Confederation of the Workers of Industry ('Confederazione dei lavoratori dell'industria') designated by the National Confederation of Stage Workers ('Federazione nazionale dei lavoratori dello spetacolo'); (f) the President of S.I.A.E.; (g) three copyright experts, designated by the Chairman of the Council of Ministers; (h) the member of the Office of the Chairman of the Council of Ministers in a decree of the Office of the Chairman of the Council of Ministers and shall remain in office for a period of four years.

659. The Council shall meet in ordinary session each year upon a date fixed by the Office of the Chairman of the Council of Ministers, and in extraordinary session on all occasions when so requested by the said President.

660. The Council may be convened: (a) in general assembly; (b) in Special Committees.

All members of the Council shall participate in general assemblies. The Special Committees shall, from time to time, be constituted for the study of given questions, as directed by the Chairman.

The Chairman of the Council of Ministers' upon the proposal of the Chairman of the Council may also invite to meetings, but without the right to vote, persons other than members of the Council who may be especially competent on the questions to be considered.

661. The secretariat shall be provided by the Director of the Office of Literary Scientific and Industrial Property, established under the Office of the Chairman of the Council of Ministers.

662. The members of the Council shall receive attendance fees for each day of sitting, in accordance with current regulations governing such matters.

Chapter 2. Legal Protection of Software

§1. The Legal Protection of Computer Programs

663. Legislative decree no. 518 of 29 December 1992, entitled 'Implementation of Directive 91/250/EEC on the legal protection of computer programs', added, into Article 2, point 8) of Law n. 633 of 22 April 1941, concerning the 'protection of copyright and the exercise of other related rights', the term *computer programs* between the works protected in Italy by copyright law.

664. Article 2 of Law 633/41 now specifically includes in the protection: '[...] 8) computer programs, expressed in any form as long as the result of original intellectual creation. Are excluded from the protection afforded by this law the ideas and principles which underlie any element of a program, including those which underlie its interfaces. The term program includes the preparatory material for the design of the program'.

665. Objects of protection, provided that the work is *original* as a result of intellectual creation, are the program and all the preparatory material used for the design of the same; on the contrary, are expressly excluded from the protection afforded by these rules ideas and possibly innovative principles.

666. Concerning the identification of the requirement of *originality* in the software, however, it is worth noting that the Italian case law has embraced the so-called minimal creative intellectual approach to the work, extending that protection to programs with a *minimal* degree of creativity.

667. Already in 1986, the Supreme Court had occasion to point out that software writers produce a creative result, and as such is protectable under the standards established for the protection of copyright, every time they 'give new contributions in the field of information, express original solutions to problems of data processing, in a better way than before certain content and ideas, even if barely noticeable' (Cass. Pen., sect. III, 24 November 1986).

668. The author of the software (as the author of any original work which falls between those works listed in Article 2 of the. 633/41) becomes, together with the creation of the work, and regardless of the completion of any administrative or bureaucratic formalities, the original proprietor of a complex of moral and patrimonial rights related to the work itself.

669. The author's moral rights, including the right to recognition of the authorship and the integrity, are not in the disponibility of the author and, as such, indispensable, inalienable and imprescriptible.

The acts involving moral rights are null and unproductive of legal effect.

670. The property rights (or the financial exploitation of the work), on the contrary, are full available and may be subject to total or partial sale.

671. Article 64-*bis* of Law 633/41 includes, among the rights of economic utilization specifically related to computer programs: (i) the right to reproduce the program by any means or in any form, in whole or in part, on a permanent or temporary support; (ii) the right to translate, adapt, transform and modify the program; (iii) the right to distribute to the public in any form the original or copies of the same program.

672. Article 64-*bis* of Law 633/41 states that the exclusive rights conferred by the Copyright Law to computer programs include the right to make or authorize: (a) the reproduction, permanent or temporary, total or partial, of the computer program by any means or in any form. Insofar as loading, displaying, running, transmission or storage of the computer program require a reproduction, such acts are subject to the authorization of the copyright holder; (b) translation, adaptation, arrangement and any other modification of the computer program and the reproduction of the results thereof, without prejudice to the rights of those who alter the program; (c) any form of distribution to the public, including the rental of the original computer program or of copies thereof.

The first sale of a copy of the program in the European Union by the rightholder or with his consent shall exhaust the distribution right of that copy within the community, except the right to control further rental of the program or a copy thereof.

§2. The Patentability of Software

673. In the Italian legal framework, intellectual creations (such as software) fall into two distinct categories: that of *industrial inventions* (Articles 2584 et seq. of the Italian Civil Code), protected by patents system, and that of *intellectual property* (Articles 2575 et seq.), protected by copyright.

674. The aspect that, more than any other, differs in Italy the patent protection from the protection afforded by copyright law is that, while in the case of patent protection is the *subject of the idea* as a basis of the invention, the copyright protects the intellectual work in its specific form of *expression.*

675. In the late eighties and early nineties, it was long debated also in Italy about the correct legal regime applicable to computer programs, reaching, at least at European level (Directive 91/250/EEC), the conclusion that the copyright was the most suitable mean for the protection of software, since it can effectively protect the individual program in its concrete form of expression, but without imposing too severe limitations to the diffusion of innovative ideas and, with them, to technological and scientific progress.

676. As we have already noted, in Italy the legislative decree of 29 December 1992, n. 518, conforming to the prevailing approach to regulation 'copyright-like', has included the protection of computer programs within Law n. 633 of 1941 on copyright.

677. Within the European Community legal framework, the patentability of software is, in general, excluded from the European Patent Convention of Monaco of 5 October 1973 (CBE), entitled 'Convention on the Grant of European Patents'.

Under Article 52 of that Convention (the contents of which, as we are concerned, is now part of Article 45 of the new Italian Industrial Property Code), in fact, computer programs, 'taken as such, not fall into the category of new inventions, capable of industrial application, which can be patented'.

678. The words 'taken as such' (or, as indicated in the Italian Code of Industrial Property, 'as such') by which the limit is restricted to the patentability of computer programs, however, has allowed in recent years, the granting of several patents relating to programs, in cases of software interacting with specific hardware devices, closely related to a particular industrial invention (this is the case, e.g., the software that manages and pilots the peculiar features of a device mower or, again, the program that governs the chip implanted in a tennis shoe, in order to adapt the shape of the sole to the particular morphology of the ground).

679. The debate over whether or not to extend patent protection to computer programs is, however, very lively.

The arguments of those who insist about the inadequacy of the protection afforded by the current legislation regarding copyright counterpoint strictly the opinion of those who stress the negative impact that patent protection applied to computer programs would have on research and scientific progress.

On 6 July 2005, the European Parliament has rejected a proposal for a Directive on the patentability of computer-implemented inventions.

§3. The Legislation Governing Illegal Duplication of Software

680. The issue of illegal copying of computer programs ('piracy') is, certainly, an argument that, in recent years, has affected the various legislative measures concerning the protection of copyright and the legal protection of software.

681. The first legislation that is specifically devoted to regulate the phenomenon of illegal duplication of software in Italy was legislative decree no. 518 of 29 December 1992: with Article 10 of this Decree was introduced, in the body of Law 633/41, Article 171-*bis* regarding illegal duplication of computer programs.

682. Article 171-*bis*, in its original formulation, provided that whoever unlawfully duplicates *for gain* computer programs or, for the same purpose, imports, distributes, sells, holds for commercial or business leases computer programs not marked by the Italian Society of Authors and Publishers (SIAE) is subject to the penalty of imprisonment from six months to three years and a fine of between 500,000 (EUR 250) and 6,000,000 Liras (EUR 3,000).

683. This provision, which for years has represented a milestone in the field of criminal protection of copyright in Italy, has subsequently been significantly modified by Article 13 of Law n. 445 of 18 August 2000, under which the new and currently existing text of Article 171-*bis* of Law 633/41, provides: that whoever unlawfully duplicates, *for profit*, computer programs or, for the same purpose, imports, distributes, sells, holds for commercial or business leases or computer programs not marked by the Italian Society of Authors and Publishers (SIAE) is subject to the penalty of imprisonment from six months to three years and a fine of EUR 2,582 to EUR 15,493.

684. The new rule, certainly not trivial, introduced by Law 248/2000, is evident in the replacement text of Article 171-*bis* of the original phrase 'for gain', with the new – and potentially broader significance – expression 'for profit'.

685. With the existence of the term of the previous provision of the law, in fact, the interpreters were divided between those who accepted the concept of 'financial gain' intended as any generic financial advantage that the agent had intended to pursue his own conduct, insisting to encompass also the so-called cost savings resulting from the failure of the original product purchase (Court of Turin, 5 October 2000, n. 1407), and who, on the contrary, with emphasis on the necessary nature of the *positive increase in capital gain*, includes only the activities aimed to obtain a concept of 'profit' (Cagliari Pret. 3 December 1996).

686. The new formulation of Article 171-*bis* seems to have solved any possible divergence of interpretation on this point.

687. According to the main Italian case law, replacing the words 'for gain' with the words 'for profit' and eliminating, therefore, the controversial concept of gain, the Legislator evidently intended broadly sanction the scope of Article 171-*bis* of Law on Copyright (Cass. Pen., Section III, 33303/2001).

688. In conclusion, the existing law governing protection of copyright considers criminally relevant, according to Article 171-*bis*, not only the possibility of unauthorized duplication of software aimed at a growing wealth of the agent but also the conduct of those who illegally duplicate a computer program intending to take advantage of the savings resulting from not purchasing the original software.

§4. Technological Protection Measures

689. In compliance with the provisions established by Directive 200/29/CE, with Law 9 April 2003, n. 68, 'Implementation of Directive 2001/29/EC on the harmonization of certain aspects of copyright and related rights in the information society' was inserted, into the body of Law 633/41, a new Title (II-b) called 'technological protection measures'.

690. Under Article 102-*quater*, paragraph 1, of Law 633/41, the holders of copyright and related rights (and the makers of databases) can be affixed to the works effective technological protection measures that include all the technology, device or component that, in the normal course of its operation, is designed to prevent or restrict acts not authorized by the rightholders.

691. The text of the new Article 102-*quater* of Law 633/41 is clear: the holders of copyright and related rights may affix to the works effective technological measures that include all the technology, device or component that, in the normal course of its operation, is designed to prevent or restrict acts not authorized by the owners' rights.

The technological protection measures are considered effective when the work or the use of the copyrighted material is controlled by the rightholders through application of an access device or protection process, such as encryption, scrambling or transformation of the work or other protected material, or is restricted by a copy control mechanism, which achieves the protection objective.

692. Technological measures of protection taken into account by the copyright law consist of hardware and/or software that, when applied to the work, allows to adjust the accessibility to the work or regulate the manner of use.

The first category of technological protection measures can be represented, for example, by all those systems used to limit the access to certain content only to authorized users.

Fall, otherwise, in the category of technological protection measures used to regulate the permitted use of works, those devices which prevent the unauthorized copying of protected works.

693. The CSS (Content Scrambling System), commonly used to protect audiovisual content distributed on DVD, is a typical example of an effective technological measure applied to protect intellectual property.

Other examples of technological protection measures widely used in the marketing of protected content are the SafeDisc system, widely used for software distribution on optical media, the so-called Serial Copy Management System, which helps to prevent the creation of digital copies or, again, the system FairPlay, mainly used for the online distribution of music files.

694. Anyone who, for personal use and for profit, imports, distributes, sells, rents, sells for whatever reason, advertises for sale or lease, or possess for commercial purposes, equipment, products or components, or provides services that have the predominant purpose or commercial use to circumvent the technological protection measures, which are primarily designed, produced, adapted or made for the purpose of enabling or facilitating the circumvention of those measures, shall be punished under Article 171-*ter* of the Law on Copyright, with imprisonment from six months to three years and a fine from EUR 2,582 to EUR 15,493.

§5. The Backup Software in the Law of Copyright

695. The Italian legislation on copyright, alongside rights specifically granted to authors of creative works, protects also the rights and freedoms due to the *users* of such works.

696. With respect to computer programs, in particular, Articles. 64-*bis* and *ter* of Law 633/41, listed a series of activities (so-called free utilizations) that, notwithstanding the general principles in force, may be made without further authorization from the holder of rights.

697. Under Article 64-*ter*, paragraph 2, of the Law on Copyright, cannot be prevented by contract who has the right to use one copy of the computer program, to make a backup copy of the program if such copy is required for the daily use.

698. As specified in the Act, a 'backup' (which is different from copying or private reproduction) allows the legitimate user of the program to protect it from possible malfunctions that may render unusable the original software.

§6. File-Sharing

699. The term 'file-sharing' is used to indicate the conduct of those who, using special software and communication protocols, use computer networks to transmit, receive and share digital content.

In Italy, exchanging files via telecommunications networks is not, of course, in itself, an unlawful conduct.

700. The negative connotation that is generally attributed to the term 'file–sharing', as well as the legal relevance that such conduct can take, depends from the fact that, often, these operations transmit and receive files with content protected by copyright law.

701. The Italian law has recently been reformed by Law n. 43 of 31 March 2005 concerning urgent measures for the university and cultural activities.

702. There are basically three legal provisions in Italy that are particularly relevant in the case of file-sharing.

703. First of all, under Article. 171, letter a-*bis*), shall be punished by a fine of EUR 51 to EUR 2,065 anyone, without being entitled to any purpose or in any form available to the public, runs into a system of computer networks, without connections to any other user, an intellectual work protected, or part of it.

704. Article 171, letter a-*bis*) of Law 633/41 states that is liable to a fine of between 100,000 (EUR 51) and 4,000,000 Liras (EUR 2,065), any person who *makes available to the public*, with connections of any kind, an intellectual work protected, or part thereof.

705. Last but not least, is punished with imprisonment from one to four years and a fine of EUR 2,582 to EUR 15,493, anyone who, in violation of Article 16 (exclusive right of communication to the public), *for profit*, communicates to the public an intellectual work protected by copyright, or part of it.

706. Under current Italian legislation, therefore, not all activities generically related to alleged file-sharing assume the same legal weight.

It is possible, in particular, to identify at least three different conducts, each related to one of the specific cases outlined by the rules just considered: (i) simple receive (download) of content protected by copyright and subsequent illegal use of the same, with violation of the provision in Article 174-b, l. 633/41, and subsequent *administrative sanction*; (ii) simple input (upload) or sharing (upload and download), without being entitled to copyright-protected content in a system of computer networks, and violation of the provision in Article 171, letter. a-*bis*), l. 633/41, and the consequent penalty of a fine; (iii) input (upload) or sharing (upload and download) for profit, without having the right, of content protected by copyright in a system of computer networks, and violation of the provision in Article 171-*ter*, paragraph 2, letter. a-*bis*) with the consequent penalty of imprisonment and a fine.

Chapter 3. Legal Protection of Databases

§1. Introduction

707. Databases, at least in a wide sense, have existed since the dawn of civilization as archives of information of various natures. During the last twenty years, in coincidence with the development of informational technologies and, most recently, online ones, a progressive increase of the interest in the realization and use of these goods has occurred. Indeed, the advent of electronic memories has transformed in a substantial way the intrinsic characteristics of databases so that they have become goods of primary significance.

At the time, as the database became a product of the enterprise, the first necessity felt was to supply it with a protection against possible forms of unfair competition. Legislation has oriented itself in this direction since the beginning.[200]

The regulation of competition has limited the (albeit necessary) competitive relationship that exists between the subject that claims protection and the part that is believed to have committed the damaging behaviour. The proprietor of the information cannot do anything against subjects that are oriented towards a different segment of the market, even if they are using his database for the products and services supplied. It is therefore on the urge of the enterprises in the sector that the EU legislation and national legislation oriented themselves towards a form of protection apt to offer some instruments that can be exerted *erga omnes*, similar to copyright.

708. Ordinary provisions on intellectual achievements, however, could at most protect databases with an original selection of information or an original disposition of them.[201] In the absence of both of these, the underlying claim attaches to the investment of the entrepreneur, which is distinct from traditional copyright, even though economic rights of authors and others that claim a connected right normally requires the existence of a creative and original work.[202]

---

200. One of the first settlements in Italy considered to be an act of unfair competition concerned the use of a database that contained the names of possible clients supplied by the *ex sole* director and partner of a competitor enterprise. On the point *see* Tribunale di Genova, 19 giugno 1993, *Diritto dell'informazione e dell'informatica*, 1993, p. 1117.

201. The Corte di Cassazione expressed itself in favour of the protection of the database as an intellectual achievement, 19 Jul. 1990, No. 7397, *Massimario delle giurisprudenza italiana*, 1990, ruling: 'Provided that the listing of works protected with copyright – *ex* Art. 2575 c.c. and Arts 1 and 2 of the L. 633/41 – has to be meant as an exemplification and not a strict list, while the requirement of originality of the work pertains to the form of exposition and not to the content exposed, also news of public domain can be the object of a work susceptible of protection according to the regulation on the matter of copyright when they are expresses in a form that is characterized, in any way, by a sign of the author's personal elaboration. Therefore, the protection typical of copyright is applicable in the case of a catalogue of goods (as it is, after all, in case of a calendar or of a list of other and various kind), when the exposition is characterized by the presence of significant elements of creativity, consisting in the placement and organization of the news on the basis of criteria that have a certain originality and not on the basis of simple alphabetical or chronological criteria'.

202. The L. 633/41 contains a significant exception: mere photographs. The reproduction with a photographic or similar technique that does not produce a creative work is, indeed, anyway protected, by recognizing some rights of the photographer including the right to a fair remuneration.

The same tenor belongs to some of the rulings of the jurisprudence on merits. On this point the ruling (the first in Italy) of the judges of the capital city is famous: 'A database can be qualified as an intangible good of creative character; it can therefore be protected by the regulation on copyright' (Court of Rome, 14 dicembre 1989, *Diritto dell'informazione e dell'informatica*, 1990, p. 219).

§2. The Juridical Definition of Database

709. The first expressed statutory recognition of databases in the national ambit consists in the ratification of the TRIPS, incorporated into Italian law with L. 747/94. Article 10 of Appendix 1.C of the TRIPS sets out the principle of protection of databases as intellectual creations as long as the selection or the organization of their content represents an intellectual achievement.

710. At an international level, subsequently, Article 5 of the WCT superseded this, providing: 'The compilations of data or of other material, in any form, that due to the selection or the disposition of their content represent intellectual creations are protected as such. The protection does not cover the data and the material itself and does not compromise the copyright possibly existing on the data or on the material contained in the compilation.'

711. A particularly articulate answer to the instances of protection of databases has been supplied by the Community Legislature with the enactment of Directive 1996/9/CE, adopted at national level with L. 24 April 1998, n. 128, containing provisions for the fulfilment of duties deriving from Italian membership in the European Communities, implemented with D.Lgs. 169/99.[203]

After the 1999 amendment, Article 1, L. 633/41 provides now that copyrights protect 'those databases that due to the choice or disposition of the material represent an intellectual creation of the author'. The complete definition of the object of copyright protection is contained in Article 2, n. 9 of L. 633/41, that specifies that in the protection are included: 'databases . . . meant as collections of works, data or other independent elements systematically or methodically disposed and individually accessible thanks to electronic means or in other ways'.

§3. The Original Database

712. The collections of works, data and other independent elements, systematically or methodically disposed and individually accessible through electronic means or in another way, are an intellectual achievement when the choice or the disposition of the material is original and creative. To assess if copyright protection can be granted to a database, no other criteria are applied.

203. *See* L. Chimienti, *Banche di dati e diritto d'autore* (Milano, Giuffrè, 1999).

713. In the case of a selective database (namely creative and original for the choice of the content), creativity is considered intrinsic in the originality of the informative data. This consists of a collection of data (independent, systematically or methodically disposed and individually accessible) that has not been the object of the exertion of a right to economic use before and therefore, for example, has never been communicated, published or diffused. The creativity of the selection will also subsist when the information, not original in itself, does not appear in any analogue collection.

714. The database is also an intellectual achievement where it is creative and original due to the disposition of its content. Even prior to the amendment in 1999, jurisprudence had emphasized – in compliance with the principle of the protection of representation of ideas (and beyond ideas as such) – the relevancy of originality and creativity in the organization of simple ideas and notions, disregarding the fact that these are used to express informative data of various kinds, as long as they were processed and organized in a personal and autonomous way.[204]

715. There is no consensus regarding the level of creativity and originality required to give rise to copyright in a database. Those who consider the existence of any element of structuring of the material sufficient to include the database among the protected works clash with those who emphasize the need to impose a minimum threshold of originality, thus excluding from the protection regime collections that are not the outcome of a processing activity worthy of protection.[205]

I. The Subjects of the Right

716. The original title of the acquisition of copyright on the database consists, according to Article 6, L. 633/1941, of the creation of the work as a particular expression of intellectual effort. If the database is created by more than one subject, the provisions on the matter of joint works and works in common apply, respectively contained in Articles 7 and 10 of L. 633/41.

Article 12-*bis*, L. 633/1941, implementing Directive 91/250/CEE on the matter of programs for processors and now integrated with reference to databases, assigns to the employer the right to the economic use of the creations of the employee realized in the execution of his tasks and according to the instructions given by the

204. *See* Corte di Cassazione, 2 Dec. 1993, No. 11953, Rivista di diritto industriale, 1994, p. 157 (with annotation by P. Frassi, 'La tutela delle compilazioni di informazioni attraverso il diritto d'autore'). Concerning originality requirements, *see* decisions C-241/91, C-242/91, Radio Telefis Eireann, Indipendent Television publications Ltd., *Intellectual property Owners Inc. v. Commissione delle Comunità europee*, Magill TV Guide Ltd., AIDA, 1995, 261 (con nota di L. Zagato) e la sentenza della Corte Suprema degli Stati Uniti, 27 marzo 1991, Feist Publications Inc. v Rural Telephone Service Company Inc., Foro italiano, 1992, IV, colonna 37. *See also* R.A. Gorman, 'The Feist case: reflections on a pathbreaking copyright decision', Rutgers Computer & Technology law Journal, No. 18, 1992, pp. 731 et seq.

205. *See* V. Di Cataldo, 'Banche-dati e diritto *sui generis*: la fattispecie costitutiva', AIDA, 1997, p. 22.

employer himself.[206] The *ratio* of the provision is to protect the investment of those subjects that have a fundamental role in the existence itself of the so-called culture industry.

II. The Content of the Right

717. The faculties assigned to the proprietor of copyright on original databases are covered in Section VII of Chapter IV, Title I (Articles 64-*quinquies* to 64-*sexies*), L. 633/41, introduced by D.Lgs. 169/1999.

According to Article 64-*quinquies*, paragraph 1, L. 633/41, the author has the exclusive right to perform or use:

- the permanent or temporary, total or partial, reproduction of the database with any means and in any form;
- the translation, adjustment, a different disposition and every other modification, besides any reproduction, distribution, communication, presentation or demonstration in public of the results of these operations;
- the distribution to the public of the original or of copies of the database;
- the presentation, demonstration or communication in public of the database, included its transmission performed with any means and in any form.

718. The legitimate user of the database or of a copy of it cannot be prevented from performing activities of reproduction (permanent or temporary, total or partial, with any means and in any form) and of reproduction, distribution, communication, presentation or demonstration in public of the results of the translation, of the adjustment, of a different disposition and of any other modification of the database, if these activities are necessary for the access to the content, intended for its normal use. The legitimate user authorized to use only a part of the collection can exercise the mentioned activities only on that part.

719. The author's right on a database – as well as the right of the constitutor[207] – is subject to the principle of community exhaustion. This means that the first sale of the database or a copy of it within the European Union by the proprietor of the right, or with his consent, extinguishes the power to control, within the Union itself, the successive sales.

On this point, it is necessary to signal that the online transmission of a database constitutes a performance of services and not a delivery of goods. In consequence, it is not included in the scope of application of the principle of exhaustion. Directive 1996/9/CE provides for the non-application of community exhaustion to online databases included in the sector of service performances, as opposed to databases fixed on material supports. Although the national statutory provisions implementing

206. Besides this hypothesis, the attribution *ex lege* of the right to the employer is set out for programs for processors and works of industrial design.
207. Regarding which *see infra* §4.

1996/9/CE do not expressly set out anything with reference to the online transmission of databases, any possible doubt on the point has been, as observed beforehand, definitively solved with the modifications introduced by D.Lgs. 68/03.

§4. The Right of the Constitutor

I. The Subject of the Right

720. The constitutor of a database is the person who performs significant investment for the realization of a database, or for its verification or presentation, by committing, for this purpose, financial means, time and work.

The necessary costs in order to consider the investment relevant cannot be valued in an absolute way. It is therefore necessary to consider the medium costs of the sector, of other persons, or of the same person in preceding or contemporary times. In the calculation of the resources committed all the costs for the realization, beginning from those necessary for the collection of data, its processing and subsequent treatment will be included.

721. In the perspective of the protection and promotion of the European Community market, the right of the constitutor is recognized only with regard to the citizens of a Member State of the European Union or usual residents on its territory. If the constitutor is an enterprise or a corporation, in order to ascertain the existence of the right, it is necessary to verify that the enterprise or corporation has been created according to the legislation of a Member State of the European Union and that it has its major activities, its central administration or the premise of its main activity within the Union. If the corporation or enterprise has only major activities within the Union, an effective and continuing tie between the exercised activity and the economy of one of the Member States has to subsist.

The provision of Article 102-*bis*, L. 633/41 on the necessary tie between the constitutor and the territory of the European Union is in line with the principle of the established performer, introduced at a general level for the appliance of the community regulations in contracts concerning electronic commerce, contained in Directive 2000/31/CE (implemented in Italy with D.Lgs. 9 April 2003, n. 70).[208] The investor will thereby only be able to use the patent assigned to him by the legislation if he is an established performer, namely a subject that effectively exercises *sine die* an economic activity through a firm establishment in the EU, while the simple presence on the territory of the community of the technical means or of the technologies necessary to perform the service is not a sufficient premise for the subsistence of the right.

208. Published in G.U. 14 Apr. 2003, n. 87, SO.

II. The Content of the Right

722. In a completely independent way from the protection of a database according to copyright (therefore also in cases of databases that are non-creative and not original), Article 102-*bis* of L. 633/41 identifies for a right belonging to the constitutor to forbid extraction works, i.e. reuse of the whole or of a substantial part of the database. This new exclusive right, regulated by Chapter III of Directive 1996/9/CE (Article 7-11) and, in the national ambit, by Title II-*bis* of L. 633/41 (Article 102-*bis and* 102-*ter*), is named, respectively, sui generis right and right of the constitutor.[209]

723. The object of the right of the constitutor is the 'substantial' content of the database: the constitutor can forbid acts of extraction and reuse of the whole, or of a substantial part of, content of the database that is the outcome of significant investments. Extraction means 'the permanent or temporary transfer of the whole or of a substantial part of the content of a database on another support with any mean or in any form' (Article 102-*bis*, letter b), L. 633/41); reuse is defined as 'any form placed at public disposal of the whole or of a substantial part of the content of a database through the distribution of copies, the leasing, the transmission performed through any means and in any form' (Article 102-*bis*, letter c), L. 633/41).

724. The fact that the legitimate user of a database cannot perform operations that are in contrast with the normal management of the database or that cause an unjust damage to its constitutor does not entitle the constitutor to forbid the actions of extraction or reuse of non-substantial parts, evaluated in qualitative and quantitative terms, performed by the legitimate user. Also in this case, if the user is authorized to use only a part of the database, he can extract or reuse non-substantial parts without the consent of the constitutor, with reference to the specific part that is covered by the authorization.

725. As observed beforehand, the right of the constitutor is subject to the principle of community exhaustion. In this sense, the same considerations formulated on the online transmission of the database apply.

III. The Duration of the Right

726. The duration of the right of the constitutor is fixed at fifteen years, accruing from 1 January of the year successive to the date of completion of the constitution of the database or of its placing at public disposal.

727. Article 102-*bis*, paragraph 8, L. 633/41 provides furthermore that if substantial modifications or integrations are made to the content of the database, and these imply new relevant investments, 'from the moment of the completion or of

---

209. *See* V. Di Cataldo, 'Banche-dati e diritto *sui generis*: la durata', AIDA, 1997, pp. 20-28.

the first placing at public disposal of the database modified or integrated this way, and as such expressly identified, an autonomous deadline of the duration of the protection accrues'.

The mere update of a database, even if it does not cause a substantial modification of the methodological structure of the collection, but determines a substantial integration of the database, then the deadline of the duration of protection will accrue again from the date that the modification was made. The duration of database rights seems weak – at least from a temporal point of view, since the right lasts just fifteen years – but in fact it has an undetermined duration, and can potentially be infinite, in clear contrast with the principle of the exhaustion of the right to economic use in the ambit of copyright.[210]

§5. The Derogations

728. The right of the author of the database and the right of the constitutor are subject to derogations, whereby the author or the constitutor cannot oppose the use of the database.[211] With D.Lgs. 169/99, the Italian legislature has reached a drafting of the provisions that limits the principle of exclusivity, the application scope of which is narrower than that at the EU level with Directive 96/9/CE, most of all with reference to the right of the constitutor.

729. The Italian legislation does not implement, first of all, the community provisions that refer to the derogations related to the right of the author and of the constitutor and that set out the free use for private purposes of a non-electronic database. This could, in some cases, be included in the free uses for personal purposes introduced by D.Lgs. 68/03.[212]

730. The second derogation contained in the Community Directive has as its object the use of the database for educational purposes or scientific research. If this requirement is fulfilled, the community provision excludes the application of the principle of authorization, as long as the legitimate user signals the source from which the informative data have been taken and provided that their use is limited to what is justified by the non-commercial purpose pursued.

The provisions contained in Article 64-*sexies*, paragraph 1, letter a), L. 633/41 provide that the derogation to copyright for the purposes of education or scientific research does not permit permanent reproduction of the whole or a substantial part of the content without express authorization by the proprietor of the right.

731. With regard to the scope of exclusion of the right of the constitutor, for purposes of public security or for an administrative or jurisdictional procedure, these have been adopted in the domestic legislation only with the enforcement of D.Lgs. 68/03.

210. *See* M.C. Cardarelli, 'Il diritto *sui generis*: la durata', AIDA, 1997, pp. 64-85.
211. These derogations add to those examined beforehand on the matter of copyright (*see* Ch. 1, §5).
212. *See also* Ch. 1, §5.

Chapter 4. Legal Protection of Computer Chips

§1. Legal Protection of Computer Chips

732. The debate on the juridical protection of microcircuits started in the Country that had seen the birth and the development of this technology: the United States. This lively debate had great influence in the Italian legal framework, too.

Confronting the necessity of protection of microchips, American jurisprudence was reluctant to dilate the principles of copyright to the point of including semiconductors.[213]

The producer industries were soliciting the creation of a statute 'sui generis' since they believed that neither protection by means of copyright nor protection by means of patent would fit the requirements of such a specialized technical sector and that the provisions on trade secrets, unfair competition, trademark and contractual protection could prove to be insufficient.[214]

The desired statute had to guarantee the producer of the microcircuit immediate protection, uniform in the whole national territory and possibly extended abroad. This protection had to be limited, however, in order to allow the use of chips by other entrepreneurs, once the initial investments had been repaid, and to not prevent the circulation of the ideas underlying the new technology.[215]

733. On the basis of these premises, on 11 November 1984, the Semiconductor Chip Protection Act was enacted: this was the model that inspired other national legislation.

The American statute provided, for the protection of the national product, that an equivalent protection would be granted to topographies and related foreign products if the condition of reciprocity was respected.

However, an interim protection with the deadline of 17 November 1987 was granted to the states adhering to CEE, until these states could adopt an ad hoc legislation.[216]

This caused an acceleration in the search for a legislative solution at the EC level, resulting in Directive 87/54/CEE of the Council of the European Economic Community of 16 December 1986 that contained a detailed regulation on the matter of legal protection of semiconductor products' topographies, which was very similar to that of the United States.[217]

213. *See* V. Franceschelli, Prime riflessioni sul progetto di legge di iniziativa governativa per la tutela del software e del firmware, in Diritto dell'informazione e dell'informatica, 1987.

214. *See* E. Giannantonio, cited.

215. *See* E. Giannantonio, cited.

216. *See*, in particular, A. Musso, La tutela giuridica delle topografie dei prodotti a semiconduttori, Rivista di diritto industriale, 1990.

217. It has to be added that the Directive likewise specifies that 'the protection of topographies of semiconductor products, in compliance with the present directive, should not frustrate other forms of protection' already existing in the respective juridical systems, as for example those 'related to the right on patents and to the rights on utility patterns' or those 'on the matter of copyright'. On this point *see* G. Olivieri, La nuova legge sulla tutela dei 'microchips' in Diritto dell'informazione e dell'informatica, 1990.

734. Japan, being likewise an important producer of microchips, on the example set by the United States, passed Law n. 43 of 1985.

735. With regard to Italy, the EC Directive was implemented (after the prescribed deadline) in the law of 21 February 1989, n. 70, which contained 'provisions for the juridical protection of the topographies of semiconductor products'.

Before the enactment of this statute, there had been a government bill regarding the protection of software and firmware.[218]

Regarding software, this has been the object of many court rulings that tended to frame its protection in the scope of the statute on copyright.[219]

The above-mentioned jurisprudential stance did not gain the agreement of the legislature, part of which was in favour of the protection of this particular kind of software by means of patent.

This doctrine, indeed, preferred to consider firmware the 'creation of a process',[220] as it is a complex of programs indissolubly tied to the functioning of a machine and able to accomplish certain results that constitute the solution of technical problems.

736. The enforcement of the mentioned statute allowed a protection sui generis, that, although based partly on the statutory provisions on copyright and partly on the statutory provisions on patenting, drew closer, however, to the statutory provisions on inventions and utility patterns.[221]

Law n. 70 of 1989 consists of twenty-five articles.

---

218. 'Norme per la tutela dei programmi per elaboratore e delle topografie di prodotti a semiconduttori', IX legislatura, 1987, Doc. 751-A. On this point *see* V. Franceschelli, cited.

219. *See*, in particular, Pret. Milano, 1 ottobre 1987 and Pret. Roma, 4 luglio 1988, that qualify the firmware as intellectual achievement. For a commentary on the first, V. Franceschelli, Dal software al firmware: nuove frontiere della protezione giuridica dei prodotti informatici, in Rivista di diritto industriale, 1988, who states 'it is a solution . . . that deserves being subscribed to. After all the firmware is nothing but a software the peculiarity of which consists only in the particular way it is memorized: on microchips the first, on magnetic supports the second'. For the second, and a contrario, B.M. Gutierrez, cited, who, in favour of patentability, believes that 'the materiality and the technical functionality of the firmware forbid its exclusion from the category of the 'creations of process'. Analogue opinion has R. Pardolesi, Software di base e diritto d'autore: una tutela criptobrevettuale?, note to Pret. Roma del 4 luglio 1988 in Il Foro Italiano, 1988, who hopes for a legislative intervention and while waiting for this states that 'the only appreciable alternative would consist in applying to operative programs the regulation on patents'. Nor 'does the impracticability at this stage of the patents' regulation legitimate a retreat/diversion on copyright'.

220. C. Ciampi, *Il problema della proteggibilità del software nell'ordinamento giuridico italiano e straniero*, in G. Alpa, La tutela giuridica del software, Milano, 1984. *See also* B.M. Gutierrez and R. Pardolesi, cited work.

221. It must here be specified that the enforcement of the new legislation left open the discussion in doctrine on the possibility that the property provided through the statute on the protection of the topography could be summed up with the protection of what the topography represents, namely of the program, by means of copyright (hypothesis of the 'double track'). On this point G. Olivieri, cited, comments as follows: 'The suggestion, however, is not convincing . . . the thesis in exam seems to entrust the provisions on copyright with the task of protecting . . . the contents, namely those "concepts processes, systems, techniques or information" embodied in the topography that, due to expressed will of the Legislator, are not object of exclusive rights . . .'.

737. Article 1 has a definitional content. The meaning of some expressions that are used throughout the statute is clarified. In particular, a 'semiconductor product' is defined as 'every finished or intermediate product: (a) consisting of a complex of material that includes a layer of semiconductor material; (b) that contains one or more layers made of conductor, isolating or semiconductor material, placed according to a three-dimensional prearranged layout; (c) destined to perform, exclusively or together with other tasks, an electronic function'.

738. The 'topography' of a semiconductor product consists of 'a series of correlated drawings, however fixed or codified: (a) representing the three-dimensional layout of the layers the semiconductor product is made of and (b) series in which each image reproduces wholly or partly a surface of the semiconductor product at any stage of its production'.

739. With regard to the object of protection, Article 2 provides that 'the topographies deriving from the intellectual creative effort of their author, that are not common or familiar in the context of the semiconductor products' industry, can be object of exclusive right'. Furthermore, topographies deriving from the combination of common or familiar elements can be the object of protection, as long as they satisfy the requirements defined by the first paragraph of Article 2.[222]

740. The interpretation of Article 2 can be problematic with reference to the meaning that should be given to the word 'familiarity'. In order to be an object of protection, topographies have to derive from the intellectual creative effort of their author. They have to be original (as compared to the knowledge of the time).

Neither the Italian legislature nor the American legislature specified what should be considered 'originality' with reference to these particular products.

741. The notion of 'originality' elaborated for the inventions cannot be applied. In the case of these, originality, or intrinsic novelty, is an 'unexpected advantage' with respect to the technical knowledge of the time. For topographies, it is not possible to talk of an unexpected result, but the aim will be to protect the intellectual effort employed to create a product that, although distinguished from others already existing in the market, is anyway included in the scope of the technical knowledge of the time.[223]

742. On the basis of Article 3, the exclusive rights on semiconductor belong to the author and his partners. However, where the topography is created by an

---

222. 'The topography resulting from the combination of others already known, therefore, could be considered "original", and thus protectable, as long as – and proportionally – it proves able to solve a different problem, namely, to perform a new electronic function.' G. Olivieri, cited.

223. *See* E. Giannantonio, cited work, and G. Olivieri, who states: 'The expressed purpose of the regulation is to protect and stimulate the investments made by the industries of the sector, so that completely compliant with such purpose appears the choice to protect the topography of a microchip every time this is not of "routine" – it is not included, namely, among those commonly employed to create the products of the sector – but is instead the result of a responsible and expensive research activity.' Cited work.

employee, the right to protection, except when the contract provides differently, belongs to the employer of the author. If it is the result of the execution of a different work contract,[224] the right to protection belongs, except when the contract provides differently, to the principal in the contract.

743. Article 4 provides that these rights consist of the following entitlements:

– to reproduce in any way or form, wholly or partially, the topography;
– to exploit commercially or to hold or distribute for trading purposes or to import a topography or a semiconductor product on which a topography is fixed.

744. The rights over topographies and semiconductor products are alienable and transferable.

They are, therefore, exclusive rights on immaterial goods, equivalent to those that protect intellectual achievements or inventions. However, they differ from them, since the object of protection is a utility product and not a work of art, and on the other hand lacks the originality required from inventions.

745. The same Article 4 introduces a limit to the protection granted to these rights, so-called reverse engineering.[225]

746. Exclusive rights do not extend themselves to reproductions performed experimentally, for the purposes of teaching, analysis and evaluation of the topography and of the concepts, procedures, systems and techniques included in the topography itself. Coherently and analogously to what is provided by Article 2 of Law 633/41 for software, paragraph 3 of Article 2 declares that the protection does not include 'concepts, processes, systems, techniques or codified information, embodied in the topographies'.

747. The creation of a 'derived' topography subsequent to an activity of reverse engineering, therefore, is not an act of counterfeiting. However, concretely, it can be not very easy to distinguish the result of an operation of reverse engineering from a mere copy with some slight modifications.

748. In this case, the subject who has exerted his faculty of reverse engineering will have to demonstrate in the first place that his work has a sufficient degree of

224. 'The contract other than that of subordinate work to which the provision refers to results substantially to be the so-called research contract, that is included in the scheme of the intellectual work performance, if carried out by a single professional, or in the scheme of contract work, if carried out by a society or organization' A. Musso, cited.

225. As it was clarified during the preparatory works of the Congress of the United States, reverse engineering refers to 'the work and the effort to comprehend the functioning of the circuit to render it more functional' that breeds not a mere copy but a new product, even if only slightly modified. E. Giannantonio, cited.

creativity and that it has allowed an increase of the functionalities of the product,[226] and, second, that the topography is the result of an autonomous work of research and proportional investments.[227]

Counterfeiting is excluded, likewise, where reproductions are made for private use: the provision derives from Article 5, paragraph 2 of the CEE Directive, that specifies 'for non-commercial purposes'.

749. Another limit is the so-called principle of exhaustion of rights subsequent to the first act of commercial exploitation: the rights get exhausted with the first commercial exploitation carried out by the proprietor or with his consent (Article 4, paragraph 5). The consequence is the free circulation of the product across national territory, without the proprietor being able to claim a right against purchaser third parties, with the exception of limiting agreements, that have a merely mandatory effect.

750. Protection will be granted to each topography provided that within two years from the date of the first commercial exploitation anywhere in the world, its registration has been requested in Italy (Article 7).

751. The registration procedure, modelled on the chart of the one set out for industrial inventions, provides the competency of the Ufficio centrale dei brevetti ('UCB' – the Central Patent Office) that checks both the formal regularity of the request and the subsistence of the substantial requirements necessary according to the law, including originality.

752. The registration request must be accompanied by the plans and documents necessary to enable the evaluation of the requirements of 'novelty' and 'creative activity' (Article 9 e 11).

753. If the UCB does not recognize the subsistence of the formal or substantial requirements for the registration, the applicant can lodge an appeal within thirty days to the Commissione dei Ricorsi (Commission of Appeals), under Article 71 of the Legge Invenzioni (Statute on Inventions).

754. The above-mentioned articles have raised some doubts since the present technical structure of the UCB does not allow a deep examination of the registration requests from a substantial point of view, but only a summary resolution on them.[228]

755. Due to a presumption, the subject requesting the registration will be the proprietor of the rights and will be entitled to exercise them.

---

226. On this topic *see* A. Musso and E. Giannantonio, cited works.
227. G. Olivieri, cited work.
228. *See* V.C. Arcari, Un brevetto che protegge il chip, in Il Sole 24 Ore, 16 febbraio 1989: 'The exam of the drawings of a circuit is a very complicated operation because it requires the use of an equipment that the appointed organization does not own and the creation of a database containing all the already patented drawings'.

The length of the protection is ten years,[229] beginning from one of the following dates:

(1) the end of the commercial year during which the topography or the semiconductor product on which the topography is fixed have been for the first time commercially exploited in any part of the world;
(2) the end of the commercial year in which the registration request has been filed in the due form.

756. Article 16 contains the so-called reservation mention[230] providing: 'The topography, the semiconductor product and its external wrapping can carry a mention made of: (a) the symbol T enclosed in a circle; (b) the date on which the topography has been object of commercial exploitation for the first time; (c) the name, the trade-name or the initials of the proprietor of the right.

This mention demonstrates the occurred registration, the claim of the propriety or the intent of requesting the registration . . .'.

The legislation points out as counterfeiting acts and as acts violating exclusive rights:

– the reproduction of the topography in any way and by any means;
– the fixing of the topography on a semiconductor product by any means;
– the use, importation and possession, for purposes of trading or distribution, of the semiconductor product on which the topography is fixed (Article 17).

757. A legal action of protection in favour of the proprietor of the right is provided. After the registration of the topography or the injunction of the person who has filed the request, a person who performs the counterfeiting acts above can be required to compensate the damages caused to the proprietor (Article 18).

758. The same Article 18 provides two cases in which the right to a fair retribution is granted:

– where the counterfeiting acts occur between the first act of commercial exploitation of the semiconductor product with reservation and the registration of the topography;
– where the acts mentioned in points (a) and (b) of Article 17 occur after the first act of commercial exploitation of a semiconductor product without reservation.

229. Article 6: 'Length of the protection'.
230. 'It is the execution of a suggestion contained in Art. 9 of the Directive, that provides: – When the legislation of the Member States provides that semiconductor products produced by using protected topographies can carry a mark, the mark to use will be a capital "T" – Italy imitates thus for the first time the Anglo-Saxon system, that characterizes protected work with specific and known marks, like the "C" of Copyright', V. Franceschelli, Prime riflessioni sul progetto di legge di iniziativa governativa per la tutela del software e del firmware, cited.

759. In this second case, the author of the counterfeiting has the right to obtain a licence on fair conditions to continue the exploitation of the topography within the limits of the use performed before this was registered.

760. The Italian statutory provisions, in the wake of the Semiconductor Chip Protection Act, protect the subject who has purchased a semiconductor product in good faith and without having knowledge of the rights existing burdening it (Article 19). The importation, distribution, trading or use of counterfeit products is not considered counterfeiting when these acts are performed in good faith.

In these cases, the prosecution of the undertaken activity within the limits of the contracts entered into and of the existing stocks is allowed, but the proprietor has the right to a fair retribution.

From the procedural point of view, the statute provides that action to ascertain the counterfeiting, to obtain compensation for damage or fair retribution cannot be started before the registration and can be promoted only for acts performed in the three years preceding the action itself (Article 20, comma 1).

761. A literal interpretation of the provision could seem to suggest that the counterfeiting action cannot be initiated unless the administrative act that accepts the registration request has been issued, whereas the exercise of the mentioned action cannot take place if the proceeding is pending in front of the UCB. However, due to the very long waiting time for the grant of the certificate by UCB, there is a need for protection of the property at an earlier stage.[231]

The consequence is the availability of a protective claim while the registration proceeding is pending that legitimates the exercise of the action as soon as the request for protection has been made by the proprietor.[232]

According to Articles 20 and 21, the main measures of protection provided are the seizure, the description and the urgent measures contained in Part III, Chapter V, of the Code of Civil Procedure, namely the judiciary seizure, the conservative seizure and the unnamed measures provided by Article 700 cod. proc. civ.

762. However, the instruments, devices and other accessories containing semiconductor products, being part of the structure of or being issued to earth vehicles, naval vehicles, spacecrafts or aircrafts that temporarily or accidentally enter in the Italian territorial, maritime or air space, cannot become the object of counterfeiting actions or be subject to precautionary measures (Article 20, comma 4).

763. With regard, finally, to the territorial ambit of the protection granted by the statute, in addition to the national and EC territory and to those states that subordinate the application of their own legislation to foreigners to the reciprocity of treatment towards their own citizens, provisions contained in D.Lgs. n. 198 of 1996

231. This need, already felt in other sectors of industrial property, has been taken into account by the Italian legislature on the topic of industrial inventions and by the European Legislature, which has provided a provisory protection for the applicant to the European patent ex Art. 67 C.B.E. A. Musso cited.

232. *See*, in particular, A. Musso, cit.

modified Article 5 of the Statute to bring it into line with the Accordo TRIPS (TRIPS Agreement), to which Italy is a party.[233] This agreement binds the members to take measures for the protection of foreign topographies of the adhering countries on the basis of what is provided by the Washington Convention on intellectual property on the matter of semiconductors.

233. After the modifications introduced, Art. 5 now provides that 'The exclusive rights container in Art. 4 are recognized when: . . . c) at the time of the first commercial exploitation or of the registration request the proprietor of the topography is: . . . (2) citizen or juridical person of another State part of the agreement on the features of intellectual property rights related to commerce, adopted in Marrakech on 15 Apr. 1994 or of a convention that regulates the protection of a topography Italy has adhered to; (3) citizen or juridical person or resident or owning a serious and effective factory for the creation of topographies or for the production of integrated circuits in the territory of one of the States mentioned by points 1 and 2; . . .'. *See* G. Guglielmetti, Adeguamento della legislazione interna in materia di proprietà industriale alle prescrizioni obbligatorie dell'accordo relativo agli aspetti dei diritti di proprietà intellettuale concernenti il commercio- Uruguay Round (D.Lg. 19 marzo 1996, n. 198), Le nuove leggi civili commentate, 1998.

Chapter 5. Other Intellectual Property Rights in the ICT Sector

§1. Rights Connected with the Exercise of Copyright

764. Without prejudice to the rights granted to the author pursuant to Part I of the Italian Copyright Law, the producer of a phonographic record or of any other similar contrivance for reproducing sounds or voices shall have the exclusive right, for the period and under the conditions laid down in the articles of the Law, to reproduce, by whatever duplication process, and distribute the said record or contrivance of his production.

765. The right of distribution shall not be limited to the territory of the European Union, unless the first sale of the phonogram was carried out or authorized by the producer in a country of the European Union.

766. The producer of the phonographic record or of any similar contrivance for reproducing sounds or voices, as well as the artists who interpreted or performed the interpretation or the performance recorded or reproduced on the said contrivances, shall be entitled, independently of the rights of distribution, lease and loan pertaining to them, to remuneration in exchange for the utilization, for purposes of gain, of the record or of the similar contrivance through broadcasting, cinematography, television, in public dancing parties, in public premises and on the occasion of any further public utilization of the said contrivances.

767. The producer shall be entitled to exercise the aforesaid right and shall share out the remuneration among the artists who acted, interpreted or performed the work.

768. Except when agreed otherwise by the parties, the said remuneration shall be calculated, paid and distributed pursuant to the Regulation.

769. The amount of such remuneration and the shares of distribution, as well as the relative formalities, shall be determined according to the provisions of the regulations.

770. No remuneration shall be required in respect of the utilization for instructional or propaganda purposes by the State administration, or by institutions authorized by the State for such purposes.

771. The artists who interpret or perform and the producer of the phonogram which was utilized shall be entitled to fair remuneration, including when the utilization was not effected for purposes of gain.

772. Except when agreed otherwise by the parties, the said remuneration shall be calculated, paid and distributed pursuant to the Regulation.

773. The producer shall be entitled to oppose any utilization of a record or contrivance for producing sounds or voices if effected under conditions of such a nature as seriously to prejudice his industrial interests.

774. Upon application of the interested party, the 'Office of the Chairman of the Council of Ministers' pending a decision of the judicial authority, may nevertheless authorize the use of the record or like contrivance for reproducing sounds or voices, after technical investigation and the ordering, where necessary, of steps to eliminate any factors which would detract from the standard of the performance.

775. The duration of the rights specified in this part shall be fifty years from the time of fixation.

776. Nonetheless, if during that period the phonogram is lawfully published under the provisions of Article 12, paragraph 3, the duration of the rights shall be fifty years following the date of first publication.

777. Copies of a phonograph record or like contrivance for reproducing sounds or voices shall not be commercially distributed unless they bear, indelibly imposed upon the said record or contrivance, the indications specified in Article 62, insofar as they are applicable.

778. The person who, by direct recording of sounds or voices, undertakes the making of the original record or like contrivance for reproducing sounds or voices shall be considered the producer.

779. The place of production shall be considered to be that in which the direct original recording was created.

780. The producer of cinematographic or audiovisual works or of sequences of motion pictures shall have the exclusive power: (i) to authorize reproduction, whether direct or indirect, of the original works and of the copies thereof; (ii) to authorize distribution, by whatever means including by sale, of the original works and of the copies thereof; the right of distribution shall not be limited to the territory of the European Union, unless the first sale was effected or authorized by the producer in a country belonging to the European Union; (iii) to authorize lease and loan of the original works and of the copies thereof; sale or distribution, in whatever form, shall not limit the right of lease and loan; (iv) to authorize the making available to the public of the original and of the copies thereof, in such a way that members of the public may access them in the time and from the place individually chosen by them. This right shall not be exhausted by any act of making available to the public.

781. The rights shall end on the expiration of a period of fifty years from the time of fixation. If the cinematographic or audiovisual work or the sequence of moving images is published or communicated to the public during that period, the said rights shall expire 50 years from the first publication or, if earlier, from the first such communication to the public of the cinematographic or audiovisual work or of the sequence of moving images.

782. Without prejudice to the rights granted by this law to authors, to producers of phonographic records and similar contrivances, to producers of cinematographic or audiovisual works or of sequences of motion pictures, to artists who interpret or perform, those subject carrying out broadcasting activities by radio or television shall have the exclusive power: (i) to authorize the recording of broadcasts effected by wire or air: this right shall not be granted to cable distributors who rebroadcast, by cable, the broadcasts of other broadcasting organization; (ii) to authorize reproduction, whether direct or indirect, of the recordings of their communication to the public provided the latter is carried out in a place which is accessible upon payment of an entrance fee; (iii) to authorize distribution of the recordings of their own broadcasts as well as their communication to the public provided the latter is carried out in a place which is accessible upon payment of an entrance fee; (iv) to authorize distribution of the recording of their own broadcasts: this power shall not be limited to the territory of the European Union unless the first sale was effected or allowed by the person having the said power in a country of the European Union.

783. The subjects shall also have the exclusive right of utilization of the recordings of their own broadcasts for further broadcasts or rebroadcasts or for further recordings.

'Broadcasts' shall mean broadcasts by radio and television. 'By wire or air' shall include broadcasts by cable and via satellite.

The rights shall continue for fifty years since the end of the calendar year in which the first diffusion of a broadcast was effected.

784. Artists who interpret or perform shall be all those actors, singers, musicians, dancers and any other persons who play, sing, recite or perform, in whatever manner, intellectual works, whether protected or of public domain.

785. The artists who interpret or perform shall have the exclusive power, regardless of any remuneration to which they may be entitled to their live artistic performances: (i) to authorize recording of their artistic performances; (ii) to authorize reproduction, whether direct or indirect, of the recordings of their artistic performances; (iii) to authorize broadcasting by air and communication to the public, in whatever form and manner, of their live artist performances, unless the latter were intended for broadcasting by radio or television or are already the subject or a recording for broadcasting purposes. If the recording is represented by a phonographic record or any similar contrivance, and where it is utilized for purposes of gain, the artists who interpret or perform shall be entitled to the remuneration as per Article 73; if the recording is not utilized for purposes of gain, the artists who interpret or perform shall be entitled to the fair remuneration as per Article 73-*bis*; (iv) to authorize distribution of the recordings of their artistic performances: this right shall not be limited to the territory of the European Union, unless the first sale was effected by the person having the aforesaid right, or with the latter's consent, in a country of the European Union; (v) to authorize lease or loan of the recordings of their artistic performances and of the reproductions thereof: the artists who interpret or perform shall retain, even when granting the right of lease to a producer of phonograms or cinematographic or audiovisual works or of sequences of motion pictures, the right to obtain fair remuneration for the lease contracts made by the said producer with third parties. Any contrary stipulation shall be void.

786. Artists who act, interpret or perform shall be entitled to oppose any diffusion transmission or reproduction of their recitation or performance which might be prejudicial to their honour or reputation.

787. For the purposes of the application of these provisions, the following shall be included within the definition of artists who act, interpret or perform: (i) persons who, in the performance of any dramatic, literary or musical work or composition, play an important artistic part, even if subsidiary to the leading performers; (ii) the conductors of an orchestra or choir; (iii) entire orchestras or choirs, provided that the orchestral or choral part of the performance has artistic value in itself and is not a mere accompaniment.

788. Artists who act, interpret or perform the leading parts in a dramatic, literary or musical work or composition shall be entitled to have their names indicated in the diffusion or transmission of their recitation or performance and applied in an indelible manner to any phonograph record, cinematographic film or other like a contrivance.

789. Unless where agreed otherwise by the parties, it is presumed that the artists who interpret or perform alienated their right to authorize lease at the time of stipulation of a contract for the production of a cinematographic or audiovisual work or a sequence of motion pictures, without prejudice to the right to fair remuneration.

790. Unless where agreed otherwise by the parties, it is presumed that the artists who interpret or perform alienated their rights of recording, reproduction, broadcasting and distribution at the time of stipulation of a contract for the production of a cinematographic or audiovisual work or sequences of motion pictures.

791. The fair remuneration shall be determined pursuant to the provisions of the Regulation.

792. The rights shall continue for fifty years since the end of the calendar year in which the performance, the representation or the recitation took place. If a fixation of the performance is published or communicated to the public during that time, the duration of the rights shall be fifty years as from the first such publication or, if earlier, from the first such communication to the public of the fixation.

793. The author of sketches of theatrical scenes which do not constitute an intellectual work covered by copyright shall have a right to remuneration when such sketch is further used in theatres other than that for which it was composed.

This right shall continue for five years from the first performance in which the sketch was used.

794. Pictures of persons, or aspects elements or features of natural or social life, obtained by photographic or analogous processes, including reproductions of works of graphic art and stills of cinematographic film, shall be considered to be photographs for the purposes of the application of the provisions of this part.

795. Photographs of writings, documents, business papers, material objects, technical drawings and similar products shall not be so considered.

796. The exclusive right of reproduction, diffusion and circulation of a photograph shall, insofar as portraits are concerned, and without prejudice to any copyright in works of graphic art reproduced in photographs, belong to the photographer.

797. However, if the work has been produced in the course of the fulfilment of a contract of employment or of work then, within the limits of the object and purpose of the contract, the exclusive right shall belong to the employer.
In the absence of agreement to the contrary, the same shall apply in favour of the person who commissions photographs of objects in his possession, subject to the payment of an equitable remuneration to the photographer by any person who commercially utilize the reproduction.
The Chairman of the Council of Ministers in accordance with the provisions specified in the Regulation, fixes suitable rates for the remuneration to be paid by any person who so utilizes the photograph.

798. In the absence of agreement to the contrary, transfer of the negative or similar means of reproduction of a photograph shall involve the transfer of the rights, provided that such rights are the property of the transferor.

799. The copies of the photograph must bear the following indications: (i) the name of the photographer or the name of the firm to which he belongs, or of the person who commissioned the photograph; (ii) the year of production of the photograph; (iii) the name of the author of the work of art which has been photographed.
When the copies do not bear the said indications, their reproduction shall not be deemed wrongful and the remuneration shall not become due unless the photographer proves bad faith on the part of the reproducer.

800. The production of photographs in anthologies destined for scholastic use and, in general, in scientific or didactic works shall be lawful, subject to the payment of equitable remuneration which shall be determined in the manner provided in the Regulations.

801. In any reproduction, the name of the photographer and the year of making shall be indicated if such are given upon the photograph which has been reproduced.

802. The reproduction of photographs published in newspapers or other periodicals, and which concern persons or current events or matters of public interest, shall be lawful, subject to the payment of equitable remuneration.

803. The exclusive right in respect of photographs shall continue for twenty years from the making of the photograph.

804. Letters, collections of letters, family and personal memoranda and other writings of a like nature, having a confidential character or associated with the intimacy of private life, may not be published, reproduced or in any manner brought to the knowledge of the public without the consent of the author and, in the case of letters and collections of letters, the consent also of the addressee.

After the death of the author or of the addressee, the consent of the spouse and children or, if none exist, the consent of the parents shall be required; if there is no spouse, child or parent, the consent of the brothers and sisters or, if none exist, the consent of the direct ascendants and descendants to the fourth degree shall be required.

When the persons indicated in the preceding paragraph are two or more in number and disputes arise between them, the judicial authority shall decide the matter, after having heard the public prosecutor.

The wishes of the deceased person, when expressed in writing, shall in all cases be respected.

805. The consent shall not be necessary when knowledge of the contents of such written matter is required for the purposes of civil or penal proceedings, or in connection with the defence of the honour or reputation of the person or family concerned.

806. The provisions of the preceding parts shall apply also to letters constituting works protected by copyright, even after they have fallen into the public domain.

Such provisions shall not apply to official documents and letters and documents and letters of interest to the State.

807. The portrait of a person may not be displayed, reproduced or commercially distributed without the *consent* of such person.

808. The consent of the person portrayed shall not be necessary when the reproduction of the portrait is justified by his notoriety or his holding of public office, or by the needs of justice or the police, or for scientific, didactic, or cultural reasons, or when reproduction is associated with facts, events and ceremonies which are of public interest or have taken place in public.

The portrait may not, however, be displayed or commercially distributed when its display or commercial distribution would prejudice the honour, reputation or dignity of the person portrayed.

809. In the absence of agreement to the contrary, a commissioned photographic portrait may be published, reproduced or caused to be reproduced by the person photographed or by his heirs or successors in title, without the consent of the photographer, subject to the payment of equitable remuneration to the photographer by any person making commercial use of the reproduction.

If the name of the photographer appears upon the original photograph such name must be indicated.

810. The author of engineering projects and other analogous works which constitute original solutions of technical problems shall in addition to the exclusive right of reproduction of the plans and drawings of the actual projects has the right to equitable remuneration from any person who, with gainful intent and without the consent of the author, realizes the technical project concerned.

In order to exercise his right to remuneration, the author must insert upon the plan or drawing a declaration of reservation of the right and must deposit the plan or drawing with the Office of the Chairman of the Council of Ministers in accordance with the provisions of the Regulations.

The right to remuneration shall continue for twenty years from the date of the deposit prescribed in the second paragraph.

811. The title of a work, when it uniquely identifies the work, may not be reproduced in connection with any other work without the consent of the author.

This prohibition shall not extend to works which are of a kind or character so far removed as to exclude all possibility of confusion.

The reproduction of headings used in periodical publications to give unique identification to the normal and characteristic features appearing thereunder shall, under like conditions, also be prohibited.

The title of a newspaper, magazine or other periodical publication may not be reproduced in other works of the same kind or character unless two years have expired since the cessation of its publication.

812. The reproduction of information and news shall be lawful, provided it is not effected by way of acts which are contrary to fair practice in journalism and provided the source is given.

The following shall be deemed to be unlawful acts: (i) the reproduction or the broadcasting, without authorization, of bulletins of information distributed by press or information agencies, before the lapse of sixteen hours from the distribution of the actual bulletins and, in any case, before their publication in a newspaper or other periodical authorized by such agency. For this purpose and in order for the said agencies to have a right of action against persons who make unlawful utilization, bulletins must bear a precise indication of the day and hour of their issue; (ii) the systematic reproduction of published or broadcast information or news, with gainful intent, by newspapers or other periodicals or by broadcasting organizations.

813. The reproduction or imitation of other works of the same kind, or of headings, emblems, ornamentations, arrangements of printing signs or characters or any other particularity of form or colour in the external appearance of an intellectual work, when the said reproduction or imitation is capable of creating confusion between works or authors, shall be forbidden as an act of unfair competition.

§2. Common Provisions

814. A general public register of works protected by the Italian Copyright Law shall be established in the Office of the Chairman of the Council of Ministers.

The S.I.A.E. shall be responsible for the maintenance of a special public register for cinematographic works.

Works which are subject to the requirement of deposit shall be registered in the said registers, together with an indication of the name of the author, the producer, of the date of publication and other particulars specified in the Regulations.

The S.I.A.E. shall further be in charge of the keeping of a special public register for computer programs. In the said register there shall be registered the name of the person to whom the exclusive rights of economic utilization belong and the release date of the program – *release* meaning the first act of exercise of the said exclusive rights.

In the absence of proof to the contrary, registration shall be accepted as proof of the existence of the work and the fact of its publication. The authors and producers indicated in the register shall be deemed, in the absence of proof to the contrary, to be the authors and producers of the works attributed to them. In the case of cinematographic works, the presumption shall be applicable to the annotations made in the Register.

The keeping of the public registers shall be governed by the Regulations.

The registers may be kept by using computer equipment and instrumentation.

815. At the instance of the interested party legal instruments executed between living persons, transferring in whole or in part rights recognized by the Copyright Law, or establishing rights of enjoyment or guarantee thereof, as well as instruments serving to divide or to associate such rights, may also be registered in the form prescribed by the Regulations.

Such registration shall also have such legal or administrative effects as the provisions of the Copyright Law or other special laws accord to registration.

816. The authors and producers of works and products protected by the Law, or their successors in title, shall deposit with the Office of the Chairman of the Council of Ministers one specimen or copy of the work or product, within the period and in the manner specified in the Regulations.

In the case of dramatico-musical or symphonic works of which the orchestral parts have not been printed, it shall be sufficient to deposit one copy or specimen of the version for voice and piano or for piano only.

With respect to computer programs, the said deposit shall be optional and subject to charge.

Photographs shall not be subject to the obligation of deposit.

817. Failure to deposit shall not prejudice the acquisition or exercise of copyright in respect of works protected under the provisions of the Law, or under the provisions of international conventions.

The Chairman of the Council of Ministers shall be entitled to seize a specimen or copy of a work which has not been deposited as required by the Regulations.

§3. TRANSFER OF THE RIGHTS OF UTILIZATION

818. The rights of utilization belonging to the authors of intellectual works, as well as the connected rights having a patrimonial character, may be acquired, alienated or transferred under all methods and forms allowed by law, subject to the application of the rules contained in the Italian Copyright Law.

819. An author who has attained the age of 16 shall be deemed capable of fulfilling all legal acts relating to works created by him and of instituting any action in respect thereof.

820. In the absence of agreement to the contrary, the transfer of one or more copies of the work shall not involve the transfer of the rights of utilization.

However, the transfer of a mould, an engraved plate or any similar medium used to reproduce a work of art shall, in the absence of agreement to the contrary, be deemed to include the right to reproduce the work provided such right belongs to the transferor.

821. The transfer of rights of utilization must be established *in writing*.

822. The right of publication of an intellectual work and the rights of utilization of a published work, insofar as they belong personally to the author, may not be the subject of any pledge seizure or sequestration, either by contractual act or by way of forced execution.

Copies of the work and the proceeds of utilization may, however, be the subject of a pledge, or be seized or sequestered, according to the rules of the Code of Civil Procedure.

823. The rights belonging to the author, with the exception of the right to publish a work during his lifetime, may be expropriated for reasons of State interest.

824. Expropriation shall be authorized by Presidential Decree at the instance of the Chairman of the Council of Ministers acting in conjunction with the Minister of Public Instruction and in consultation with the Council of State.

The indemnity due to the dispossessed person shall be specified in the decree of expropriation or a subsequent decree.

The Decree shall have executive force against successors in title and as against third parties who are the holders of physical objects necessary for the exercise of the expropriated rights.

825. Recourse before the Council of State in its judicial capacity shall be admitted against a decree of expropriation for reasons of State interest, but disputes concerning the amount of the indemnity shall be within the competence of the ordinary courts.

§4. Transmission Mortis Causa

826. After the death of the author, the rights of utilization of the work, if not otherwise disposed of by the author himself, shall remain undivided between the heirs for a period of three years from the date of death, unless the judicial authority, at the instance of one or more of the co-heirs, agrees, for serious reasons, that division shall be effected without delay.

When the said period has expired, the heirs may, by common accord, decide that the rights shall continue to be held in common for such period as may be fixed by them, within the limits specified by the provisions contained in the Codes.

Such community shall be regulated by the provisions of the Civil Code and by those which follow.

827. The administration and representation of the community interests shall be conferred upon one of the co-heirs, or upon some person outside the succession.

If the co-heirs fail to appoint an administrator, or if they do not agree upon such appointment within one year from the effective date of the succession, the administration shall, upon the request of one of the co-heirs or of the S.I.A.E., be conferred upon the S.I.A.E. by decree of the tribunal of the place where probate was granted.

The same procedure shall be followed in the case of the appointment of a new administrator.

828. The administrator shall take charge of the management of the rights of utilization of the work.

He shall not, however, authorize new editions, translation or their elaborations, nor the adaptation of the work to cinematography, broadcasting or recording upon mechanical contrivances, except with the consent of heirs representing more than half of the value of the estate, and subject to such measures as may be taken by the judicial authority to safeguard the minority in accordance with the rules of the Civil Code relating to communities.

§5. Publishing Contracts

829. The contract by which the author grants to a publisher the exercise of the right of publication of an intellectual work by way of printing, for the account and at the cost of such publisher, shall be regulated apart from the special provisions contained in the Codes, by the general provisions of the Copyright Law and by the special provisions which follow.

830. The contract may have for its object all the rights of utilization which belong to the author within the field of publication, or certain of them, with such provisions and for such duration as may be provided by the laws in force at the time of the contract.

In the absence of a stipulation to the contrary, it shall be presumed that the rights transferred are exclusive.

Future rights which may be granted by subsequent laws and which involve the protection of copyright wider in scope or longer in duration cannot be included in the transfer.

In the absence of an express stipulation, alienation shall not extend to the rights of utilization in later elaborations and transformations to which the work may lend itself, including adaptations to cinematography, broadcasting and recording upon mechanical contrivances.

In the absence of an agreement to the contrary, the alienation of one or more of the rights of utilization shall not imply the transfer of other rights which are not necessarily dependent upon the right transferred, even if they are included in the same category of exclusive rights.

831. If the contract relates to works which have not at that date been created, the following rules shall be observed: (i) any contract shall be void which has for its object all the works or all the works of a certain category which the author may create, without limit of time; ii) without prejudice to the rules governing contracts for works and employment, contracts which relate to the alienation of exclusive rights in respect of works to be created may not extend for a term in excess of ten years; (iii) if the work to be created has been determined, but the term within which such work shall be delivered has not been fixed the publisher may at any time request the judicial authority to fix such term. If the term has been fixed, the judicial authority may extend it.

832. If after a substantial and self-sufficient portion has been completed and delivered, the author should die, or should find himself unable to complete the work, the publisher shall be entitled to elect to regard the contract as rescinded, or upon making a proportionate payment to consider it as having been fulfilled insofar as concerns the delivered portion, unless the author has manifested or manifests a wish that the work should not be published unless entirely completed.

If cancellation of the contract takes place at the request of the author or his heirs, the uncompleted work may not be assigned to other persons, under penalty of damages.

833. A publishing contract may be based upon the number of editions or upon a certain period of time.

A contract based upon the number of editions shall be deemed to confer upon the publisher the right to make one or more editions during a period of twenty years from the date of delivery of the completed manuscript.

The number of editions and the number of copies of each edition shall be specified in the contract. However, alternatives may be provided for, either in respect of the number of editions and copies or in respect of the remuneration based thereon.

In the absence of such indications, it shall be understood that the contract has for its object a single edition of not more than 2,000 copies.

A publication contract based upon a period of time shall be deemed to confer upon the publisher the right to produce the number of editions which he may consider necessary within the time specified, which period shall not exceed twenty years, and shall specify a minimum number of copies of each edition, to be produced; in the absence of such indication the contract shall be void. The maximum period of twenty years shall not apply to contracts concerning encyclopaedias and dictionaries; sketches, drawings, vignettes, illustrations, photographs and similar works, for industrial use; cartographical works; dramatico-musical and symphonic works.

In both forms of contract, the publisher shall be free to spread the editions over such number of reprints as he may consider suitable.

834. Copies of the work shall be countersigned in accordance with the rules established by the Regulations.

835. If several editions are contemplated by the contract, the publisher shall, within a reasonable advance period, be obliged to notify the author of the probable time of exhaustion of the current edition.

He shall, at the same time, declare to the author whether or not he intends to proceed with a new edition.

If the publisher has declared that he will renounce the making of a new edition, or if, having declared his wish to proceed with a new edition, he does not so proceed within a period of two years from the notification of such declaration, the contract shall be regarded as rescinded.

The author shall be entitled to damages in respect of the non-production of the new edition unless the publisher shows an adequate justification.

836. The author shall be required: (i) to deliver the work under the conditions specified in the contract and form which will not make printing unduly difficult or costly; ii) to guarantee, for the entire period of the contract, the undisturbed enjoyment of the rights granted.

In addition, the author shall have both the obligation and the right to correct printers' proofs, in accordance with the conditions established by custom.

837. The publisher shall be required: (i) to reproduce the work and put it into commercial circulation in conformity with the original and according to rules of good publishing practice, with the name of the author, or as an anonymous or pseudonymous work if so provided in the contract; ii) to pay the stipulated remuneration to the author.

838. The publication or reproduction of the work shall take place within the period fixed by the contract; such period shall not be more than two years from the date of effective delivery to the publisher of the complete and final copy of the work.

If no period is specified in the contract, publication or reproduction of the work shall take place within two years of written request made to the publisher. The judicial authority may, however, fix a shorter period when such is justified by the nature of the work or by any other special circumstance.

Any stipulation renouncing the fixing of a period or specifying a period in excess of the maximum referred to above shall be void.

The maximum period of two years shall not apply to collective works.

839. If a person acquiring the right of publication or reproduction does not effect publication or reproduction of the work within the period specified by the contract or by the judge, the author shall be entitled to demand that the contract be cancelled.

The judicial authority may grant to the person acquiring the right an extension of time, not exceeding one half of the aforesaid period and subject, where necessary, to a suitable guarantee. The judicial authority may also restrict the decision on cancellation to part only of the provisions of the contract.

In the case of total cancellation, the person who acquired the right must return the original of the work and shall be obligated to make good any damage, unless he proves that the failure to publish or reproduce took place despite the exercise of due diligence.

840. Until such time as the work is published by printing, the author may introduce therein any modifications which he considers suitable, provided that they do not alter the character and purpose of the work, and provided he bears any major expenses occasioned by the modifications.

The author shall have the same right in relation to new editions. The publisher shall consult the author on this matter before proceeding with new editions. In the absence of agreement between the parties, the period for carrying out modifications shall be fixed by the judicial authority.

If the nature of the work requires it to be brought up-to-date prior to any new edition, and the author refuses so to do, the publisher may have it brought up-to-date by other persons, provided that the new edition shall indicate and distinguish the work of such persons.

841. The remuneration of the author shall consist of a share of the proceeds which, in the absence of agreement to the contrary, shall be calculated upon a percentage basis of the retail price of the copies sold. However, his remuneration may be represented by a lump sum for editions of dictionaries, encyclopaedias, anthologies and other works produced in collaboration; translations, newspaper and magazine articles; discourses or lectures; scientific works; cartographical works; musical or dramatico-musical works; works of art.

In contracts providing for the sharing of proceeds, the publisher shall be required to render an annual account of copies sold.

842. In publishing contracts, the retail price shall be fixed by the publisher, after prior notice to the author. The author may object to the price fixed or modified by the publisher if it is such as would gravely prejudice the interests of the author or the dissemination of the work.

843. The publisher shall not transfer the rights he has acquired to other persons without the consent of the author unless there is an agreement to the contrary or a change of ownership of the business.

However, in the latter event, the publisher may not transfer his rights if such transfer would be prejudicial to the reputation of the author or the dissemination of the work.

844. If the work does not find a sufficient market at the price fixed, the publisher, before selling the remaining copies below cost price, or as waste, shall ask the author if he wishes to acquire the copies at a price calculated upon the amount obtainable by their sale at such price or as waste.

845. Publishing contracts shall terminate: (i) upon expiration of the contractual period; ii) when their fulfilment is impossible by reason of the failure of the work; (iii) when the author dies before completion of the work; (iv) when the work cannot be published, reproduced or commercially distributed by reason of a judicial decision or a provision of law; (v) in case of cancellation of the contract; (vi) in any case where the work has been withdrawn from commerce.

846. The bankruptcy of the publisher shall not cause the cancellation of the publishing contract.

The publishing contract shall, however, be revoked if the liquidator, within one year of the declaration of bankruptcy, does not continue to carry on the publishing business or does not transfer it to some other publisher.

§6. Contracts for Public Performances

847. The contract by which the author grants the right to perform in public a dramatic, dramatico-musical, choreographic, pantomimic or other work destined for performance shall, in addition to the general provisions contained in the Codes, be governed by the general provisions of the Copyright Law and by the special provisions which follow.

In the absence of provision to the contrary, the grant of any such right shall be neither exclusive nor transferable.

848. The author shall be obliged: (i) to deliver the text of the work if it has not already been published in printed form; (ii) to guarantee, for the duration of the contract, the undisturbed enjoyment of the rights granted.

849. The grantee shall be obliged: (i) to perform the work without additions, deletions or variations therein which have not been agreed to by the author, and with previous announcement to the public, in the customary manner, of the title of the work and the name of the author and any translator or arranger of the work: ii) to allow the author to supervise the performance; (iii) not to change, without serious reasons, the principal interpreters of the work and the directors of the orchestras and choirs, if appointed in agreement with the author.

850. If the grantee of the right of performance, notwithstanding the request of the author, fails to continue to perform the work after a first performance or a first cycle of performances, the author of the musical or literary portion who demonstrates the fault of the grantee shall be entitled to request the cancellation of the contract.

851. A contract for the performance of a musical composition shall be governed by the provisions of the Copyright Law, insofar as they are applicable to the nature and object of such contract.

§7. WITHDRAWAL OF THE WORK FROM COMMERCE

852. The author, whenever serious moral reasons arise, shall be entitled to withdraw the work from commerce, subject to liability to indemnify any persons who have acquired rights to reproduce, diffuse, perform or circulate such work.

853. This right is personal and is not transmissible.

In order to exercise this right, the author shall notify his intention to the persons to whom he has transferred the said rights and to the Office of the Chairman of the Council of Ministers shall give public notice of such intention in the manner established by the Regulations.

Within a period of one year from the last date of notification and publication, the interested parties may have recourse to the judicial authority to oppose the exercise of the claim of the author or to obtain liquidation and compensation for damages.

854. The judicial authority, if it finds that the grave moral reasons invoked by the author exist, shall exhibit the reproduction, diffusion, performance or circulation the work, subject to the payment of an indemnity in favour of the interested parties and shall fix the amount of such indemnity and the period for its payment.

Before the expiration of the period specified in the final paragraph of the preceding Article, the judicial authority, upon request and if it finds that urgent reasons exist, may provisionally decree such prohibition after such security as it may deem necessary has been furnished.

If the indemnity is not paid within the period fixed by the judicial authority, the effect of the Decree shall automatically cease.

The continuation of the reproduction, diffusion, performance or circulation of the work after expiration of the period allowed for recourse to the judicial authority, as specified in the final paragraph of the foregoing Article, or after any decree suspending trading in the work, shall be subject to the civil and penal sanctions of the Copyright Law for infringement of copyright.

§8. RIGHTS OF THE AUTHOR IN RESPECT OF INCREASE IN VALUE OF WORKS OF ART

855. The authors of works of art in the form of paintings, sculptures, drawings and prints and the authors of original manuscripts shall be entitled to a percentage of the amount by which the price of the first public sale of original copies of such works and manuscripts exceeds the price of first alienation, and such excess shall be presumed.

The organizer of the sale, the vendor and the purchaser shall, however, be entitled to prove that such public sale was not preceded by any act of alienation for valuable consideration, or that the price of first alienation was not less than that obtained in the public sale.

856. The authors of the works shall also be entitled to a *percentage* of the higher value than the original copies of their works ultimately acquire in successive public sales, such higher value being the difference between the price at the last public sale and the price at the public sale which immediately preceded it.

857. Proof of the price paid for a work and of the conditions specified shall be the responsibility of the authors.

858. The percentage shall be reduced to 5% if the vendor proves, in turn, that he acquired the copy at a price not less than half of that realized by him.
These provisions shall not apply to anonymous or pseudonymous works.

859. For the purposes of the protection, replicas made by the author shall also be considered as original works, but not reproductions otherwise produced.
In respect of prints, those which have been derived from original engravings, signed by the author, shall be considered as original works.

Chapter 6. Internet Domain Name Registration

§1. The Italian Registry

860. The *Italian Registry* is the Registry of 'dot it' Internet domains.
'Dot it' is the domain name extension of Italy. Only the Registry can accept request, change or delete one or more '.it' domains.

861. At the request of users, the Registry associates a name with the long and difficult-to-memorize numerical addresses needed to navigate on the Web. The association is stored in an archive (Dbna, database of assigned names) that all computers connected to the Web must query in order to reach a '.it' domain. This service is called DNS (Domain Name System), and it regulates, in a transparent manner, how the Internet operates.

862. In 1987, Icann instructed the CNR (Consiglio Nazionale delle Ricerche – Italian National Research Council) to manage .it extensions. And that is how the .it Registry was founded, which is based at the Institute of Informatics and Telematics of the CNR in Pisa.

863. In December 1987, Iana (Internet Assigned Numbers Authority) recognized the ccTLD.it and entrusted its management to the Italian National Research Council given the technical and scientific expertise gained of its researchers, who had been among the first in Europe to adopt the IP protocol.

864. The service of registration and maintenance of Italian domains was initially carried out by the CNUCE (another institute of the CNR). In 1997, this responsibility passed to the Institute for Applied Telematics (IAT-CNR) and, thereafter, to the Institute of Informatics and Telematics (IIT-CNR), founded in 2002 by the merger between IAT and the Institute of Computational Mathematics.

865. The spread of .it domain names has followed in tandem the more general development of the Internet in Italy.
For the first ten years, the use of the Web remained confined to the worlds of academia and research, and domain registration was a niche phenomenon.
The explosion of the World Wide Web took place in Italy in the late 1990s. The process of registering .it domain names saw a massive rise.

866. The Registry has gradually expanded its operational structure and, correspondingly, has tailored the regulatory and technological instruments to the new needs of the operators and the market.

867. After the elimination of the limit on the number of domains registered (in 2000 for companies, in 2004 for natural persons), the number of new registration requests for .it domains has gradually gone up to around 20,000 per month.

868. The Italian Registry today is the fifth country code top-level domain in Europe in terms of the number of domains registered.

869. The introduction of synchronous registration in September 2009 marked another turning point in the world of Italian Internet domains.

870. Through the Extensible Provisioning Protocol (EPP), in fact, each Registrar can operate directly on the database of domains, in real time and without submitting any documentation to the Registry – either paper or electronic.

The elimination of forms and waiting times, combined with a flexible architecture, means that the 'synchronous' procedure is an efficient state-of-the-art registration system.

Operators can enhance their business and at the same time promote the dot.it domains. Thanks to the synchronous system, the average number of registrations has increased from 25,000 to over 35,000 new domains every month.

871. In October 2010, the number of Italian domains reached two million Internet domains, twice as many as there were only five years previously.

Another milestone is that the CNR, which has always been a leader in the history of Italian network, has once again confirmed that Pisa, the home of the Institute for Informatics and Telematics, which manages the Italian Registry, is the cradle of computer science in Italy.

The year 2012 is a year of celebration. Twenty-five years have passed since the Italian Registry began its history at CNUCE (an institute of the Italian National Research Council – CNR).

Since December 1987 the Registry has been managing the registration and maintenance of dot.it domain names. It all began with the birth of cnr.it (the first domain in the Italian network, which actually began as cnuce.cnr.it, the name of the first institute of the CNR).

The Registry was delegated to carry out its duties by the Internet Assigned Numbers Authority, now ICANN (Internet Corporation for Assigned Names and Numbers), which has historically been responsible for assigning IP addresses at an international level along with the operational management of the DNS.

872. Heading up the Registry is the Director of the Institute of Informatics and Telematics of CNR (Iit-Cnr), who brings in the Management Committee to coordinate the various activities and the Rules Committee for the formulation of the Regulations for the assignment and maintenance of domain names.

The Management Committee consists of the heads of the five units under which the Registry is organized.

873. The assignment of domain can be the subject of dispute between one or more entities who claim the right to it.

The .it Registry does not take part in resolving the dispute, but provides its users with a specific tool: *the challenge procedure*. This 'freezes' the allocation of the domain until the dispute has been resolved and allows those who have initiated the challenge to exercise a right of first refusal on any new assignment.

874. Opening a challenge does not allow a domain already registered by another party to be automatically obtained, but gives access to two procedures – rather than going to Court – for the resolution of the dispute: amicable composition and a reallocation procedure.

A challenge can be initiated by sending the Registry a written request with details of the sender, the domain name that is being challenged, the background and the rights that are presumed as being impaired.

§2. General Rules

875. In Italy, regulations drafted by the *Naming Authority* contain the rules for the assignation of domain names under the Italian Country Code Top-Level Domain, 'it'.[234]

The regulations define the 'rules and technical procedures for registration' and are accompanied by technical manuals (such as 'Guidelines for Managing Tasks and Operations on Domain Names in ccTLD 'it'') that detail each operation referred to in the regulations and specify the competences and actions of the people involved.

General principles concerning registration in Italy are as follows (contained in the 'Regulations for the Assignation and Management of Domain Names in the ccTLD "it"', Version 7.1, 3 November 2014) ('TLD Regulations'):[235] (a) by the very nature of resolving domain names on the Internet (via the Domain Name System, 'DNS'), it is only possible to use a domain name if this has been registered in the international hierarchy of domain names (Regulation 1.2.3(1) TLD Regulations); (b) a domain name is assigned on a first come, first served basis – a domain name cannot be booked in advance and is assigned directly to a registrant (Regulation 1.2.3(2-3) TLD Regulations); (c) the Registry guarantees the technical and administrative infrastructure for the service of resolving '.it' ccTLD domain names, in accordance with the technical norms in force (Regulation 1.2.3(4) TLD Regulations); (e) The Registry does not tolerate 'cybersquatting', that is to say the systematic buying up and hoarding of domain names (Regulation 1.2.3(5) TLD Regulations); (f) the registration of a domain name under the '.it' ccTLD is permitted only to persons who have citizenship, residence or a registered office in the countries of the European Economic Area (EEA), the Vatican, the Republic of San Marino and Switzerland (Regulation 1.2.3(6) TLD Regulations); (g) a domain name is assigned to the Registrant only after the applicant has provided their data, accepted the conditions and responsibilities established for the registration of a domain name in the ccTLD .it terms set forth in the Regulations and is aware of their responsibilities (Regulation 1.2.3(7) TLD Regulations).

876. An integral part of the regulations are the 'Regulations for Resolution of Disputes in the ccTLD' and are accompanied by technical manuals (guidelines for

---

234. *See* <www.nic.it/en/domini/regolamento.html>.

235. *See* 'Regulations for the Assignation and management of domain names in the ccTLD 'it', Version 7.1, 3 Nov. 2014, <www.nic.it/en/docs/assignment-and-management-domain-names-cctdl-it-regulations-version-7-1>'.

the resolution of disputes in ccTLD 'it') that detail each operation referred to in these regulations and specify the competences and actions of the people involved.[236]

877. Before registering a domain name in Italy, a registrant has to verify the name's availability by using the DataBase of Assigned Names (DBAN), where the Registry stores all data regarding domain names already assigned. To check if a domain name has been already registered under the ccTLD 'it', it is possible to search the IT-NIC domains database. If the domain name is available, one must then request the Registry to register a new .it domain name through an accredited 'Registrar' (Registrar is an intermediary for the Registry for all the registrations of domain names, as well as for the maintenance of the information in the DBAN Registry). The Registrar also carries out any subsequent transactions for the same domain name. The Registrant has sole responsibility for requesting the registration and use of the domain name.

878. The Registrant is obliged to promptly notify the Registrar, referenced in the registration of the domain name, of any variation of their data released during registration or the last operation performed on the domain name that led to the updating of the data in the DBAN.

879. According to Italian law, the assignee of a domain name is responsible for the registration and assignation of the domain name, as well as any services activated on the domain name (Regulation 1.2.3 of the TLD Regulations). Disagreements with the Registry are subject to Italian law, although the Registry cannot be held responsible for syntax or semantic errors contained in the data received during the phases of the assignation and the maintenance of domain names, except in the case of a grave mistake on the part of the Registry (ibid.).

880. The 'Regulations for the Resolution of Disputes in the Country Code Top-Level Domain 'it' (henceforth the 'Dispute Regulations'), provide a non-court dispute resolution mechanism for disputes arising from the assignation and use of domain names for the ccTLD 'it'. The Dispute Regulations provide the possibility of arbitration; a procedure for the reassignation of domain names subject to challenge procedure; a technical procedure for the reassignation of domains; and general principles of equity and equal accessibility to the service.

881. With the rules and instruments of the Dispute Regulations, Internet users have access to rapid and economical dispute resolution mechanisms that are consistent with the principles of equity and equal accessibility to the DNS and the Internet in general.

Informal arbitration, by means of arbitrators nominated by each party, is entered into voluntarily. This procedure is available for disputes concerning the assignation of domain names.

---

236. *See* 'Regulations for the resolution of disputes in the ccTLD 'it' Version 2.1', 3 November 2014, <https://www.nic.it/en/docs/dispute-resolution-cctld-it-regulations-version-2-1>.

The Dispute Regulations establish, as far as the services broadly speaking supplied by the Registry are concerned, an administrative procedure for reassigning domain names, under which all holders of ccTLD 'it' domain names are subject. This procedure is not of a jurisdictional nature and can therefore be halted by any of the parties at any time by a petition to the ordinary courts.

§3. Arbitration

882. The assignee of a domain name registered with the *Registry* can submit any dispute arising from the assignation of the domain name to informal arbitration, in accordance with the *Dispute Regulations*, on the understanding that the decisions reached by the *Board of Arbitrators* are legally binding.

Recourse to the arbitration clause, to be signed by the parties, can be made at the time of registration of a domain name, or at a later time by means of the appropriate form available on the *Registry's* website.

883. A list of arbitrators is kept by the *Registry*, which comprises the names of experts on the subject of domain names. Application proposals by Internet experts are presented to the *Registry* and are submitted to a *Rules Committee* for evaluation. The list of arbitrators is nominated by the *Registry* and is available on the *Registry's* website. The *Board of Arbitrators* is composed of three arbitrators, one being chosen by each of the two parties and the third, who acts as chairperson of the *Board of Arbitrators*, being chosen by the two arbitrators nominated by the parties.

The party wishing to commence the arbitration procedure must nominate its arbitrator by means of recorded delivery letter, addressed to the opposite party, the arbitrator he or she intends to nominate, and the *Registry*. The letter must indicate which arbitrator was chosen from the list, as well as the matter to be put to the *Board of Arbitrators*, the factual and legal reasons on which the matter is founded, the party's conclusions on the dispute, the domicile and e-mail address of the party and an invitation to the other party to nominate another arbitrator from the list. The party to whom the invitation to nominate an arbitrator is addressed must then, within ten working days of receiving the original letter, nominate its own arbitrator. Should the party fail to do so, the inviting party can then ask the *Registry* to nominate an arbitrator, and the *Registry* will proceed with the nomination within five working days of the request. The parties are then notified of the nomination via e-mail.

The party arbitrators thus nominated then choose a chairperson for the *Board of Arbitrators* within five working days of the nomination of the second arbitrator. Should such a nomination not be made within this period, a diligent party may ask the *Registry* to nominate the third arbitrator. This nomination by the *Registry* must also be made within five working days, of which the parties are notified via e-mail.

The *Board of Arbitrators* is deemed constituted from the day following the acceptance of the task on the part of the chairperson of the *Board*.

The arbitrators must announce their decision within ninety days of the constitution of the *Board*.

884. The arbitrators seek to pass an amicable judgment according to equity, on the basis of the Dispute Regulations, and according to Italian law.

The chairperson of the *Board of Arbitrators* notifies the parties and the *Registry* of the decision of the Board by means of a recorded delivery letter. The decisions of the *Board* are kept at the *Registry* and made available to the members of the arbitration list. The arbitration decision is also made public, except if otherwise requested by either of the parties. The decision of the Board of Arbitrators is final.

Decisions of the *Board of Arbitrators* are put into effect by the Registry within five working days of receipt of the notice of a decision.

§4. The Italian Procedure for the Reassignation of Domain Names

885. Registered domain names subject to a challenge procedure, in accordance with Article 5.1 of the 'Regulations for the Assignation and Management of Domain Names under the ccTLD 'it'' may, at the request of the challenger, be subject to the procedure for reassignation. The procedure for reassignation is applicable to any domain name registered under the ccTLD 'it'.

886. The aim of this procedure is to verify the title to use, or legal disposability of, the domain name and that the domain has not been registered or maintained in bad faith. The only possible result of the procedure is the reassignation or non-reassignation of the domain name. The procedure is not of a jurisdictional nature and, as such, does not prevent the parties from appealing, even at a later date, to a court of law or arbitration.

887. The procedure for reassignation is conducted by special organizations called *Dispute Resolving Services* (DRS) who must, subject to the opinion of the *Rules Committee*, meet the requirements of the Registry.

The choice of DRS for carrying out the procedure is made by the party who initiates the procedure and at whose sole expense the costs are charged.

The procedure cannot take place if another judgment concerning the domain name being challenged is already pending before an ordinary judge, if relief is awarded in accordance with Article 806 of the Italian Civil Procedural Code, or if the domain name is an issue before a Board of Arbitrators acting under Article 2 of the Dispute Regulations (above).

Should a judgment by an ordinary judge, or the decision of an arbitration procedure in accordance with Article 806 of the Italian Civil Procedural Code, or by a Board of Arbitrators acting under Article 2 of the Dispute Regulations, be presented while a procedure for reassignation is still pending, the procedure must be extinguished.

888. The Registry, in agreement with the *Rules Committee* (above), checks that the DRSs who apply to conduct the reassignation procedure have the prerequisites necessary for conducting it and supervises their work, in accordance with the standards contained in the 'Procedure for Qualifying Out-of-Court Dispute Resolution Service Providers Within the Context of the ccTLD .it'.

In the case of repeated violations of the standards by a dispute resolution service provider, the *Registry* can exonerate it from the performance of the procedures, subject to the opinion of the *Steering Committee* of the .it Registry or other similar body.

889. The procedure is applied to domain names for which a third party ('Petitioner') claims: (a) that the domain name subject to a challenge is *identical* to, or it is such as to mislead people into believing that it is, a trademark or other distinctive company sign to which the petitioner lays claim, or the petitioner's own name and surname; (b) that the current assignee ('resistant') has *no right or title* in relation to the domain name being challenged; and lastly (c) that the domain name has been registered and is being used in *bad faith.*

If the petitioner proves that the above three conditions exist, and the resistant cannot in turn prove that he or she has a right or title to the domain name being challenged, the domain name will then be transferred to the petitioner.

As regards to the second condition, the resistant is deemed to have a right or title to the domain name being challenged if he or she can prove: (i) that before receiving notice of the challenge, the resistant used or was objectively preparing to use the domain name, or a name corresponding to the domain name, for the public offer of goods or services; or (ii) that the resistant is known personally as an association or commercial organization by the name corresponding to the registered domain name, even if he or she has not registered the related trademark; or (iii) that he or she is making lawful use of the domain name for non-commercial or commercial purposes, without the intention of misleading the petitioner's clients or of infringing a registered trademark.

890. The following circumstances, if proved, are considered as proof of the registration and use of a domain in bad faith (Regulation 3.7 of the *Regulations for the Resolution of disputes in the cc TLD 'it'*): (i) circumstances that lead one to believe that the domain name has been registered with the primary aim of being sold, assigned for use, or in any way transferred to the petitioner, or to a title holder of a name which is the subject of a right recognized or established by Italian or European Union Law, or to a competitor of the petitioner, for a consideration, money or otherwise, which exceeds the costs reasonably incurred by the resistant for the registration and maintenance of the domain name; (ii) the circumstance in which the domain name has been registered by the resistant in order to prevent the holder of the right to a name, trademark, denomination, geographic denomination or other distinctive sign recognized by Italian or European Union Law from using such a name, denomination, trademark or other distinctive sign in a corresponding domain name for activities in competition with those of the petitioner or, for public bodies, judiciary or other organs of the State, in such a way as to mislead citizens looking for information regarding the activities of such institutions; (iii) the circumstance in which the domain name has been registered by the resistant with the primary aim of damaging a competitor's business, or of usurping the name and surname of the petitioner; (iv) the circumstance in which the domain name has been used with the intention of attracting Internet users, for the purpose of obtaining profit, giving rise to possible confusion with a name which is the subject of a right recognized or established by Italian or European Union Law or with the name of a public body; (v) the circumstance in which the registered domain name is a proper noun or name of a public or private body, and for which there is no demonstrable connection between the holder of the domain name and the registered domain name.

The above list is for the purposes of illustration and is not exhaustive.

The *Board of Experts* may also examine evidence of other examples of bad faith in the registration and use of a domain name.

891. A list of pending reassignation procedures and the decisions from previous procedures are publicized on the Registry's website and on the website of the DRS to which the deciding Board belongs except when, in exceptional cases (including those where the Board maintains that the publication of a decision might gravely damage the image of one or both of the parties to the dispute), the Board justifiably decides not to make the whole or part of a decision public (Regulation 3.11 of the regulations for the resolution of disputes in the cc TLD 'it')).

Part III. ICT Contracts

Chapter 1. Hardware Contracts

§1. Introduction

892. There are no special features peculiar to hardware-supply and leasing contracts (the latter now becoming less and less widespread in parallel with the steady decrease in hardware prices).

Without a specific legislative framework in place in Italy, these contracts are made to fall within the purview of the law regulating the sale of movable goods (Article 1470 and following Italian Civil Code), as well as their letting or renting (Article 1571 and following of the Italian Civil Code), and this law is made to operate in conjunction with integrations and exceptions provided for in the clauses of standardized contracts.[237]

These integrations and changes describe technical standards; hardware compatibility with different kinds of operating environments or software which the user may already have installed; time and mode of delivery, installation, testing and set-up; the characteristics needed for the places in which the product is to be installed; any additional obligations which the supplier is bound by (such as instructing personnel); and the terms and duration of the warranty designed to protect users in the event of malfunctions.

In addition to the provisions of above, if one of the parties can be considered as a 'consumer' and the other one can be qualified as a 'professional' by means of Article 3 and following of D.Lgs. 206/2005 (also known as the Italian Consumer Code), special rules for consumer's protection apply.[238]

893. Hardware procurement contracts and the mode of their performance are known to cause contention when it comes to establishing the exact moment of delivery to a customer. The forms used by large-scale suppliers (a practice that retailers are picking up fast on) carry a clause under which delivery is complete as soon as the equipment is deposited 'on the street-level ground floor' of the address of delivery, at which time liability for damage transfers from the supplier to the customer. This clause runs contrary to a well-established judicial line by which 'the obligation to deliver can be understood as fulfilled only when the buyer is put in a condition,

237. *See* E. Bonazzi & C. Triberti, *Guida ai contratti di informatica*, vol. 2, UNICOPLI, 2007.
238. *See* G. Finocchiaro, *I contratti ad oggetto informatico*, Padua, 1993.

not only to actually have the product placed in his or her property, but also to operate it according to its intended use'.[239] Plainly, a customer cannot begin to enjoy a hardware product before this product is installed – and, if need be, tested – and hence delivery cannot be understood to be complete any time before these activities are brought to completion.

The technical nature and complexity of hardware is such that the testing of any such product takes on a special importance in the performance of a hardware-supply contract.[240]

In this regard, it is generally the practice in contract-making to require that if the product is tested successfully, the customer and the tester underwrite a declaration by which the customer formally accepts the product's delivery and thereby relieves the supplier of all responsibility for any malfunctions at the time of delivery.

By contrast, if product testing fails, the supplier will have to take the measures necessary to enable the system software and hardware to run properly, and if these actions fail the customer will be fully entitled to request that the supplier replaces, free of charge, all the components necessary to make the machine operative, or that the price initially agreed is marked down if the machine is to be accepted as is.

894. Another delicate matter is how to proceed when writing into a contract the manufacturer's pledge to stand behind the product in the event of any malfunctioning. Computer-product suppliers like to limit these warranties by wedging into the contract a number of clauses that damage the consumer and violate the provisions set forth in Articles 1490 and following and 1512 of Italian Civil Code.

A study exposes a fact that is cause for concern, namely: some of the contracts used in this industry carry clauses that limit the supplier's warranty to an assurance that the product exhibits the technical specifications the supplier promised it would have, but expressly suppressing all other forms of warranty, so that any malfunctioning and any consequent product inoperability of any duration, as well as any unsuitability of the product for the use the customer is to make of it, are not covered.

Judicial precedents,[241] in the rare instances in which a decision has been made on the use and sale of computer systems, simply reiterate the legislation already in place to regulate any legal transaction or juridical act (act in the law), so that the supplier's liability is said to subsist only if the product's technical specifications as promised differ significantly from the specifications of the product as delivered.

895. Hardware-lease contracts, however, were once widespread but, on account of the steady fall in hardware prices, are no longer used much except to regulate transactions between the private sector and the Public Administration. For this reason, we will attend to this matter only briefly.

---

239. Cass. Civ., 22 Oct. 1995, no. 11234. The principle expressed has been confirmed in recent years also by Cass. Civ., 11 Sept. 2014, no. 19161.

240. *See* G. Finocchiaro & F. Delfini, *I contratti ad oggetto informatico*, Padua, 1993.

241. Cass. Civ., 15 June 2000, no. 8153.

This kind of contract falls under the purview of the legislation regulating the renting or letting of movable goods, which is modified – and, where possible, exceptions to it are made – by contracting parties acting in their autonomy as juridical persons. Here, too, it has become the practice to make wide use of standardized contracts and forms drawn up unilaterally by the lessor, and no particular interpretive issues emerge.[242]

The only sticking point is the terms and conditions to be built into the warranty and the lessor's consequent liability in the event of malfunctions that should impair the system's performance or even make it impossible for the lessee to use the system at all.

It is the contract-making practice here that limits warranties so that when any system component needs to be repaired or replaced – a task which our legislation on letting and renting entrusts to the lessor – a further contract takes effect: a maintenance and service contract that attaches to the main lease contract and sets out the agreement specific to this task.

242. *See* M.G. Losano, 'Le radici europee dell'elaboratore elettronico', *Le scienze*, no. 89, 1976 and G. Finocchiaro & F. Delfini, *I contratti ad oggetto informatico*, Padua, 1993.

Chapter 2. Software Contracts

§1. Licence Agreements

896. Under a software-licensing agreement, the author of a work sells irrevocably such rights as entitling a third party to use the work for an economic activity. As discussed in Chapter 2, these rights are currently regulated in detail under Article 64-*bis* and following of the author's rights (copyright) law as modified by Legislative Decree (D.Lgs.) no. 518/92.

These contracts have not taken a firm foothold in the industry, because the author of a software program (be it a big software house or a single entrepreneur or freelance programmer) does not stand to gain much by effecting a full transfer of the rights to the economic use of that program, for it typically takes a considerable investment and a great expenditure of resources to develop a software product.

Further, licence contracts have not come under any extensive legal study, the reason being that this type of economic arrangement, besides finding only a limited diffusion, is already regulated in large part by Law no. 633/41, on intellectual property, under Articles 107-111. Article 110 in this subset makes it necessary to have written evidence that a licence agreement has been made.

Even here in Italy, the expression *licenza d'uso* (the standard rendition of 'licence agreement') is now widely understood to designate those arrangements by which a licensor grants to a licensee (or end user) the right to use a software product, or a single copy of it, against the payment of a given sum.

897. Prior to this, without sufficiently specific legislation by which to regulate the use of software, and in view of the peculiar clauses written into standardized licence agreements, jurists in Italy had discussed at length how to frame such transactions: they would sometimes advance the thesis that these constitute a renting or letting, and less often a kind of sale.

The above-mentioned D.Lgs. no. 518/92 not only brings software within the group of intellectual property creations protected by copyright legislation but also works out in detail the exclusive rights that a copyright holder has over a software program as well as the use that can be made of this program. Now, in consequence of this piece of legislation, the question as to whether licensing is properly a letting/renting or a sale has lost much of its import. This is because the software licence agreement – given the content of Article 64-*bis* and following, and independently of the legal terminology chosen to designate it – is now largely regulated by the legislation in question (by D.Lgs. no. 518/92). Nevertheless, the question of the legal type with which to categorize licensing agreements, and so the question of the kind of regulation these agreements should be made subject to, does not effectively lose all its significance: the question comes into play should the contracting parties omit to specify an element essential to the arrangement, or should it become necessary to ascertain the validity of clauses limiting the licensor's liability or clauses making exceptions to warranty requirements as set out by legislation.

Considering that each licensing agreement takes as its object a single copy of the software program licensed, and that under a standard contract the licensee does not purchase the software but only acquires a title to its use, it seems best to assimilate the licence agreement to a letting or renting agreement (rather than to a sales contract). Consider, too, that the letting or renting contract scheme is often explicitly referred to in some of the forms used to execute a licence agreement.

898. In compliance with the Law on Copyright – Article 64-*bis* and the following, already discussed in the chapter on the legal protection of software – a software licence agreement enables the software's author to retain an exclusive right to make (full or partial and permanent or temporary) copies of the software; to translate, adapt or transform it; and to distribute it in any form. Users, on their part, are entitled to copy, translate, adapt and transform the program only to the extent that these activities are necessary to render the program functional according to its intended use; users can also make a backup copy of the program, but only if this is necessary to observe, study or test the program's operation.[243]

Moreover, it is standard business practice to integrate the content of these agreements with clauses designed to extend in various ways the rights reserved to the licensor, limiting at the same time the licensor's liability and duty to warrant the product.

We see this, for example, with the licensee's right to make copies of the software for private use in addition to the backup copy expressly authorized by law, and with this person's obligation to run the software on a single computer, often identified in the agreement itself. The licensor, however, is not bound by any liability or requirement to warrant the product for any errors or interruptions it may cause or if it proves unfit to meet the user's needs or to allow certain functions.

Furthermore, the licensee is generally prohibited from sub-licensing the program and from using it in any further way not specified in the agreement except with the licensor's prior written consent pursuant to Article 1594 c.c., by which a rent contract cannot be transferred to a third party without the renter's consent.

All the user can do in case a problem comes up is to request a refund in the amount paid for the licence, or request the defective software to be repaired or replaced, or again request the sum fixed in advance to cover the licensor's limited liability.

899. There is a kind of arrangement, called a shrink-wrap licence agreement, which is peculiar at least in what concerns its mode of creation, and which is specifically designed for the sale of standardized software.[244]

The agreement is called a shrink-wrap licence agreement because the product is shrink-wrapped in clear plastic so that the terms and conditions of use can be read before purchasing the product and without unpacking it. The first of such clauses cautions expressly that by opening the package you accept in full the licence agreement that follows. If you have purchased the product and do not accept the agreement, you must refrain from opening the package and hence return it promptly to the retailer or the software house requesting a full refund in the amount paid for the product.

243. *See* G. Finocchiaro & F. Delfini, *I contratti ad oggetto informatico*, Padua, 1993.

244. *See* Musti, 'Il contratto di licenza d'uso del software', *CeI*, no. 3, 1998 and D'Arrigo, 'Prospettive della c.d. 'licenza a strappo' nel nostro ordinamento', *Diritto informazione e informatica*, 1996.

Another clause, likewise appearing in print on the package, requires the purchaser to fill out a registration card and mail it to the manufacturer to get software updates and enjoy the warranty accorded. The same clause requires that the user, upon receiving the first update, destroys the software's previous version and accompanying documentation as well as any copy and modified versions made of the software.

Shrink-wrap agreements have been subject to question, especially in the past, with doubts cast on the notion that an agreement is validly accepted the moment someone tears open a package; another point was the purchaser's ability (or lack thereof) to reject any terms and conditions found inside the package and therefore undiscoverable before opening the package itself. Now judicial decision-making is overcoming these problems by seizing on general principles and criteria that allow a bona fide interpretation of contracts.[245]

§2. Software-Development Contracts

900. The expression 'software-development contract' designates a variety of transactions in business practice, so what ends up getting called by this name may be an arrangement that one can bring under the purview of contracting (giving out contract awards: *contratto d'appalto*) or under the purview of contracts for the performance of intellectual services (*contratto di prestazione d'opera intellettuale*).

The importance and complexity of software-development contracts suggests that we should consider the question by dealing in turn with:

(a) the object (purpose) and performance of the contract;
(b) its legal status or qualification;
(c) its possible defects of form or substance; and
(d) the ownership of the software developed.

901. (a) Object and Performance of the Contract: software-development contracts are framed to enable researching, designing and bringing out software tailored to the needs of a specific client.

The need to develop purpose-specific software suited to diverse and complex tasks is to account for one of the main features distinctive of this kind of contract, namely: the multiple interconnected phases it builds and the collaboration that in varying degrees it sets up between client and developer.

Thus, for example, if a company needs a software program to automate the management of its inventory, the contractor, in collaboration with the client, will have to analyse the flow of merchandise in and out of the warehouse and identify the problems involved in this activity. The contractor will work out a range of design solutions and, always according to the client's response, will proceed to develop, instal, and test-run the software commissioned and finally train the client's personnel to use the new system.

245. Cass. Civ., 11 Sept. 2014 no. 19161.

Specifically, there will be an initial project phase in which the client explains its needs to the software house, which in turn will undertake to give such specifications a technical rendering, thereby outlining in rough form a number of possible solutions.

The client will thus be able to evaluate the solutions proposed and instruct the software house to pursue a given direction; the two will then collaborate in drawing up the project that will become the object of a second phase.

In phase three, the software house, after obtaining from the client all the authorizations necessary to go ahead with the project, will develop the software according to the technical and functional specifications agreed upon.

Lastly, in phase four – implementation – the software previously developed is installed on the client's computer system and tested, and the personnel is trained to use the program.

Commercial practice is such that, given the complexity involved in performing software-development contracts, the parties generally agree to write into the contract, for each project phase, a work-plan that sets out in detail the steps to be undertaken in the course of the phase in question, along with deadlines and with technical and functional specifications describing the software's constituent modules. These phase-specific agreements will become integral to the main contract and play a vital role should any disagreement emerge as to the manner of performing the contract.

902. (b) The Contract's Legal Standing: the contract scheme which a software-development contract ought to be brought under will depend in large measure on the characteristics of the party who undertakes to develop the software in question. Indeed if this party is an entrepreneur, the contract will be brought under the purview of contracting legislation (*appalto*) and hence will be regulated by Article 1655 and following of the Italian Civil Code, but if this party is a private person, the relationship can be framed, at this person's choice, as either a contracting enterprise or a performance of intellectual services, in which case the contract will be regulated by Article 2230 and following of the Italian Civil Code.

Here, in default of a specific agreement by the parties, the contract will look like a contracting transaction (*contratto d'appalto*) set up as a business venture and as a performance of intellectual services if the contract is performed by a single programmer doing the bulk of the work.

As we will see shortly, immediate consequences follow depending on whether the contract is looked upon as a contracting transaction or as a performance of intellectual services: the developer will incur different obligations and will therefore be subject to different kinds of responsibility.

Thus, a contract awarded under a contracting scheme (*contratto d'appalto*) is goal-oriented, namely obliging the contractor (*appaltatore*) to achieve a certain result and put through for the client a given project. In a contract for the performance of intellectual services, by contrast, the developer (*prestatore d'opera*) pledges exclusively to make every effort to achieve the result specified and is not bound to succeed in this as well.

903. (c) Contract Defects: as was noted earlier, it is often only by approximation, and with a margin of vagueness, that software-development contracts can set out the software solution to be developed: this is due to the difficulty in confronting the client for an accurate description to the developer of the problems to be solved, combined with the developer's interest in keeping the object of the contract as indefinite as possible, so as to have an escape route in the event of a failure to deliver on the promise made.

Plainly, indeed, in absence of contract documentation setting out accurately the object of the contract, the client will be in difficulty to subsequently challenge the developer on any alleged failure of consideration: the developer can always take up the line of defence that what is actually to account for the alleged failure is an insufficiently circumscribed description of the client's needs, or that no express guarantee was ever made that the software would meet the client's specific needs.

Judicial decision-makers – when faced with the objective difficulties involved in setting out criteria for assessing claims of failure of consideration in this kind of contract – are generally minded to invoke the general principles of the legal system relative to proper conduct and good faith.

The responsibilities the developer incurs for faulty performance are weaved tightly with the transaction-type the contract in question must fall under.

In particular, when the commitment undertaken by the software house can be subsumed under the transaction-type relative to contracting, it will be necessary to refer to the legislative provisions on failure of consideration and non-performance, set out in Articles 1667 and 1668 of the Italian Civil Code. These state that the client, to take advantage of a contract warranty, must appraise the developer of the non-performance no later than sixty days since its discovery and must act on the claim within two years of receiving the product. Moreover, the same provisions state as well that the warranty is not due if the client accepted the product delivered or was aware of the non-performance involved, or was in a condition to come to know of it, except if the developer, acting in bad faith, failed to disclose such non-performance.

When, however, the contract must be subsumed under a scheme for the performance of intellectual services, it will be necessary to refer to the legislative provisions specific to this scheme, namely, Article 2236 of the Italian Civil Code, which states the following: if the performance in question makes it necessary to overcome complex technical difficulties, the vendor (*prestatore d'opera*) will not be held accountable for any damages consequent on faulty performance, except where intentional wrongdoing or gross negligence are involved.

Considering that software-development contracts always make it rather easy to prove the special complexity of the duties assumed, we may well understand how these contracts, making specific reference to Article 2236 of the Italian Civil Code, often enable the developer to elude all sorts of liability.

Returning now to the case of a software-development contract subsumable under contract work or service delivery (*appalto d'opera o di servizi*), we will need to look at the rather recurrent question of latent defects.

Article 1667 of the Italian Civil Code states that a client's free acceptance of a product relieves the contractor of liability solely for patent defects (discoverable by reasonable inspection), and not for latent ones.

This provision acquires special relevance with software contracts, for it is widely known among computer users that a flaw in a software program (a 'bug', in computer lingo) will often surface only a long time after the program is first installed (and perhaps tested).

Here, the first problem peculiar to software-development contracts is the need to establish what has to be considered as a latent defect, and consequently under what circumstances the software house or contractor, despite obtaining the client's acceptance of a product after the product was tested, continues to be liable towards the client for any flaws or deformities from standard operation that should make the software partly or completely inadequate to meet the client's needs.

Second, judicial decisions have adopted the view according to which all defects must be found latent that cannot be discovered by anyone not specifically trained in computer science and programming, that is, by the layperson.[246]

Here, the client, in compliance with the general provisions on contract law set forth in the Italian Civil Code, will be entitled to request a product or service equal to what was agreed on, or else to request a price reduction; again, the client will be entitled to rescind the contract if the flaw or discrepancy involved is such that it renders the product completely inadequate for its purpose.

904. (d) Ownership of the Software: another aspect of software-development contracts worthy of fuller consideration is the ownership of or title to their copyright (or author's right), in view of the fact that the user/client and developer/contractor are both generally interested in securing such ownership (or title) with the exclusion of the other party.

The client has every interest in obtaining this exclusively, thereby recouping some of the expenses incurred in the process of getting the software developed. By securing exclusive ownership, the client can license the product to others or simply turn to advantage the competitive edge consequent to his right to be the only one to use the software solution developed specifically to facilitate the same client's activity.

The software house, on its part, will try to retain a privilege to exploit the economic opportunities afforded by the know-how acquired in the course of the complex development activity undertaken for the client, using this know-how as a knowledge base for future marketable software solutions worked out for other clients.

The end result of this conflict of interests varies widely from contract to contract and is largely dependent on the bargaining power that each party has.[247] Thus, the parties may agree that the software's owner – the one entitled to exploit the program economically – is the client; or else a client having title to those rights may agree that the contractor, too, can exploit the program economically, both parties making a mutual commitment to recognize each other's royalties.

Lastly, the parties may agree that the client is entitled only to use the program and, to the contractor's benefit, shall waive every other right.

---

246. Cass. Civ., 7 June 2017, no. 14199 and Cass. Civ., 22 Nov. 2013, no. 26233.
247. T.A.R. Roma, 21 Mar. 2017 no. 3742.

Chapter 3. Turnkey Contracts

§1. Contracts for the Supply of Information Systems

905. The supply of computer systems is effected under a complex contract scheme – encompassing hardware supply, licensing and software development – through which one party undertakes to deliver to another a hardware system and a software solution that are jointly adequate to meet the client's specific needs.

This type of contract, though in wide use, raises delicate questions as to how to proceed when establishing its legal standing or qualification, its content and the specific obligations undertaken by the supplier.

The reason why these questions have become an issue is that suppliers have a practice of splitting up their obligation (to supply a turnkey information system) into a number of separate agreements each having its own consideration and object, most often circumscribed only in rough approximation.

This way, if the supplier should fail to comply with some or all of the obligations incurred under any one of the separate agreements, and even if, as is often the case, such non-performance prevents the client from using the entire computer system, the client will then have little chance of terminating the other agreements made, and hence little chance of getting a refund.

Even so, judicial decision has begun, albeit timidly, to recognize the unity of the contract-type on which contracts for the supply of information systems are based, so that when a failure to perform one agreement makes the entire system inoperable, there is then a valid ground for terminating all the other standing agreements made with the supplier.

In other words, judicial decision holds that the separate agreements made are to be understood as functionally connected: while each agreement retains its autonomous object, the agreements collectively have the joint purpose of effecting and regulating a single economic undertaking.

It follows from this that every defect affecting a single agreement (invalidity, inefficacy, termination, etc.) will affect the other agreements as well, by virtue of the Latin precept *simul stabunt, simul cadent.*

Moreover, always according to judicial decisions – because an information system is not simply a collection of items and devices sold separately, but is rather, from the standpoint of the contractual relationship, an articulated and indivisible whole – the contract-type in question comes into being by way of an 'objective connection', meaning a connection independent of the parties' will and hence not susceptible to being eliminated even by an express manifestation of an intent to do so.

The recognition of this connection of negotiation often proves to be decisive in these contracts when it comes to protecting the client from contract defects or non-performance on the part of the contractor.

If the information system provided by the supplier proves inadequate to meet the client's requirements as set out in the agreements made, the client will be in a position to challenge the supplier for failure to attain the promised results, and hence for failure to perform the overall contract, consequently earning a legitimate claim to termination and damages.

§2. SYSTEMS-INTEGRATION CONTRACTS

906. The systems-integration contract is among the most recent, albeit already dated, kinds of information-system contract to have been used in business practice in Italy.

Systems-integration contracts are complex because they are marked by the concurrence of different elements distinctive of several of the other information-system contracts previously looked at. Chief among these elements are software development and licensing and the sale and renting or letting of hardware and information systems.

Systems integration, the object of this contract-type, consists of building to client specification an information system (or part of one) and enabling specific functions based on the joint operation of user and system provider.

As was seen to be the case with software-development contracts, here, too, a correct performance of the agreements made cannot stand free of the parties' continuing collaboration, because only the client is in a position to fully know the needs that have to be satisfied and the exact functions and technical specifications of the software and hardware components already in place.

The legal nature of systems-integration contracts is also related to that of software-development contracts (a connection that will shortly be found to exist with outsourcing contracts as well). Namely, judicial decision is bent on bringing these transactions, too, under the scheme of contracting, to such an extent that in the Anglo-Saxon systems, contracting transactions are made subject to a 'no pass, no pay' guarantees and hence to the regulatory framework of turnkey contracts.

This (again in connection with what was previously observed about software-development contracts) seems unassailable since we have again a widely established business practice to formalize the overall contract by underwriting a set of separate agreements each taking a purpose and object of its own.

Thus, even without an express statement by the parties, these constituent agreements must all be understood to have a functional connection (and even a genealogical one in given circumstances) and to be collectively framed to enable the parties to exhaustively set out the terms of their relationship, a relationship born of the very need to achieve a concrete result established in advance, namely systems integration.

Because of a substantial similarity with reference to the legal issues involved in the different stages that make up the performance of a systems-integration contract (from setting out system specifications to final testing), it seems best to consider these stages by looking at what was previously said about software-development contracts, especially with regard to copyright ownership, system implementation and customization, and the need to establish at the outset, in an accurate and analytic fashion, the criteria the parties will be guided by throughout the course of their relationship under the contract.

Chapter 4. Maintenance Contracts

§1. Maintenance and Servicing Contracts

907. Contracts designed for the maintenance and servicing of hardware, and even more so of software, have become fundamentally important in commercial practice and now figure prominently among investments of businesses operating in the information technology sector.

As we will see shortly, the expression 'maintenance and service contracts' actually designates, from a strictly legal standpoint, contract-types that take a wide range of different objects.

As has been stated effectively, 'maintenance services represent, for the user, the basic way to get the most out of the investment made. For the supplier, on the other hand, after sale services are double-edged: they make up a formidable promotional tool, but when problems and dissatisfaction arise, they become a source of endless inconveniences and controversies, such that some can tarnish the product's image and future marketability'.[248]

Now, the different kinds of maintenance offered in these contracts can be compared by drawing a distinction between static or corrective maintenance, on the one hand, and dynamic or ameliorative maintenance, on the other.

The first category comprises what is known as 'debugging', meaning by this all those activities aimed to rid a software program of its flaws and necessary to bring the product in line with the technical and functional standards originally represented to the user, client and purchaser; the second category takes in all the activities designed to modify, update and improve the program, enabling functions not originally represented which prove necessary only later or which clients later demand to meet the changed needs.

Contract-making practice in Italy has spawned a wide variety of forms by which maintenance and service can be delivered. These include over-the-phone assistance, access to specially designed local or remote diagnostic programs and, for problems of a more serious nature, even on-site assistance parallel to that guaranteed with the purchase of traditional, old-economy products.

Maintenance often makes it necessary to change or integrate a program's source code.

908. As it is known, however, and as was previously observed while discussing the legal protection of software, save a few exceptions set out in the law, there can be no intervention on a source code without a prior express authorization by its author, or by the copyright holder of the program involved.

This requirement comes into force with dynamic or ameliorative maintenance even more than with corrective maintenance.

This is to be accounted for by looking at Italy's copyright law (as amended by D.Lgs. 518/1992). Article 64-*ter* of this law, on static maintenance, says that the end

248. *See* C. Rossello, I contratti dell'informatica nella nuova disciplina del software, Milan, 1997.

user of a particular software program need not seek any authorization from the program's copyright holder to undertake the activities specified under the foregoing:

> Article 64-*bis*, letters *a* and *b*. Now, these activities include not only loading the program and its copyright notice but also changing the source code if the program does not otherwise 'enable the functions it was designed to enable […] including among these the fixing of errors'.

On the mainstream interpretation of this provision, corrective maintenance is an activity instrumental and necessary to safeguard the user's right to keep using the program for what it was meant to do.

Another legal aspect that has practical import is the difficulty involved in sorting out whether corrective maintenance falls under the purview of the main contract or makes up an object of its own under one of the separate agreements.

909. A further legal question closely bound up with maintenance contracts is the disclosure of the source code. For, as it often turns out, the user's formally recognized right to intervene (or get others to intervene) in the program stands the risk of being undermined by non-disclosure of the source code.

In fact, as previously observed, under Article 64-*quater* of our copyright law (an article brought into force by D.Lgs. 518/92), there is a single exceptional circumstance that allows a licensee to lift a copyright holder's exclusive access to a software program's decompilation data and that is if such data prove indispensable to obtaining information necessary to effect the interoperability of an autonomously created computer program, and only as long as the following conditions are met:

(a) the said activities are undertaken by the licensee, or by others entitled to use a copy of the program, or by someone acting on their behalf, or by someone authorized to this end;
(b) the data necessary to effect interoperability is not already immediately accessible by the subjects indicated at point (a) above;
(c) the said activities are confined to those parts of the original program where intervention is necessary to obtain interoperability.

The need to obviate this problem has given place in recent years to the practice of writing into licensing and software-development contract (and others like them) clauses by which the program's source code must be deposited with a notary public or with a third person selected by agreement of the parties.

Chapter 5. Facilities-Management Contracts

§1. Contracts for Outsourcing Information Systems

910. This contract-type is rather widespread in commercial and corporate practice. Under this arrangement, the provider of a computer service assumes the responsibility of managing for a corporate client an appreciably articulated series of information-system processes and procedures not directly pertaining to the client's core business but instrumental to it.

A number of reasons may compel outsourcing the management of a business' information system. For example, there may be a need to improve IT services, to streamline a business activity dependent on such services or, for example, to develop and offer to clients new products and services that renders it necessary to manage the company's information system more efficiently and competitively than through insourcing.

These goals are pursued in commercial and corporate practice in Italy by recourse to outsourcing schemes that differ from one another in several respects and yet, as will be seen shortly, can be made to fall juridically within the same negotiation category. These schemes are respectively called 'simple outsourcing', 'transfer outsourcing', 'joint-venture outsourcing' and 'group outsourcing'.

In simple outsourcing, the management of a company's computer system is contracted out, in whole or in part, to a computer-service provider (or vendor). In transfer outsourcing, an entire sector of a company's activity and assets (computer systems, personnel, contracts, etc.) are turned over to a vendor entrusted (under an outsourcing contract) with providing the computer services connected with that activity. In joint-venture outsourcing, a computer-system sector is turned over to a joint-venture entity set-up for the express purpose of running that sector; in line with the joint-venture scheme, the client and the vendor share the capital of the entity in question. In group outsourcing, finally, the information-system services are turned over to a company entirely owned by the customer.

911. As noted earlier, the element common to all these types of agreements is their object, namely, the task of managing a company's computer system. In the Italian legal system, a long-winded process of jurisprudential debate and judicial decision has established that outsourcing contracts should generally be made to fall under the contract-service scheme (*appalto di servizi*).[249]

Under this scheme, the service provider is typically entrusted with overseeing all of the customer's computer operations and tasks, which range from managing and maintaining all applications and operating systems to designing, developing, implementing and running the entire information system.

The very amplitude and heterogeneity of the objects these contracts can take is such that it is often hard to establish exactly the scope of the duties incurred by a service provider who enters a contract of this kind.

---

249. Cass. Civ., 2 Oct. 2006, no. 21287.

912. Another aspect peculiar to outsourcing contracts is that the parties, in the process of drawing up a contract, will need to describe as accurately as they can a set of minimum standards for the services to be provided, for only this way will it be possible to make an accurate assessment as to whether the service provider is meeting its obligations under the contract fully.

Indeed, absent such provisions, the amplitude and heterogeneity of the contract's object will generally make it difficult for the customer to challenge the service provider for non-compliance.

The characteristics peculiar to the object of an outsourcing contract affect the ways (now widely established in commercial practice) through which a monetary value is assigned to the contract's consideration. The customer is generally required to remit to the service provider a payment consisting of a fixed sum established in advance (but which can be adjusted, within a given range, to the ups and downs of the currency's purchasing power) and a variable sum anchored to the 'amount' of service performed.

913. A final characteristic peculiar to outsourcing contracts is their long duration. This is because turning over an entire corporate sector or function to a service provider is a process difficult to undo, entailing as it does a radical shakeup of the outsourcing company.

This is the case especially with the specific outsourcing contracts in question (the kinds whose object is an information-system service) and that is due to the all-encompassing nature of the services entrusted to the provider as well as to the extreme delicacy of such tasks and to the responsibility that comes with them.

The same consideration explains the central role that rescinding clauses play in this kind of outsourcing contract.

The client company's main objective (even when its relations with the service provider get strained) is often to ensure the contract's performance rather than to cause the contract to be cancelled. Indeed, any break in the client/vendor relationship can slow down and even suspend the computer services provided and therefore impair significantly the client company's ability to function efficiently.

Rescission is here going to be a measure of last resort, and the contract clauses relative to it must regulate accurately the post-contract phase, too, in which the service provider is required to cooperate in passing its know-how and responsibilities on to the client's newly selected provider, or must work directly with the client if the client should decide to take back under its own responsibility the previously outsourced services.

Chapter 6. Network Services

§1. Internet and Network Services

914. This is a category that has as its object heterogeneous services, which have in common the employment of the Internet. Among the contracts that have these services as their object, the Internet access contract is particularly relevant: not only does it constitute the necessary premise to make use of every other service available online but also does it usually includes a series of accessory services of great utility for the user. With the contract in question a certain supplier, denominated 'service provider' or more generically 'provider', guarantees the user a connection to the Internet network.

In commercial practice, it is possible to identify Internet access contacts at both definite and indefinite times, with the consideration commensurate to the connection length or otherwise *forfait* (lump sum), namely a fixed price independent of the length of the connection. The connection is usually performed through the phone network, but more evolved services can also be accomplished through other means (optical fibres, satellite networks, etc.). Usually the user has to endow himself with an adequate device that allows the connection to the Internet (for example, a modem); sometimes this is supplied by the provider in free loan for use, therefore with a separate and accessory agreement that binds the user only to the restitution of this good once the Internet access contract is terminated.

Among the further services that are usually rendered by the provider is the allotment of one or more e-mail accounts and the concession of a space on the server to manage messages. Not infrequently, there is concession of a further space that the user can employ to create one or more web pages. Generally, the quantity of space supplied by the provider is not unlimited but determined in the contract. Other services can include software download, database consultation, employment of online tools for the creation of web pages, access to discussion groups, to chat rooms and so on. Such services can be the object of separate contacts, whether these are made with the same provider of the Internet access or with other network operators.

915. Since the Italian legislature has not provided a specific regulation on the matter of network services, the interpreter will have to identify from time to time the contractual type among those that the Civil Code disciplines that fits the specific service best. In order to do this, the interpreter will principally consider the characteristic performance supplied with the contract, namely, the main duty of the debtor. If, then, to take an example from the services cited beforehand, a party pledges to supply software through the Internet to the other by rendering it available to download on its website, the contract will be regulated according to provisions on software use licence or sale[250] and not on contract work. Here the relevant performance is the sale or enjoyment of possession of a good – the software – while the access to the supplier's site and the download service represent only the means

250. *See* para. 2 in this chapter.

through which the parties perform the contract and are therefore irrelevant for the purpose of the legal categorization of the agreement.

916. If identifying the characteristic performance of a service offered through the Internet can seem quite easy, it is not always simple to include the legal act in a determined contractual type. For example, regarding Internet access contracts, Italian jurists are divided between those that consider only the provisions on contract work applicable[251] (Article 1655 and following of the Italian Civil Code) and those who consider the provisions on supply contracts[252] (Article 1559 and following of the Italian Civil Code) concurrent to and also prevailing over contract work provisions. This last stance, in particular, identified in the juridical act in question a duration performance (since the provider is the subject that has to ensure the user the connection to the network for the whole length of the contract), typical of supply contracts and not of contract work. This thesis would be confirmed by the mention in Article 1677 of the Italian Civil Code of provisions on supply contracts, which should prevail with respect to any other provision due the enactment in Article 1570 of the Italian Civil Code: 'The provisions that regulate the contract to which the single performances correspond, apply also to supply contracts, since they are compatible with the foregoing provisions.' According to this section, it would be pointless to oppose the fact that the supply contract has as its object only the supply of things (Article 1559 of the Italian Civil Code) and thus it does not include the performance of *facere* (doing) services, typical of the provider. This technical obstacle could be easily circumvented by considering the technological evolution that would allow the interpreter to include in the notion both the product (*opus*) and the service.[253]

917. According to the first stance, instead, the Internet access contract should be regulated only by the provisions on contract work, since the main obligation of the provider consists of supplying the user those services that are peculiar to his organization,[254] a fact that would explicitly recall the definition of contract work contained in Article 1655 of the Italian civil code, according to which '[..] *a party assumes, with the necessary organization of means* [..], *the accomplishment of a work or a service* [..]'. It should be concluded, thus, that also the main accessory services fall under the regulation that is typical of contract work since they are part of the provider's organizational structure. Therefore, to return to the previous example, the service through which the provider renders available to the user a space on the server to manage e-mail or to create a website would not frame a lease contract with a portion of the provider's hard disk as its object, but a service delivery contract.[255] For this purpose it is claimed that the provider holds at all times the control of his hard disk – not delivering any good to the user, as it is instead

251. L. Albertini, I contratti di accesso ad internet, in Giust. Civ., 1997, II; G. De Nova, I contratti di accesso ad internet, in AIDA, 1996.
252. The most recent is D. Bocchini, *Il contratto di accesso ad internet*, in *Diritto dell'informazione e dell'informatica*, Giuffrè 2003, n. 3, p. 471 e segg.
253. Ibid., 475.
254. *See* G. De Nova, *I contratti di accesso ad internet*, in AIDA, 1996, 42.
255. Trib. Roma, 23 Nov. 1998.

requested by provisions on lease contracts – and that the characteristic performance consists exclusively of guaranteeing access to e-mail or the introduction of the website into the Internet, therefore in supplying a service.[256]

918. Leaving aside the juridical qualification of the contract in question, those clauses that exonerate the provider from any liability with regard to the contents put online by the user deserve particular attention.

With such clauses, indeed, the supplier aims at safeguarding himself from possible third parties' claims in case the information spread through his services are illicit or violate other people's rights.

Even if their validity and effectiveness has been long discussed, these clauses now find support in Decree 9 April 2003, n. 70, that implements Directive 31/2000/CE on electronic commerce.

The ordinance in question, in Articles 14, 15 and 16, allows the provider to exert his role of mere intermediary with respect to the illicit activities carried out by the user and the consequent liability towards damaged third parties. It is understood that the user has a duty, due to the mentioned clauses, to indemnify the provider both in substance and in procedure against any claim.

Still, the validity of those contractual settlements that provide the faculty for the supplier to remove without advance notice the contents put online by the user that are considered illicit – therefore to carry out, in effect, censorship – has to be assessed.

Except in the case of blatant unlawfulness of the information and due to the silence of Legislative Decree 70/2003 on this point, it is suggested here that the general principles of contractual good faith (Article 1375 of the Italian Civil Code) and of fair behaviour (Article 1175 of the Italian Civil Code) should operate: the provider should, therefore, give advance notice to the user of the supposed unlawfulness of the information, in order to let him produce evidence against it.

Otherwise, if the content put online should prove to be illicit – for example, after a judicial investigation – the provider could be held to compensate the damage, for having infringed his contractual duties. Recent case law is still oriented to this point.[257] In fact, as confirmed by the Italian Supreme Court, the responsibility of the service providers, unlike content providers, applies only on an exceptional basis. The formers will continue not to be responsible for content uploaded by users, unless such providers, having become aware of the illegal nature of the content, upon communication from the competent authorities, do not act immediately to remove the information or to disable access.[258]

---

256. *See* G. De Nova, *I contratti di accesso ad internet*, in AIDA, 1996, 43.
257. Tribunale Milano, 18 June 2018.
258. Cass. Civ., 2016, no. 54946.

Chapter 7. Government Contracts

§1. Introduction

919. The administration 'in substantial sense', as juridical activity aimed at the care of public interests, expresses itself through contracts of common law.[259]

In the common administrative experience, the contracts through which the administration assures certain performances (supply provision, services distribution, etc.), by third parties, for the payment of sums of money, emerge as instruments of substantial administration.

920. The area of contracts, in the ambit of the administrative activity, represents a very wide area. The contracts of Public Administrations, in their phases of formation, execution and successive and possible contentious episodes, show a regulation that greatly differs from one of the analogous common-law contracts stipulated between private parties.

921. The relevant statutory provisions are contained in the following statutes:

- Royal decree (R.D.) no. 2440/1923, containing provisions on the administration of the capital and general accountancy of the State.
- R.D. no. 827/1924, containing provisions for the execution of the statute on the administration of the capital and general accountancy of the State.
- D.Lgs. no. 39/ 1993, containing provisions on the matter of informational automatized systems of Public Administrations.
- Law (L.) no. 537/1993, containing provisions on public contracts.
- D.Lgs. no. 82/2005, also known as 'Codice dell'amministrazione digitale', containing provisions on the digitalization of the Italian Public Administration.
- D.L. no. 83/2012 ('Urgent Measures for the Growth of the Country') containing, among others, the institution of the 'Agenzia per l'Italia Digitale', the Italian Agency for digitalization.
- L. no. 208/2015, also known as 'Legge di stabilità 2016' containing provisions on the formation of the annual and multi-annual State budget.
- D.Lgs. no. 50/2016, also known as 'nuovo Codice dei contratti pubblici' containing provisions on public contracts.

922. The purchase of goods and services by the Public Administration requires, with priority, the identification of the most adequate procedure, under the profiles of inexpensiveness, efficiency and efficacy, to adopt in the specific purchase.

These statutory provisions set out a framework that addresses both the 'procedural' phase of public procurements (resolution to negotiate, choice of the contracting party, award, with the related phases of approval and control) and their 'contractual' phase (namely all those acts that begin with the stipulation of the contract and end with the performance or non-performance of contractual duties).

---

259. *See* A. Sandulli 1953; P. Michiara 1997; E. Santoro 1999; G. Corso 2010.

923. The procedure when a Public Administration plans to purchase supplies and services from the market, in the specific case of informational nature, can be usefully analysed by referring to the provisions of D.Lgs. no. 50/2016 and of R.D. no. 827/1924.

Preliminarily, it is convenient to recall Article 37 of the R.D. no. 827/1924 which provides that all contracts from which a revenue or an expenditure of the State derive have to be preceded by public auctions and possibly divided in lots, when this division appears advantageous. The Royal Decree provides cases in which it is possible to proceed to a private bidding (Articles 38, 39), to a competition contract work (Article 40) and finally to contracts with private negotiation (Article 41).

924. The main procedures of award and consigning, provided by D.Lgs. no. 50/2016, are the following:

(a) open procedure (public auction) – Article 60;
(b) restricted procedure (private bidding and contract competition work) – Article 61;
(c) negotiated procedure (private negotiation) – Article 63.

925. (a) The open procedure can be defined as the award procedure in which every interested enterprise can formulate an offer. Among the points in favour of the choice of this procedure is the wider participation of competitors. This should guarantee strong competition, with consequent advantages for the administration. Under the operational profile 'a self-selection' between the potential competitors occurs on the basis of the minimum requirements provided for the participation in the competition and on the basis of a careful evaluation made by each competitor of the ability of accomplishing the object of the competition. Another aspect in favour is in the higher speed of the procedure, since, usually, a single commission is nominated to proceed to the comparison of the offers and the award. Article 3 of R.D. 2440/1923 requires public auctions for active contracts of the Public Administration. Passive contracts (for the purchase of supplies or performances of services) may adopt the restricted procedure.

The auction notice is similar to an 'invitation to make an offer' (Cass. S.U., 10 July 1956, no. 2551). With this, the Public Administration binds itself to observe, in the course of the competition, a certain standard procedure and delimits the object and the essential conditions of the future contract. The call, indeed, has to indicate the main characteristics of the contract, the type of procedure that will be followed for the award, the requirements to be admitted to the competition and the method of fulfilment of these requirements necessary for admission to the tender. The award represents the closing act of the procedure for the selection of the individual contracting party and takes place through the minutes with which the administration discloses the most advantageous offer and assigns the contract work to the best bidder. The award has the nature of an administrative act, through which the winner is ascertained and the relationship of consideration between the winner and the administration is made, on the basis of the mutual duties set out by statutes, specifications and terms of the competition. The award 'is not merely a preparatory act of the successive negotiation; it is instead the closing act of the whole procedure of the competition with which the Public Administration expresses its will to create, by adhering to the offer received, that determined juridical tie' (Corte Conti, 14 April 1988, no. 1930; Cass. 17 June 1991, no. 6846).

926. (b) The restricted procedures (private bidding and competition contract work) can be defined as procedures of award preceded by a phase of preselection carried out on the basis of the technical, economic and financial capabilities of the competitors. Only the enterprises invited by the awarding administration can make an offer. In the private bidding, the goods or service object of the competition is, usually, precisely identified in all its features, in the competition contract documentation. The object of the competition is outlined in its essential elements, and the competitors have the onus to offer detailed technical projects, pointing out the conditions and prices at which they are willing to perform the contract work. The restricted procedure is adopted where the administration needs 'the collaboration of firms considered particularly adequate to realize projects that, for their technical, artistic and scientific complexity or novelty, require a deeper knowledge and a more refined inventive or constructive ability'. (Cons. Giust. Amm. 7 Jan. 1987, no. 1). The private bidding is a competition in which only those who have been expressly invited by the administration may participate, who fulfil certain requirements, after a preliminary and discretionary choice. It takes place through the formulation, by the invited enterprises, of secret biddings. The administration chooses the offer that most satisfies the criterion it has chosen itself. In the private bidding, in place of the call for bids, the opening act of the procedure is the invitation, which has the same content as the call but is addressed to specific receivers.

The competition contract work is a procedure of a licensing kind, during which the various offers of projects are evaluated, and one of them chosen, with reference to the public interest that is being addressed in the specific case.

Participation in the competition contract work is usually restricted, on the basis of invitations; however it can also be open, but this happens very rarely. The procedure of comparing competition contract work is a procedure with discretionary content and a strong technical component. The comparative evaluation of the offers that have arrived, made by a commission appointed by the administration, 'has to be done both under the economic profile, with regard to the capability and reliability of the competitors; and with reference to the firm compliance of the results emerged from the competition with the pursued purposes'. (Cons. St., V, 26 Oct. 1987, no. 656). The moment of the stipulation of the contract remains autonomous with respect to the procedure aimed at the identification of the best offer, while the contractual tie is born with the stipulation of the contract.

927. (c) The negotiated procedure (private negotiation) can be defined as the consignment procedure during which the awarding administration consults the enterprises it has chosen itself and negotiates the terms of the contract with one or more of them. The formation of the contract, in this case, instead of occurring through an administrative procedure aimed at choosing the contracting party, takes place through private negotiation, namely according to common law. The negotiation is provided by the legislation in force as an exceptional method of formation of the contract. It is allowed in the following cases:

- if the auction is deserted;
- if the object of the contract has such peculiarities, under the technical-productive profile, that it allows the exclusive consideration of several specific firms;
- if there are such reasons of urgency that 'the delay of auctions and biddings cannot be tolerated';
- in any other case in which there are special and exceptional circumstances, due to which the forms of the competition cannot be followed.

This procedure is characterized by the broad discretionary power that the administration has.

928. The administration that is negotiating will form its will through types of proceedings that require that the reasons which induced the administration to start negotiation are made clear, making an external process of syndication possible.

This phenomenon is 'public evidence', by which, the formation of the administration's will has to consist of at least one act of an administrative nature that emphasizes the reasons for the contractual operation that is being undertaken, even if that is in the contractual matter itself, in order to allow external control.

929. The contract, even if stipulated through private negotiation, always finds its source in an administrative act with which the contract project, as well as the method that has to be followed for the choice of the contracting third party (namely the resolution to negotiate), is set out.

The resolution to negotiate is a programmatic act and represents the premise of the effective contractual proceeding. In the relationships with third parties, indeed, since it is a programmatic act, it is considered internal (Cass. Civ., 30 Oct. 1987, no. 8010 and Cass. Civ., 19 Nov. 2014, no. 24654). As specified by the Consiglio di Stato: 'a resolution to negotiate does not have to be necessarily and previously manifested in a determined formal act' (Cons. St., VI, 29 July 1991, no. 492).

930. The procedures end with the stipulation of the contract, the layout of which is already known to both the winning subject and the other participants to the competition. Public procurement contracts require written form; otherwise they are void. The contract that embodies the agreement between the Public Administration and the winner to constitute and regulate the economic and juridical relationship between them, related to the contract work that is the object of the award procedure, has to comply with the essential requirements of the statutory provisions. The contract can be drafted online, according to Article 44 of D.Lgs. 50/2016.

§2. INFORMATIONAL CONTRACTS

931. The purchase of informational goods and services in the public ambit is subject to special regulation, partially repealing the provisions on the general accountancy of the State and the provisions that regulate the purchase of goods and services by Public Administrations in general. This regulation is contained in D.Lgs. no. 82/05, D.L. no. 83/2012 and L. no. 208/2015.

932. In addition to the contracting administration, the other subjects involved in public contracts procedures are principally: (i) AgID and (ii) CONSIP Spa.

933. (i) According to Article 19 D.L. no. 83/2012, AgID is subject to the supervision of the President of the Council of Ministers, the Minister of Economy and Finance, the Minister for Public Administration and Simplification, the Minister of Economic Development and the Minister of Education, University and Research.

As far as concerns public contracts, AgID prepares the three-year plan (hereinafter also 'the Plan') for information technology in Public Administration that is approved by the President of the Council of Ministers (i.e., the current three-year plan is between 2017 and 2019).[260] The Plan contains, for each administration or category of administrations, the list of IT and connectivity goods and services and related costs, divided into expenses to be incurred for innovation and expenses for current operations, identifying also the goods and services whose acquisition is of particular strategic importance.[261]

The purpose of the Plan is to suggest a technical-organizational solution to cope with the information needs, upon evaluation of the costs, benefits and risks related to the performance of the contract. This offers, in a preventive way, useful elements for the layout and the effective possibility of realization of a project of informatization. The Plan, therefore, constitutes the fundamental tool for service innovation and rationalization of the ICT expenditure in the Public Administration.[262]

934. (ii) According to Article 20 paragraph 4 D.L. no. 83/2012, Consip Spa (Concessionaria Servizi Informativi Pubblici – Concessionaire of Public Informational Services) is a public law company which has, among others, the power to formulate opinions on the economic and technical congruence of the interventions and contracts relating to the acquisition of IT goods and services, to monitoring the execution of the aforementioned interventions and contracts (Article 3, paragraph 2, lett. c) of D.Lgs. 1 Dec. 2009, no. 177).

935. Informational contracts can be divided into two categories:

(1) Supplies: purchase, lease, leasing of hardware, software licence of use.

---

260. Art. 513 L. no. 208/2015.
261. *See* http://www.lapadigitale.it/wp-content/uploads/Piano-triennale-informatica-PA.pdf, consulted on 28 Jan. 2019.
262. *See* AgID Circular no. 2/2016.

(2) Services: software development, maintenance and technical assistance related to machineries, monitoring, staff training. With reference to the services requested by the Public Administration, these can be divided into services appointed to third parties related to activities of advice and programming and technical services.

936. Furthermore, contracts concerning an informational object have a complex contractual object that includes both supplies and services. In these cases, since a 'mixed contract' is framed, the applicable regulation is identified on the basis of the principles of economic accessoriness and prevalence. With reference to the length of the contract, some standards have been identified: an ordinary standard, according to which the length of the contracts is fixed each time by the will of the parties or is provided by the general conditions; a standard of first application, according to which the length is flexible and serves to allow the administration to begin the organization of the activity; and finally a transitory standard, according to which the Public Administration, at the first application of the Decree, can request the contracting enterprises to revise the contract, or of some clauses, during the course of its execution to suit the purposes and the principles of the Decree on the basis of the circumstances and criteria defined by AgID.

937. As a special rule for public ICT contracts, Article 512 of L. no. 208/2015 provides that Public Administrations provide their supplies exclusively through the purchase and trading instruments of Consip Spa or other public entities such as the aggregating subjects ('soggetti aggregatori') and the regional purchasing centres. This procedure has been established in order to specifically guarantee the optimization and rationalization of the purchases regarding IT goods and connectivity services.

938. According to Article 513 L. no. 208/2015, Consip Spa (or the aggregating subjects concerned) has the duty to programme purchases of IT goods and connectivity services, consistent with the aggregate demand referred to in the aforementioned Plan. By doing so, Consip has to previously consult the AgID.

The Audit Court ('Corte dei Conti') also recognized ICT goods and services as a special category of merchandise subject to specific provisions of law, and thus they compel Public Administrations to recur to Consip Spa or the aggregating subjects to purchase them.[263]

939. In case of goods and services whose acquisition is of particular strategic importance as indicated in the Plan, the central government and peripheral administrations, excluding schools of all levels, educational institutions and university institutions, as well as the national public welfare and social assistance institutions and tax agency pursuant to Legislative Decree 30 July 1999, n. 300, are entitled to recur only to Consip Spa.

263. Corte dei Conti, 27 Apr. 2016, DEL. no. 52/2016.

940. As particularly concerns IT programs, Article 68 paragraph 1 D.Lgs. 82/2005 provides that Public Administrations, in compliance with D.Lgs. 39/1993, acquire, computer programs following a comparative assessment of a technical and economic type among the following solutions available on the market:

(a) development of IT programs on behalf and at the expense of the administration on the basis of the requirements indicated by the same client administration;
(b) reuse of computer programs developed for and at the expense of the same or other administrations;
(c) acquisition of proprietary computer programs through the use of a user licence;
(d) acquisition of computer programs with open-source code;
(e) acquisition by combination of the methods referred to in points (a) to (d).

941. According to Article 68 paragraph 1-*bis* D.Lgs. 82/2005, to this end, the Public Administrations perform a comparative assessment of the different solutions available on the basis of the following criteria:

(a) total cost of the program or solution as a purchase, implementation, maintenance and support cost;
(b) the level of use of data formats and open-type interfaces as well as standards capable of ensuring interoperability and application cooperation between the various IT systems of the Public Administration;
(c) guarantees of the supplier in terms of security levels, in compliance with the legislation on personal data protection, service levels taking into account the type of software acquired.

942. In the view to optimize the public expense, the law admits the purchase of acquisition of proprietary computer programs only where it is not possible to access solutions already available within the Public Administration, or free software or open-source codes, adequate to the needs to be satisfied (Article 68 paragraph 1-*ter* D.Lgs. 82/2005). Such an assessment is carried out according to the methods and criteria defined by the AgID.

943. In addition, according to Article 69 D.Lgs. 82/2005, the Public Administrations that are holders of computer programs realized on specific indications of the public client have the obligation to make available the relevant source code, complete with the documentation and released in public directory under an open licence, in free use to other Public Administrations or to legal entities that intend to adapt them to their needs, unless justified reasons of order and public security, national defence and election consultations. This provision is in order to facilitate the reuse of computer programs owned by Public Administrations.

944. An exception to the above-mentioned rule for IT good and services is made by the following Article 516 L. no. 208/2015. In fact, the administrations and the companies referred to in paragraph 512 may proceed with procurement outside the procedures above-referred exclusively following a specific motivated authorization from the administrative top management, if the good or service is not available or suitable to meet the specific needs of the administration. The exception also applies in cases of necessity and urgency, however functional to ensure the continuity of administrative management. In such cases, the proceeding administration shall make a communication to the National Anti-Corruption Authority (ANAC) and the AgID.[264]

264. Corte dei Conti, 27 Apr. 2016, DEL. no. 52/2016.

Part IV. Electronic Transactions

Chapter 1. Legal Status of Electronic Transactions

§1. Introduction

945. Among the many activities that are included in the concept of electronic commerce, there is no doubt that the transactions performed online have a central and basic role and, therefore, the negotiation and the conclusion of agreements of a contractual nature.[265]

As already discussed,[266] L. 59/1997 introduced the principle of the full validity of contracts stipulated through an informational or online means; Article 15, paragraph 2 of which provides that 'the acts, data and documents formed by the Public Administration and by private subjects through informational and telematic instruments, the contracts stipulated in the same forms, as well as their storage and transmission with informational and telematic instruments, are valid and relevant for every effect of law'.[267]

946. Nothing prevents the valid conclusion of a contract through informational and online instruments, but this raises specific questions with reference to the formation and conclusion of the contractual agreement, with regard to its content and form, as well as to the identification of the time and place of the conclusion of the contract.[268]

---

265. On the matter of the definition of electronic commerce and of services of the Information Society *see supra*, *General introduction*, para. 4, *E-commerce: facts and figures*.
266. *See supra*, *General introduction*, para. 4, *E-Commerce: Facts and Figures*.
267. L. 15 Mar. 1997, n. 59, '*Delega al Governo per il conferimento di funzioni e compiti alle regioni ed enti locali, per la riforma della pubblica amministrazione e per la semplificazione amministrativa*', G.U. 17 Mar. 1997, n. 63. *See also* Art. 8, para. 1 D.Lgs. 23 Jan. 2002, n. 10, '*Attuazione della direttiva 1999/93/CE relativa ad un quadro comunitario per le firme elettroniche*', G.U. 15 Feb. 2002, n. 39, and Art. 11, para. 2 D.P.R. 28 Dec. 2000, n. 445, '*Testo unico delle disposizioni legislative e regolamentari in materia di documentazione amministrativa*', G.U. 20 Feb. 2001, n. 42. The national legislature has in this way anticipated the EC Legislature, in such a way that, when implementing Directive 2000/31/CE, it has not been considered necessary to restate the concept expressed in Art. 9, para. 1 of the directive.
268. The Italian doctrine usually distinguishes between the category of the so-called telematic [online] contracts, namely contracts clinched through the employment of telematic [online] instruments between subjects that are in different places, and of the 'digital contracts', which are as well clinched in digital form thanks to the use of informational instruments, but that do not occur necessarily between subjects that act at a distance. A digital contract can be, for example, the one clinched between parties simultaneously present, that form the contractual document with the aid

947. In the Italian ambit, the general regulation in point has to be searched for first of all in the Civil Code that provides a general section dedicated to the provisions applicable to any contractual type (regarding the essential elements of the contract, the regulation relating to its conclusion, etc.).[269] To this are also added, in the civil code, specific provisions dedicated to the so-called standard contracts, namely contractual types for which the legislature provides a particular regulation.[270]

948. What is relevant, for the purpose of conclusion of the contract, is the common will of the parties, namely the full coincidence between the declarations of will coming from the contracting subjects: this will, on the basis of the general principle of freedom to contract, is the element that founds the establishing of the contractual tie and can be manifested both in an expressed way (orally, in written form or with any other sign), and tacitly (so-called businesslike behaviour, namely the behaviour held by the party that, without declaring expressly its will, carries out the contract).

949. The principle of freedom to contract assures that the parties can decide which kind of contract to make, determine freely its content (within the limits of law), and if they wish, conclude a so-called innominate contract, one not corresponding to any of the contractual types provided by the law.

950. With regard to the contractual agreement, this can be formed simultaneously (at the same moment in time), or through successive phases. The basic principle is contained in Article 1326 c.c.: 'The contract is clinched at the moment in which the subject that has made the offer has the knowledge of the acceptance of the other party.' The acceptance must be fully compliant with the offer; otherwise it will stand in turn as a new offer. This provision is therefore applied regardless of the means that the parties use to conclude the contract. The following Article 1335 c.c. introduces the so-called presumption of knowledge, the principle on the basis of which the offer and the acceptance (as well as their possible revocation) are considered known at the moment they reach the address of the receiver, unless the party proves that, not due to his negligence, it was impossible for him to receive the news.

---

of a computer and sign it with the respective electronic signatures. A further category different, since super-ordinated to the telematic and also the digital contracts, is the category of the 'contract through electronic means' which the EC Legislature refers to in Directive 2000/31/CE, meaning agreements can conducted at a distance with devices that are not necessarily telematic [online]. The present treatment is however mainly dedicated to the contract defined as 'telematic', and in particular to those (also referred to as 'virtual contracts') clinched at a distance through two specific telematic [online] channels: the World Wide Web and the electronic mail. These last contacts, indeed, certainly represent the contractual type of greater interest in the actual context of e-commerce.

269. Civil Code (Regio decreto 16 marzo 1942 – XX, n. 262), Libro quarto, Titolo II, indexed '*Dei contratti in generale*', Arts 1321-1469. The contract is defined by Art. 1321 Italian Civil Code as 'the agreement between two or more parties to establish, regulate or extinguish between them a patrimonial juridical relationship'. Following, the Civil Code will be mentioned with the acronym 'c.c'.

270. Codice civile, Libro quarto, Titolo III, indexed 'Dei singoli contratti', Arts 1470-1986, among which there is the sale contract (Art. 1470 e ss.).

951. The application of the provisions of the code to online contracts (or virtual contracts if preferred), and more in general to the contract clinched through an electronic means,[271] poses various specific questions tied to its nature, being *inter absentes* (namely, clinched without the parties being simultaneously physically present) and due to the fact that the contracting parties communicated at a distance through an online (telematic) instrument.

952. The first problem to be considered is the identification of the contracting parties. Since the parties are operating at a distance and in different places, they are not able to identify with certainty their counterpart. They are also unable to ascertain that the relating declaration has arrived intact. Therefore it is necessary to determine the imputability and the integrity of the contractual declarations transmitted by electronic means and their juridical value.[272]

953. As discussed,[273] the effect of the contractual declaration, determination of its genuineness and its validity, is connected with the form of the contract.[274]

954. With regard to both the juridical binding character of the contractual declaration and the form of the contract itself, the employment of electronic signatures and in particular of qualified digital signatures can appear decisive, since they are able to render juridically certain the origin and integrity of both the contractual offer and the related acceptance, allowing the parties to lawfully rely on the occurred conclusion and validity of the contract.[275]

---

271. *See* Art. 13, para. 1 of D.Lgs. 9 Apr. 2003, n. 70, 'Attuazione della direttiva 2000/31/CE relativa a taluni aspetti giuridici dei servizi della società dell'informazione, in particolare il commercio elettronico, nel mercato interno', G.U. 14 Apr. 2003, n. 87.
272. A different stance regards the transactions that occur through the so-called EDI (Electronic Data Interchange), largely employed in negotiations that are business to business. In such cases, the identification of the counterpart/counterparts is usually performed beforehand, when the framework contract that regulates the whole system is stipulated (in written form). Here, therefore, it is possible to find expressed consideration of the various technical and most of all juridical aspects related to the transmission of electronic documents (their validity, the place and time of the clinching of possible contracts, the liability of the parties, the applicable law and the place of jurisdiction, etc.). *See* G. Finocchiaro, *I contratti informatici, in Trattato di diritto commerciale e diritto pubblico dell'economia* (directed by F. Galgano), vol. XXII, CEDAM, Padova, 1997.
273. *See supra*, General introduction, para. 4, *E-commerce: facts and figures*.
274. In general, the principle of the freedom of form of the contract allows the parties (except in the cases expressly provided for by the law) to determine the form to give to the agreement, that will be fully valid even if, for example, the contract is concluded orally. When required, the written form of the contract can be requested *ad substantiam*, in case it is the requirement for the validity itself of the contract (as, for example, for the transfer of the propriety of estates according to Art. 1350 c.c.), or *ad probationem*, namely not for the validity of the contract, but in case to give proof of its existence (that can be supplied neither by witnesses nor through presumptions: for example, the insurance contract provided by Art. 1888 c.c.).
275. In national ambit, the various measures on informational documents and electronic signatures have merged in the '*Testo unico in materia di documentazione amministrativa*' (Consolidation on the matter of administrative documentation) enacted in 2001, that has been modified by D.Lgs. 10/2002 implementing the Directive 1999/93/CE. The D.P.R. 445/2000 has thus been modified again by the D.P.R. 7 Apr. 2003, n. 137, '*Regolamento recante disposizioni di coordinamento in materia di firme elettroniche a norma dell'articolo 13 del decreto legislativo 23 Jan. 2002, n. 10*', G.U. 17 Jun.

955. While advising to refer to the specific treatment of the matter,[276] it is here sufficient to observe that, due to the validity recognized in the informational document signed with an electronic signature (in particular, with a digital signature or with another type of qualified electronic signature, Articles 10 and 11 D.P.R. 445/2000) it is possible to conclude a contract through online (telematic) means, for which written form is expressly requested.[277]

956. Where, instead, no use of an electronic signature occurs, the validity of the online (telematic) declaration (namely, its imputability to another subject) will therefore have to be evaluated on the basis of the reliance engendered by the person making the declaration regarding his own identity, reliance that will be regarded as reasonable and therefore relevant, only if it is substantiated by objective elements that allow a verification by the other contracting party. It is held that the principle elaborated in the past in relation to the use of the telex can be applied here: according to this, the reliability of the declaration (in the case *de quo* contained in an informational document) is tied to the reliability of the 'warden' of the technical device that the declaration is sent through.[278]

957. Coming to the formation of the online (telematic) contract, the possible means through which the conclusion of the agreement can be reached are various.

958. The contract can first of all be concluded through the exchange of electronic mail messages between the parties, according to the standard layout ex Article 1326 c.c. mentioned above.[279]

959. When, instead, the conclusion of the contract occurs online, through the World Wide Web, there are essentially two methods.

960. The first method, which is very widespread, is that in which a website contains an offer supplied with all the essential elements of the contract to the conclusion of which it is aimed. The website will be classified as a real contractual offer

---

2003, n. 138; with regard to the new techical rules for the generation, apposition and verification of digital signatures *see* the D.P.C.M. 13 Jan. 2004, '*Regole tecniche per la formazione, la trasmissione, la conservazione, la duplicazione, la riproduzione e la validazione, anche temporale, dei documenti informatici*', G.U. 27 Apr. 2004, n. 98.

276. *See infra*, Part IV, para. 2, Regulations of electronic signatures and certification services.

277. Both ad substantiam, and ad probationem: *see supra*, note n. 10. On the juridical validity of the informational document *see* as last stance Cass. 6 Sep. 2001, n. 11445.

278. *See* F. Delfini, *Il Commercio elettronico*, CEDAM, Padova, 2004, p. 74 e ss.

279. With regard to the relevance of electronic mail and of the subjects that use it for purposes of qualification of the activity as service of the information society, and therefore, in the Italian ambit, to its relevance for the purpose of the application of D.Lgs. 70/2003, *see* the Considerando n. 18 of the Directive 2000/31/CE.

and, in particular, as a public offering ex Article 1336 c.c. This consists of a contractual offer to the world, *incertas personas*, addressed to an undetermined category of subjects or any way to such a number of them to exclude the personal character of the offer itself.[280]

961. Where the website does not contain the essential elements of the future contract, but only some of them, there will not be a public offering, but an invitation to offer or propose. According to this contractual layout (not always easily distinguishable from the public offering), the subject that answers the invitation will not accept a contractual offer but will make an offer himself and the operator of the website will be free to decide whether to accept the user's offer effectively concluding an agreement or not, resulting in no contractual agreement.

962. With regard to the conclusion of the online (telematic) contract in the World Wide Web, the method that occurs more often consists in manifesting the acceptance of the contractual offer through the so-called point and click, namely the acceptance expressed through the press of the so-called contractual button.[281]

The general juridical validity of such form of expression of the will to clinch a contract in a free form is acknowledged by the dominant doctrine.[282]

963. This relevance, however, finds an obstacle when the contract requests a determined form or, as it often happens, the contractual conditions are provided by only one of the parties and they contain so-called vexatious covenants.

The form of the contract has already been discussed. With regard to the general conditions of the contract, Article 1341, paragraph 1 c.c., provides that if such general conditions are prearranged by one of the contracting parties only (therefore, without any negotiation), these will be effective towards the other only if at the time of the conclusion of the contract they were known to him or if he could have anyway known them by using due diligence. Paragraph 2 of the same article provides, therefore, that certain covenants (strictly mentioned by the law, the so-called vexatious covenants) included in the general conditions (or even in contracts clinched through forms or formularies ex Article 1342 c.c.) have to be specifically approved in written form (*ad substantiam*); otherwise they will have no effect.[283]

---

280. *See*, however, Art. 14, para. 2, of the Convention of Wien of 11 Apr. 1980 on the international sale of movable goods, where it is instead specified how 'an offer addressed to undetermined persons is only considered as an invitation to offer, unless the person that has expressed the offer has not clearly indicated otherwise'.

281. *See* V. Franceschelli, *Computer e diritto*, Maggioli, Rimini, 1989, p. 165.

282. In particular, the relevance of the contractual button is pegged to the provision of para. 4 of Art. 1326 c.c.: 'If the offeror requests a determined form for the acceptance, the acceptance is ineffective if it is given in a different form'.

283. If they are not specifically approved in written form, no effect is given to (Art. 1341, para. 2 c.c.): i) the conditions that establish, in favour of the subject that has arranged them, limitations of liability, ii) faculty of recession from the contract or to discontinue its performance, or otherwise iii) those that provide for the other contracting party lapses, iv) limitations to the faculty of interposing a demurrer, v) restrictions to the contractual freedom in the relationships with third parties, vi) tacit extension or renewal of the contract, vii) arbitration clauses or viii) derogations from the competency of the judiciary.

964. If the contract is between a professional and a consumer, the regulation provided by Article 1469-*bis* and following of the Civil Code, introduced by L. 6 February 1996, n. 52 implementing Directive 93/13/CEE, as well as the further regulation on the matter of protection of the consumer, will apply.[284]

965. The contractual button can thus be validly used when the contract has no prescribed form. When, instead, the contract is required to be in written form or the written approval of determined covenants is expressly required, the use of the contractual button appears inadequate and it will be necessary to employ (at least) an electronic signature.[285]

966. The layout of conclusion consisting in the exchange of offer and acceptance ex Article 1326 c.c. is not, however, as anticipated, the only possible one. Article 1327 c.c. provides, indeed, the hypothesis of the so-called businesslike behaviour; if, on request of the offeror or due to the nature of the deal or according to the trade usages, the performance has to be carried out without a previous answer, the contract is clinched at the time and place where the performance has begun. Such modality of clinching, however, cannot be used when the written form is required *ad substantiam.*

According to some authors, therefore, when the numbers of the credit card are typed and sent through the Web to the supplier, even without having formally accepted any contractual offer (which often occurs in the World Wide Web, typically in the contracts between consumers and commercial operators, since the resort to the use of the credit card to carry out the payment of the goods or services purchased is very widespread), the hypothesis of the clinching of the contract through a businesslike behaviour occurs.[286]

284. On the subject *see* infra, Part IV, para. 4, Protection of users of electronic services.
285. After the modifications performed on the D.P.R. 445/2000 by D.Lgs. 10/2002, the contractual button is today considered by some authors as a type of so-called weak electronic signature (*see* Art. 1, lett. *cc* and Art. 10, para. 2 D.P.R. 445/2000). The informational document (contractual offer placed on a website), signed with an electronic signature (contractual button), would thus satisfy today, according to this interpretation, the legal requirement of the written form (under the profile of the form for validity). *See* E. Tosi in *Commercio elettronico Documento informatico e firma digitale*, C. Rossello, G. Finocchiaro, E. Tosi (a cura di), Giappichelli, Torino, 2003, p. 126 and 129; *contra* F. Delfini, *Il Commercio elettronico*, CEDAM, Padova, 2004, pp. 107 and following. However, it has to be noticed how, on the probative level, the document signed with a simple electronic signature is freely assessable by the judge, with regard to its objective characteristics of quality and security (Art. 10, para. 2, second sentence, D.P.R. 445/2000). Precisely due to this circumstance and with reference also to further reasons of a different kind, the Italian doctrine appears to be inclined to a non-perfect equalization between the informational document signed with a so-called weak or a simple electronic signature and a private contract ex Art. 2702 c.c. According to a recently suggested interpretation, the informational document signed with a simple electronic signature should anyway be validly usable for the purposes of Art. 1341, para. 2 c.c., since what is required is not the private contract ex Art. 2702 c.c., but the simple written form. *See* F. Delfini, *Il Commercio elettronico*, CEDAM, Padova, 2004, p. 105.
286. The thesis is, however, controversial. According to part of the Italian doctrine (that includes A.M. Gambino, *L'accordo telematico*, Giuffrè, Milano, 1997, p. 152), such behaviour would frame an hypothesis provided by Art. 1327 c.c., but other authors are against such a reconstruction (cfr. G. Oppo, *Disumanizzazione del contratto?*, in *Riv. dir. civ.*, 1, 1998, p. 529).

967. With regard to the exact moment in which the contract can be considered as concluded, it has been said how Article 1326 c.c. provides the principle of knowledge but has to be read with reference to Article 1335 that introduces the presumption of knowledge when the declaration has reached the address of the addressee. In the ambit that interests us here, it has to be furthermore considered the provision of Article 14 D.P.R. 445/2000 that in turn introduces a further presumption: 'The informational document transmitted through online means (a telematic way) is considered sent and arrived to the addressee if transmitted to the electronic mail address this subject has declared.'[287] The informational document that represents, for example, the acceptance of a contractual offer will therefore have to be considered known to the offeror if it has arrived to his electronic address and arrived to it if sent.[288]

968. The possibility to revoke the offer and the acceptance is also connected with the identification of the time of the concluding of the contract. In general, Article 1328 c.c. provides that 'the offer can be revoked as long as the contract is not clinched', while 'the acceptance can be revoked as long as the revocation becomes known to the offeror before the acceptance does'. Due to the characteristics of the transmission of online (telematic) communication and the principles above-mentioned regarding the time of the clinching of the contract (included Article 14 D.P.R. 445/2000), it appears evident how the revocation of the offer is effectively possible, whereas the revocation of the acceptance is instead difficult to exercise concretely.[289]

969. With a difference from what has been examined now on the time of the clinching of the contract, the Italian regulations do not provide any specific provisions aimed at the identification, in general, of the place of the clinching of the contract.[290]

However, the national doctrine and jurisprudence, by appealing to the provision of Article 1326 c.c. (even if no explicit reference to the place of conclusion is found), unanimously hold that the place of the conclusion of the contract is identifiable in the place where the offeror acquires the knowledge of the acceptance. In the area of online (telematic) contracts and in light of the peculiarity of online

---

287. The tenor of Art. 14 D.P.R. 445/2000 allows the electronic address that is relevant for the purposes of the provision in exam can be 'declared' orally, being different from the election of the special domicile provided by Art. 47 c.c. that instead requires the written form.
288. The interpretation related here results as the most adherent to the tenor of the provision in exam. Cfr. *G. Finocchiaro*, *Lex Mercatoria e commercio elettronico*, in *Contratto e Impresa*, 2, 2001, CEDAM, Padova, p. 582. However, more than one interpreter believes that, actually, in Art. 14 D.P.R. 445/2000 there is the intention not to introduce a new presumption (that would worsen the position of the addressee with respect to what is provided by Art. 1335 c.c.), but to regulate only the moment of the transmission of the informational documents, by equalizing the online (telematic) transmission and delivery of the transmission and delivery in the physical world.
289. For the revocation of the public offering Art. 1336 c.c. provided that 'the revocation of the offering, if performed in the same form as the offer or in an equivalent form is effective also towards the subject that have not gained knowledge of it'.
290. The only provision that expressly considers the place of the conclusion of the contract, but with reference to a specific hypothesis, is the mentioned Art. 1327 c.c. (*see supra* in the text).

(telematic) transmission, such principle has thus brought to various interpretative suggestions, none of which can be considered settled at the moment. Among these, we remember the one that considers the online (telematic) contract clinched in the place where the server used by the offeror to receive the acceptance is physically placed or the one that identifies such place in the premise or domicile of the addressee of the acceptance (therefore regardless of the location of the used server).

970. Although the determination of the place of the clinching can be relevant,[291] its importance is, however, concretely very limited.

First of all because, with respect to the identification of the applicable statute, the Convenzione di Roma of 19 June 1980 (Convention of Rome, referred to by Article 57 of L. 218/1995) does not point out the place of clinching as a relevant criterion, but, in case of lack of choice by the contracting parties, the law of the Country to which the contract is more tightly connected will be applied.[292]

Second, when the online (telematic) contract has as parties a consumer and a professional, the provisions on the protection of the consumer will apply, both for the applicable regulation and for the determination of the place of jurisdiction (nationally as well as internationally).[293]

971. The regulation on the contract examined until now has to be further integrated with what is today provided by D.Lgs. 70/2003, in which, as provided by Directive 2000/31/CE that it implements, specific provisions on the matter of online (telematic) contracts are contained in Articles 12 and 13.[294]

---

291. For example, on the matter of the identification of the interpretative practice ex Art. 1368 c.c., as residual criterion to assess the possible jurisdiction of the Italian judge ex Art. 3, para. 2 L. 31 May 1995, n. 218 (Riforma del sistema italiano di diritto internazionale privato, G.U 3 Jun. 1995, n. 68), or for the determination of the competent court for the resolution of controversies deriving from the contractual relationship ex Art. 20 del Codice di procedura civile (R.D. 28 Oct. 1940, n. 1443, G.U. 28 Oct. 1940, n. 253): 'Facultative court for the trials related to obligation rights. For the trials related to obligation rights is also competent to judge of the place in which the obligation drawn in court was born or had to be performed'.
292. *See* Arts 3 and 4 of the Convenzione di Roma (Covention of Rome), ratified in Italy with the L. 18 Dec. 1984, n. 975, '*Convenzione sulla legge applicabile alle obbligazioni contrattuali*', G.U. 30 Jan. 1985, n. 25. To the international contract, if it is the case, will also apply the provisions of the Convezione delle Nazioni Unite (Convention of the United Nations) on the contracts of international sale of goods, adopted in Wien on 11 Apr. 1980, ratified in Italy with the L. 11 Dec. 1985, n. 765, G.U. 27 Dec. 1985, n. 303, as well as the Regulation (CE) n. 44/2001 of the Council of 22 Dec. 2000, regarding the jurisdictional competence, the recognition and the execution of the decisions on the civil and commercial matter, G.U.C.E. 16 Jan. 2001, n. L 012.
293. For example, *see* Art. 5 of the mentioned Convenzione di Roma (Convention of Rome). *See infra*, Part IV, para. 4, *Protection of users of electronic services.*
294. Art. 11 D.Lgs. 70/2003 provides: 'The present decree does not apply to:
    (a) contracts that establish or transfer rights related to estates, different from those on the matter of tenancy;
    (b) contracts that require by law the intervention of judiciary organs, public powers or professions that imply the exercise of public powers;
    (c) contracts of suretyship or of guarantees by given by people that act for purposes that are beyond their trading, enterprise or professional activities;
    (d) contract regulated by family or succession law'. It has to be noticed how the provision in exam, with a difference from what is provided by Art. 9 of the Directive 2000/31/CE, rules

972. In primis in Article 12 of D.Lgs. 70/2003, titled 'Information Aimed to the Clinching of the Contract', special informative duties are provided (besides those provided for specific goods and services, as well as those provided by Article 3 of D.Lgs. 185/1999).[295]

The performer will have to supply the following information in a clear, comprehensible and unequivocal way and before the addressee of the service sends a possible order:

(a) the various technical phases to be followed for the clinching of the contract;
(b) the way in which the clinched contract will be stored and the related modalities of access;
(c) the technical means placed at disposal of the addressee to identify and correct the errors of data insertion before the order is forwarded to the performer;
(d) the codes of conduct the performer possibly complies with and how to access them through online (telematic) means;
(e) the languages at disposal for the clinching of the contract besides Italian;
(f) the indication of the means for the resolution of controversies.

973. The duty to supply such information can be disregarded only in case of agreement between the parties, as long as these are not consumers, while it does not subsist (regardless of the subjective qualities of the contracting parties) when the contract is clinched exclusively through the exchange of electronic mail messages or equivalent individual communications.[296]

---

out the contract mentioned from the scope of application of the Decree and not, instead, from the possibility to be clinched through online (telematic) means.

295. *See* infra, Part. IV, para. 4, Protection of users of electronic services.

296. The information that now needs to be provided are in addition to the general information that the performer of the service of the information society has to render easily accessible, in a direct and permanent way, to the addressees of the service and to the competent authorities, namely (Art. 7 D.Lgs. 70/2003):

(a) the name, trade name or firm name;
(b) the domicile or premises;
(c) the details that allow to rapidly contact the performer and to directly and effectively communicate with him, included the electronic mail address;
(d) the number of inscription to the repertoire of the economic activities, REA, or to the register of enterprises;
(e) the elements of identification as well as the details of the competent Authority of vigilance in case the activity is subject to concession, licence or authorization;
(f) with regard to the regulated professions:
    (1) the fraternity or equivalent institution the performer is member of and the number;
    (2) the professional qualification and the Member State it has been issued by;
    (3) the reference to the professional regulations and the possible codes of behaviour in force in the member State of residence and the modality for their consultation;
(g) the IVA (VAT) registration number or another identification number considered equivalent in the member State, if the performer exercises an activity subject to tax;
(h) the clear and unequivocal indication of the prices and tariffs of the different services of the information society supplied, emphasizing if they are inclusive of taxes, delivery costs and other additional elements that have to be specified;

974. The covenants and the general conditions of the contract proposed to the addressee have, furthermore, to be placed at the disposal of the addressee in order to let him save them in the computer's memory and reproduce them.

975. With reference to the conclusion of the online (telematic) contract, lastly, Article 13 ('Forwarding of the Order') paragraph 1 D.Lgs. 70/2003 restates expressly the principle according to which the general provisions on the clinching of the contracts apply also to the cases in which the addressee of a good or a service of the information society forwards his order through online (telematic) means.

976. Paragraph 2 of the same article provides that, except for a different agreement between parties that are other than consumers, the performer has furthermore, without unjustified delay and through online (telematic) means, to acknowledge through a receipt the order of the addressee: this receipt must contain:

(a) a résumé of the general and particular conditions applicable to the contract;
(b) the information related to the essential characteristics of the good or of the service;
(c) the detailed indication of the price, of the payment methods, of the recess, of the delivery costs and of the applicable taxes.[297]

977. It is furthermore provided the principle according to which the electronic communication containing the order or the receipt of the order is considered as arrived when the party it is addressed to has the possibility of access to it (Article 13, comma 3 D.Lgs. 70/2003).

The provisions mentioned lastly, with reference to the receipt of the order and its content, as well as to the moment in which the order or the receipt of the order are considered as arrived, will not, however, apply to the contracts clinched exclusively through the exchange of electronic mail messages or equivalent individual communications (Article 13, paragraph 4 D.Lgs. 70/2003).[298]

(i) the indication of the activities allowed to the consumer and the addressee of the service and the details of the contract in case the activity is subject to authorization or the object of the performance is supplied on the basis of a licence of use contract.

297. The forwarding of the order receipt is a duty that does not impact in any way on the clinching of the online (telematic) contract. On the other hand, the lack of the forwarding of the order receipt is not expressly punished in D.Lgs. 70/2003, while, among others, the omission of the information provided for in Art. 12 of the Decree in exam it is, through a financial penalty (*see* Art. 21 D.Lgs. 70/2003).

298. It has to be noticed how, with a difference from what is provided by Art. 11 of the Directive 2000/31/CE, the exclusion now mentioned inexplicably regards the provision contained in para. 3 of Art. 13 D.Lgs. 70/2003, an anomaly that has probably to be ascribed to a mere error of transposition.

Chapter 2. Regulation of Electronic Signatures and Certification Services

§1. The Document and the E-Signing

978. The diffusion of information technologies and their possible use in the most diverse areas, in relations between private individuals, private individuals and the Public Administration as well as between the Public Administrations themselves, has imposed the need to give legal certainty to relations, from the point of view of the form and, more generally, of the security of legal traffic.

979. As we all know, initially the use of the Internet at its inception was free of any form of regulation. Following self-regulation phases and the use of various soft-law tools (such as recommendations, directives and use collections), the national legislator (and others) felt the need to intervene with the introduction of binding rules.

980. The Italian Legislator in the IT field, although not particularly orderly in its legislative technique (in the sense that it often brings updates and modifications through uncoordinated texts), remains however one of the most reactive to the normative solicitations both of international and of UE origin.

981. A peculiarity that needs to be underlined is that which justifies the inclusion of the issues relating to digital document and electronic signatures in the digital Public Administration framework. This is due to the fact that our Legislator, in trying to establish common rules for all (citizens, businesses and Public Administrations) has included the rules relating to these topics in the Code of digital administration, i.e. the so-called CAD, going to thus creating a single text containing at the same time civil and administrative provisions.

982. A process of dematerialization (documentary) has been underway for decades, which involves not only the relationships between private individuals but also those that involve the Public Administration.

983. The function of the document is to represent, it is a 'thing' that makes known a fact, or rather *res signata* (a perceptible object, bearing signs), so it is given to pronounce the judgment of existence of a fact, that can be subsumed under a normative type.

In other words, it has a double capacity: first of all to make present a fact of the past (hence the expression 'represent'), in *secundis* that of making its history perceptible, that is the very fact of documenting, guaranteed capacity from the lasting nature of the support on which it is documented and from the (indelible) sign traced therein.

984. While the already mentioned topic of the imputation of the document means the affixing of so-called very personal signs that cannot be reproduced by third parties, the so-called underwriting pursuant to Article 2702 Italian Civil Code suitable to make certain the traceability to a subject, a problem that in the information dimension has been solved with the provision of different electronic signatures according to the different degrees of 'resistance'.

985. With regard to the regulatory interventions issued to define the IT document, it would be of little use to list them all, but it is sufficient to hope that they followed one another in time starting from the principles of the Nineties in the tax field, for example Article 3 Legislative Decree of 12 February 1993 n. 39 on the fiscal validity of the mechanographical accounting and minimum data of the PA, passing through other administrative areas up to the criminal law with the definition of IT document contained in Article 491-*bis* Italian Penal Code: 'any IT support containing data or information having evidential value or programs specifically designed to process them', the Bassanini law in Article 15, paragraph 2, l. March 15, 1997, which states that 'the deeds, data and documents drawn up by the Public Administration and by private individuals with IT or telematic tools, the contracts stipulated in the same forms, as well as their storage and transmission with IT tools, are valid and relevant to all effects of law', to finally arrive at the definition in the CAD, Article 21 lett. p) d.lgs.82 / 2005, according to which the electronic document is 'the computer representation of legally relevant deeds or data'.

986. The most relevant current regulation of the electronic document is found mostly in chapter II, first section, CAD, Articles 20-23-*ter*., that has replaced the punctual definitions with legislative rank by referring to a secondary legislation technique, or by relying on the guidelines issued by the AgID.

The explanation of this legislative technique can be found in the legislature's attempt to keep up with technological evolution, thus trying to cut the time required for legislative production by preferring a referral to an administrative body technician certainly more agile and competent on the subject.

Another source in which we find regulation is EU Regulation n. 910/2014 (eIDAS – electronic IDentification Authentication and Signature).

987. To give a first definition, it is still useful to also review the old definition of Article 20, paragraph 1, which defined it as an 'electronic document that contains the computer representation of legally relevant deeds, facts or data'.

Paragraph 1-*bis* is also relevant and current, which provides that the electronic document satisfies the requirement of the written form and has the efficacy envisaged by Article 2702 of the Civil Code when there is a digital signature, other type of qualified electronic signature or an advanced electronic signature or, in any case, it is formed, after computer identification by its author, through a process having the requirements set by the AgID pursuant to Article 71.

The requirements are stated in such a way as to guarantee the security, integrity and non-modifiability of the document and, in a manifest and unequivocal manner, its traceability to the author.

In all other cases, the suitability of the electronic document to satisfy the requirement of the written form and its probative value are freely assessable in court, in relation to the characteristics of security, integrity and non-modifiability.

The date and time of formation of the electronic document can be opposed to third parties if affixed in accordance with the Guidelines.

The law in question assumes particular relevance with regard to the evidentiary aspect (in court) of the electronic documents as regards their signing with one of the aforementioned types of signatures, starting from the simplest, non-typed *rectius* (freely assessable by the judge), arriving up to those deemed most resistant and reliable (digital, etc.).

988. While moving on to the eIDAS regulation we see, for example, that recital 63 states that electronic documents are important for the future evolution of cross-border electronic transactions in the internal market (in a European sense), while subsequently programmatically states that 'an electronic document should not be denied the legal effects for the reason in its electronic form in order to ensure that an electronic transaction cannot be rejected for the sole reason that a document is in electronic form'.

Article 3 n. 35, also of the EU regulation under discussion, we find the definition of electronic document: 'any content stored in electronic form, in particular text or sound, visual or audiovisual recording'.

989. There are several useful definitions provided by AgID on the electronic document:

(i) It is a set of binary values whose materiality is given by the system and the IT support in which it is stored.
(ii) It can be modified or reproduced an infinite number of times, obtaining absolutely identical copies of the original.
(iii) Its content is released from support.

990. As for the forms, instead, the forms of the electronic document are several: (i) text documents, spreadsheets, XML schemas drawn up using specific software tools; (ii) documents acquired electronically or on electronic media, e-mail, documents acquired as a copy; (iii) computer records of transactions or IT processes, data provided by the user by filling in forms or forms; (iv) data set, coming from one or more databases, grouped according to a specific logical structure.

991. The characteristics, instead, of the electronic document are the following (contained in the DPCM 13.11.2014): (i) be uniquely and persistently identified; (ii) be unmodifiable, that is, formed in such a way that form and content cannot be altered and its static nature is guaranteed in the conservation phase; (iii) be produced in one of the formats suitable for conservation (*see* Annex 2 of the DPCM 13-11-2014); (iv) be stored in a computerized document management or preservation system which can also be delegated to third parties; (v) have at least a minimum set of metadata associated with it.

992. Another interesting aspect to pay attention to is the non-modifiability and integrity of the IT documents that can be reached through: (a) the creation of a 'native' IT document affixing a timestamp that is enforceable against third parties, transfer to third parties with certified e-mail with complete receipt, storage on document management systems that adopt security policies, transfer to a preservation system, for the PA with registration in the protocol register, repertoires or registers; (b) computer document from analogue document, storing documents in an IT management system that guarantees the unalterable nature of the document or in a preservation system (*see* Article 3, paragraph 5 of the Prime Ministerial Decree cit.); (c) computer registration, generation or grouping of data sets from databases, production of a static data extraction and its transfer to the conservation system.

993. From what we have just seen the following conclusions can be drawn on the nature of the electronic document, given its function, we have seen how its features are remarkable and changeable, which is why it is easier to understand the decision taken by the legislator or to opt for a updating of the subject by its very nature rapid and complex intrinsic nature, to a subject such as AgID deemed suitable to respond quickly to requests for speed and streamlined regulatory procedure with regard to technical aspects.

994. In light of this, therefore, a modern jurist cannot avoid counting among his lists of sources to be consulted if he has to deal with questions concerning IT documents, electronic signatures and everything that involves citizens and the Public Administration in its widest possible meaning with AgID, always keeping an eye on what is also the evolution of European legislation, which is increasingly becoming the driving force behind innovation in Europe (*see*, *for example*, the strategic plan for the Digital Single Market, which contains interesting aspects both on the consumer side, e-commerce, and on the PA side with the drive towards e-government).

995. Moving on to electronic signatures, we face the issue of the signing of electronic documents, or rather of technological solutions aimed at allowing their traceability to a specific subject.

In other words, it can be said that electronic signatures have the purpose of digitally replicating what in the analogue world is done with the autograph signing of a document.

However, it should immediately highlight how not all types of electronic signatures fulfil the task with the same degree of security and reliability, from which the different legal regime derives.

996. The regulatory basis of electronic signatures can be found in European Regulation eIDAS n. 910/2014, which through the strengthening of national regulations on electronic identification aims to facilitate the cross-border use of these identification means, and in the Digital Administration Code.

997. As well summarized by the AgID, here are the types of electronic signatures: (i) Electronic Signature – data in electronic form, enclosed or connected by logical association with other electronic data and used by the signatory to sign. (ii) Advanced Electronic Signature (FEA) – electronic signature that meets the following requirements: it is connected only to the signatory; it is suitable to identify the signatory; it is created using data for the creation of an electronic signature which the signatory can, with a high level of security, use under his exclusive control; it is linked to the signed data so as to allow the identification of any subsequent modification of such data. (iii) Qualified Electronic Signature (FEQ) – which in addition to those of an advanced electronic signature possesses these characteristics: it is created on a device qualified for the creation of an electronic signature; it is based on a qualified electronic certificate that has the legal effect equivalent to that of a handwritten signature. (iv) Digital Signature (FD) – is the result of an IT procedure – called validation – which guarantees the authenticity and integrity of IT documents. It gives the IT document the following characteristics: authenticity, integrity and non-repudiation.

998. Concerning Electronic Signature, Article. 3. point 10 of the eIDAS regulation defines the electronic signature as 'data in electronic form, enclosed or connected through logical association to other electronic data and used by the signatory to sign', while it was defined with Article 1, paragraph 1, letter q, of the CAD, as 'the set of data in electronic form, attached or connected by logical association to other electronic data, used as a method of computer identification'.

999. It is easy to understand how this is the simplest form of signature but at the same time also the least legally effective, in fact, since it does not provide suitable instruments to guarantee its reliability, it is freely assessable by the judge.

On reading the second standard, we see, instead, what are the characteristics on the basis of which the three types of electronic signature differ and are evaluated.

1000. Concerning the Advanced Electronic Signature, this type of signature, whose requirements are dictated by Article 26 of the reg. Eidas is the one that allows the appending subject to have direct and exclusive control of the instrument with which he is signing and at the same time to guarantee that it cannot be changed.

An example of this signature is the graphometric one affixed to a tablet in the bank or for the signing of insurance contracts if it complies with the training criteria set by the D.P.C.M. 22 February 2013.

1001. Article 1, Paragraph 1, letter q-*bis* of the CAD, defined it as 'a set of electronic data attached or connected to an electronic document that allow the identification of the signatory of the document and guarantee the unique connection to the signatory, created with means on which the signatory can keep exclusive control, linked to the data to which the signature refers in order to detect whether the data itself has subsequently been modified'.

In light of this, it can be seen that at a greater level of reliability as regards the traceability of the signature to the subscriber and the fact that it cannot be modified, the legal system recognizes a greater credibility, equating its effectiveness with that of a handwritten signature.

1002. Concerning Qualified Electronic Signature, this is a particular type of advanced electronic signature based on a qualified certificate issued by an accredited certifier and realized through a secure device for creating the signature.

With regard to its definition, Article 1, paragraph 1, letter r) of the CAD, defined the qualified signature as 'a particular type of advanced electronic signature that is based on a qualified certificate and implemented through a secure device for creating the signature'.

1003. Concerning Digital Signature, Article 1, lett. s) of the CAD defines it 'a particular type of qualified signature based on a system of cryptographic keys, a public and a private one, related to each other, which allows the holder through the private key and the recipient through the public key, respectively, to make manifest and verify the origin and integrity of an electronic document or a set of IT documents'.

As already mentioned, it meets the requirements of authenticity (guarantees the identity of the subscriber), integrity (ensures that the document is not modified after its subscription), not repudiation (the document cannot be repudiated by the subscriber, except for a false complaint).

1004. In other words, it is a type of advanced electronic signature that uses cryptography as a means of security, whose legal regime is equal to that of Article 21 and 24 CAD.

Furthermore, except in the case of authenticated subscription, together with the qualified signature it is required, under penalty of nullity, for the signing of the deeds referred to in Articles. 1350, first paragraph, nn. 1-12, if drafted on an electronic document, while n. 13 also admits the advance, finally the last period was added to Article 21, paragraph 2-*bis*, CAD, 'or are formed with the additional methods set forth in Article 20, paragraph 1-*bis*, first sentence'.

1005. In conclusion with the changes made with the two Legislative Decree n.179 / 2016 and 217/2017 to the CAD (on Article 21, paragraph 2-*bis*) through which the electronic signing of the deeds that must be done in writing, under penalty of nullity (formed on electronic document), has been envisaged, the process is completed by the Italian legislator of the equalization of electronic signatures with the handwritten signature, a similarity achieved also in the field of authentication of signatures by certain subjects if they perform the functions of public officials such as notaries, Public Administrations and lawyers.

1006. As for their legal effectiveness beyond Article 25 Eidas 'to an electronic signature the legal effects and the admissibility as evidence in judicial proceedings cannot be denied for the sole reason of its electronic form or because it does not satisfy the requirements for qualified electronic signatures', alongside Article 20, paragraph 1-*bis*, of the CAD states that 'the electronic document satisfies the requirement of the written form and has the efficacy envisaged by Article 2702 of the Civil Code when there is a digital signature, other type of qualified electronic signature or a signature advanced electronics or, in any case, it is formed, subject to the computer identification of its author, through a process having the requisites set by the AgID pursuant to Article 71 in such a way as to guarantee the security, integrity and non-modifiability of the document and, in a manifest manner and unequivocal, its traceability to the author. In all other cases, the suitability of the electronic document to satisfy the requirement of the written form and its probative value are freely assessable in court, in relation to the characteristics of security, integrity and non-modifiability'.

1007. The date and time of formation of the electronic document can be opposed to third parties if affixed in accordance with the Guidelines.

1008. An important distinction to be made, therefore, is that between documents signed with one of the electronic signatures described above and documents not bearing any electronic or simple signature.

Among the latter must be included the case of the analogical document signed in a handwritten manner and subsequently scanned in digital format, this digital document thus formed by it is not considered a signed document; in order to acquire equal value, or that of traceability to a specific subject in terms of content and paternity, it is necessary to resort to other procedural tools such as, the non-contestation by counterparty and its dispatch through a box of company e-mail or PEC.

1009. It should also be noted that as indicated in Article 21 CAD cit. even electronic signatures, simple and resistant, can be disregarded as well as the handwritten one through the verification process, or rather those who disregard to prove, for example, that a subject did not place the electronic signature by means of witness testimony without forgetting in all this, however, the obligation of diligent custody of the same pursuant to Article 32 CAD 'the holder of the signature certificate is required to ensure the custody of the signature device or of the IT authentication tools for the use of the remote signature device, and to adopt all the organizational and technical measures suitable to avoid damage to others; he is also required to personally use the signature device'.

1010. From this it follows that if a person succeeds in proving that he was not the one to affix an electronic signature, he will also have to prove that he has fulfilled the duties of diligent custody of the same; otherwise he could still incur liability for damages or anything else caused by virtue of unauthorized use of your signature.

1011. Last consideration to be made to the theme of electronic signatures is that of their temporary validity, in fact considering the speed with which the technology is developed for legal traffic safety reasons, it is advisable to expire the certificates of the signatures that should be periodically updated.

This also gives rise to the consideration that with reference to the medium tempore documents signed, the only way for them to retain their full effectiveness over time is that the documents signed in this way are kept within the digital preservation systems certified according to the criteria briefly outlined above or associate an electronic timestamp with the purpose of guaranteeing the validity of the document even after the expiry of the certificate.

1012. Therefore, as we can see, reporting the latter considerations, we can conclude that the first analysis related to the world of digital documentation and its legal validity as regards its formation, conservation as well as the aspects relating to their underwriting and efficacy, also from the evidentiary point of view, is concluded. we have a document signed with a digital signature, qualified or advanced (or equivalent), while in the case of a 'simple' electronic signature, the free evaluability of the judge who will use other possible procedural means to reinforce his / her conviction returns.

Chapter 3. Legal Aspect of Electronic Banking

§1. Foreword

1013. The use of information and communication technologies in banking activities dates back to the work carried out in the 1980s by institutions such as the Società Italiana per l'Automazione (SIA, Italian Society for Automatization) and the Commissione Interbancaria per i Problemi dell'Automazione (Inter-Bank Commission for Automatization Problems).

Today, having advanced beyond the phase of 'internal' automation of banking activity, the efforts of the banks are aimed to supply services to customers through the Web or alternative technologies of long-distance access. Such development represents an effective instrument for the banks to remain competitive in the market, by reducing the costs of the managing of services and raising, in parallel, profits. For customers, instead, the advantages connected with electronic banking are represented by far easier access to the services offered by banks and by a reduction of the charges and the costs connected with the various services and operations.

1014. After a first phase of diffidence by the customers, Internet banking, as it is often defined, has become significant.

From a survey presented in April 2004,[299] it emerges that at the end of 2003 in Italy, the number of current accounts online is about 6.3 million, with a rise of a million and a half with respect to the previous year. About half of these allow customers to carry out trading operations online. Approximately 20% of current accounts are accessible through the Web and the number of users who declare having closed their traditional countercurrent account to use the online (telematic) management is only rising. Significant increases are registered also with reference to the data that regard the use of the Web account by Italians, both to obtain information and to carry out online banking and trading operations.

§2. The Main Juridical Questions

1015. From a juridical point of view, the main questions that can emerge in the ambit of electronic banking regard: the offer of long-distance services; the conclusion of contracts; the respect of anti-money laundering regulations; the validity and proof of operations; and the possibility of identifying new forms of liability with reference, for example, to possible system discontinuances or damages suffered by customers.

It is necessary to preliminarily emphasize that the main provisions on the matter are Testo Unico Bancario (TUB, Consolidation on Banking);[300] the Istruzioni di

299. Source KPMG Business Advisory Services, *Rapporto semestrale sulla finanza on line in Italia*, presented in Milan on 1 Apr. 2004 and based on the data supplied by 59 among the main Italian Banks and Sims.

300. D.Lgs. 1 Sep. 1993, n. 385.

Vigilanza (Vigilance Instructions) of Bank of Italy;[301] the Testo Unico sull'Intermediazione Finanziaria (TUF, Consolidation on Financial Intermediation);[302] the law of 3 May 1991, n. 143;[303] il D.Lgs. 15 January 1992, n. 50.[304] It is necessary, furthermore, to remember that the reception in the Italian juridical system of Directive 2002/65/ CE concerning the long-distance commercialization of financial services to customers is awaited.[305]

To these have to be added the interpretative circulars and the implementing regulations enforced by vigilance organizations: Bank of Italy, Consob, Ufficio Italiano Cambi.

§3. The Offer of Long-Distance Services

1016. The first question that has to be analysed regards the modalities through which banks can offer their products and services through the use of long-distance communication techniques[306] and in particular, the Internet. The first statutory reference can be found in the Istruzioni di Vigilanza (Vigilance Instructions)[307] through which the Bank of Italy regulates the offer by Italian Banks of banking and financial services abroad in absence of branches (without establishment), including among them the services performed through 'informational networks', as long as '(a) the service is supplied in consequence of a commercial initiative, by the supplier on the territory of the addressee, that is not limited to the sole promotion, but contains an invitation to clinch the contract; (b) . . . the contract concerning the performance of the service can be clinched at a distance'.[308]

1017. The offer of services through the Internet by the bank, as long as it has the characteristics now mentioned, is therefore subject to the provisions on the performance of services without the establishment of branches. However, the Bank of Italy has not linked the regulation with the provisions related to the clinching of banking contracts and in particular to the duty of written form required for the conclusion of long-distance contracts.

301. Circular of the Bank of Italy n. 229, 21 Apr. 1999.
302. D.Lgs. 24 Feb. 1998, n. 58.
303. Conversion in statute, with modifications, of the Decree 3 May 1991, n. 143, containing urgent measures to limit the use of cash and bearer securities in transactions and prevent the use of the financial system for the purpose of money laundering (so-called anti-laundering statute).
304. Implementation of the Directive (CEE) n. 577/85 on the matter of contracts negotiated out of commercial premises.
305. With Law n. 306 of 31 Oct. 2003 (so-called 2003 communitarian statute) the Government has been burdened with the task of implementing a series of directives of the European Community, among which is indeed the mentioned one (the implementation of which was foreseen by the Community Legislature within 9 Oct. 2004).
306. Art. 32 of the TUF provides that by long-distance communication techniques 'are meant those techniques of contact with the customers, other than advertising, that do not imply the physical simultaneous presence of the customer and of the offering subject or a subject he has assigned'. An identical definition is given in the Vigilance Instructions of the Bank of Italy.
307. Title III, Ch. 3.
308. Para. 3, Title III, Ch. 3, s. I.

1018. The Consob, by virtue of the delegation contained in Article 32, second paragraph, TUF, has enforced specific provisions[309] that regard 'the promotion and placement of investment services, of financial instruments and of other financial products by qualified subject' providing that if they are performed through long-distance communication techniques that allow to establish a contact with single investors:

(a) with the possibility of a dialogue or of other forms of fast interaction;
(b) also without the possibility of a fast interaction, if the documents or messages sent have a contractual content,[310] have to be subject to the regulation of the offer out of sight,[311] with a relationship of genus *ad speciem* with the long-distance offer.[312]

Such reference implies the duty for the 'qualified subjects' (therefore also banks) to resort to financial promoters. Article 76 of the Regulation Consob, when confirming that this duty is limited to the offer performed through techniques 'that allow an individual communication and an immediate interaction with the investor', rules out its subsistence in the case where the contract between the parties has occurred on the initiative of the customer, without any solicitation by the bank 'with messages addressed to him'.

1019. The Commission has clarified that it is necessary to distinguish the offer through websites, for which, due to the technical characteristics of the instrument used, it is not necessary to resort to financial promoters, from those through e-mail, for which the duty remains.[313] It is specified that, if the interaction starts on the initiative of the investor, the intermediary can anyway use assigned clerks that are not financial promoters to send to the investors through e-mail:

- messages of confirmation of the dispositions given by the investor;
- on request of the investor, not solicited by the assigned clerk, the documents, even contractual, necessary for the purchase or the subscription of financial products or for the beginning of relationships that regard the performance of investment services with the intermediary itself or with third intermediaries;
- merely descriptive information on the offering subject, on the investment services or on the financial products offered.

309. Book IV of the Regulation n. 11522 of 1 Jul. 1998.
310. In substance all the general communication techniques, addressed *ad incertam personam* and that do not have a merely advertising character.
311. Provided by Book III of the same regulation.
312. *See* B. Urselli, *Internet Banking*, in G. Cassano (a cura di), *Diritto delle nuove tecnologie informatiche e dell'INTERNET*, Milano, 2002.
313. Consob communication n. DI/99052838 of 7 Jul. 1999.

§4. THE CLINCHING OF THE CONTRACT

1020. The regulation related to the clinching of financial contracts is contained in Article 117 of the TUB and in Title X, Chapter I, Section III of the Vigilance Instructions for banking contracts, in Article 23 of the TUF and in the related implementing regulations for the part concerning investment services. Furthermore, in the scope of the specific topic here discussed, the provisions on the clinching of out-of-sight and long-distance contracts, placed in Chapter II and III, Title III of the Vigilance Instructions, in D.Lgs. n. 50/1992 and in D.Lgs. n. 70 of 9 April 2003, have to be considered.[314]

1021. Both the regulations related to banking contracts and the one related to financial services provide in general that contracts have to be clinched in written form. In particular, Article 117 of the TUB and Article 23 of the TUF, by using the same formula, provide that contracts 'are drafted in written form and a copy is given to the customers'.[315]

The requirement of the written form is necessary and substantial for the validity of the contract. This formalism is meant as an instrument of transparency and protection of the weaker and more vulnerable contracting party, aimed to render evident and knowable and, in consequence, irrefutable, the content of contractual relationships, to the point that it clearly prevails on the equally felt need of speed and efficiency of commercial activities. The violation of the requirement results in the contract becoming voidable: such voidness being relative, as the action can be taken only by the customer (Article 127, paragraph 2 of the T.U.) and, therefore, realized as an instrument of protection of a private interest of the customer.

1022. With specific regard to banking contracts it is, however, spared the possibility for the CICR[316] of 'allowing particular contracts, due to grounded technical reasons, to be clinched in another form'. Since the CICR has never adopted decisions of this kind, Article 161 of the TUB is considered applicable: this provides, indirectly, the operativeness of the Decree of the Ministero del Tesoro (Minister of Treasury) of 22 April 1992 that deviates from the written form 'for the operations and services already contemplated inside contracts drafted in written form'. Therefore, Internet banking can be considered only as an applicative modality of a contract already existing between the bank and the user, and the stance according to which the elements of the electronic banking contract consist of the clinching of a 'general' contractual agreement between the bank and the customer and of the provision of the modality of performance of contractual considerations has to be

314. Implementation of the Directive 2000/31/CE related to some juridical aspects of the services of information society, in particular electronic commerce, in the internal market.

315. The copy that has to be given to the customer has to consist in the text of the contract duly signed by both the contracting parties, it is not sufficient the delivery of the sole contractual model. *See* G. Alpa, *Qualche rilievo civilistico sulla disciplina dei mercati finanziari e sulla tutela del risparmiatore, in Banca, Borsa e titoli di credito*, 1998, 372.

316. *Comitato Interministeriale per il Credito ed il Risparmio* (Interministerial committee for Credit and Savings).

accepted.[317] Such stance is confirmed by what is provided in the Vigilance Instructions of the Bank of Italy that with reference to the form of contracts clarifies that the written form is not mandatory:

(a) for operations and services performed within the completion of considerations contained in contracts drafted in written form (for example operations regulated in current account);
(b) for operations and services performed occasionally – such as, for example, payment orders in favour of third subjects, purchase or sale of foreign currency, issue of bank drafts – provided the total value of the transaction does not exceed EUR 5,000 and as long as the bank:
    (1) keeps record of the operation carried out;
    (2) delivers or timely sends written confirmation of the operation to the customer, showing the price practised, the charges and the expenses charged.
(c) for the issue of electronic currency through un-rechargeable anonymous prepaid payment cards (so-called throwaway).[318]

The Consob has equally clarified that the duty of written form subsists only for the first act of adhesion and not for all the other successive operations inherent to the same relationship.[319]

1023. The Bank of Italy emphasizes furthermore that the requirement of written form is certainly fulfilled if 'the conditions provided by the D.P.R. 28 December 2000, n. 445 are respected',[320] namely when the resort to the use of the digital signature occurs, but this specification only in part reduces the problems pointed out before, since the diffusion of these instruments among users is still very modest and, at least at the moment, no bank offers the possibility to digitally sign contracts between the bank and its customers.

1024. Every other document (bank statements, informative prospectus, etc.), the delivery of which is provided to the customer, is considered fully compliant with the regulation in force, as long as the customer has the possibility to keep it on a durable support. All other information that, according to the regulation, has to be

---

317. *See* F. Sarzana Di Sant'Ippolito, *I contratti bancari a distanza, l'Internet Banking*, in Bancamatica, n. 1-2, 2001.
318. Para. 2, second comma, Title X, Ch. 1, s. III, Vigilance Instructions, Circolare n. 229 of 21 Apr. 1999.
319. Specification contained in a communication related to the subscription of investment pools, but that has to be considered as a general principle applicable to all the contracts related to investment services. Consob communication DIS/99051449/1999.
320. Para. 4, second comma, Title X, Ch. 1, s. III, Vigilance Instructions, Circolare n. 229 of 21 Apr. 1999. On the matter of digital signature *see* M.C. Bianca, *I contratti digitali*, in *Studium Iuris*, Padova, 1998; P. Piccoli – G. Zanolini, *Il documento elettronico e la « firma digitale»*, in *Rivista del notariato*, 4/2000; G. Finocchiaro, *La firma digitale*, Bologna – Roma, 2000; C. Cevenini, *Il documento informatico e la firma digitale*, in E. Pattaro (a cura di), *Manuale di diritto dell'informatica e delle nuove tecnologie*, Bologna, 2002, 111 ss.; F. Delfini, *Il documanto informatico nella prima giurisprudenza della cassazione e il T.U. di cui alla novella del D.P.R. n. 445/ 2000*, in I Contratti, 3/2002.

given to the customer can, therefore, be transmitted through the Internet, as long as this option is not presented as automatic to the customer (that is, it has to be the consequence of a voluntary choice) and it is possible for the bank to keep a record of the correct fulfilment of the duties imposed and of the attestations received.

1025. Lastly, it has to be remembered that given that these contracts are concluded out of sight, D.Lgs. 50/1992 is in general applicable and therefore the contract has to include the provision of the right to recession within seven days from the signing, that becomes sixty days if the consumer has not received the necessary information on the existence of this right[321] (contracts regarding property securities are expressly ruled out). With reference to financial contracts, Article 30 of the TUF expressly clarifies that 'the efficacy of the contracts of placement of financial instruments or of management of individual portfolios clinched out of see or placed at a distance . . . is discontinued for seven days accruing from the date of the signing by the investor'.

1026. The implementation of Directive 2002/65/CE will cause a necessary revision of the mentioned provisions on this point, since on the one hand the exclusion of financial services from the scope of appliance of Directive 97/27/CE that concerns the general regulation on the matter of long-distance contracts[322] is expressly eliminated and on the other a longer deadline for the exercise of the right to recession is provided.[323]

§5. Electronic Banking and Anti-money Laundering Regulation: The Problem of Identification

1027. As mentioned before, the use of Internet for the long-distance commercialization of financial services poses some questions with regard to respect of the anti-money-laundering regulation.[324] As is known, intermediaries are requested to

321. *See* further on this point L. Bonzanini, *La disciplina del collocamento a distanza di prodotti finanziari*, in I Contratti, 5/1999, that emphasizes how generally the right to recession is not applied 'by many belonging to the banking sector, probably on the supposition that banks were not included in the definition of 'trade operator', or because the legislation provided by the vigilance instructions of the Banca d'Italia on the matter of out of *see* offer of banking products regulated exhaustively such matter as special regulation'.

322. That had indeed explicitly ruled out from its appliance scope contracts related to financial services (Art. 3, lett. a), listed in exemplificative way in the related all. II. The directive in point has been implemented in the Italian juridical system by D.Lgs. n. 185, 22 May 1999.

323. For a commentary on the directive *see* M. Atelli, *Commercializzazione a distanza di servizi finanziari e tutela del consumatore europeo nella direttiva 2002/65/CE*, in *Il Corriere giuridico*, 4/2003; M. Giurgola, *La direttiva 2002/65/CE sulla commercializzazione a distanza di servizi finanziari: l'epilogo di una lunga attesa*, in *Le Società: rivista di diritto e pratica commerciale, societaria e fiscale*, 1/2003; F. Roncarati, *La direttiva 2002/65/CE concernente la commercial-izzazione a distanza di servizi finanziari ai consumatori*, in *Banca impresa società*, 1/2004.

324. The fundamental legislation is represented by the Law 5 Jul. 1991, n. 197. For a complete discussion on the Italian legislation on the matter of anti-laundering, *see* R. Razzante, *La normativa antiriciclaggio in Italia*, Torino, 1999; D. Masciandaro, *Banche e riciclaggio*, Milano, 1994; F. Capriglione, *L'antiriciclaggio tra prevenzione sociale e disinquinamento del settore finanziario*, in

personally identify their customers both on the occasion of deposits of more than EUR 12,500[325] and in the hypothesis of continuous relationships, including the opening of an account or a deposit.

1028. The duties of identification now outlined represent one of the main obstacles on the matter of the clinching of long-distance financial contracts, also in light of the clarifications of the Comitato Antiriciclaggio (Anti-money-laundering Committee) according to which 'in principle the identification of a customer . . . has to be performed by the intermediary in presence of the same customer'[326] and of the Decree of the Minister of Treasury of 19 December 1991 that provides that identification data related to the opening of accounts, deposits or other continuing relationships have to be acquired in presence of the proprietor of the relationship or of the mandatory, if they are not proprietors of other relationships with the same intermediary.

1029. Given the general principle of direct identification, the same authorities have successively provided some derogations. For purposes that are of interest here it must be pointed out that the Comitato Antiriciclaggio has recognized that 'in particular cases the intermediary is allowed to use the identification data acquired by another intermediary, provided that this data result from a document with which this second subject declares, under his own responsibility, having performed the identification'.[327]

1030. With reference, then, to the possibility of clinching determined contracts through mail, the deviation has been allowed and has to be considered applicable by analogy also to the other banking and financial contracts, where the customer is someone the intermediary has already had relationships with. For the efficacy of the underlying relationship, indeed, 'the provision allows to rescind from the verification of the recognition document and the acquisition of the related details',[328] as long as the customer has a valid identification document.

These derogations realize the appliance of the principles of long-distance identification, contained in the Decree of the Ministero del Tesoro of 29 October 1993, and of simplified identification, contained in the 1991 decree, and represent an effective modality of fulfilment of the identification duties provided by Article 2 of Law 197/1991, for contracts concluded through the Internet. They are, however, derogations that require the existence of a pre-existing relationship or the intervention of a third party held to the fulfilment of such duties.

Banca borsa e titoli di credito, Milano, 1998, n. 4; U. Belviso, *Gli intermediary finanziari*, in Giurisprudenza commerciale, Milano, I, 2000; D. Masciandaro, *Criminalità e intermediazione finanziaria*, Milano, 1996.

325. *See* D.M. 17 ottobre 2002, publ. in G.U. n. 290 dell'11 dicembre 2002, that has brought up to EUR 12,500 the limit of EUR 10,329.14 that derived from the conversion in euro of the original amount of 20 million lire.
326. Anti-money-laundering Committee, opinion of 21 Dec. 1995, n. 30.
327. Anti-laundering Committee, cited opinion.
328. Anti-laundering Committee, *Contratti di finanziamento per corrispondenza ed obblighi di identificazione di cui all'art. 2 della Legge 5 luglio 1991*, opinion of 8 Nov. 1996, n. 49.

What is reported represents a significant limit to the possibility of employing online (telematic) technologies in the formative phase of the contractual relationship.

1031. The Ufficio Italiano Cambi, by acknowledging the development of the new financial, security and insurance products, as well as the fast technical evolution of distribution and placement instruments, has recognized the necessity to outline an operational scenery sufficiently certain for the identification of the behaviours that the intermediaries have to observe when identifying customers if they employ online (telematic) instruments.[329] On the basis of the stance expressed in the European Community (*see*, *for example*, by the European Commission, the draft of Directive 14 July 1999),[330] the UIC has expressly stated the possibility of using interpretation to 'adjust the appliance of the regulation in force to the evolution of the operative forms'.

1032. In particular, starting from the consideration that the draft of the abovementioned directive includes the payment performed through credit transfer among the criteria to have the certainty of the origin of the accounts, and considering that the Decrees of the Ministero del Tesoro do not provide any particular requirements of form for the issue of the attestations related to the long-distance identifications, the UIC has specified that 'the use of a credit transfer on an account, presupposing the occurred identification of the subscriber by the transferring bank at the time of the opening of the account, would render unnecessary its repetition by the requesting intermediary'. In order to be a valid attestation, the credit transfer has to comply with the following conditions:

- the credit transfer has to be performed on a continuing relationship for which the customer has been properly identified;
- the 'contracting intermediary' (that has to perform the long-distance identification), once received the communication of identification data from the customer, has to assign to this an identification code to communicate to the bank that, in turn, will have to report it on the credit transfer sent to the intermediary;
- all the following operations have to transit on the original supporting account, in order to have the certainty that they are always performed by the same subject, so that the duty of identification provided for every operation to have effect on the same relationship will be fulfilled.

A further method of long-distance identification, alternative to the credit transfer, is identified by the UIC in the compilation of a form containing the identification data of the customer, stamped and signed by the attesting intermediary.[331]

329. Ufficio Italiano Cambi, 'Parere in materia di identificazione a distanza', 31 Jan. 2000.

330. Draft for directive COM(1999)352 def., in modification of the directive 91/308/ CEE related to the prevention of the use of the financial system for illicit activities' money laundering.

331. Method certainly not adequate to the mentioned needs of speed and dematerialization.

1033. In the perspective of favouring the functionality of the system through the employment of online (telematic) technologies, the UIC has expressed itself on the possibility for intermediaries to use a digital signature, investigating the limits within which this can be an instrument adequate to attesting the identification, for anti-laundering purposes, of a subject that operates with long-distance communication techniques. Since in general the auditors are not included among the subjects obligated by the observance of the anti-laundering regulation and, specifically, the identification required to them for the issue of a digital signature does not necessarily require the presence *de visu* of the requesting subject (leaving to the auditor the choice of the procedure to follow), the digital signature can be considered an adequate instrument to attest the occurred identification in long-distance operations only when it is issued after a procedure that respects the general principles on the matter of anti-laundering. For this purpose, the operative handbook (in which the procedure adopted by the certifying subject is identified) is therefore required to provide that the identification has to occur in the presence of the customer, that the measures of revocation or discontinuance of the digital signature have to be disclosed and that on the occasion of the renewal of the signature, the identity of the customer has to be verified once again.

1034. To this has to be added the fact that Law 197/1991 provides that the identification has to occur through '*assigned staff*', this expression meaning 'subjects tied to the intermediary by a relationship of subordinate work or by a relationship of collaboration provided by statutory provisions or by a proper convention in which are specified the duties' of Law 197/1991.[332] Therefore, in order to let the intermediary resort to identification performed by the auditor, it is necessary for him to stipulate a proper convention with this. It has yet to be specified that the intermediary remains anyway the only liable party for violations of the anti-laundering regulation and thus he is held responsible to verify the work of the auditor.

332. For a deep analysis on the problems related to long-distance identification through digital signature and an accurate critic on the opinion expressed by UIC, *see* F. Bravo, *Le convenzioni con gli enti certificatori di firma digitale*, in *I Contratti*, N. 5/2003.

Chapter 4. Protection of Users of Electronic Services

§1. Protection of Users of Electronic Services

1035. The exigency of protection of the consumer, meant in general as a physical person that acts beyond a professional role or activity,[333] rises from the consideration of how he appears the 'weak contracting party' with respect to the professional operator, primarily due to the different level of information he has access to.

If the exigencies of protection of the consumer affirmed themselves before the development of electronic commerce, it is precisely with reference to this (the so-called *e-commerce business to consumer*) that this topic finds today one of the most significant battlefields: in transactions performed online. Indeed, the imbalance between the positions of the contracting parties is intensified, due to the technological barrier that can thwart or prevent the consumer not only from identifying with certainty the counterpart but also from knowing (and often negotiating) the contractual conditions, from adequately examining and/or evaluating the good or service that is the object of the agreement, from understanding the mechanisms of functioning of the informational and online (telematic) instrument and the related legal (juridical) consequences.[334]

1036. The EU Legislature has always been particularly sensitive and active with regard to the protection of the consumer, so that the consistent *corpus* of national regulations dedicated to it is largely derived from EC legislation.[335]

1037. The first national measure of interest for the purposes of the present treatment, still in force, dates back to 1992. D.Lgs. of 15 January 1992, n. 50, 'Attuazione della direttiva n. 85/577/CEE in materia di contratti negoziati fuori dei locali

333. Although similar in part, there have been many legal definitions of consumer introduced through time. The one contained in Art. 2, lett. e) of D.Lgs. 9 Apr. 2003, n. 70, Attuazione della direttiva 2000/31/CE refers to '*relativa a taluni aspetti giuridici dei servizi della società dell'informazione, in particolare il commercio elettronico, nel mercato interno*', G.U. 14 Apr. 2003, n. 87: any physical person that acts 'with purposes not referable to the trade, enterprise or professional activity possibly exercised'.

334. On the subject *see*, *ex multis*, A. Palazzo, U. Ruffolo (a cura di), *La tutela del navigatore in Internet*, Milano, Giuffrè, 2002; S. Sica, P. Stanzone (a cura di), *Commercio elettronico e categorie civilistiche*, Milano, Giuffrè, 2002; V. Franceschelli (a cura di), *Commercio elettronico*, Milano, Giuffrè, 2001; C. Rossello, G. Finocchiaro, E. Tosi (a cura di), *Commercio elettronico Documento informatico e firma digitale*, Giappichelli, Torino, 2003; F. Delfini, *Il Commercio elettronico*, CEDAM, Padova, 2004.

335. After all, the protection of the interests of the consumers is expressly recalled among the aims of the EU (*see* Art. 153 EC Treaty). The centrality of the topic has been expressly confirmed, with specific reference to electronic commerce and to the services of the information society, in Art. 3 of the Directive 2000/31/CE and thus in Art. 5 of D.Lgs. 70/2003. The Italian doctrine, also, has not failed to assess how the stratification of the legislation on the matter of protection of the consumer, first at a European level, then at a national one, poses today, due to the lack of an adequate coordination between the various measures, many interpretative questions; a situation that could hopefully change with the enforcement of the consolidation on the matter of consumerism, the final approval of which could be imminent (*see infra*).

commerciali',[336] although not primarily dedicated to online (telematic) contracts, expressly provides, indeed, its appliance also to contracts regarding the supply of good or the performance of services 'clinched through the use of informational or telematic instruments'.[337]

1038. The salient elements of the Decree under examination consist of the introduction of the (inalienable) right to recession for the consumer (Article 4 D.Lgs. 50/1992) and the related informative duties that burden the trade operator, as well as in the provision of unavoidable territorial competence of the judge of the place of residence or domicile of the consumer, if located on the State territory, for possible civil controversies (Article 12 D.Lgs. 50/1992).

1039. Having introduced the definitions of 'consumer' and 'trade operator',[338] the field of application of the Decree is then delimited to cases in which a contract regarding the supply of goods or the performance of services is stipulated between a consumer and a trade operator out of the commercial premises of the second,[339] while expressly excluded are contracts regarding estates, foodstuffs, drinks or other products of domestic use delivered at frequent and regular times, insurance contracts and the contracts related to stock exchange securities (Article 3 D.Lgs. 50/1992).

1040. The terms and modalities for the exertion of the right to recession (as anticipated, the right cannot in any case be the object of renunciation by the consumer, Article 10 D.Lgs. 50/1992) are provided by Article 6 of the Decree: in general, within seven days from the reception of the goods or from the date of signing of the order note, the consumer will have to send the trade operator a communication in which he declares the will to recede from the contract, without the necessity

---

336. G.U. 3 Feb. 1992, n. 27.
337. Art. 9 (other special forms of sale), para. 1 D.Lgs. 50/1992. It has to be noticed how Art. 11 itself, para. 2 D.P.R. 28 Dec. 2000, n. 445, *Testo unico delle disposizioni legislative e regolamentari in materia di documentazione amministrativa* (Consolidation of the statutory and regulamentary provisions on the matter of administrative documentation), G.U. 20 Feb. 2001, n. 42, provides that to contracts concluded with informational instruments or through online (telematic) means through the use of a qualified electronic signature 'apply the provisions in force on the matter of contracts negotiated out of the trade premises'. The reference operated (today implicitly) to D.Lgs. 50/1992 by Art. 11, para. 2 D.P.R. 445/2000 has been the object of various interpretations. The doctrine appears at the moment to consider its value as merely strengthening and of reference with regard to the applicability of such discipline also when the contractual will is concretized in an informational document signed with a qualified signature. *See* C. Rossello, in *Commercio elettronico Documento informatico e firma digitale*, C. Rossello, G. Finocchiaro, E. Tosi (a cura di), *cited work*, p. 419; F. Delfini, *Il Commercio elettronico*, *cited work*, pp. 244-245.
338. Respectively (Art. 2 D.Lgs. 50/1992): the physical person that acts for purposes that can be considered extraneous to his professional activity; the physical or juridical person that acts in the scope of his trading or professional activity, as well as the person that acts in the name and on behalf of a trade operator.
339. *See* Art. 1 D.Lgs. 50/1992.

to adduce any justification or reason. The communication can occur through registered letter with return receipt, or through telegram, telex or telefax, provided that within the following forty-eight hours a confirmation is given through a registered letter with a reception notice.

With the reception of the communication of the recession by the trade operator, the parties are free from the respective contractual duties, except, of course, if the contract has been partly or totally performed. In these cases, the consumer, within seven days, will have to give the good received back to the trade operator, while the trade operator will be held to refund what has already been paid by the consumer within thirty days from the reception of the communication related to the recession (Article 8 D.Lgs. 50/1992).

The right to recession cannot be exerted if the delivered goods are not any more substantially intact, or for performances, in hypotheses of contracts regarding services, that have already been carried out (Article 7 D.Lgs. 50/1992).

1041. The trade operator is also burdened with the duty to inform the consumer, in written form and before the concluding of the contract, of the existence in his favour of the right to recession, as well as on the terms, modalities and other conditions for its exercise (Article 5 D.Lgs. 50/1992).[340]

1042. The opportunity to apply the provisions of D.Lgs 50/1992 to the hypotheses of electronic commerce has caused the rise, however, of some perplexities. The question, in particular, is whether the online (telematic) sale really frames a contract 'negotiated out of the commercial premises' or not. Actually, the consumer, on his own initiative (telematically), reaches the virtual spaces of the vendor online and, therefore, he seemingly does not suffer the vendor's commercial aggressiveness.

1043. More adherent to reality and the characteristics of electronic commerce is the regulation introduced with D.Lgs. 22 May 1999, n. 185, '*Attuazione della direttiva 97/7/CE relativa alla protezione dei consumatori in materia di contratti a distanza*'.[341]

The reasons that have caused a new intervention on the topic can be chosen among a great number, considering that they pre-exist Directive 97/7/CE. Long-distance commerce, characterized by the employment of communication techniques included in the ambit of a sale or service performance organization, would not allow the consumer to base his contractual decisions on a sufficiently faithful picture. In particular, the worry of the provision of adequate instruments for the protection of consumers in the ambit of trans-frontier commerce emerges. The purpose is not only to protect the contracting party that is potentially weaker but also to create within

340. In case the trade operator has omitted to supply the consumer with the information on the right to recession or anyway has supplied it in a way that does not allow the correct exertion of the right, the deadline within which it is possible to exert it will be sixty days from the date of clinching of the contract or from the date of reception of the good (Art. 6 D.Lgs. 50/1992).

341. G.U. 21 Jun. 1999, n. 143 (rectification G.U. 30 Sep. 1999, n. 230).

the European Union a feeling of trust towards the new modalities of negotiation, guaranteeing a clear and homogeneous juridical frame of reference.

1044. The Italian decree that implements the directive faithfully traces the community text, and even, as it will be seen, introduces some innovations aimed at elevating the level of protection of the consumer.

1045. Article 1 of D.Lgs. 185/99 contains, first of all, the definitions: the consumer is described as 'the physical person that acts for purposes not ascribable to a professional activity possibly exercised'; the long-distance contract is 'the contract clinched between a supplier (a subject that acts in the scope of his professional activity) and a consumer with a long-range system, organized by the supplier, that employs, for the determination of the content of the contract and its clinching, exclusively one or more long-range communication techniques'; lastly, 'long-range communication techniques' refers to 'any means that, without the simultaneous physical presence of the supplier and the consumer, can be employed for the clinching of the contract . . .'.

1046. The first protection measure identified consists of a duty of an informative kind towards the consumer. The consumer has to receive, before the conclusion of the long-distance contract, the following information (Article 3 D.Lgs. 185/1999):

- identity and address of the supplier;
- essential characteristics of the good or service that is the object of the contract;
- the price, including all the taxes and rates, the expenses and the modalities for delivery and payment and every other form of performance of the contract;
- the length of the validity of the offer and the price;
- the existence of the right to recession or its exclusion;
- the modalities and times for returning or collecting of the good in case the right to recession is exerted;
- the cost relating to the employment of the communication technique used when the cost is calculated on a parameter different from the basic tariff;
- the minimum length of the contract in case of contracts with a continuous or periodical completion.

This information, connected in an unequivocal way to the intention of proposing a contract of commercial nature, has to be supplied, according to the principles of trade loyalty, in a clear and comprehensible way, with the most adequate means according to the communication technique employed by the supplier (Article 3).[342]

342. In particular, in case of telephonic communication, the identity of the supplier and the commercial purpose of the telephone call have to be strictly declared at the beginning of the conversation; otherwise (with an innovation with respect to the text of the Directive 97/7/CE) the contract will be void (Art. 3, para. 3 D.Lgs. 185/1999). On the matter of the regulation on electronic commerce provided by D.Lgs. 70/2003, when a consumer is involved, in particular about the informative duties and the forwarding of the order receipt, *see* what is reported *supra*, Part IV, para. 1, *Legal status of electronic transaction*.

Article 3, paragraph 4, D.Lgs. 185/1999 provides that, in case of personal communication, the information has to be supplied in Italian if the consumer so requests.

The information listed, and some other information,[343] must be confirmed to the consumer in written form or, at his choice, on another durable support at his disposal, before or at the time of the completion of the contract (Article 4 D.Lgs. 185/1999).

1047. The regulation provided by the Decree does not apply to long-distance contracts (Article 2 D.Lgs. 185/1999):

- related to financial services;
- clinched through automatic dispensers;
- clinched with telecommunication operators that employ public telephones;
- clinched for the construction or the sale of estates or that have as their object rights related to estates;
- clinched on the occasion of an auction.

1048. The protection of the consumer in the matter of long-distance contracts finds, once again, its fundamental regulation in the provision of the right to recession for the consumer, as a form of compensation for his position of weakness and informative *deficit*. Article 5 D.Lgs. 185/1999 provides that, within ten working days, without any specification of the reasons and without any penalty, the consumer can recess from any long-distance contract, simply by forwarding a written communication to the geographical address of the premises of the supplier, through a registered letter with a reception notice.[344] The only expenses the consumer has to suffer for the exertion of the right to recession will be the expenses aimed at the restitution of the goods to the sender when this is expressly provided by the long-distance contract.

If the delivery of the good has occurred, the consumer will of course be obligated to return it or to place it at the disposal of the supplier or the person designated, according to the modalities and times provided by the contract. The deadline for the restitution of the goods cannot in any way be shorter than ten working days, accruing from the date of reception of the good. The supplier, on his part, will have to

343. In particular (Art. 4 D.Lgs. 185/1999): (a) an information on the conditions and the modalities of the exertion of the right to recession; (b) the geographical address of the premises of the supplier the consumer can submit claims to; (c) the information on the after-sale service and on the existing commercial guarantees; (d) the terms for the recession from the contract in case the duration is undetermined or exceeds a year.

344. The deadline for the exertion of the right to recession has thus been raised with respect to the seven working days provided by the EC text (*see* Art. 6, para. 1 Directive 97/7/CE) and will accrue: (a) for goods, from the day of their reception by the consumer; (b) for services, from the day of the clinching of the contract. This goes as long as the informational duties contained in 4 D.Lgs. 185/1999 and above-mentioned have been fulfilled: otherwise the deadline will accrue from the day in which they have been fulfilled if this fulfilment occurs after the clinching of the contract and provided it does not occur after the deadline of three months from the clinching. In case the supplier has omitted to give the mandatory information, the deadline for the right to recession is raised to three months, accruing (a) for goods, from the day of their reception by the consumer and (b) for services, from the day of the clinching of the contract.

attend for free to the refund of what has possibly been paid by the consumer in the shortest time possible and anyway within thirty days from the time of his knowledge of the exertion of the right to recession by the consumer.

1049. Unless the parties reach a different agreement between themselves, the possibility to exert the right to recession is ruled out in a series of situations related to contracts (Article 5, paragraph 3 D.Lgs. 185/1999):

(a) of supply of services the execution of which has already begun, with the agreement of the consumer, before the expiration of ten days deadline;
(b) of supply of goods or services the price of which is connected with fluctuations of the financial market rates that the supplier cannot control;
(c) of supply of goods tailored or clearly personalized or that, due to their nature, cannot be returned or risk to deteriorate or decay rapidly;
(d) of supply of sealed audiovisual products or informational software, opened by the consumer;
(e) of supply of newspapers, periodicals and magazines;
(f) of services of bets and lotteries.

1050. The contract will have to be performed by the supplier within thirty days accruing from the day following the transmission of the order by the consumer (Article 6 D.Lgs. 185/1999).[345]

1051. The provisions related to the informative duties, the written confirmation of the information and the right to recession, as well as to the performance by the supplier, do not apply, however, to:

- contracts of supply of foodstuff, drinks or other goods for domestic use of current consumption delivered at the domicile of the consumer, at his place of residence or work, by distributors that perform frequent and regular rounds;
- contracts of supply of services related to housing, transport, refreshment or free time, when at the act of clinching of the contract the supplier binds himself to such performances at a certain date or determinate period.

1052. Also, the principle according to which the consumer is not bound to any performance for unrequested supplies is set out, and actually they are forbidden if they imply a request of payment. In any case, the lack of answer can never be interpreted as a tacit consent of the consumer (Article 9 D.Lgs. 185/1999).[346]

---

345. Art. 6 itself, para. 2 D.Lgs. 185/1999 provides that in case of non-performance of the order by the supplier, due to unavailability, even temporary, of the good or service requested, the supplier, within the deadline of thirty days, has to inform the consumer and attend to the refund of the sums possibly already paid for the payment of the supply. Except in case of consent of the consumer, that has to be expressed before or at the time of the clinching of the contract, the supplier cannot complete the contract by performing a supply different from the one agreed upon, even if of equivalent or superior value and quality.
346. A partly similar provision, in fact, had been already introduced in D.Lgs. 31 Mar. 1998, n. 114, *Riforma della disciplina relativa al settore del commercio, a norma dell'articolo 4*, comma 4, della

1053. For the safeguard of the consumer, Article 11 D.Lgs. 185/1999 provides that the rights set out by the Decree are inalienable (and any agreement against its dispositions is void) and that they have to be recognized in favour of the consumer, even if the parties have chosen to subject the contract to a regulation other than the Italian one.[347]

1054. On the matter of the criterion on the basis of which the Court competent for civil controversies related to long-distance contracts has to be determined, in compliance with what is provided by Article 12 of D.Lgs. 50/1992, the competent territorial judge will be that of the place where the consumer has his residence or domicile, as long as he is located on the territory of the State (Article 14 D.Lgs. 185/1999).

1055. Article 13 D.Lgs. 185/1999 provides the possibility for the consumers' and users' associations to take legal actions for the protection of the consumers' general interests with reference to the subject matter of the Decree.[348]

---

legge 15 Mar. 1997, n. 59, G.U. 24 Apr. 1998, n. 95. Art. 18, para. 2 of the mentioned decree, dedicated to the 'Sale through mail, television or other communication systems' (included, therefore, the telematic instrument) provides, indeed, the prohibition to 'send good to the consumer unless after a specific request. The dispatch of samples of products or of gifts, without expenses or ties for the consumer is allowed'. The following Art. 19 of D.Lgs. 114/1998 is instead dedicated to the 'Sales performed at the domicile of the consumer'. The Minister of Industry, with reference to the mentioned decree, has successively dedicated a proper circular (Circolare 1 Jun. 2000, n. 3487/c) precisely on the regulation of the sale of goods through electronic means (namely 'electronic commerce'). After clarifying the fact that the regulation contained in the l D.Lgs. 114/1998, in particular Art. 18, applies also to the hypotheses of *e-commerce* in which one of the parts is a final consumer, it expressly signals that to such transactions clinched through the Internet both the provisions of D.Lgs, 50/ 1992 (in fact, expressly recalled by Art. 18 of the Decree), and of D.Lgs. 185/1999 apply.

347. In compliance with Directive 97/7/CE, D.Lgs. 185/1999 dedicates specific provisions to the 'Payment through card' (Art. 8) and to the 'Limits to the employment of some forms of long-distance communication' (Art. 10). In case the supplier violates the provisions set out for the protection of the consumer, Art. 12 of D.Lgs. 185/99 provides, besides the possible penal relevancy of the fact, an administrative financial penalty from EUR 516 up to 5,164, limits, that can be doubled in case of recidivism. The most recent doctrine, with specific reference to the possible omission of the informative duties towards the consumer contained in Art. 3 D.Lgs. 185/1999, has proposed also the applicability of Artt. 1439 ('Dolo', 'malice') and 1440 ('Dolo incidente', 'incident malice') of the Civil Code (Regio decreto 16 marzo 1942 – XX, n. 262, from now on 'c.c.'): therefore, respectively the voidability of the contract in case the omission has been determinant for the clinching of the contract (that without the omission would not have been clinched) and the compensation for the damage, in case, vice versa, the omission has not been determinant for the consent, although without it an agreement with different conditions would have been concluded.

348. D.Lgs. 185/1999 recalls on this regard Art. 3 of the L. 30 Jul. 1998, n. 281, *Disciplina dei diritti dei consumatori e degli utenti*, G.U. 14 Aug. 1998, n. 189, a statute that provides this faculty for the associations of consumers in general for the protection of the general interests of the consumers. This regulation declares also the fundamental rights of consumers and users (Art. 1, para. 2 L. 281/1998): (a) health protection; (b) security and quality of goods and services; (c) adequate information and correct advertising; (d) consumers' education and information; (e) fairness, transparency and equity in contractual relationships concerning goods and services; (f) promotion and development of free, voluntary and democratic associations between consumers and users; (g) provision of public services according to standards of quality and efficiency.

1056. Lastly, it must be pointed out that Article 15 D.Lgs. 185/1999 expressly provides that, until the enforcement of a consolidation of coordination with D.Lgs. 50/1992, to the special forms of sale provided by D.Lgs. 50/1992 and by Articles 18 and 19 of D.Lgs. 114/1998, apply the provisions more favourable to the consumer contained precisely in D.Lgs. 185/1999.

1057. To the dispositions now remembered, specifically dedicated to contracts clinched at a distance, has to be added the general regulation on the matter of contracts clinched between consumers and professionals, once again wanted by the EC Legislature. This consists, in particular, of the regulation related to the so-called abusive covenants provided by Articles 1469-*bis* – 1469-*sexies* c.c., as introduced by the Law of 6 February 1996, n. 52, that implemented Directive 93/13/CEE.[349]

1058. In the contract clinched between the consumer (the physical person who acts for purposes that are beyond an enterprise or professional activity possibly exercised) and the professional (a physical or legal person, public or private, who acts in the scope of his enterprise or professional activity) the covenants that, even if not against good faith, determine a significant disequilibrium, burdening the consumer, of the rights and duties deriving from the contract, are considered vexatious covenants (1469-*bis* c.c.).

The vexatiousness of a covenant has to be evaluated considering the nature of the good or service that is the object of the contract, the circumstances existing at the time of its clinching and the contractual covenants as a whole, but it does not pertain to the determination of the object of the contract nor the adequateness of the consideration for the goods and services, as long as these are identified in a clear and comprehensible way.

1059. Covenants that reproduce statutory provisions or international conventions, as well as those, with the burden of proof on the professional, that have been the object of personal negotiation are not vexatious (1469-*ter* c.c.).

1060. Article 1469-*bis* c.c. contains a series of covenants that are presumed vexatious until proved otherwise and, except for some derogations, in case of the performance of financial services.[350]

Vexatious covenants are ineffective while the contract remains effective. The ineffectiveness works only to the advantage of the consumer and can be found by the judge (1469-*quinquies* c.c.).

---

349. L. 6 Feb. 1996, n. 52, *Disposizioni per l'adempimento di obblighi derivanti dall'appartenenza dell'Italia alle Comunità europee – Legge comunitaria* 1994, G.U. 10 febbraio 1996, n. 34, that has implemented (Art. 25) the directive 93/13/CEE. The provisions in exam add to those, of general application, contained in Arts 1341 e 1342 c.c., respectively on the matter of general conditions of contract and of contracts clinched though forms and formularies, already discussed (*see supra*, Part IV, para. 1, *Legal status of electronic transaction*).

350. The twenty hypotheses of vexatious covenants provided by Art. 1469-*bis* c.c. are inspired and in line with those identified by the EC Legislature (as a list of example, not exhaustive) in the Enclosure to the Directive 93/13/CEE.

1061. Covenants are ineffective, even if they have been negotiated, if their object or their effect is:

(1) to exclude or limit the liability of the professional in case of death or damage to the person of the consumer, derived from a fact or omission of the professional;
(2) to exclude or limit the legal actions of the consumer against the professional or another part in case of total or partial non-fidelity or malpractice by the professional;
(3) to foresee the adhesion of the consumer as extended to covenants that he has not had, in fact, the possibility of knowing before concluding the contract.

In case of contracts in which all the covenants, or some of them, are proposed to the consumer in written form, such covenants always have to be drafted in a clear and comprehensible way, and in case of doubt on the sense of one covenant, the interpretation more favourable to the consumer prevails (1469 *quater* c.c.).

1062. It is furthermore set out that the ineffectiveness of any contractual covenant that, by providing the applicability to the contract of a regulation of a country out of the EC, has the effect of depriving the consumer of the protection guaranteed to him by Article 1469-*bis* – 1469-*sexies* c.c., when the contract is more closely connected with the territory of an EC Member State (Article 1469-*quinquies* c.c.).

1063. Also, the associations representative of consumers and professionals and the chambers of commerce, industry, crafts and agriculture are allowed to sue the professional or the association of professionals that employ general conditions of contract and ask the competent judge to inhibit the use of conditions the abusiveness of which has been ascertained (Article 1469-*sexies* c.c.).

1064. Contracts that are *business to consumer* offer more and more profiles of internationality, resulting in the extreme relevance of the identification of the applicable law and the competent court. On this matter, besides the provisions already mentioned, can be applied (on the basis of the reference mark contained in Article 57 of L. 31 of May 1995, n. 218[351]) the provisions of the Convention of Rome, 1980, on the law applicable to contractual obligations[352] (in particular of Article 5

351. L. 31 May 1995, n. 218, Riforma del sistema italiano di diritto internazionale privato, G.U. 3 Jun. 1995, n. 68.
352. *Convenzione di Roma* (Convention of Rome), ratified in Italy with the L. 18 dicembre 1984, n. 975, *Convenzione sulla legge applicabile alle obbligazioni contrattuali* (Convention on the regulation applicable to contractual duties), G.U. 30 Jan. 1985, n. 25. Art. 5 provides indeed that, in any case, the choice of the parts on the applicable regulation cannot have as its result the deprivation of the consumer of the protection guaranteed to him by the mandatory provisions of the legislation of the Country he usually resides in:

– if the clinching of the contract has been preceded in this country by a specific proposal or by an advert and if the consumer has performed in the same country the acts necessary for the clinching of the contract or of the Convention, titled 'Contract Clinched by the Consumers'), as well as those of Regulation (CE) n. 44/2001 of the Council, 22 December 2000, regarding the jurisdictional competence, the recognition and the execution of the ruling on civil and commercial matters.[353]

1065. Lastly, it has to be pointed out how, in fulfilling the delegation contained in Article 7 of L. 29 July 2003, n. 229,[354] the Italian Consiglio dei Ministri (Council of Ministers) has approved preliminarily, during the meeting held on 28 October 2004, on motion of the Ministro delle attività produttive (Minister of the productive activities) a layout of a government decree that should contain the '*Codice delle disposizioni in materia di tutela dei consumatori – Codice del consumo*' ('Code of the Dispositions on the Matter of Protection of Consumers – Code of Consumption'). The Code, now entered in its final phase of approval and thus near to its enforcement, is a significant operation of reorganization and coordination of the many national provisions on the matter of consumerism. In the intentions of the legislature, through the instrument of this consolidation the interpretative problems and the lacking link between the various measures that followed each other through time will be solved and, at the same time, a full harmonization of the national regulations with the European stances will be reached.[355]

- if the other party or its representative has received the order of the consumer in the Country of residence or
- if the contract represents a sale of goods and if the consumer has gone from the Country of residence to a foreign country and has performed the order, as long as the travel has been organized by the vendor to exhort the consumer to purchase.

In the absence of a choice, such contracts are subject to the regulation of the Country in which the consumer has his usual residence, provided the mentioned conditions recur.

353. Regulation (CE) n. 44/2001 of the Council of 22 Dec. 2000, concerning the jurisdictional competence, the recognition and execution of decisions on civil and commercial matters, G.U.C.E. 16 gennaio 2001, n. L. 012, that substitutes, among the Member States, the Convention of Brussels, 1968 (Art. 68 Regulation CE n. 44/2001). Section 4 of the Regulation is dedicated, in particular, to the jurisdictional competence on the matter of contracts clinched with consumers and provides that the action can be taken by the consumer in front of the judges of the Member State in the territory of which the other part is domiciled, or in front of the judges of the place where the consumer is domiciled, while the action of the other contracting party can be taken only in front of the judges of the Member State in the territory of which the consumer is domiciled (Art. 16 Regulation (CE) n. 44/2001).

354. L. 29 Jul. 2003, n. 229, Interventi in materia di qualità della regolazione, riassetto normativo e codificazione. – Legge di semplificazione 2001, G.U. 25 Aug. 2003, n. 196.

355. The draft of the Code diffused at the end of 2003 consisted of 147 articles. The further national regulations relevant on the matter of protection of the consumer, at the moment in force, but largely destined to merge in the 'Code of consumption' are: L. 10 Apr. 1991, n. 126, *Norme per l'informazione al consumatore, G.U. 16 Apr. 1991, n. 89; D.Lgs. 25 Jan. 1992, n. 74, Attuazione della direttiva 84/450/CEE, come modificata dalla direttiva 97/55/ CE in materia di pubblicità ingannevole e comparativa, G.U. 13 Feb. 1992, n. 36 (errata corrige in G.U. 2 May 2000, n. 100); D.Lgs. 17 Mar. 1995, n. 111, Attuazione della direttiva n. 90/314/CEE concernente i viaggi, le vacanze ed i circuiti 'tutto compreso', G.U. 14 Apr. 1995, n. 88; D.Lgs. 9 Nov. 1998, n. 427, Attuazione della direttiva 94/47/CE concernente la tutela dell'acquirente per taluni aspetti dei contratti relativi all'acquisizione di un diritto di godimento a tempo parziale di beni immobili, G.U. 14 Dec. 1998, n. 291; D.Lgs. 25 Feb. 2000, n. 84, Attuazione della direttiva 98/6/CE relativa alla protezione dei consumatori in materia di indicazione dei prezzi offerti ai medesimi, G.U.*

11 Apr. 2000, n. 85; D.Lgs. 2 Feb. 2002, n. 24, Attuazione dalla direttiva 1999/44/CE su taluni aspetti della vendita e delle garanzie di consumo, G.U. 8 Mar. 2002, n. 57; on the matter of the long-distance commercialization of financial services or insurance products, *see* the reference marks reported *supra*, *General introduction*, para. 4, *E-commerce: facts and figures.*

Part V. Non-contractual Liability

Chapter 1. Negligence

§1. Liability and Negligence

1066. The liability for wrongdoing, or extra-contractual liability, is assuming a growing role in the context of activities carried out on the Internet. The difficulties connected with the identification of the offenders, in particular, favour the multiplying of illicit activities, which are facilitated also by more and more sophisticated information technologies.

Some wrongdoing which would have been unthinkable only a few years ago are today fully accomplishable, thanks to the aid of powerful software and fast communication channels. One of the most recent examples, that endangered the cultural sector, is the illicit diffusion of intellectual works, reducible to the size of a few megabytes by means of compression programs and transferable in a very short time using high-speed access.

1067. In Italy, there is not yet a regulation on extra-contractual liability specifically dedicated to Internet. It will therefore be necessary to refer to the general provisions set by the Civil Code for wrongdoing,[356] dwelling, even if shortly, on the principles that discipline the topic.

The main provision is represented in Article 2043 of the Civil Code, according to which 'any willful or negligent act that causes others an unjust damage obliges the person who has performed the act to compensate the damage'. The source of compensation is therefore an act or omission. A positive act is one that becomes manifest in 'doing', for example the activity of duplication of a software. An omission takes place because of the inaction of a person who is obliged to act, for example, a provider who, despite the order from authorities, does not remove information of illicit origin that is contained in his website.

1068. It has to be noticed that the omission is considered a wrongdoing only if the subject has a legal duty to act to avoid the damage. To continue with the example just cited, an Internet user who notices illicit copyright information contained on another's site and does not report the fact will not share any liability for damage caused to the lawful proprietor of the right on that information, since he has no duty in this sense.

---

356. Civil Code, Book IV ('Delle obbligazioni'), Title IX ('Dei fatti illeciti'), Arts 2043-2059.

1069. To be compensated, the plaintiff must show that the damage he suffered was unjustly caused; that is, an interest that the juridical system considers worthy of protection has to be harmed. The evaluation of the worthiness of the interest is usually performed by the legislature through statutes at the moment in which the right to damage compensation is recognized; whereas, when there is no expressed law provision, the evaluation will be carried out by the judge according to his free assessment, in consideration of the circumstances of the fact.

1070. Another element that is necessary to frame compensation is the causal relationship between the illicit fact and the damage: the damage has to be a direct consequence of the act or omission.

1071. Another fundamental principle on the matter of extra-contractual wrongdoing regards the subjective profile of the offender: to be held responsible, he has to have performed the act wilfully or with negligence.

'Wilfulness' consists of the intention to cause the damaging event, as in the case of a hacker who damages an informational system by infecting it with an informational virus. In this case what is relevant is the will to cause the damage (e.g., the destruction of the data contained in the informational system). It has to be noted that, in this context, wilfulness assumes a different connotation from the one provided in the area of defects of the consent (Articles 1439 and 1440 of the Civil Code) that consists of fraud perpetrated by one party towards the other.

'Negligence' is instead the lack of diligence, prudence or skilfulness. Here, the damaging event is unwanted but caused as consequence of negligent, imprudent or unskilful behaviour, for example, a supplier of an informative service that publishes on his site a piece of news that is later discovered to be slanderous, without bothering to check its veracity.

1072. To obtain compensation, the damaged person has to prove the wilfulness or the negligence of the offender. The difference with contractual liability is evident. For example, a creditor can indict in contract, in the event of non-performance, and the debtor has to substantiate that the performance has become impossible due to a cause not indictable to him; instead, regarding non-contractual liability for wrongdoing, the burden of proof is shifted, since the creditor (damaged) is the one who has to demonstrate that the debtor (offender) has to compensate the damage.

1073. The type of compensation also differs between contractual liability, which is limited only to the patrimonial damage, whereas compensation for extra-contractual liability can be extended to non-patrimonial damage (the so-called moral damage), although this happens, according to Article 2059 Civil Code, '. . . *only in the cases provided by statutes*'.

Normally, compensation for wrongdoing is only patrimonial, i.e. susceptible to economic evaluation. Compensation implies an obligation to 'give' that has as its object a sum of money that represents the monetary equivalent of the damage caused.

1074. Article 2058 of the Civil Code nevertheless provides that the damaged party can ask if it proves to be possible according to the nature of the damage and not excessively onerous for the debtor, '. . . *the restoration in specific form*', from which an obligation of 'doing' instead of the typical one of 'giving' can arise.

1075. The patrimonial damage consists of accruing damage that represents the loss suffered by the damaged party, and lost profit, namely the missing profit. For example, the supplier of an Internet service harmed by an informational virus will have a right to the compensation of the expense necessary to restore the service (accruing damage), as well as the sums that, during the period of service inactivity, he has not gained due to non-usage (missing profit).

1076. Not all damages, however, are compensable: there must be a causal relationship that connects the damage and the wrongdoing in a direct and immediate way, as provided regarding obligations in general, by Article 1223 of the Civil Code: '*The compensation of a damage due to nonperformance . . . has to include both the loss suffered by the creditor and the missing profit, as long as they are its immediate and direct consequence*'.

1077. The case in point provided by Article 2043 does not exhaust the criteria for liability for wrongdoing: the Code provides many exceptions to the general rule, traditionally traced to the cases of indirect liability, on one hand, and of objective liability, on the other.

1078. The first group includes cases in which the person held liable is different from the one who performed the act: in particular among these, there is the liability of employers, owners and principals '. . . *for the damages caused by the wrongdoing of their servants and assistants in the exercise of the tasks they are assigned to*' (Article 2049 of the Civil Code). The effect of this provision is that, for example, the employer answers, usually jointly with his subordinate, for and wrongdoing performed by subordinate employees.

The rule is justified by the fact that the principal, by appropriating the result of the work of others, has to assume the related risks, including that of the subordinate employee causing damage to third parties while carrying out his tasks.

1079. The second group includes the situation in which the offender answers even in the absence of wilfulness or negligence. The peculiarity lies therefore in the irrelevance of the subjective element of the wrongdoing.

For example, liability for the exercise of dangerous activities, regulated by Article 2050 Civil Code, is irrespective of wrongdoing or negligence: '*Anyone who causes a damage to others while performing an activity that is dangerous due to its nature or to the nature of the employed means, has to compensate it, if he does not prove to have taken all the adequate measures to avoid the damage.*' Various special statutes, such as Law 31 of December 1996, n. 675, and D.Lgs 196/03 on personal data processing,[357] carry an express reference to the provision.

It is necessary to emphasize that in these cases the discharging proof does not concern the act, but rather the nature of the dangerous activity: the offender therefore has to demonstrate that he has taken every precaution offered related to the activity performed.

1080. After this necessary general foreword, it is now convenient to dwell on the aspects of extra-contractual liability that affect the Internet more closely. Jurists distinguish between wrongdoing performed through the Internet and wrongdoing performed against the Internet. In the first group, the means employed is not relevant and the Internet is only one of the possible channels through which the illicit activity is performed. Typical examples are defamation or illegal duplication of software. In the second group are those illicit behaviours aimed against typical Internet activities and that often assume penal relevance: for example, the diffusion of informational viruses or the damaging of online (telematic) systems.

1081. Furthermore, some recognize a *tertium genus* – wrongdoing *of* Internet – that unites the conducts performed by network managers, conceivable only in the virtual context of the Internet: irregular registration of a domain's name, linking unlawful activities, unlawful use of meta-tags and so on.[358]

1082. Particular attention has to be turned to the Internet subjects, namely those who carry out activities connected to its use. On the basis of the nature and purposes of such activities, indeed, it is possible to determine if a subject is liable or not, in an extra-contractual way, for certain types of wrongdoing. The roles that these subjects fall under are network operators, service providers, content providers and end users. The next two chapters regard network operators and service providers. Concerning the other two, a particular mention is deserved of the situation in which the end user, besides exploiting the services released by other operators, becomes a supplier of contents himself. In this case he will be liable, on a par with every other professional content provider, for every possible unlawful activity connected to the supply, for example, a user exploiting webspace granted by the service provider, who renders available to the public a series of photographic works

357. Art. 18: '*Anyone who causes others damage because of personal data processing has to compensate it according to art. 2050 cod. civ.*'. The same provision is contained in Art. 15 of the Legislative Decree 30 Jun. 2003, n. 196 'Codice in materia di protezione dei dati personali', that took effect from 1 Jan. 2004 and that repealed Law 31 Dec. 1996 n. 675. Some authors believe that the reference to Art. 2050 Italian Civil Code only causes the shift of the proof burden and not the inclusion of the informational activity connected to the processing among the dangerous activities. *See* U. Ruffolo, Dati personali: trattamento e responsabilità, in V. Cuffaro, V. Ricciuto, V. Zeno Zencovich, *Trattamento dei dati e tutela della persona*, Milano, 1998.

358. In this sense S. Sica, G. Comandè *Il commercio elettronico*, Giappichelli, 2001, p. 220, that distinguishes wrongdoing *of* Internet, *against* Internet and *through* Internet.

protected by copyright, or those who directly render their hard disk available to other users by means of a program and through peer-to-peer connections, to allow the download/upload of music files, as happened in the famous *Napster* case.[359]

359. 1. Ended with the ruling of 12 Feb. 2001 n. 16401 by the US Court of Appeals for the Ninth Circuit.

Chapter 2. Liability of Network Operators

§1. Liability of Network Operators

1083. By 'network operators' we refer to those who manage the infrastructures of which the Internet is composed.

Their role is to supply the communication lines to the Internet, namely, to borrow an expression coined by American jurisprudence, the cables and channels for its functioning.

1084. The main infrastructures, the spinal column of the Internet (*backbone*) are, for example, transoceanic cables that connect European and American networks. The telephonic line is also among the Internet's communication lines and still accounts for the major part of data traffic in Italy and many other countries. Other infrastructures are radio links, satellite networks and optical fibres.

1085. The fundamental characteristic that marks network operators is their neutrality with respect to the content of the information transferred. This is simply transported from one point of the network to another as a mere flow of data, without the operators perceiving its intrinsic value. Their position in relation to wrongdoing performed on the Internet can therefore be assimilated to that of voice telephone operators, who, since attending to direct transport and commutation of voices in real time, are not considered liable for statements made by those talking.

1086. This reasoning, as obvious as it may seem, is confirmed by statutory provisions: the Ministerial Decree of Poste e delle Telecomunicazioni of 13 July 1995, n. 385,[360] in regulating the content and modalities of information supply and exploitation of *audiotex* and *videotex* services – in many respects similar to the services supplied on the Internet – provides, in Article 18 n. 2, that '*the net manager assumes only the liability connected to the transport of information* . . .' and not that concerning the content or the modalities of service distribution. Liability for these rests with the '*suppliers of information or services and managers of service centers*', wholly comparable to content providers, to go on in the analogy.

1087. To this we must add what is provided by Legislative Decree of 9 April 2003, n. 70, which implemented the EC Directive 31/2000/CE on electronic commerce,[361] which, in Article 14, contains the principle by which the subjects that carry out the mere transport of information – so-called intermediary workers – are not liable for their content.

1088. Possible profiles of extra-contractual liability on the part of network operators should rather be searched for in the relationship with the other subjects of the network, in particular service providers, namely those that provide access to Internet to content suppliers and end users. The regulation of such relationships

360. Published in G.U. General Series 18 Sep. 1995, n. 218.
361. In Suppl. Ord. N. 61/L of 14 Apr. 2003 to G.U. n. 87 of 14 Apr. 2003.

assumes a great significance in Italy since the manager of the public telecommunications network is also service provider: this circumstance places the manager in a dominant position with respect to the competition that could be thwarted by unjust or non-competitive access conditions compared to those of the manager itself.[362]

1089. First, it has to be pointed out that D.Lgs. of 17 March 1995, n. 103, which implemented EC Directive 90/388/CEE, regulated the offer of telecommunication services besides voice telephony, liberalizing, among others, the Internet access service.[363] The service provider is included among those suppliers who are allowed, according to Article 2 of the mentioned decreto, '*access to the public network to supply, through commuted connections or through connections directed to the above- said network, telecommunication services different from vocal telephony . . .*'.

1090. The following d.P.R. 19 September 1997, n. 318, '*Regolamento per l'attuazione di direttive comunitarie nel settore delle telecomunicazioni*'[364] has then provided, in Article 2, the principle according to which 'The installation, running and supply of telecommunication networks as well as the supply of services related to them accessible for the public are activities of preeminent public interest, the execution of which is based on: a) free competitiveness and plurality of operators, in full respect of the principles of objectiveness, transparency, non-discrimination and proportionality . . . .' It seems that service providers have to be included among these activities of preeminent public interest, in particular among those regulating the supply of services related to the telecommunication sector.[365]

1091. There is no doubt, therefore, that the manager of the telecommunication network has the duty to negotiate with the providers that ask for access: for this purpose, every refusal or proposal of access under excessively onerous conditions can be the object of claims as laid down in Article 8 of the above-mentioned D.Lgs. 103/1995. Should the refusal be legitimate, the non-closing of the access contract will constitute a violation of Article 1337 Civil Code, from which, according to jurisprudence's dominant stance,[366] liability for wrongdoing derives. The compensation of the damage will be limited to negative interest, in its double aspect of accruing

---

362. For a review on this topic, *see* the report of the Competition and Market Controller Authority at <www.agcm.it/agcm_ita/relaz/relaz_02.NSF>.
363. G.U. General Series 6 Apr. 1995 n. 81.
364. G.U. 22 Sep. 1997 n. 221.
365. *See* F. Signorelli, *Profili di responsabilità del provider nell'E-Commerce*, in AA.VV. *Il Commercio elettronico*, Giuffrè 2001, p. 558.
366. Among the last rulings, *see* Cass. 14 Feb. 2000 n. 1632 and Cass. 29 Apr. 1999 n. 4299. Consistent with in doctrine Bianca, *Diritto civile III*, *Il contratto*, Milano 1984. *Contra*, in the sense that *culpa in contraendo* has a contractual nature, Trib. Milano, 11 gen. 1988, in *Nuova Giur. Civ. Commentata*, 1988, I, 499 and, in doctrine, Scognamiglio, *Dei contatti in generale*, Comm. Scialoja e Branca, 1970.

damage – represented by the expenses pointlessly undertaken in the pre-contractual phase – and loss of profit represented by the loss of contractual opportunities with other end users.[367]

1092. The non-contractual issues of unfair competition and abuse of a dominant position in the relationship between the subjects in question can arise when the manager, even if guaranteeing service providers access to the Internet, does not offer them adequate conditions to operate in the service market in a condition of parity. In particular, many have emphasized how the policy carried out by the manager, a subject in a dominant position in the market of Internet access, is apt to reduce the competitive capability of other operators, determining therefore a significant alteration of competitiveness in the markets of data transmission and Internet access services.[368] An example in this sense is supplied by the recent report made by the main service-providers' associations, according to which the network manager, in offering to the public a certain Internet access service[369] without having beforehand supplied a corresponding wholesale offer[370] to the other operators, has in fact prevented these from offering analogous competitive services in the market.[371]

1093. The protection available to the service provider in such cases is principally of administrative and jurisdictional nature:

- The first, carried out through the intervention of the Telecommunication Controller Authority[372] and the Competitiveness and Market Controller Authority,[373] intended to stop unfair competition acts performed by the telecommunication network manager.
- The second, of a litigious nature, tends to obtain compensation on the basis of the general principles related to liability for wrongdoing, in the above-said boundaries.

---

367. On the damage deriving from the loss of *chances*, *see* Corte Cass., sez. II, 13 Dec. 1994 n. 10649.
368. *See*, on this point, the report of the Competition and Market Controller Authority relative to year 2001, available at <www.agcm.it>.
369. Access to the Internet through ADSL technology.
370. In jargon *Wholesale* offer, that stands next to the *retail* offer.
371. For more details on the matter, *see* the site of the 'Associazione Italiana Internet Providers', at <www.aiip.it/com03_12_2002.htm>.
372. Established with the L. 31 Jul. 1997, n. 249 (G.U. Suppl. ord. 31 luglio 1997, n. 177).
373. Established with the L. 10 Oct. 1990, n. 247 (G.U. Serie Gen. 13 ottobre 1990, n. 240).

Chapter 3. Liability of Service Providers

§1. Foreword

1094. The *Internet Service Provider* (ISP) is the link between telecommunication managers, on one side, and, on the other, end users, whether these are suppliers of goods, suppliers of services, public or private organizations, institutions, universities, associations or foundations, consumers, etc.

Particularly, the ISP can supply services of various types connected with the use of telematic communication networks with TCP/IP (Transfer Control Protocol/Internet Protocol). Among these services is Internet access, as well as, among the most frequent:

- e-mail service;
- organization and managing of online (telematic) discussion forums; and
- '*hosting*', with which the provider renders available to the user portions of memory on his processors (the host server), in order to allow the memorization and visualization of websites, therefore rendering the information therein contained accessible, consultable, memorizable or downloadable from any part of the world where there is a connection to Internet, except for possible restrictions prearranged through particular technical means (e.g., a password).

1095. Through the services offered by the ISP, users can carry out various activities, many of which are the object of rights provided by specific constitutional guarantees. For example, freedom of expression, thought and freedom of the press, guaranteed by Article 21 of the Italian Constitution, the first paragraph of which explicitly provides that 'Everyone has the right to freely express their thoughts through spoken or written words and *every other mean of diffusion*,' with the obvious limits set out due to the respect of the right of others, in particular with reference to honour and to reputation (included the so-called commercial reputation). The management of an economic undertaking, protected by Article 41 of the Constitution, by force of which the activities aimed at the supply of goods or the performance of services can be carried out through Internet-working systems, is subject to the borders provided by the second paragraph, which establishes that the principles of non-contradiction with social utility and with respect to security, freedom and human dignity cannot tolerate infringements.

1096. This first public law organization indicates the necessity to regulate the sector in order to avoid the performance, through the service of undoubted public significance offered by ISPs, of wrongdoing of various natures, punished both civilly and penally, including defamation, unfair competition, copyright infringement, etc.

However, the need to protect third parties' rights against possible wrongdoing by those accessing Internet services has also to be tempered with the need to protect the market, promote technological development and protect ISPs' rights. Towards these, indeed, it would be excessively burdensome to provide strict, objective liability if not tempered by possible exemptions, with the risk of frustrating the abovementioned freedom of economical undertaking. The statutory choices, therefore, have to stand on considerations of law policies and on the basis of considerations that can emerge from an economic analysis of the law.

1097. To simplify the point, it is convenient to keep in mind that to burden ISPs excessively with juridical liabilities for damages accruing due to the use of the services they offer could compromise the position of the ISPs in the potential global market of the information society, with an ensuing impossibility to bear the economic expenses caused by the translation of the consequences of the wrongdoing suffered by the offended subjects. All this would make it difficult for ISPs to remain in the market and would, therefore, have repercussions for end users that, through Internet access suppliers and through the further services performed, are unable to render effective those constitutional rights above briefly mentioned. Attention has to be paid also to the exploitation of the right of expression of thought through the press, seriously limited until recently:

- by the notable costs to sustain for the diffusion of messages, through traditional means, to a significant number of people;
- the necessity to register the periodical press; and
- the necessity to fulfil the previous inscription in the roll and/or record of publicists and journalists.

Many of these limitations have lost their relevance with the advent of the Internet, with the possibility to carry out journalistic activity through online (telematic) systems, at very low costs and the potentially planetary diffusion of information or of other forms of expression of thought, with an effect that is even greater than that of the traditional means of the press.

§2. Jurisprudence's Stances on the Topic of ISP's Liability

1098. On the basis of these premises, our discussion turns to what the statutory provisions to regulate the position of ISPs should be, with reference to wrongdoing performed by subjects who exploit their services.

For this purpose, it is proper to keep in mind that the first cases were solved in a non-unanimous manner by American jurisprudence that was the first jurisdiction called on to rule on cases in point concerning the unlawful use of the Internet.

1099. Among the relevant rulings, the one given in the outcome of the case *Cubby Inc. v. Compuserve*,[374] concerning the diffusion, in a discussion forum, of defamatory pieces of news and false information on a commercial entrepreneur, deserves to be mentioned. In the case in question that constitutes a leading case on the matter that is the object of the present dissertation, the liability of the ISP was

374. *Cubby Inc. v. Compuserve*, 776, F. Supp. 135 (S.D. NY 1991).

denied, due to the impossibility, on its behalf, to exercise an effective control on the information that passed through its processors. It must be noted that the liability of the service provider was not excluded beforehand, but only since the exercise of the controls in question became effectively impossible. It seems to be possible to infer, however, that this impossibility is a refutable presumption, by force of the reasoning according to which usually an ISP, particularly one of great size, is not able to control the flow of information input on the Internet through the services he offers, in the same way that a telecommunications manager (e.g., in the case of voice telephony) or a bookseller is not considered liable for the wrongdoing performed by third parties by using the telephonic line or the publications in paper form. Likewise, therefore, the ISP should not be considered liable for the wrongdoing performed by someone who uses the services it offers.

1100. The above-mentioned jurisprudential ruling stands on the assimilation of the figure of the provider to a distributor of information. In this regard, it has to be remembered that, before the statutory reform of the telecommunications sector, that took place in 1996, liability of the subjects who, other from the author, affect the diffusion of offensive messages was divided into three categories: *publisher liability*, *distributor liability* and *common carrier liability*. As it has been authoritatively stated, 'with a good dose of approximation it can be said that: for the first standard of liability, typically applied to publishers, one has to answer only for not having exercised the control on the published material; for the second standard of liability, typically applied to booksellers and newsagents, one has to answer only if aware or reasonably apt to be aware of the unlawfulness of the distributed material; for the third standard of liability, typically applied to phone companies, one never has to answer, not even if aware of the unlawful messages transmitted'.

1101. Another jurisprudential stance is perceived with reference to the case *Stratton Oakmont Inc. and Daniel Porush v. Prodigy Service Company*,[375] the ruling of which appears to resume the reasoning's expressed in the case *Cubby Inc. v. Compuserve*, however reaching an opposing solution, with the consideration that, even if no duties of control burden the ISP on wrongdoing performed by its users, in fact, the provider itself offered, on its initiative, adequate information filter systems and supplementary services of control of the contents. This reasoning induced the judging body to assimilate the ISP's position, in the case in question, to that typical of the publisher (*publisher liability*), subject to duties of editorial control of the published material, therefore diverging from the model of *distributor liability* that could otherwise be framed in most hypotheses.

1102. A further decision, in the well-known case *Zeran v. America Online*,[376] delivered after the enforcement of the *Communication Decency Act* of February

375. *Stratton Oakmont Inc. and Daniel Porush v. Prodigy Service Company*, n. 31063/94, NY Supreme Court, 10 May 1995.

376. *Zeran v. America Online Inc.*, 958 F. Supp. 1124 (1997), aff'd, 129 F.3d 327 (4th Cir. 1997), cert. denied, US, 118 S. Ct. 2341 (1998). *See* R. Natoli, cited work, p. 83 and ss.

1996, ruled out the liability of the provider with reference to defamatory information, the existence and unlawfulness of which he had been informed of with the request of consequent removal and correction. In the case in question, therefore, the analogy for the ISP is not only to the *publisher* but also to the *distributor*, denied, therefore, attributing him a sort of immunity.[377]

1103. Other rulings on the topic of liability of the provider have been delivered in the matter of infringement of intellectual property copyright. *Playboy Inc. v. Frena*,[378] regarded the diffusion on a BBS (*Bulletin Board System*) of photographic images property of Playboy Inc., as copyright infringement. The liability of the provider, in the case in question, was judged subsistent aside from every investigation on the possibilities of control both on the content of information present on the BBS and the awareness of the unlawfulness of these.[379] Courts have therefore recognized direct and objective liability of the ISP ('direct liability').

1104. On the matter of copyright infringement, we mention also the ruling delivered in the case *Sega Entertainment Ltd v. Maphia*,[380] where the principle of the ISP's liability was newly declared, but in a different form. The case did not concern objective and direct liability of the provider, but his contributory liability was established, based on the presupposition that the provider was aware of the wrongdoing performed through the services he himself had prearranged.[381]

1105. The stances expressed by American jurisprudence seem useful to comprehend the peculiarity of the decisions delivered by Italian judges.

As a matter of principle, in the Italian system, the analogy of the provider to the publisher, with the related consequences on the applicable liability regime, is ruled out. The ruling of the Penal Court of Oristano, 25 May 2000,[382] recognized the impossibility of applying the 'provisions set out for defamation by means of the press and for radio-phonic or television broadcastings to defamation performed through Internet, since this is a totally peculiar information media to which, on penal matters, the regulation set out for the press, the radio or the television cannot be extended by analogy'. The principle applies also to the civil sector where, by

377. The decision ruled in second instance, in the mentioned case *Zeran v. America Online Inc.*, stood on the interpretation of the Sez. 230(*b*) of the *Communication Decency Act (1996)*, that, among the purposes of the statute, includes the following: '*to promote the continued development of the Internet*'; '*to preserve the vibrant and competitive free market that presently exists for the Internet and other interactive computer services, unfettered by Federal or State regulation*'. In consequence, the judge concluded that '*by its plain language, [that] creates a federal immunity to any case of action that would make service providers liable for information originating with a third-party of the service*'. *See* R. Natoli, cited work, p. 86.

378. *Playboy Inc. v. Frena*, 839 F. Supp. 1552 (M.D. Flo. 1993).

379. L. Bugiolacchi, *Principi e questioni aperte in materia di responsabilità extracontrattuale dell'Internet Provider. Una sintesi di diritto comparato, in Il diritto dell'informazione e dell'informatica*, Milano, 2000, n. 6, pp. 838 and ss., *see* in general.

380. *Sega Entertainment Ltd v. Maphia*, 857, F. Supp., 679 (N.D. Cal., 1994).

381. L. Bugiolacchi, cited work, p. 842.

382. *See Diritto dell' informazione e dell'informatica*, Milano, 2000, p. 653, with note by P. Costanzo.

force of the joint provision of Article 2059 Civil Code and 185 c.p., the compensation for non-patrimonial damage is excluded.[383]

1106. The first rulings delivered by Italian civil jurisprudence appear to show the consequences of the debate started in the United States. We have to remember the ordinance delivered by the Court of Cuneo on 23 June 1997 (*Giur. Piemontese*, 1997, 493), that literally recalls some reasonings analogous to those underlying the decision of the *Zeran* case and concludes that:

> The Service provider is in fact, unless wanting to determine an almost total paralysis of the traffic, unable to limit or control towards which sites the subject called in jargon *navigator* will direct his cybernetic sails to. On the other hand, it would be like asking the manager of a telephonic line to answer for the content of conversations – or of faxes – that one of his users holds with the people called.[384]

Therefore, 'The Service provider that limits himself to allowing the access to the net, as well as the space on his own server for the publication of informative services carried out by the information supplier, is not liable in the event of copyright infringements that this performs.'[385]

1107. In case of defamation through Internet, Italian jurisprudence has expressed a similar stance with regard to defamatory messages addressed against a banking

383. The Ordinance of the Tribunal of Napoli, 8 August 1997, ruled in the trial *Soc. Pomicino v. Soc. Geredil* et al., deserves to be mentioned. For the purpose of the repression of anticompetitive and not defamatory behaviours, the judge considers 'the Internet network ... the same of a press product', with the consequence 'that the owner of a domain name in Internet has the duties of the owner of a communication legal entity'. It has to be noticed how the ruling specifies that liabilities burden, in the first place, the owner of the domain name ('eventual wrongdoings integrated by the content of the pages inserted in the site managed by the owner of a domain name on the Internet are chargeable to this subject: this subject is indeed burdened by a duty of careful verification of the lawful propriety of the distinctive mark used by the advertiser and of previous control on the content of the message, in order to assure that the advert is evident, truthful and correct. This principle stands still even if the owner of the domain name limits himself to the technical maintenance of the site, while the creation, management and trading negotiation of the pages to put online is assigned to a third party'), to successively declare a principle of joint liability of the owner of the website, towards which are reaffirmed duties of vigilance ('In the telematic Internet network, the proprietor of a site is bound to keep watch in order to identify acts of unfair competition performed through the publication of adverts; therefore, in case he does not comply due to willfulness or negligence with these duties, the above-mentioned proprietor of the Internet site is jointly liable of the wrongdoing'.). It must be noted that this ruling reached the extreme conclusion of considering the judicial order of shutting down the website as an adequate remedy in hypotheses of unfair competition performed through the appropriation of valuable features and the diffusion of confidential news through the Internet network. Cf. *Giust. Civ.*, 1998, I, 259, with note by Albertini; *Resp. Civ. e Prev.*, 1998, 173, with note by Sanzo; *Dir. Informazione e Informatica*, 1997, 970; *Dir. e Giur.*, 1997, 472, with note by Catalano; *Riv. Dir. Ind.*, 1999, II, 38, with note by Capra.

384. Trib. di Cuneo, Ord. 23 Jun. 1997. *See* F. Signorelli, *Profili di responsabilità del provider nell'e-commerce*, in V. Franceschelli (edited by), *Commercio elettronico*, Milano, 2001, p. 570.

385. Trib. di Cuneo, Ord. 23 Jun. 1997. *See* F. Signorelli, cited work, p. 571.

company and diffused through the Internet by means of the insertion in a newsgroup, by considering non-recognizable the liability of the provider (therefore holding as justified the exception of lack of passive legitimation) with the reasoning that, being in a non-moderated forum, the service provider could not exercise any control on single interventions, limiting itself to rendering available to the users a 'virtual' space of discussion (electronic board).[386]

1108. More in the same judgment (*V.L. v. Netweb*), the Court of Napoli, first in a monocratic composition and later in a collegiate composition after a claim, has delivered two opposing ordinances that emphasize the dialectic between the two stances that have emerged on the matter of an ISP's liability.

The first ordinance states the subsistence of the liability of the provider by hinging on juridical considerations that are new with respect to those that emerged in the debate in the United States. More precisely, in the wake of a doctrinal stance that includes authoritative jurists,[387] the ruling in question moves from the regulation on the matter of protection of the person in personal data processing, introduced in the Italian juridical system in response to a European Community solicitation, by declaring the principle according to which 'In case of defamation performed through the contents of an Internet site, the joint liability of the provider subsists, even if he has limited himself to simply host on his own servers the content of the web-pages prepared by the client, by force of Article 18 of Law n. 675 del 1996, that extends the rule contained in Article 2050 Italian civil code to the subject that processes personal data.'[388] The assumption, of which we will give more account in the continuation, has been refuted before the courts, where, in deference to the principle that by now seems to be consolidated even despite the statutory provision on the matter of privacy protection, the general principle of non-liability of the ISP has been once again affirmed, on the model of the '*distributor liability*'

386. Trib. di Roma, Ord. 4 Jul. 1998. Cf. F. Signorelli, cited work, p. 571, according to which the reasoning gives 'immediate satisfaction of a clear principle universally accepted', that consists in considering a subject 'liable of a wrongdoing (apart from some specific and well defined exceptions), inasmuch as this is direct and immediate consequence of an action or omission of that subject and is directly referable to his behavior'. The assumption, however, appears not to consider the functions of the civil liability identified by the most recent civil doctrine, that is careful to the considerations of economic analysis of the law that suggest to prefer, in the new socio-economic context, regimes of objective liability that are apt to allow a better redistribution of the risks introduced in the market and a more equilibrated reallocation of the consequences of the wrongdoing, regardless of considerations on the subjective criteria of indictment, based on negligence or wilfulness.

387. Among all, *see* V. Zeno-Zencovich, *Profili attivi e passivi della responsabilità dell'utente in Internet*, in A. Palazzo – U. Ruffolo (ed.), *La tutela del navigatore in Internet*, Milano, 2002, pp. 142 e 143; G. Giacobbe, *La responsabilità civile per l'uso di Internet*, in V. Ricciuto – N. Zorzi (edited by), *Il contratto telematico*, Padova, 2002, p. 222.

388. Trib. Napoli, Ord. 8 Jul. 2002, *V.L. v. T.V., Netweb S.p.A.*, in *Giurisprudenza napoletana*, 2002, 11, 427. It has to be kept in mind that the Law 675/96, together with other primary and secondary provisions enforced in the sector *de quo*, has successively flowed, with modifications, in d.lgs. 30 giugno 2003, n. 196 (published in G.U.R.I. 29 Jul. 2003, serie generale n. 174, S.O. n. 123/L; enforced on 1 Jan. 2004), known as the T.U. o Code on the protection of personal data. Art. 18 of the Law 665/96, mentioned in the ruling cited in the present text to which the note refers, has now flowed in Art. 15, co. 1, of the Code.

above emphasized, being understood, therefore, to recognize liability in cases in which the provider is aware of the wrongdoing performed by his own users and does not take steps to eliminate it.[389]

1109. Finally, it has to be emphasized how the principle of '*distributor liability*' applied in the context of defamation appears to apply by analogy also with reference to other types of extra-contractual wrongdoing. For example, in unfair competition, Italian jurisprudence shows the courts to be inclined to extend the borders of the providers' liability only in the case of awareness on the part of the ISP or where the ISP had sufficient evidence of wrongdoing without taking steps to remove it.[390]

§3. Doctrinal Stances on the Topic of ISP's Liability (Mentions)

1110. Jurisprudential stances we have accounted for above are echoes of corresponding doctrinal positions that, however, present themselves richer and more articulated in the reasonings adduced. In our brief review, we have to remember how the complete non-liability of the ISP has been declared by Franzosi.[391] In this

389. *See* Trib. Napoli, Ord. 4 Sep. 2002, *Netweb S.p.A. v. V.L.* (in *Giurisprudenza napoletana*, 2002, 11, 427), where it is stated: 'In order to consider the *provider*, who limits himself to hosting on his servers the contents of an Internet site created by a customer, liable for the illicit activities performed by the customer, it is not possible to recognize an hypothesis of presumed guilt, but it is necessary for the guilt to exists concretely, recognizable, for example, when having become acknowledged of the defamatory content of some web pages he does not immediately operate to stop its diffusion on the net'.

390. *See*, in particular, Trib. Roma, 22 Mar. 1999, *Ina v. Soc. I.Net* (in *Il diritto dell'informazione dell'informatica*, 2000, 66, with note by Sammarco; *Riv. dir. comm.*, 1999, II, 273 with note by Visconti), where it is stated 'Even if he does not have the duty to check the illicit content of the communications and messages that are introduced in a site, the *provider* that performs the connection in the net is liable due to negligence if the content of the communications he has to transmit appears blatantly illicit, since, by performing the connection, he concurs to the wrongdoing because he gives a causal contribution to its perpetration. In the case in point, the *provider* had concurred to the wrongdoing consisting in an act of unfair competition for not having recognized, according to due diligence, the use of a well-known acronym by an unauthorized subject'; as well as Trib. Napoli, 28 Dec. 2001, *Philips S.p.A. v. Infostrada S.p.A., Telecom Italia S.p.A., et al.* (in *Il diritto dell'informazione e dell'informatica*, 2002, 1, 94), according to which 'The registration of a registered mark as a domain name on the Internet and the use of it into *meta tags* or *web pages* by the non-proprietor for a trading and promotional purpose integrate an illicit conduct that is included in unfair competition, for which the *provider* is liable as co-responsible if the knowledge of the abuse exists and he does not intervene to eliminate it'. Lastly, *see* Trib. Monza, Ord. 14 May 2001, *Doctor Glass Group s.r.l. v. Nexia s.a.s. di Villa Daniele s.a.s.* et al. (in *Giurisprudenza milanese*, 8/9, 2001, p. 320), where it is stated: 'The liability 'due to the position' of the *provider* has to be excluded, since he can be called to answer of wrongdoings performed on the Net only when he has direct knowledge of the wrongdoing or could anyway be able to gain this knowledge through due diligence'.

391. M. Franzosi, in AIDA, Milano, 1997, p. 249. According to the author, the obligation of the *provider*, contractually deduced, would consist of the supply of the connection to Internet and in the disposability of the devices necessary to guarantee the permanence for the time stipulated, without the possibility to identify further obligations (except if due a different and explicit stipulation) or to derive from these any sort of liability for the illicit performed by one's customers.

regard, for example, the figure of the provider has been compared not only to that of the network operator (telecommunications operator or manager) but also to that of motorway managers, who cannot be held liable in case of wrongdoing performed, respectively, by telecommunications service users or by drivers who access through the toll.

1111. Others, however, recognize a joint liability of the ISP with respect to that of the author of the wrongdoing, due to the fact that the first, as manager of the offered services, cannot be defined as a mere organization of a technical instrument, since he assumes a 'role of filter between user and public'.[392]

1112. The declaration of a liability of ISPs, however, has been considered by others necessary to awaken responsibility for the activities performed on the telematic network, most of all if we consider the difficulties in identifying the authors of wrongdoing in the hypothesis in which there is not a control on the effective identity of the subject that requests the access.[393] On this point, some have questioned who should compensate for damage caused by a user anonymously registered and, therefore, not recognizable in his real identity.[394] Let us think of the hypothesis in which a subject accesses the Internet by using an ID and a password of others, as well as the further hypothesis in which a subject registers online by providing a false identity. In particular, it has been questioned if the provider could appeal to an exemption of liability by pleading that the damaging event does not ensue directly from his conduct.[395] In considering that also anonymity can constitute a constitutionally protected right,[396] it has been suggested to distinguish between absolute anonymity and partial anonymity,[397] and to grant only to the second a form of protection,[398] with a clear intent of *moral responsibility*.

392. G. Giacobbe, *La responsabilità civile per l'uso di Internet*, in V. Ricciuto – N. Zorzi (edited by), *Il contratto telematico*, Padova, 2002, p. 222.
393. In the international panorama, *see* O. Hance, *Internet e la legge*, Milano, p. 170.
394. G.M. Riccio, *Diritto all'anonimato e responsabilità civile del provider*, in L. Nivarra – V. Ricciuto (a cura di), cited work, pp. 25 and ss.
395. G.M. Riccio, cited work, pp. 25 and ss.
396. Typical is the example coming once more from the law of the USA, where the provision of the *Communication Decency Act* that forbids Internet users to adopt a false identity has been declared conflicting with the principle of *freedom of speech* contained in the First Amendment of the Constitution. *See*, *amplius*, G.M. Riccio, cited work, p. 39.
397. In total anonymity the identity of the subject sending a communication or expressing his thoughts is unknown both to the receivers and the perceivers of the information, and also to the *provider* that renders possible the communication or the diffusion of the same information. Vice versa, in partial anonymity the identity of the subject is known only to the *provider* and not to the receivers.
398. *See* G.M. Riccio, cited work, p. 39, where the author emphasizes that 'this way is achieved the possibility to trace the real identity of the agent, that will be called to answer directly of the damages eventually consequent to his actions'.

1113. Under another profile, the application of provisions on the press has appeared in any way not apt to be pledged. On this point, *see* Zeno-Zencovich[399] and Costanzo.[400]

1114. Based on the provisions that protect the person in personal data processing, contained in Article 18 of Law 675/96 (now substituted by Article 15, co. 1, of the Code on personal data protection), aggravated or objective liability[401] on the part of ISPs is established by Article 2050 of the Civil Code, for the exercise of dangerous activities. It is barely necessary to mention that this article, by force of which 'anyone who causes damages to others in the exercise of an activity that is dangerous for its nature or for the nature of the means used, is held to compensate if he does not prove to have adopted every caution adequate to avoid the damage', is indeed recalled by Article 18 of the cited Law 675 (now Article 15, co. 1, of the Code on personal data protection), where it is provided that 'whoever causes damages to others by effect of a personal data processing is held to compensate according to Article 2050 of the civil code'. Even if the doctrinal stance is not at all unanimous on the applicability of the provision to the activity carried out by the provider, since dissenting opinions have been expressed,[402] the clear statutory setting appears strict and does not leave appreciable margins of exemption, most of all if we consider that the article considers bound to compensation 'whoever' causes damages by effect of personal data processing and that for the expression '*processing*' an almost all-encompassing definition is given: this contemplates 'any operation or complex of operations . . . concerning the collection, the record, the organization, the storage, the consultation, the elaboration, the modification, the selection, the extraction, the comparison, the use, the interconnection, the blockage, the communication, the diffusion, the deletion, and the destruction of data'.[403]

399. V. Zeno-Zencovich, *Alla telematica non si applica la legge sulla stampa, in Il diritto dell'informazione e dell'informatica*, Milano, 1998, pp. 15 and ss.

400. P. Costanzo, *Libertà di manifestazione del pensiero e pubblicazione in Internet*, in *Il diritto dell'informazione e dell'informatica*, Milano, 1998, pp. 373 and ss., by criticizing some stances that, even if denying the duty of control for the provider, consider the criteria aimed to the identification of abuses of the right to chronicle applicable to what is 'published' on the Internet.

401. The hypothesis of liability provided in the Italian juridical system by Art. 2050 Italian Civil Code, diffusely considered as an hypothesis of aggravated liability with the shift of the burden of proof on the adoption of every measure adequate to avoiding the damage, has been considered an hypothesis of objective liability by a well-known and authoritative doctrine, on the consideration that the proof the legislature requests is so onerous that it ends up being coincident with the demonstration of a fortuitous circumstance or a circumstance beyond one's control, regardless of the existence of subjective indicting criteria like wilfulness or negligence. *See* G. Alpa, *La responsabilità civile*, Milano.

402. On this point the consideration made by L. Bugiolacchi, cited work, p. 835, seems interesting: the author, although not excluding the liability of the *provider, ex* Art. 2050 c.c. (as referred to by Art. 18 of the Law 675/96) for the information and data he introduces, believes, however, that the scope of application of the provision has to be restricted when the activity of apposition of every security measure adequate to avoiding the damage (that statutory provisions request) is not possible, and this with specific reference 'to the content of the informative data input on the net by other subjects than the *provider* that manages the *server* and on which the same *providers* are not able to carry out a preventive or successive control'.

403. *See* Art. 1, lett. *b)*, Law 675/796, now substituted by Art. 4, co. 1, lett. *a)*, of the Code of personal data protection.

Among the Italian jurists who recognized the hypotheses of liability now briefly outlined there are Zeno-Zencovich[404] and Giacobbe.[405]

§4. The Liability of the ISP after the Implementation of the European Community Directive on Electronic Commerce

1115. The discourse on ISPs' liability, as we can infer, involves considerations that regard the functions that should be performed by the juridical regime on the matter of extra-contractual liability. In particular, it has to be kept in mind that, in case of a wrongdoing exceeding the contract, if the provision contained in Article 2043 of the Civil Code applies, the economic consequences of the wrongdoing would burden the damaged subject in all those cases in which it is not possible to recognize the subsistence of the subjective elements of wilfulness or negligence, or in all those cases in which the damaged subject is not able to fulfil the burden of proof on the mentioned elements.

1116. The general criterion, according to which one should answer for a damage only if the event took place due to wilfulness or negligence, is usually represented with the Latin phrase '*nullum crimen, nulla poena, sine culpa*' (no criminal liability should exist in the absence of fault) that sanctions the author of the wrongdoing. This way, the principle of liability based on subjective indictment criteria, by rendering compensable only the damage related to cases in point where the fact is connoted by wilfulness or negligence, associates to the compensative function sanctions and is, at the same time, preventive of the performance of the wrongdoing. By accomplishing brief and elementary considerations of legal economic analysis, we can clearly infer how the liability modelled according to the dictate of Article 2043 of the Civil Code implies that possible damages deriving from the performance of an activity carried out by a certain subject, even if in absence of a wilful or negligent conduct, end up harming the damaged subject, without him having any redress. The damage caused would end up remaining where it fell, burdening a subject that has not caused it. In an evolved social-economic context that knows multiple forms of organization for the performance of more and more complex activities, with the possibility to effect a translation of the risks introduced in the market and, more in general, in the social context, through the mechanism of insurance, co-assurance

404. V. Zeno-Zencovich, *Profili attivi e passivi della responsabilità dell'utente in Internet*, in A. Palazzo – U. Ruffolo (edited by), *La tutela del navigatore in Internet*, Milano, 2002, p. 143.

405. G. Giacobbe, *La responsabilità civile per l'uso di Internet*, in V. Ricciuto – N. Zorzi (edited by), *Il contratto telematico*, Padova, 2002, p. 222, according to which the possibility of talking of objective liability has to be excluded, since on the *provider* has to be identified the burden of a real specific duty of verification, compatible, following this reconstruction, with the provision of Art. 2050 c.c. It is necessary to remember that those who consider the liability provided by Art. 2050 c.c. as an hypothesis of objective liability, also emphasized, since a long time ago, the applicability of Art. 2050 c.c. as rule for extra-contractual damage by *computer*, and this even before the enforcement of the Law 675/96. Cf. G. Alpa, *Note per un progetto di legge sulle banche dati*, il G. Alpa (edited by), Computer e responsabilità civile, Milano, 1985, p. 143; G. Alpa, *Responsabilità extracontrattuale ed elaboratore elettronico*, in *Il diritto dell'informazione e dell'informatica*, Milano, 1986, p. 388; as cited in L. Bugiolacchi, cited work, p. 835.

and reinsurance, the question is whether the principle of extra-contractual liability based on subjective indictment is appropriate in terms of efficiency and social justice.[406]

1117. The different requirements of responsibility provided by the Italian Civil Code – among these, 2050, recalled also by Article 18 of Law 675/96 (now Article 15, co. 1, of the code on personal data protection) – appear clearly based on indictment criteria that are different from those considered by Article 2043 of the Civil Code, since there strict (objective) no-fault liability is outlined.[407]

1118. Having to choose, for interpretative purposes, which provisions are applicable in case of contractual wrongdoing performed through the Internet and which, in relation to this, is the position of the ISP, we cannot avoid considering the consequences, under the juridical profile, of the different ways to intend the provisions of the Civil Code we are now commenting on. In particular, we have discussed if Article 2043 of the Civil Code should have the function of general provision for wrongdoing exceeding the contract, against which the other forms of liability (for conduct of others, aggravated or objective) would be regarded as exceptions. The adhesion to this approach would imply inapplicability by analogy with the provisions different from those based on subjective indictment criteria.

---

406. Let us note that the judgment on the compliance with the criterion of social justice, far from assuming in that context an ideological value, impacts significantly on the sense of 'trust' that a subject can bestow on the organized activity of the businessmen. Therefore the choice of the type of liability to adopt for cases in point economically or socially worthy of particular attention, as it is for the hypothesis of illicit facts referable to the use of new technologies, should be made according to the impact on the whole social, economic and juridical system.

407. *See* G. Alpa, *La responsabilità civile*, Milano, 1999, pp. 757 and ss.; as well as P.G. Monateri, *Manuale della responsabilità civile*, Torino, 2001, p. 358. In summarizing, due to the necessity to synthesize the present dissertation, it has to be remembered that recent doctrinal stances tend to include in the scope of objective liability the various hypotheses of liability contained in Art. 2047 and following of the Civil Code, with particular reference to the liability of the ward of an incapable person, the tutor, the parent, the owner or mandant, the warden of goods, the owner of animals (or the subject that employs them), the proprietor of buildings in ruin, the subject exercising dangerous activities. On the point, *see* P.G. Monateri, last work cited, pp. 289-448. It has to be recognized, however, that jurisprudence has since long assumed a position opposed to that assumed by the doctrine, by carrying out a merely formal reconduction of the mentioned liabilities to hypotheses of negligence variously qualified (*see culpa in vigilando*, *culpa in educando*, *culpa in eligendo*, *culpa in omittendo*, etc.), although not only the absence of any textual reference to a subjective criterion of direct indictment, but even an opposing *voluntas legis*, valuable also through a logical and systematic interpretation, is recognized. On the point, indeed, there has been someone who has effectively defined the jurisprudential stance with the epithet of '*declamatory*', standing on positions that respect the formal data completely regardless of the effective content of the provisions under examination. *See* De Vogli, *L'art. 2051 c.c. tra declamazione e regole operazionali*, in *Danno e resp.*, 1999, 209, as cited in L. Bugiolacchi, cited work, p. 832, note n. 15. Anyway it has to be observed that now also the jurisprudence shows the will to adhere to the interpretation made for a long time by the legislature, as it is possible to infer from the ruling C. Cass. 5031/98, as well as, less recently, from C. Cass., sez. un., sent. 12019/91 (Cf. G. Alpa, *Responsabilità per rischio da cose in custodia*, in *Nuova giur. civ. comm.*, 1992, I, 82). On the point, *see* L. Bugiolacchi, cited work, p. 832.

1119. Recent doctrinal stances, instead, by considering the juridical relevance of provisions based on different criteria of liability indictment and thus reaching a largely systematic interpretation, emphasize how in actuality, in the Italian juridical system, it is not at all possible to recognize in Article 2043 the general rule of civil liability, since the system of civil liability is 'multicentric'. In other words, there is a variety of indictment criteria that are different but of the same grade, without one being considered as prevailing over the others. Considering the whole regime of extra-contractual liability leads to reassessing and extending the application of provisions based on objective criteria of liability. That appears particularly significant in a context susceptible to being perfectly framed in the juridical categories we are traditionally used to, as in cases of civil wrongdoing that concern the information society. In particular, with reference to the liability of the provider, provisions that leave aside the investigation on the profiles of guiltiness would have wider application.

1120. It appears evident how the choice of the applicable regime ends up being a choice of legislative policy[408] and, as such, to be affected during the stage of statutory production. This is what happened with the recent intervention of the Italian legislature, with the enforcement of D.Lgs. 70/2003, implementing EC Directive 2000/31/CE, the aim of which is to effect an harmonization in the national market with regard to the services of the information society (directive on electronic commerce).

This way, provisions ad hoc on the matter of liability of the provider were enforced, with the effect not only of supplying new solutions but also of introducing new criteria in the jurisprudential production and in the doctrinal debate in course. From such provisions, the text of which is integrally provided in note, some relevant principles, briefly discussed below, can be extracted.[409]

1121. Although the provisions *de quibus* introduce clear and wide hypotheses of liability exemption in favour of the provider, the *principle of presumption of liability* of the ISP appears applicable.

1122. The proof of the subsistence of liability under these provisions burdens the subject. We have therefore the declaration of the *principle of the shift of the burden of proof* with regard to justifying circumstances imposing, through the wording of the provisions, for the exemption of liability, a strict control over the subsistence of the required ('the worker is not liable . . . as long as [. . .]').

1123. In consideration of the delicate task of the ISP, that assumes a neuralgic function for the subsistence of the whole online (telematic) communication system, the minimization of liability is aimed to avoid limiting the development not only of

408. V. Zeno-Zencovich, *Internet tra diritto penale e diritto civile, in Il diritto dell'informazione e dell'informatica*, Milano, 1999, p. 1055. *See also*, L. Bugiolacchi, cited work, p. 858.

409. *See* Art. 14 (*Responsabilità nell'attività di semplice trasporto* – Mere conduit), Art. 15 (*Responsabilità nell'attività di memorizzazione temporanea* – caching) and 'Art. 16 (*Responsabilità nell'attività di memorizzazione di informazioni* – hosting).

e-commerce but also of the whole phenomenon of Internet working, through which users can exploit non-economic activities of constitutional significance. We observe therefore the declaration of the further *principle of exemption of liability of the provider* only in the hypothesis in which his intervention in the transmission or memorization of data is merely technical, accompanied by the *principle of peremptoriness of justifying conditions.*

1124. Particularly significant is, furthermore, the *principle of absence of a general duty of control on behalf of the ISP* towards possible wrongdoing performed by its own clients through the services it supplies. The statutory dictate explicitly denies that the provider should be held to search facts or circumstances pointing to the presence of unlawful activities, avoiding therefore to make it assume a censorial role, that would be inadmissible in a democratic society.[410] In this regard it has to be emphasized that a possible duty of control on the performance of wrongdoing would substantiate the obligation to carry out an activity that would not only be onerous under the economic profile but also of difficult execution on both the practical level (since this would presuppose the juridical competences necessary to the identification of wrongdoing) and the juridical level (since providers would need inspective powers that would be intolerable because they would infringe the most elementary constitutional guarantees).[411]

The principle mentioned just now, however, is tempered by the duty for the provider to inform public authorities of alleged wrongdoing of which he has become in any way aware, performed by the addressees of its own services.

1125. The different duty of revealing to public authorities information that allows the identification of the addressee of the services, in order to prevent or to repress wrongdoing performed through the Internet, appears to comply with the *principle of partial anonymity*, an account of which has been given in the brief doctrinal review in the previous paragraph.

1126. Finally, the statutory provision consecrates also the *principle of liability of the provider* with reference to unlawful contents in the context of non-performance of the duties of information to public authorities or non-compliance with court orders or orders by the administrative authority with functions of vigilance.

---

410. It has to be noted, indeed, that among the main objections moved against the thesis that declares a liability of the ISP for the wrongdoing performed by one's customers, one recognized the grounded risk of the introduction of a 'censorship', that the *provider* would be induced to exercise in order to avoid possible liabilities.

411. *See also*, on the point, Trib. di Prato, Ord. 15 Oct. 2001, *E.T. Group s.r.l. v. Tex Net Telecomunicazioni s.r.l.* (in *Il foro toscano*, 2002, 1, 100, with note by Rason), where it has been stated that if the *provider* prevents certain e-mail messages from reaching the subjects registered on someone else's *mailing list* 'he is performing (besides a violation of the contractual duties towards his e-mail user) a wrongdoing towards the transmitting enterprise. Such blockage activity can be considered lawful only if justified by the performance of a contractual duty'.

1127. From what we can infer with reference to the reading of the introduced statutory provisions, the effort of the legislature to balance opposing juridical and economic interests that are relevant in the sector that is the object of the present discourse is clear. The result shows itself to be worthy, even if, on one side, it does not completely eliminate the questions already arisen in doctrine and, on the other, it poses new criteria on which doctrine and jurisprudence will have the opportunity to challenge themselves subsequently, pending a definitive adjustment of the regulations. While deferring to another stage further and more exhaustive considerations that we here omit, as a mere example it has to be first of all emphasized that the recent legislation does not intervene in the matter already regulated by Law 675/96 that provides for the protection of the person with reference to personal data processing. It seems therefore correct to assert that the question of the applicability of Article 2050 c.c. and Article 18 of Law 675/96 appears still open.[412] Other criteria, the relevance of which the legislature has not yet shown to have understood, regard the specific hypothesis of unlawful fact inherent in the use of '*software agents*'[413] that are destined to impose a reassessment of the rules and the principles of liability that exceeds the contract applicable to the matter that is the object of the present discourse.

§5. ISP Liability in the Social Network and Platform Economy

1128. Subjects offering remote services, by electronic means, at the request of a recipient, 'normally for remuneration' are defined in European legislation as 'information society services' and are regulated by Directive 31/2000 relative to 'certain aspects legal aspects of information society services, in particular electronic commerce and the internal market', the so-called Directive on electronic commerce, implemented by the Italian legislator with legislative decree 70/2003.

1129. Aimed at fostering the development of e-commerce and the free circulation of information society services and goods in the single market, the Directive aims to reduce the possibilities for Member States to introduce establishment or liability regimes for the information processed that decreases the growth of these services and their circulation in the single market, establishing a first common legal framework.

---

412. In favour of the applicability of the articles mentioned in the text, even with the advent of the new regulation, *see* V. Zeno-Zencovich, *Profili attivi e passivi della responsabilità dell'utente in Internet*, in A. Palazzo – U. Ruffolo (edited by), *La tutela del navigatore in Internet*, Milano, 2002, pp. 142 and 143.

413. With reference to the specificity of the juridical issues related to the *software agents*, *see* G. Sartor, *Gli agenti software: nuovi soggetti del cyberdiritto?*, in *Contratto e impresa*, Padova, 2002, 2, 466 and following. On the matter, but with the denial of the feature *od specificità*, *see also* G. Finocchiaro, *La conclusione del contratto telematico mediante i «software agents»: un falso problema giuridico?*, in *Contratto e impresa*, Padova, 2002, 2, 501 and following.

1130. Directive 31/2000 still constitutes the main normative reference with regard to the responsibility of the provider of information society services for the information stored by it on behalf of the user, so-called provider liability or secondary liability.

More precisely, it is the responsibility of the subjects who carry out 'the transmission of information through a communication network, the provision of access to a communication network or the storage of information provided by a recipient of services' and is provided for by the Directive absence of a general obligation to monitor the information processed.

1131. Article 15 of the Directive establishes, in fact, that the Member States must not impose on the providers of such services, better specified in Articles 12, 13 and 14, 'a general obligation of surveillance on the information they transmit or memorize nor a general obligation of actively seek facts or circumstances that indicate the presence of illegal activities'.

1132. The second paragraph of the same article specifies that the Member States can, however, provide that the providers of such services 'are required to inform the competent public authority without delay of alleged illegal activities or information of the recipients of their services or to communicate to the competent authorities, at their request, information allowing identification of the recipients of their services with which they have data storage agreements'.

1133. The third paragraph provides, in the version implemented by the Italian Legislator, that the provider is civilly liable if, following a request to this effect by the judicial or administrative authority, he has not acted promptly to prevent access to the content, as well as if, having become aware of the unlawful or prejudicial nature of one third of the content, it has not informed the competent authorities.

1134. These principles, applicable to the provider's liability, can be summarized as follows: (i) the provider does not have an obligation to monitor the contents that it preserves, disseminates or transmits; (ii) it is not required to actively search for illegal activities; (iii) if he learns of illegal activities he must inform the authorities without delay; (iv) if the authorities require him to provide information or to disable access to some content, the provider must act without delay.

1135. The services imagined by the European legislator, almost twenty years ago, in providing this discipline, were divided into three categories, respectively described and governed by Articles 12, 13 and 14 of the Directive, based on the activities they carried out.

1136. The activity of mere conduit, according to the Directive, consists in 'transmitting, on a communication network, information provided by a recipient of the service, or in providing access to the communication network'.

The provider that carries out this activity is not held responsible for the information transmitted as long as it does not give rise to the transmission, does not select the recipient and does not modify the information transmitted.

1137. The caching activity consists, instead, in 'transmitting, on a communication network, information provided by a recipient of the service' and in carrying out an 'automatic, intermediate and temporary storage of such information carried out for the sole purpose of making the subsequent forwarding to other recipients at their request'.

In this case, the provider is not responsible as long as it does not modify the information, carries out the activity in accordance with the provisions on access to information and updating of the same, does not interfere on the lawful use of technologies to obtain information on the use of information and provided that he acts promptly on such information if he becomes aware of the fact that they have been removed from the place in which they were previously on the network or that access to them has been disabled due to spontaneous intervention or by order of the authorities, of the recipient of the service.

1138. Finally, the hosting activity consists of the 'memorization of information provided by a recipient of the service' and has raised the major problems of interpretation.

This category includes activities that are very different from each other, from managing a personal blog in relation to user comments, search engines and social networks.

However, the jurisprudence has tried on several occasions to attribute to the provider some form of responsibility with respect to the offences committed by the users, believing that this subject could not be considered completely extraneous to the activities of the users. This led to the elaboration of a fundamental distinction between active provider and passive provider, aimed at reaffirming the responsibility of some types of providers.

1139. The distinction is based on Recital 42 of Directive 31/2000, in which it is stated that the exclusion of liability applies exclusively to the 'case in which the activity of information society service provider is limited to the technical process', or carry out a 'purely technical, automatic and passive' activity, without knowledge or control of the information transmitted or stored. It follows that if the provider performs an 'active role' on the managed contents that it is not merely technical, or if it has actual knowledge of the illegal content, the exclusion of liability does not work.

1140. The service provider to whom, in the years of drafting the Directive, the Legislator thought could be, at most, the provider of information storage space such as the space for the creation of a personal blog or a website open to users' comments, far from the complexity and the possibilities of interactions between users allowed by today's platforms.

The service offered today goes well beyond the mere memorization of information, and through the structuring and analysis of the information itself it comes to offer something more.

Think of the social network, the search engine or the brokerage platform and you will notice that these are complex services, often difficult to distinguish from one another, where information uploaded by users becomes an integral part of the business model.

Not only that, the possibilities of storing content by users are structured, regulated and sometimes controlled by platforms. And, in the case of the platforms being analysed, this activity enters into the conclusion of a contract.

1141. It is also evident that in the current scenario the expression 'purely technical, automatic and passive' loses much of its meaning.

Created to distinguish the activities that required human intervention from automated activities, it is ill-suited to the extensive use of algorithms which, although operating automatically, cannot be said to be neutral or 'merely passive'.

1142. The principle of the absence of a surveillance obligation has thus begun to suffer some first important erosions by the Courts. Consider, for example, the case of *Delfi v. Estonia*, but above all to the *Google Spain* case.

1143. Recently, also, the Italian Court of Cassation, in the reconstruction of the provider's responsibility, has specified that for the knowability of the crime the legal knowledge is sufficient and, therefore, the communication of the owner of the injured right, unless proved otherwise, as well as that, for the purpose of recognizing the unlawfulness of the content, it is sufficient that it 'be reasonably ascertainable' and that the subject 'is grossly negligent for not having positively rediscounted it, in the same way as the degree of diligence that it is reasonable to expect from an operator network professional at a given historical moment'.

1144. It is believed, however, that the strongest signal of the beginning of the sunset of this vision, which gives way to the responsibility of these subjects, is to be found in the most recent European legislative proposals.

1145. In the Communication 'Tackling Illegal Content Online. Towards an Enhanced Responsibility of Online Platforms', the Commission stated that the platforms are the main point of access to information on the Internet and therefore have a significant social responsibility, having to protect users and society itself and prevent criminals and to the people involved in illegal activities to exploit their services: 'Online action should take decisive steps to address this problem, as part of the responsibility which flows from their central role in society.'

1146. The platforms have become interlocutors of the European institutions, invited to the collaboration for the contrast of the illegal activities committed online by the users, sitting at the tables where the new normative proposals were elaborated.

There was no structured intervention, but action was taken by sectors, developing regulatory instruments (directives and regulations), but also codes of conduct and forms of collaboration between platforms and institutions.

1147. The Commission has, in fact, always repeated the applicability of the regime under Directive 31/2000, identifying, however, sectors in which it requires platforms for 'cooperation'. In the aforementioned Communication, the Commission recalls the regime under the Directive, but placing the accent on Recital 47, where it specifies that the impossibility for Member States to impose on lenders a general surveillance obligation 'does not concern the obligations of surveillance in specific cases and, in particular, it does not affect the orders issued by the national authorities according to the respective laws'.

From this provision, the Commission draws the possibility to request, instead, with regard to some 'specific cases', with respect to which it introduces or intends to introduce, with different instruments and more or less impacting on the responsibility of the provider, some forms of intervention.

1148. The most relevant interventions and proposals for intervention with regard to platform responsibility concern, in particular, the following topics: terrorism, e-evidence, hate speech, fake news, audiovisual, media service, copyright.

1149. With regard to 'terrorism', the European Union has issued Directive 541/2017 (Directive on the fight against terrorism and which replaces the Council Framework Decision 2002/475 / JHA and amends Council Decision 2005/671 / JHA), which lists a series of crimes which, if committed with the aim of severely intimidating the population, to unduly compel public authorities or an international organization to perform or refrain from performing any act or in order to seriously destabilize or destroy the fundamental political, constitutional, economic or social structures of a country or an international organization are considered terrorist crimes.

1150. Among the provisions therein, which invite Member States to take the necessary measures to ensure that the conduct described therein is punishable as a crime, there is also the 'public provocation to commit acts of terrorism'.

The Directive was followed by a regulation proposal specifically aimed at preventing the dissemination of online terrorist content, which concerns the content uploaded by users on online platforms and which, first of all, requires that providers can and must intervene, where provided, without, however, losing the benefits of the exemption from liability for users' uploaded content, as per Directive 31/2000.

1151. Not unlike the proposed Regulation on European orders for the production and preservation of electronic evidence in criminal matters, the so-called E-evidence Regulation, which aims 'to adapt the cooperation mechanisms to the digital age, supplying the judicial authorities and of contrast the tools to keep up with the current methods of communication of criminals and combat modern forms of crime'.

The objective of the proposal is 'to establish the rules according to which a competent European Union judicial authority can, through a European production or conservation order, order a service provider offering services in the Union to produce or keep electronic evidence'. These are instruments that can only be used in cross-border situations, i.e. in cases where the service provider is established or represented in another Member State.

1152. In particular, it provides for the possibility of requesting 'European production orders' and 'European conservation orders' for service providers that provide electronic communication services, information society services (hosting services), name services to domain and IP numbering. Under this proposal, 'service providers become the central pivot of the system, acting as a "valve" capable of regulating the entry of a given order from the issuing authority of a Member State in the order in which the researched data are physically preserved'.

1153. Regarding the issue of the hate speech, in May 2016, the European Commission, Facebook, Twitter, YouTube and Microsoft developed a Code of Conduct (Code of Conduct on Countering Illegal Hate Speech Online) to counter the spread of expressions of hatred online and which provides for: the implementation of clear and effective procedures for reporting users of illegal content and for their removal; the commitment to check the users' reports concerning hate speech within 24 hours of receipt and to remove the content where they are harmful; better information to users about the types of content not allowed and the procedures for removing them; cooperation and dialogue with the European Commission to counter these phenomena.

1154. Also with regard to the 'fake news', or online disinformation, it was decided to proceed by adopting a code of conduct, the first version of which, however, received a negative opinion from the group of experts appointed by the Commission.

1155. With regard to audiovisual media services, for which a Directive already existed, it was decided to intervene by modifying it, through the proposal for a Directive 'amending Directive 2010/13 / EU relating to the coordination of certain legislative, regulatory and administrative provisions of the States members concerning the provision of audiovisual media services in view of the evolution of market realities', now approaching entry into force.

It introduces, limiting itself to the issues under analysis, a new Chapter IX-*bis* to the 'Audiovisual Media Services Directive', concerning the provisions applicable to 'platform services for video sharing'.

Where the platform has as its 'main objective' or as the objective of a section of the service the supply of videos generated by users, the new rules introduced regarding audiovisual media services will also be applied. Among the newly introduced regulations, limiting the analysis to those of interest, Article 25 of the Directive provides that, without prejudice to the principles set out in Directive 31/2000, such platforms adopt measures to: 'a) protect minors from contents that could harm the physical, mental or moral development of minors; (b) protect all citizens from contents that instigate violence or hatred towards a group of people or a member of such a group defined with reference to sex, race, color, religion, ancestry, national or ethnic origin'.

1156. Also with regard to the protection of copyright, the proposal for a Directive on copyright in the digital single market, much debated and recently approved, provides for the adoption of measures for the platforms, in agreement with the holders of the rights, 'aimed at guaranteeing the functioning of the agreements concluded with them for the use of their works or other material or aimed at preventing that certain works or other material identified by the holders of the rights through collaboration with the same lenders are made available on their services'.

The platforms must also inform the holders of the rights of the implemented measures and, 'if appropriate', report 'adequately' on the recognition and use of the works and other material; provide for the adoption of complaint and appeal mechanisms; adopt 'adequate and proportionate technologies for the recognition of contents, taking into account, among other things, the nature of services, the availability of technologies and their effectiveness in light of technological developments'.

1157. The responsibility of the platform for user content, so-called secondary liability, is therefore structured as follows: there is the principle of irresponsibility as per Directive 31/2000, which does not apply where the platform operator performs a selection / modification of the contents (if not in an automated way), and it is flanked by a series of exceptions with respect to which the provider is required to intervene or invited to do so, with the blessing of the Commission which specifies that in such cases of adoption of measures on a voluntary basis the intervention on the contents will not lead to the loss of the principle of irresponsibility set out in the Directive.

1158. The result is a confused picture, so much so that the European Commission itself has affirmed that 'it is not always easy to trace the limit of the intervention that intermediaries can operate on the contents they transmit, store or host, beyond which they lose the benefit of exemption from liability under the e-commerce Directive'.

The traditional distinctions between active and passive providers – in addition to the aforementioned problem concerning the difficult distinction in the case of automated but not passive and neutral operations – are becoming meaningless.

It would therefore seem to derive a leopard-like mechanism: irresponsibility as a rule, which jumps in the case of direct intervention, unless this intervention is aimed at repressing one of the phenomena for which the Commission encourages intervention.

1159. From the existing complexity emerges the need for a European legislative intervention that can move beyond Directive 31/2000 and provide a single regulation concerning the management of the contents by the platforms. In the Communication 'Tackling Illegal Content Online. Towards an Enhanced Responsibility of Online Platforms' the Commission has begun to outline some common principles.

1160. First, the platforms are required to intervene when they become aware of illegal content and that this can happen: following the receipt of orders from judicial or administrative authorities, communications from competent authorities, 'specialized trusted fluggers' (or subjects who are entrusted by the platform with the task of verifying the contents), holders of intellectual property rights, user reports, following activities of the same platform. Simplifying and focusing on the subjects, we could relist them as follows: reporting by public authorities, reporting by private parties, platform on its behalf.

1161. The Communication also establishes that the platforms must establish procedures for the reporting of the contents by the users, which are simple and user-friendly, which allow to categorize the reports making the user know why he believes the content is illegal. They must also be transparent about the procedures for managing notifications, elaborate specific reports and provide for notification and contestation of removal decisions, in order to guarantee the protection of the right to freedom of expression and fundamental rights.

1162. It should also be noted that the platforms may also include cases of removal of legitimate content that, however, conflict with their terms of service. In this case, they are required to be transparent and to specify their policies in a clear and sufficient manner.

Chapter 4. Product Liability

§1. Product Liability in the Italian Juridical System (Mentions)

1163. In the Italian juridical system, after arduous legislative efforts aimed to guarantee compensation for damage caused by a faulty product even in absence of a specific statute, the gap has been filled through the enforcement of D.P.R. n. 224 of 1988, implementing EC Directive 85/374/CEE, successively modified by D.Lgs. n. 25 of 2001, in turn enforced for the implementation of Directive 1999/34/CE.

1164. Under a subjective profile, the regulation allows to obtain compensation from a quite vast number of subjects, through the formulation of the wide category of the 'producer', defined to include the manufacturer of the finished product or of a part of it, the producer of raw material, the agriculturist, the breeder, the fisher, the hunter or any other person who effectively presents himself as a producer by placing his own trademark or other distinctive sign on the product or on the packaging. The category of the subject held to answer, already vast in itself, is also extended to the commercial importer of the product in the EC, as long as purposes of distribution subsist (among which have to be included sale, leasing and financial leasing), as well as to anybody who effectively presents himself as an importer in the EC, by force of the apposition of his own name, trademark or other distinctive sign on the product or on the packaging. Where the producer is not identified, liability cannot generally be excluded, in respect of certain formalities provided by Article 4 of D.P.R. 224/88, by the supplier or commercial distributor of the product, who can, however, discharge himself from liability or obtain the exclusion from the possible trial by indicating the producer or his own direct supplier, as long as the conditions provided by the same Article 4, reference to which is made, occur. The definition of beneficiaries of the regulation is lacking. The text generically refers to them by using the adjunct 'damaged subjects'.[414]

1165. The producer, as above identified, is liable for damages caused by faults of the product, defined by Article 2 of D.P.R. 224/88, only for the purposes of the regulation under examination, 'every good, even if incorporated in another good or estate', with the specification that 'also electricity is considered as a good'. Therefore the hypothesis of damage caused by 'estates',[415] by 'services' and by 'immaterial goods' appears excluded from the regulation *de qua*. In the context of

---

414. The reference to the *status* of the consumer has been omitted in order to avoid interpretations aimed to the restriction of the range of applicability of the provisions in question only to the hypotheses of subsistence of negotial relationships intervened or *in fieri*. Let us think of the position of the so-called *bystanders*.

415. On the point, *see* O. Troiano, *Comm. all'art.* 2, in *Commentario del D.P.R. 224/98* edited by Pardolesi, in *Le nuove leggi civili commentate*, 1989, p. 510; as well as A. Lupoli, *La responsabilità per danno da prodotti difettosi*, in *Diritto dei consumatori e nuove tecnologie* edited by F. Bocchini, Torino, 2003, II, pp. 51 and 52, where it is emphasized that the ratio of the exclusion of estates stands on the fact that since these goods cannot circulate, they cannot constitute any obstacle to the free trade in the common market and therefore are out of the purposes pursued by the directive that the D.P.R. 224/88 implements.

information society, the exclusion of these last two categories, on which we will dwell later, assumes a particular significance.

1166. In order to assert product liability, it is necessary to recognize the requisite of defectiveness, whereby the product itself does not offer 'the security that can legitimately be expected, considering all circumstances'.[416] With relation to the 'legitimate expectations of security', as a criterion used to identify the defectiveness of the product, the following articulation has been suggested: information faults; planning faults; fabrication faults.

1167. Defectiveness of the product due to *information faults* occurs when the expectations of security are compromised by the presentation of the product itself, with regard to the directions that accompany it, to the instructions, to the representation and, more in general, of its circulation. In this case, the judgment on the faultiness of the product does not depend on the intrinsic characteristics of the good. This is not contradicted by the necessity that the assessment of the fault should be assessed in relation to the normal use the good is 'reasonably destined' to. Liability cannot be recognized, instead, with relation to behaviours not 'reasonably' predictable, which exclude the possibility to assess the faultiness of the product for the lack of a 'legitimate' expectation on security.

1168. The product liability for faults in the planning of goods, instead, regards the situation in which the faultiness is recognizable in every piece of a certain series.[417] The fault in question, however, cannot be assessed only on the basis of the circumstance that an 'upgraded product' has been released.[418]

1169. Finally, fabrication faults concern single pieces of a produced series[419] and, more precisely, when one or more pieces of a perfectly regular series turn out faulty.[420] In this case, liability subsists apart from the compliance with information duties and the faultiness is established by the mere confrontation with products belonging to the same productive series.

1170. Liability does not subsist in the following six situations provided by Article 6 of D.P.R. 224/88:

(1) failure to release the product;
(2) non-existence of the fault at the time the product was released;
(3) fabrication of the product for other purposes than sale or other forms of distribution for valuable consideration, or fabrication or distribution of the product out of the exercise of the professional activity;

416. *See* Art. 5, co. 1, D.P.R. 224/88.
417. P.G. Monateri, cited work, p. 519.
418. *See* Art. 5, co. 2, D.P.R. 224/88.
419. P.G. Monateri, cited work, p. 519.
420. A. Lupoli, cited work, p. 57.

(4) conformity of the fault with exigencies of compliance with a binding regulation or with a mandatory ordinance;
(5) non-consideration of the faultiness of the product at the time of its release on the basis of the scientific and technical knowledge of that time;
(6) faultiness only caused by the conception of the product in which the component part or the raw material has been incorporated, with regard to the liability of the producer or the supplier of the component part or of the raw material, or faultiness caused by 'the compliance of these with the instructions given by the producer that employed them'.

1171. With regard to the probative regime, the burden of proof is on the damaged subject regarding the defect and the causal relationship between the defect and damage as well. The producer, instead, is burdened with the proof of the justifying circumstances outlined above, keeping in mind that with relation to the second hypothesis the legislature considers sufficient the demonstration in probabilistic terms that the fault, in consideration of the circumstances, was not yet existing at the time of the release of the product.

1172. Compensation, on the basis of the regulation in question, is only available for three categories of damage: death; personal injury; and destruction or deterioration of a thing different from the faulty product. In this last hypothesis, however, the damaged thing has to be 'of the kind normally and specially destined to private use and likewise principally used by the damaged subject', and the compensation is limited by the presence of a cap equal to the sum of 750,000 lire (EUR 387.34).

1173. Compensation is proportionally reduced for concurrent negligent acts of the injured person, while liability is totally excluded if the victim voluntarily exposed himself to the danger deriving from the fault of the product, being aware of it.

1174. At the end of this brief scrutiny, it is necessary to observe, furthermore, that by force of the expressed dictate of Article 15, co. 1, D.P.R. 224/88, the provisions examined until now do not exclude, neither limit, the rights deriving from other statutes, so a concurrent claim alongside other fault-based regimes of liability provided in the Italian juridical system, such as those contained in Article 2043 Civil Code and following, should be possible.

§2. Liability for Damage Caused by Informational Instruments

1175. After these brief mentions of the general regulation of product liability,[421] we now want to dwell on the possibilities of application of the statute *de qua* in case the damage is a consequence of the use of informational instruments.

---

421. For a detailed analysis of the producer's liability in the Italian juridical system, *see*, among all, G. Alpa, *La responsabilità civile*, Milano, 1999, p. 833 e ss.; *see also* C. Castronovo, *La nuova responsabilità civile*, Milano, 1997, pp. 299 e ss.

In this regard it is mandatory, in the first place, to investigate if these can be included in the notion of 'product' provided by D.P.R. 224/88 and above enunciated.

Italian legislation has challenged the subject, thus proposing, in the course of time, different solutions. With reference to *hardware*, as a matter of fact, the regulation of the liability of the producer has appeared obvious, due to the physical characteristics of the good considered. Regarding software, it had been difficult to declare it as having the nature of 'goods', an essential characteristic for the purposes of applicability of D.P.R. 224/88.

1176. Some accredited doctrinal stances moved from the consideration that the *software*, as an intellectual creation protected by copyright, would have the character of immateriality and, thus, could not be included in the definition of 'product' provided by the regulation in question. This position was supported also by reasonings on the technical nature of the software, consisting of a complex of logical instructions supplied to a processor in a programming language.

1177. Another doctrinal stance, instead, approaches the problem from a different point of view, emphasizing how the development of software should often be traced to the notion of 'service', rather than to that of 'product' requested by the statute to ground the liability in question. In this regard, some suggested distinguishing between hypotheses in which the software has been commissioned ad hoc (by means of development contracts related to the specific exigencies of the buyer) and different hypotheses in which the software has been created to meet the general exigences of the customers (*software standard*).[422] In this last case, the process of commercialization and mass distribution the software is exposed to would justify the applicability of the regulation in question, removing the software from the category of 'service'.

1178. A further theory has suggested that software, although being a complex of logical instructions, is usually sold jointly with support, so that with this it forms a whole that should be considered a 'good' and, thus, a 'product', by force of Article 2 of D.P.R. 224/88.

1179. With regard to these considerations, nevertheless, we have to emphasize how the advent of the Internet has brought other distribution systems of informational products that are not tied to a physical support. Yet, software cannot be used without hardware. Apart from the modalities with which the software is released, therefore, the indivisible tie with the hardware and running the program always involves 'physical effects once introduced in a computer',[423] which leaves no doubt as to the applicability of D.P.R. 224/88 to software products, the 'physicality' of

422. C. Rossello, *La responsabilità da inadeguato funzionamento di programmi per elaboratore elettronico: aspetti e problematiche dell'esperienza nordamericana*, in Rivista critica di diritto privato, 1984, p. 123; *see also*, with a deeper consideration of other solutions, C. Rossello, *Software difettoso e responsabilità da prodotto*, in *Economia e diritto del terziario*, 1993, p. 975.

423. A. Lupoli, cited work, p. 70.

which should be emphasized. 'The physicality of the *software* has been confirmed by the EC Commission, that has solved every doubt on this regard, by considering applicable to it the Directive on the liability of the producer in the same way as it applies to handmade or artistic products.'[424]

1180. In adding further considerations of a more technical nature, it has to be observed that the logical instructions the software consists of, since formulated in a certain programming language, end up constituting the '*source code*', successively translated in an '*object code*'. Object code can be directly run on the processor through the assumption of a certain circuit order of one's logical-arithmetical unit, allowing the processing of electronic signals, that are characterized by the use of flows of electrons not to perform motive power, develop heat, etc., but to transmit signals used for purposes of data communication.[425] This flow of electrons that constitutes the means of transmission of data in binary code through the opening or closing of electric circuits appears to allow the inclusion of the informational instrument in the notion of 'product' contained in Article 2 of D.P.R. 224/88, precisely by force of the textual reference to *electricity*, considered in this context as the flow of electrons aimed to obtain the transmission of data in binary codes (*bit*) according to the instructions of the software, inseparably tied to the hardware at the time of its running.

424. *See* A. Lupoli, cited work, p. 70, with reference to the written Interrogation n. 706/88, with answer on 15 Nov. 1988, in G.U.C.E. C 114/42 of 8 May 1989.
425. R. Borruso, *L'informatica per il giurista*, Milano, 1990, p. 2. It has to be noticed that the author, in another work titled *Computer e diritto*, Milano, 1988, II, p. 396, even if with reference to the discusses issue of the patentability of the software, concludes 'the materiality cannot be denied, anyway, for the 'object code' inserted in the central memory of the *computer*'.

Part VI. Privacy Protection

Chapter 1. Regulation of Personal Data Processing

§1. History of Privacy Protection in Italy

1181. The current privacy legislation in Italy is the result, as in many European Countries, of a process of layered normative creation, starting from the first Directive, that of 1995, and coming up to the 2016 Regulation.

In a nutshell, but we will see better in the following lines, the first rule in Italy on the subject of data protection was enacted in 1996 (Law n. 675 of 1996).

Law 675 was repealed in 2003 by the Privacy Code (Legislative Decree N. 196 of 2003) which was significantly modified (and reduced) in 2018 by Legislative Decree n. 101 which adapted the old Italian legislation to the advent of the GDPR.

On the other side, the Italian Constitution contains no express guarantee of the right to privacy, so the aforementioned norms are, today, the landmark for the interpreter.

The jurisprudential debate over the existence of a right to privacy date back to the Fifties, in particular concerning the case of the tenor Enrico Caruso.

The family asked to protect some particular aspects of the life of the tenor, but in this case, the Court of Cassation (the Supreme Court in Italy) did not find any violation in spreading information that was lawfully obtained.

1182. The perspective changes in the Sixties when a publisher would like to publish a book based on the correspondence between Benito Mussolini and Claretta Petacci.

In this case, the Petacci's relatives went in a trial to defend the honour and reputation of their relative, and the Court decided that the publishing of that book could violate a fundamental right of every person that is the right of self-determination.

Since the fact is not of interest for the public and Mrs Petacci did not give the consent to publish her correspondence, the judge concluded for not allowing the book to be published.

1183. But the attention to privacy *stricto sensu* and its legal regulation dates back to the mid-nineties.

First, in 1970, the 'Workers' Statute' (Law n. 300 of 20 May 1970) disciplined, in Articles 4 and 8, the problem of the remote control of the worker and his privacy in the workplace but did not discuss, in general, the privacy problem in the Italian society. This norm is still alive.

1184. Another important step on the way of privacy right in Italy is the sentence of the so-called *Esfandiari* case, regarding the princess Soraya that was photographed with a man in her property.

In this case, the Court of Cassation (CCass, civil section, Judgement 2129/1975, 27 May 1975) recognized a right of privacy for the princess, because the fact is not of interest for the public.

1185. Last but not least, in Italy, in 2010, there was the conviction of three Google executives for violating the Italian Data Protection Law: the case regarded the online posting of a video showing a disabled person being bullied and insulted.

The case was decided on 24 February 2010 by the Italian Judge Oscar Magi: four Google executives were acquitted with regard to the charge of defamation, but three of them were sentenced to a six-months suspended-jail for violation of the Italian data protection law.

1186. Initially, the right to privacy protected a person's private life and domicile; over time, as technology evolved, it was extended to protect the ability of individuals to determine what sort of information about themselves is collected and how that information is used.

1187. In 1996, to comply with the provisions established by the European Union, Italy had to pass a general law governing privacy and data protection: Law n. 675 of 31 December 1996. It was the first law of this kind in Italy. It was repealed in 2003, but it has a very important cultural and historical value.

1188. This law, relating to the protection of persons and other subjects regarding the processing of personal data, was the ratification of Directive 95/46/EU on the protection of individuals with regard to the processing of personal data and the free movement of such data, according to the Schengen Agreement, ratified in Italy with Law n. 388 of 30 September 1993.

1189. On 27 June 2003, it was approved by the Italian Council of Ministers the Personal Data Protection Code (Legislat. Decree no. 196 of June 2003) which has implemented both the provisions of Directive 95/46/EU on Data Protection and Directive n. 2002/58/EC of 12 July 2002 concerning the processing of personal data and the protection of privacy in the electronic communications sector. The Privacy Code 'survived' the advent of GDPR and now is still in force in some of its original parts not in contrast with GDPR.

1190. The Privacy Code, in its original (2003) version, was divided into three parts.[426] The first part described the general data protection principles that apply to all organizations. The second part provided additional measures to be undertaken by

426. For a general overview of the privacy evolution in Italy *see* C. M. Bianca, F. D. Busnelli (ed.), 'La protezione dei dati personali. Commentario al D. Lgs. 30 giugno 2003, 196' (CEDAM, Padova, 2007); P. Cendon (ed.), 'Libera circolazione e protezione dei dati personali' (Giuffrè, Milano, 2006); V. Cuffaro – R. D'Orazio – V. Ricchiuto (ed.), 'Il codice del trattamento dei dati personali'

organizations in certain areas as, for example, healthcare, telecommunications, banking and finance or human resources. Part three related to sanctions and remedies.

1191. Proceeding to a brief analysis of the old introductory part of the Privacy Code (we will see that several principles still live today in the GDPR norms), there were three main sections of the text:

(i) a first part with general provisions that described the key principles of the whole discipline of the right to protection of personal data;
(ii) the guarantee of privacy as a fundamental right, and
(iii) the principle of necessity of data processing, aimed at minimizing the use of personal data, providing that the computer systems and software must be configured only for the pursuit of goals allowed, thus excluding the treatment whenever it is possible to pursue these goals through the use of anonymous data or procedures that would enable the identification only when needed.

1192. The Code was amended by the decree adapting the national legal system to the GDPR 2016/679 (Legislative Decree N. 101 of 10 August 2018).

1193. Accordingly, several of its provisions were amended or repealed and sections were added.

The decree has made use of the margin of manoeuvre afforded by the GDPR to Member States as regards, in particular, processing activities based on legal obligations or for purposes in the public interest (Article 6(1), letters c) and e)); processing of biometric, genetic and health-related data (Article 9(4) and Article 36(5)); processing activities covered by Chapter IX of the GDPR (journalism, labour, research, archiving, etc.).

As a result, several provisions of the 2003 Code were left in place as they were found not to be in conflict or overlap with the GDPR and to provide added value for the relevant stakeholders based on the implementing experience of the past fifteen years.

§2. The Personal Data Protection Code of 2003 (Before the GDPR Advent) and the Main Definitions in the Italian Legal Framework

1194. With Legislative Decree n. 196, dated 30 June 2003, it was introduced in Italy the Data Protection Code (or 'Privacy Code').

1195. Article 1 of the Code ('Right to the Protection of Personal Data') stated that everyone has the right to protection of their personal data.

(Giappichelli, Torino, 2007); R. Pardolesi (ed.), 'Diritto alla riservatezza e circolazione dei dati personali' (Giuffrè, Milano, 2003); S. Rodotà, 'Intervista su privacy e libertà' (Laterza, Bari, 2005); G. Santaniello (ed.), 'La protezione dei dati personali' (CEDAM, Padova, 2005); C. Cossu 'Dal caso Soraya alla nuova legge sulla tutela della riservatezza' in *Contr. e impr.*, 1, 49, 1998.

1196. Article 2 ('Purposes') established that the law shall ensure that personal data are processed by respecting data subjects' rights, fundamental freedoms and dignity, particularly with regard to confidentiality, personal identity and the right to personal data protection.

1197. The processing of personal data must be regulated by affording a high level of protection for the rights and freedoms referred to in the Code, in compliance with the principles of simplification, harmonization and effectiveness of the mechanisms by which data subjects can exercise such rights, and data controllers can fulfil the relevant obligations.

1198. Article 3 of the Code ('Data Minimisation Principle') stated that information systems and software shall be configured by minimizing the use of personal data and identification data, in such a way as to rule out their processing if the purposes sought in the individual cases can be achieved by using either anonymous data or suitable arrangements to allow identifying data subjects only in cases of necessity.

1199. For the purposes of the Code, Article 4 ('Definitions') was really important because it defined the taxonomy of privacy in Italian legal system, and these definitions are often used by other laws that involve, at any level, a data processing.

The first definition is about the 'processing' of data that shall mean any operation, or set of operations (carried out with or without the help of electronic or automated means), concerning the collection, recording, organization, keeping, interrogation, elaboration, modification, selection, retrieval, comparison, utilization, interconnection, blocking, communication, dissemination, erasure and destruction of data, whether the latter are contained or not in a data bank.

1200. The second definition is about 'personal data' that shall mean any information relating to natural persons that are (or can be) identified, even indirectly, by reference to any other information including a personal identification number.

1201. 'Identification data' shall mean personal data allowing a data subject to be directly identified, and 'sensitive data' shall mean personal data allowing the disclosure of racial or ethnic origin, religious, philosophical or other beliefs, political opinions, membership of parties, trade unions, associations or organizations of a religious, philosophical, political or trade-union character, as well as personal data disclosing health and sex life.

1202. 'Judicial data' are personal data concerning the criminal record office, the register of offence-related administrative sanctions and the relevant current charges or the status of being either defendant or the subject of investigations pursuant to the Criminal Procedure Code.

1203. At last, 'anonymous data' are any data that either in origin or on account of its having been processed cannot be associated with any identified or identifiable data subject.

1204. The subjects considered by the Decree are four:

(i) 'data controller', any natural or legal person, Public Administration, body, association or other entity that is competent, also jointly with another data controller, to determine purposes and methods of the processing of personal data and the relevant means, including security matters;
(ii) 'data processor', any natural or legal person, Public Administration, body, association or other agency that processes personal data on the controller's behalf;
(iii) 'persons in charge of the processing', the natural persons that have been authorized by the data controller or processor to carry out processing operations; and
(iv) 'data subject', any natural person that is the subject of the personal data.

1205. From a technical point of view, 'communication' shall mean disclosing personal data to one or more identified entities other than the data subject, the data controller's representative in the State's territory, the data processor and persons in charge of the processing in any form whatsoever, including by making available or interrogating such data.

1206. 'Dissemination' consists in disclosing personal data to unidentified entities, in any form whatsoever, including by making available or interrogating such data.

1207. 'Blocking' shall mean keeping personal data by temporarily suspending any other processing operation.

1208. Regarding communication activities, 'electronic communication' shall mean any information exchanged or conveyed between a finite number of parties by means of a publicly available electronic communications service.

1209. This does not include any information conveyed as part of a broadcasting service to the public over an electronic communications network except to the extent that the information can be related to the identifiable or identified subscriber or user receiving the information.

1210. 'Call', in the text of the Code, means a connection established by means of a publicly available telephone service allowing two-way communication in real time.

1211. 'Electronic communications network' shall mean transmission systems and switching or routing equipment and other resources which permit the conveyance of signals by wire, by radio, by optical or by other electromagnetic means, including satellite networks, fixed (circuit- and packet-switched, including Internet) and mobile terrestrial networks, networks used for radio and television broadcasting, electricity cable systems, to the extent that they are used for the purpose of transmitting signals, and cable television networks, irrespective of the type of information conveyed.

1212. 'Public communications network' is an electronic communications network used wholly or mainly for the provision of publicly available electronic communications services which support the transfer of information between network termination points.

1213. 'Electronic communications service' is a service which consists wholly or mainly in the conveyance of signals on electronic communications networks, including telecommunications services and transmission services in networks used for broadcasting.

1214. Concerning the users, 'subscriber' shall mean any natural or legal person, body or association who or which is party to a contract with the provider of publicly available electronic communications services for the supply of such services, or is anyhow the recipient of such services by means of prepaid cards.

1215. 'User' is a natural person using a publicly available electronic communications service for private or business purposes, without necessarily being a subscriber to such service.

1216. 'Traffic data' consists in any data processed for the purpose of the conveyance of a communication on an electronic communications network or for the billing thereof.

1217. 'Location data' shall mean any data processed in an electronic communications network, indicating the geographic position of the terminal equipment of a user of a publicly available electronic communications service.

1218. 'Value-added service' is any service which requires the processing of traffic data or location data other than traffic data beyond what is necessary for the transmission of a communication or the billing thereof.

1219. From a technical point of view, 'electronic mail' is defined by law as any text, voice, sound or image message sent over a public communications network, which can be stored in the network or the recipient's terminal equipment until it is collected by the recipient.

1220. 'Electronic means' shall mean computers, computer software and any electronic and/or automated device used for performing the processing.

1221. Concerning the authentication process, 'computerized authentication' shall mean a set of electronic tools and procedures to verify identity also indirectly.

1222. 'Authentication credentials' are the data and devices in the possession of a person, whether known by or uniquely related to the latter, that are used for computer authentication.

1223. 'Password' is the component of an authentication credential associated with and known to a person, consisting of a sequence of characters or other data in electronic format.

1224. 'Authorization profile' is the information uniquely associated with a person that allows determining the data that may be accessed by the said person as well as the processing operations the said person might perform.

1225. 'Authorization system' shall mean the tools and procedures enabling access to the data and the relevant processing mechanisms as a function of the requesting party's authorization profile.

1226. Finally, 'personal data breach' shall mean a security breach leading, accidentally or not, to the destruction, loss, alteration, unauthorized disclosure of or access to personal data transmitted, stored or otherwise processed in the context of the provision of a publicly available communications service.

§3. Subject Matter and Scope of Application of the Original Privacy Code

1227. The Code applied to the processing of personal data, including data held abroad, where the processing is performed by any entity established either in the State's territory or in a place that is under the State's sovereignty.

1228. The Code applied to the processing of personal data that is performed by an entity established in the territory of a country outside the European Union, where the said entity makes use in connection with the processing of equipment, whether electronic or otherwise, situated in the State's territory, unless such equipment is used only for purposes of transit through the territory of the European Union.

1229. If the Code applies, the data controller shall designate a representative established in the State's territory with a view to implementing the provisions concerning the processing of personal data.

1230. The Code shall apply to the processing of personal data carried out by natural persons for exclusively personal purposes only if the data are intended for systematic communication or dissemination.

§4. Data Subject's Rights in the Original Privacy Code

1231. Concerning the right to *access* personal data and other rights, a data subject shall have the right to obtain confirmation as to whether or not personal data concerning him/her exist, regardless of their being already recorded, and communication of such data in intelligible form.

1232. A data subject shall have the right to be *informed*: (a) of the source of the personal data; (b) of the purposes and methods of the processing; (c) of the logic applied to the processing, if the latter is carried out with the help of electronic; (d) of the identification data concerning data controller, data processors and the representative designated; (e) of the entities or categories of entity to whom or which the personal data may be communicated and who or which may get to know said data in their capacity as designated representative(s) in the State's territory, data processor(s) or person(s) in charge of the processing.

1233. A data subject shall have the right to *obtain*: (a) updating, rectification or, where interested therein, integration of the data; (b) erasure, anonymization or blocking of data that have been processed unlawfully, including data the retention of which is unnecessary for the purposes for which they have been collected or subsequently processed; (c) certification to the effect that the operations as per letters (a) and (b) have been notified, as also related to their contents, to the entities to whom or which the data were communicated or disseminated, unless this requirement proves impossible or involves a manifestly disproportionate effort compared with the right that is to be protected.

1234. A data subject has the right to *object*, in whole or in part, (i) on legitimate grounds, to the processing of personal data concerning him/her, even though they are relevant to the purpose of the collection; (ii) to the processing of personal data concerning him/her, where it is carried out for the purpose of sending advertising materials or direct selling or else for the performance of market or commercial communication surveys.

1235. Concerning the exercise of rights, the rights may be exercised by making a request without formalities to the data controller or processor, also by the agency of a person in charge of the processing. A suitable response shall be provided without delay.

1236. The mechanisms to exercise rights are simple. The request addressed to the data controller or processor may also be conveyed by means of a registered letter, facsimile or e-mail.

The Privacy Authority may specify other suitable arrangements with regard to new technological solutions.

If the request is related to the exercise of some rights, it may also be made verbally; in this case, it will be written down in summary fashion by either a person in charge of the processing or the data processor.

The rights, where related to the personal data concerning a deceased, may be exercised by any entity that is interested therein or else acts to protect a data subject or for family-related reasons deserving protection.

1237. The data subject's identity shall be verified on the basis of suitable information, also by means of available records or documents or by producing or attaching a copy of an identity document.

The person acting on instructions from the data subject must produce or attach a copy of either the proxy or the letter of attorney, which shall have been undersigned by the data subject in the presence of a person in charge thereof or else shall bear the data subject's signature and be produced jointly with a copy of an ID document from the data subject, which shall not have to be certified true pursuant to law.

The request may be worded freely without any constraints and may be renewed at intervals of not less than ninety days, unless there are well-grounded reasons.

1238. Concerning the response to data subjects, with a view to effectively exercising the rights, data controllers shall take suitable measures in order to, in particular, (a) facilitate access to personal data by the data subjects, even by means of ad hoc software allowing accurate retrieval of the data concerning individual identified or identifiable data subjects; (b) simplify the arrangements and reduce the delay for the responses, also with regard to public relations departments or offices.

1239. The data processor, or the person(s) in charge of the processing, shall be responsible for retrieval of the data, which may be communicated to the requesting party also verbally, or else displayed by electronic means, on condition that the data are easily intelligible in such cases also in the light of the nature and amount of the information.

The data shall be reproduced on paper or magnetic media, or else transmitted via electronic networks, whenever this is requested.

1240. The response provided to the data subject shall include all the personal data concerning him/her that are processed by the data controller, unless the request concerns either a specific processing operation or specific personal data or categories of personal data.

1241. If data retrieval is especially difficult, the response to the data subject's request may also consist in producing or delivering a copy of records and documents containing the personal data at stake.

If the data subject is a legal person, a body or association, the relevant request shall be made by the natural person that is legally authorized thereto based on the relevant regulations or articles of association.

1242. The right to obtain communication of the data in intelligible form does not apply to personal data concerning third parties, unless breaking down the processed data or eliminating certain items from the latter prevents the data subject's personal data from being understandable.

1243. Data are communicated in intelligible form also by using legible handwriting.

If codes or abbreviations are communicated, the criteria for understanding the relevant meanings shall be made available also by the agency of the persons in charge of the processing.

1244. Where it is not confirmed that personal data concerning the data subject exist, the data subject may be charged a *fee* which shall not be in excess of the costs actually incurred for the enquiries made in the specific case.

The fee referred to may not be in excess of the amount specified by the Privacy Authority ('Garante') in a generally applicable provision, which may also refer to a lump sum to be paid in case the data are processed by electronic means and the response is provided verbally.

Through said instrument the Garante may also provide that the fee may be charged if the personal data are contained on special media, the reproduction of which is specifically requested, or else if a considerable effort is required by one or more data controllers on account of the complexity and/or amount of the requests and existence of data concerning the data subject can be confirmed.

The fee may also be paid by bank or postal draft, or else by debit or credit card, if possible upon receipt of the relevant response and anyhow within fifteen days of said response.

§5. General Data Processing Rules in the Original Privacy Code

1245. Concerning processing arrangements and data quality, the Code states that personal data undergoing processing shall be: (i) processed lawfully and fairly; (ii) collected and recorded for specific, explicit and legitimate purposes and used in further processing operations in a way that is not inconsistent with said purposes; (iii) accurate and, when necessary, kept up-to-date; (iv) relevant, complete and not excessive in relation to the purposes for which they are collected or subsequently processed; (v) kept in a form which permits identification of the data subject for no longer than is necessary for the purposes for which the data were collected or subsequently processed.

Any personal data that is processed in breach of the relevant provisions concerning the processing of personal data may not be used.

1246. Regarding codes of conduct and professional practice, the Privacy Authority ('Garante') shall encourage, within the framework of the categories concerned and in conformity with the principle of representation, by having regard to the guidelines set out in Council of Europe recommendations on the processing of personal data, the drawing up of codes of conduct and professional practice for specific sectors, verify their compliance with laws and regulations by also taking account of the considerations made by the entities concerned, and contribute to adoption of and compliance with such codes.

The Privacy Authority shall be responsible for having the codes published in the *Official Journal of the Italian Republic*.

Compliance with the provisions included in the codes shall be a prerequisite for the processing of personal data by public and private entities to be lawful.

These provisions shall also apply to the code of conduct on the processing of data for journalistic purposes as adopted further to the encouragement provided by the Garante.

1247. Very important, in the economy of this Law, is also the topic of *information* to data subjects. The data subject, as well as any entity from whom or which personal data are collected, shall be preliminarily informed, either orally or in writing, as to: (a) the purposes and modalities of the processing for which the data are intended; (b) the obligatory or voluntary nature of providing the requested data; (c) the consequences if (s)he fails to reply; (d) the entities or categories of entity to whom or which the data may be communicated, or who/which may get to know the data in their capacity as data processors or persons in charge of the processing, and the scope of dissemination of said data; (e) the rights; (f) the identification data concerning the data controller and, where designated, the data controller's representative in the State's territory and the data processor.

If several data processors have been designated by the data controller, at least one among them shall be referred to, and either the site on the communications network or the mechanisms for easily accessing the updated list of data processors shall be specified.

1248. The *information* shall also contain the items referred to in specific provisions of the Code and may fail to include certain items if the latter are already known to the entity providing the data or their knowledge may concretely impair supervisory or control activities carried out by public bodies for purposes related to defence or State security, or else for the prevention, suppression or detection of offences.

The Garante may issue a provision to set out simplified information arrangements as regards, in particular, telephone services providing assistance and information to the public.

Whenever the personal data are not collected from the data subject, the information, also including the categories of processed data, shall be provided to the data subject at the time of recording such data or, if their communication is envisaged, no later than when the data are first communicated.

1249. The Code states also, about profiling of data subjects and their personality, that no judicial or administrative act or measure involving the assessment of a person's conduct may be based solely on the automated processing of personal data aimed at defining the data subject's profile or personality.

1250. If damage is caused on account of the processing, whoever has caused damage to another as a consequence of the processing of personal data is liable to pay damages pursuant to Article 2050 of the Italian Civil Code, which punishes the exercise of dangerous activities providing high damages compensation for non-pecuniary damages too.

1251. The end of the processing operation is, for the Law, important too: if data processing is terminated, for whatever reason, the data must be (a) destroyed; (b) assigned to another data controller, provided they are intended for processing under terms that are compatible with the purposes for which the data have been collected; (c) kept for exclusively personal purposes, without being intended for systematic communication or dissemination; (d) kept or assigned to another controller for historical, scientific or statistical purposes, in compliance with laws, regulations, community legislation and the codes of conduct and professional practice adopted in pursuance of the law.

1252. Processing of data, other than sensitive and judicial data, shall be allowed in accordance with measures and precautions that are laid down to safeguard data subjects, if the processing is likely to present specific risks to data subjects' fundamental rights and freedoms and dignity on account of the nature of the data, the arrangements applying to the processing or the effects the latter may produce.

The measures and precautions shall be laid down by the Garante on the basis of the principles set out in the Code within the framework of a check to be performed prior to start of the processing as also related to specific categories of data controller or processing, following the request, if any, submitted by the data controller.

1253. Public bodies shall only be permitted to process personal data in order to discharge their institutional tasks.

In processing the data, public bodies shall abide by the prerequisites and limitations set out in the Code, by having also regard to the different features of the data, as well as in laws and regulations.

1254. Processing of sensitive data by public bodies shall only be allowed where it is expressly authorized by a law specifying the categories of data that may be processed and the categories of operations that may be performed, as well as the substantial public interest pursued.

1255. Processing of judicial data by public bodies shall only be permitted where expressly authorized by a law or an order of the Garante specifying the purposes in the substantial public interest underlying such processing, the categories of data to be processed and the operations that may be performed.

Public bodies shall process sensitive and judicial data in accordance with arrangements aimed at preventing breaches of data subjects' rights, fundamental freedoms and dignity.

Public bodies may process exclusively such sensitive and judicial data as are indispensable for them to discharge institutional tasks that cannot be performed, on a case-by-case basis, by processing anonymous data or else personal data of a different nature.

Sensitive or judicial data that are contained in lists, registers or data banks kept with electronic means shall be processed by using encryption techniques, identification codes or any other system such as to make the data temporarily unintelligible also to the entities authorized to access them and allow identification of the data subject only in case of necessity, by having regard to amount and nature of the processed data.

Data disclosing health and sex life shall be kept separate from any other personal data that is processed for purposes for which they are not required. Data disclosing health may not be disseminated.

§6. Consent

1256. Processing of personal data by private entities or profit-seeking public bodies shall only be allowed if the data subject gives his/her express *consent.*

The data subject's *consent* may refer either to the processing as a whole or to one or more of the operations thereof.

The data subject's *consent* shall only be deemed to be effective if it is given freely and specifically with regard to a clearly identified processing operation, if it is documented in writing and if the data subject has been provided with the information referred to in the Privacy Code.

Consent shall be given *in writing* if the processing concerns sensitive data.

1257. *Consent* shall not be required if the processing: (a) is necessary to comply with an obligation imposed by a law, regulations or community legislation; (b) is necessary for the performance of obligations resulting from a contract to which the data subject is a party, or else in order to comply with specific requests made by the data subject prior to entering into a contract; (c) concerns data taken from public registers, lists, documents or records that are publicly available, without prejudice to the limitations and modalities laid down by laws, regulations and community legislation with regard to their disclosure and publicity; (d) concerns data relating to economic activities that are processed in compliance with the legislation in force as applying to business and industrial secrecy; (e) is necessary to safeguard life or bodily integrity of a third party.

1258. If this purpose concerns the data subject, and the latter cannot give his/her consent because (s)he is physically unable to do so, legally incapable or unable to distinguish right and wrong, the consent shall be given by the entity legally representing the data subject, or else by a next of kin, a family member, a person cohabiting with the data subject or, failing these, the manager of the institution where the data subject is hosted.

1259. Sensitive data may only be processed with the data subject's written consent and the Garante's prior *authorization*, by complying with the prerequisites and limitations set out in this Code as well as in laws and regulations.

The Garante shall communicate its decision concerning the request for *authorization* within forty-five days; failing a communication at the expiry of said term, the request shall be regarded as dismissed.

Along with the *authorization* or thereafter, based also on verification, the Garante may provide for measures and precautions in order to safeguard the data subject, which the data controller shall be bound to apply.

1260. Processing of judicial data by private entities and profit-seeking public bodies shall be permitted only where expressly authorized by a law or an order by the Garante, specifying the reasons in the substantial public interest underlying such processing, the categories of processed data and the operations that may be performed.

§7. Entities Performing Processing Operations

1261. Whenever processing operations are carried out by a legal person, a public administrative agency or any other body, association or organization, the data controller shall be either the entity as a whole or the department or peripheral unit having fully autonomous decision-making powers in respect of purposes and mechanisms of said processing operations as also related to security matters.

1262. The data processor may be designated by the data controller on an optional basis but, where designated, the data processor shall be selected among entities that can appropriately ensure, on account of their experience, capabilities and reliability, thorough compliance with the provisions in force applying to processing as also related to security matters.

If necessary on account of organizational requirements, several entities may be designated as data processors also by subdividing the relevant tasks.

The tasks committed to the data processor shall be detailed in writing by the data controller.

The data processor shall abide by the instructions given by the data controller in carrying out the processing and the data controller shall supervise over thorough compliance with both said instructions and the provisions referred to in the Code, also by means of regular controls.

1263. Processing operations may only be performed by persons in charge of the processing that act under the direct authority of either the data controller or the data processor by complying with the instructions received.

The aforementioned persons shall be nominated in writing by specifically referring to the scope of the processing operations that are permitted.

This requirement shall be also fulfilled if a natural person is entrusted with the task of directing a department, on a documentary basis, whereby the scope of the processing operations that may be performed by the staff working in the said department has been specified in writing.

Chapter 2. The GDPR of 2016 and the Italian Data Protection Legal Framework

§1. The General Data Protection Regulation and Its Impact on the Italian Privacy Code

1264. From 1995 until May 2018, the principal EU legal instrument on data protection was Directive 95/46/EC of the European Parliament and the Council of 24 October 1995, on the protection of individuals with regard to the processing of personal data and on the free movement of such data (Data Protection Directive).

1265. The Directive established a detailed and comprehensive data protection system in the EU, at a time when several Member States had already adopted national data protection laws. However, in accordance with the EU legal system, directives do not apply directly and must be transported into the national laws of the Member States. That fact caused a massive discretion of each Member State in transposing the directive's provisions.

Even though the Directive was meant to provide the harmonization, in practice it was transposed differently in the Member States. The results were definitions and rules interpreted differently in national laws and different severity of sanctions.

As a consequence, the Commission started the reform of EU data protection legislation.

1266. The reform led to the adoption, in 2016, of the General Data Protection Regulation ('GDRP') that replaces the Data Protection Directive of 1995.

The GDPR is now recognized as law across the EU, and it is applied from 25 May 2018: Member States had two years to ensure that it is fully implementable in their countries.

The adoption of GDPR modernized EU data protection legislation, making it fit for protecting fundamental rights in the context of digital and information technology age.

1267. The EU Commission in its Communication to the EU Parliament and the Council on the 24 January 2018 underlined that the GDPR must be the 'one single set of rules for citizens and business' subject to 'uniform and consistent application in all Member States'. Stronger rules on data protection mean that people have more control over their personal data and businesses benefit from level playing field.

In fact, 'the GDPR is the opportunity to simplify the legal environment, and so have fewer national rules and greater clarity for operations'.

1268. The GDPR develops the core principles and rights of data protection provided in for Data Protection Directive and introduces new obligations requiring organizations to implement data protection *by design* and *by default*, to comply with the principles of *accountability*, to appoint a Data Protection Officer (DPO) in certain circumstances, to comply with new rights recognized to the data subject.

§2. MAIN DEFINITIONS OF GDPR

1269. Article 1 states that the Regulation, laying down rules relating to the protection of natural persons with regard to the processing of personal data and rules relating to the free movement of personal data, protects fundamental rights and freedoms of natural persons and in particular their right to the protection of personal data.

The free movement of personal data within the Union shall be neither restricted nor prohibited for reasons connected with the protection of natural persons with regard to the processing of personal data.

1270. For the purposes of the Code, Article 4 ('Definitions') contains relevant definitions.

Concerning types of data, 'personal data' means any information relating to an identified or identifiable natural person (data subject), such as a name, an identification number, location data, an online identifier or to one or more factors specific to the physical, physiological, genetic, mental, economic, cultural or social identity of that natural person.

'Genetic data' means personal data relating to the inherited or acquired genetic characteristics of a natural person which give unique information about the physiology or the health of that natural person and which result, in particular, from an analysis of a biological sample from the natural person in question.

'Biometric data' means personal data resulting from specific technical processing relating to the physical, physiological or behavioural characteristics of a natural person, which allow or confirm the unique identification of that natural person, such as facial images or dactyloscopic data.

'Data concerning health' means personal data related to the physical or mental health of a natural person, including the provision of health care services, which reveal information about his or her health status.

1271. The GDPR refers to sensitive personal data as '*special categories of personal data*' (see Article 9), as personal data revealing racial or ethnic origin, political opinions, religious or philosophical beliefs, or trade union membership, and the processing of genetic data, biometric data for the purpose of uniquely identifying a natural person, data concerning health or data concerning a natural person's sex life or sexual orientation.

1272. The subjects considered by Article 4 are:

i) 'controller', the natural or legal person, public authority, agency or other body which, alone or jointly with others, that determines the purposes and means of the processing of personal data;
ii) 'processor', a natural or legal person, public authority, agency or other body which that processes personal data on behalf of the controller;
iii) 'data subject' an identifiable natural person is one who can be identified, directly or indirectly, in particular by reference to an identifier such as a name, an identification number, location data, an online identifier or to one

or more factors specific to the physical, physiological, genetic, mental, economic, cultural or social identity of that natural person;

iv) 'recipient', a natural or legal person, public authority, agency or another body, to which the personal data are disclosed, whether a third party or not,

v) 'third party', a natural or legal person, public authority, agency or body other than the data subject, controller, processor and persons who, under the direct authority of the controller or processor, are authorised to process personal data;

vi) 'representative', a natural or legal person established in the Union who, designated by the controller or processor in writing pursuant to *Article 27* represents the controller or processor with regard to their respective obligations under this Regulation

1273. In the text of GDPR, 'enterprise' means a natural or legal person engaged in an economic activity, irrespective of its legal form, including partnerships or associations regularly engaged in an economic activity.

'Group of undertakings' means a controlling undertaking and its controlled undertakings.

'Supervisory Authority' means an independent public authority which is established by a Member State.

1274. From a technical point of view, 'processing' means any operation or set of operations which is performed on personal data or on sets of personal data, whether or not by automated means, such as collection, recording, organization, structuring, storage, adaptation or alteration, retrieval, consultation, use, disclosure by transmission, dissemination or otherwise making available, alignment or combination, restriction, erasure or destruction.

'Restriction of processing' means the marking of stored personal data with the aim of limiting their processing in the future.

'Profiling' means any form of automated processing of personal data consisting of the use of personal data to evaluate certain personal aspects relating to a natural person, in particular to analyse or predict aspects concerning that natural person's performance at work, economic situation, health, personal preferences, interests, reliability, behaviour, location or movements.

'Pseudonymization' means the processing of personal data in such a manner that the personal data can no longer be attributed to a specific data subject without the use of additional information, provided that such additional information is kept separately and is subject to technical and organizational measures to ensure that the personal data are not attributed to an identified or identifiable natural person.

'Filing system' means any structured set of personal data which are accessible according to specific criteria, whether centralized, decentralized or dispersed on a functional or geographical basis.

'Cross-border processing' means either: (a) processing of personal data which takes place in the context of the activities of establishments in more than one Member State of a controller or processor in the Union where the controller or processor is established in more than one Member State; or (b) processing of personal data which takes place in the context of the activities of a single establishment of a controller or processor in the Union but which substantially affects or is likely to substantially affect data subjects in more than one Member State.

1275. 'Consent' of the data subject, in the text of Article 4, means any freely given, specific, informed and unambiguous indication of the data subject's wishes by which he or she, by a statement or by a clear affirmative action, signifies agreement to the processing of personal data relating to him or her.
'Personal data breach' means a breach of security leading to the accidental or unlawful destruction, loss, alteration, unauthorized disclosure of, or access to, personal data transmitted, stored or otherwise processed.

§3. Subject Matter and Scope of Application of the GDPR

1276. As stated above, the GDPR applies to 'personal data' meaning any information relating to an identifiable person who can be directly or indirectly identified in particular by reference to an identifier.
This definition provides for a wide range of personal identifiers to constitute personal data, including name, identification number, location data or online identifier, reflecting changes in technology and the way organizations collect information about people.

1277. The GDPR applies both to automated personal data and to manual filing systems where personal data are accessible according to specific criteria. This could include chronologically ordered sets of manual records containing personal data.

1278. The Regulation has comprehensive rules on territorial scope. The GDPR applies to process carried out by organizations operating within the EU. It also applies to organizations outside the EU that offers goods or services to data subjects in the EU or monitor their behaviour.

1279. The GDPR does not applies to certain activities including processing covered by the Law Enforcement Directive processing for national security purposes and processing carried out by individuals purely for personal/household activities.

§4. Main Principles: Article 5, Accountability, Privacy by Design and Privacy by Default

1280. Article 5 requires that personal data shall be:

(1) processed lawfully, fairly and in a transparent manner in relation to the data subject ('lawfulness, fairness and transparency');
(2) collected for specified, explicit and legitimate purposes and not further processed in a manner that is incompatible with those purposes; further processing for archiving purposes in the public interest, scientific or historical research purposes or statistical purposes not be considered to be incompatible with the initial purposes ('purpose limitation');
(3) adequate, relevant and limited to what is necessary in relation to the purposes for which they are processed ('data minimization');
(4) accurate and, where necessary, kept up-to-date; every reasonable step must be taken to ensure that personal data that are inaccurate, having regard to the purposes for which they are processed, are erased or rectified without delay ('accuracy');
(5) kept in a form which permits identification of data subjects for no longer than is necessary for the purposes for which the personal data are processed; personal data may be stored for longer periods insofar as the personal data will be processed solely for archiving purposes in the public interest, scientific or historical research purposes or statistical purposes subject to implementation of the appropriate technical and organizational measures required by this Regulation in order to safeguard the rights and freedoms of the data subject ('storage limitation');
(6) processed in a manner that ensures appropriate security of the personal data, including protection against unauthorized or unlawful processing and against accidental loss, destruction or damage, using appropriate technical or organizational measures ('integrity and confidentiality').

1281. Article 5(2) adds that the controller shall be responsible for, and be able to demonstrate compliance with, paragraph 1 ('accountability').

1282. Article 5 sets out seven key principles which lie at the heart of the GDPR. They are set out right at the start of the legislation and inform everything that follows.

1283. Compliance with the spirit of these principles is a fundamental building block for good data protection practice.

1284. Another important principle is the one stated in Article 24 that underlines the responsibility of the controller ('accountability').

Taking into account the nature, scope, context and purposes of processing as well as the risks of varying likelihood and severity for the rights and freedoms of natural persons, the controller shall implement appropriate technical and organizational measures to ensure and to be able to demonstrate that processing is performed in accordance with this Regulation. Those measures shall be reviewed and updated where necessary.

1285. Accountability is one of the data protection principles that makes the data controller responsible for complying with GDPR provisions and says that the data controller must be able to demonstrate his compliance.

1286. The data controller needs to put in place appropriate technical and organizational measures to meet the requirements of accountability. There are some measures that the data controller can adopt including, for example, implementing data protection policy, maintaining documentation of processing activities, taking a 'data protection by design and by default' approach, implementing appropriate security measures, appointing a data protection officer (DPO) and recording, where necessary, personal data breaches.

1287. Accountability obligations are ongoing: the data controller must review and update the measures adopted.

1288. Article 25 states that taking into account the state of the art, the cost of implementation and the nature, scope, context and purposes of processing as well as the risks of varying likelihood and severity for rights and freedoms of natural persons posed by the processing, the controller shall, both at the time of the determination of the means for processing and at the time of the processing itself, implement appropriate technical and organizational measures, such as pseudonymization, which are designed to implement data protection principles, such as data minimization, in an effective manner and to integrate the necessary safeguards into the processing in order to meet the requirements of this Regulation and protect the rights of data subjects.

1289. Article 25(2) adds that the controller shall implement appropriate technical and organizational measures for ensuring that, by default, only personal data which are necessary for each specific purpose of the processing are processed. That obligation applies to the amount of personal data collected, the extent of their processing, the period of their storage and their accessibility. In particular, such measures shall ensure that by default personal data are not made accessible without the individual's intervention to an indefinite number of natural persons.

1290. Article 25 requires appropriate technical and organizational measures to implement the data protection principles and safeguard of individual rights. This principle is data protection by design and by default.

1291. In essence, the principle means that the data controller has to integrate or bake in data protection into processing activities and business practices, from the design stage to the lifecycle.

§5. Italian New Privacy Legislation and the Relationship Between the 'Old' Privacy Code and the New GDPR Framework

1292. Even though the GDPR is directly applicable, Member States have to update their existing national data protection laws, to fully align with the regulation.

1293. In fact, during the final term to align with the GDPR, new local legislation on data protection is being published on the Italian Official Gazette (G.U.).

1294. In particular, the annual European Delegation Law (Law n. 163/2017, Article 13) conferred a mandate on the Government to issue one or more legislative decrees, by 21st May 2018, which shall:

(a) repeal or amend the rules of Legislative Decree 196/2003 ('Privacy Code') which are non-compatible with the GDPR;
(b) coordinate the system of administrative fines set forth by the Privacy Code with the one in the GDPR by introducing other criminal penalties, which shall be effective, proportionate and dissuasive;
(c) coordinate any other national law regulating data protection issues with the GDPR;
(d) provide for the necessary conferral of powers to the Italian Data Protection Authority in order to integrate and complement the data protection legal framework through its administrative provisions, authorizations and decisions of general application.

1295. At the beginning of August 2018, so after the term of the definitive entry into force of the GDPR (25 May 2018), legislative decree n. 101/2018 was issued by the Government (cfr. G.U., 4 September 2018).

1296. Legislative decree no. 101 of 10 August 2018, amending and adapting the Italian Privacy Code to the GDPR, has been issued on 4 September 2018 in the Official Journal and entered into force on 19 September 2018.

1297. As Olivi states, the analysis of the Decree reveals a legislative technique aimed at developing most of the 'open clauses' contained in the GDPR, i.e. those allowing member states to specify further certain aspects of the provisions concerned (for instance, those related to children's consent and the processing of special categories of personal data).[427]

1298. Children who have reached the age of 14 years can validly express their consent to data processing in relation to the offer of information society services.

---

427. *See* G. Olivi, Italy: Italian Data Protection Code Reformed To Enact GDPR. What Is New?, Dentons, 28 Sep. 2018, http://www.mondaq.com/italy/x/740422/data+protection/Italian+Data+Protection+Code+Reformed+To+Enact+GDPR+What+Is+New.

The holder of parental responsibility over the child must give consent where the child is below the age of 14 years.

In this regard, the GDPR sets the minimum age of 16 years old but allows Member States to fix a lower age for granting valid consent.[428]

1299. Biometric, genetic and health-related data can be processed if specific safeguard measures (including security measures, such as encryption and pseudonymization) are implemented.

The Italian Authority (*Garante*) will establish such safeguards at least on a two-yearly basis.[429]

1300. The processing of judicial data is allowed based only on a law or regulatory provision providing for appropriate safeguards for data subjects. Lacking these law provisions, the requirements for the lawful processing of judicial data shall be determined through a Decree of the Ministry of Justice.[430]

1301. The data controller or data processor, in the context of their organizational structure, may delegate to natural persons, expressly designated, specific tasks and functions related to the processing activities to be carried out.

The introduction of this provision in the Privacy Code, Olivi notes, reflects Article 29 of the GDPR which refers to *'any person acting under the authority of the controller or of the processor'*, thus leaving room for persons authorized to carry out some tasks related to processing activities, giving them appropriate instructions.[431]

1302. The Authority will lay down ethical rules for personal data processing carried out by both public and private bodies in the employment context, pursuant to Article 88 of the GDPR.[432]

1303. The most relevant changes to the Privacy Code concern, notes Olivi, sanctions, both administrative and criminal.

Administrative sanctions recall those established by the GDPR, specifically: the Decree states that Article 83(4) of the GDPR (imposing administrative fines up to

---

428. *See* G. Olivi, Italy: Italian Data Protection Code Reformed To Enact GDPR. What Is New?, Dentons, 28 Sep. 2018, http://www.mondaq.com/italy/x/740422/data+protection/Italian+Data+Protection+Code+Reformed+To+Enact+GDPR+What+Is+New.
429. *See* G. Olivi, Italy: Italian Data Protection Code Reformed To Enact GDPR. What Is New?, Dentons, 28 September 2018, http://www.mondaq.com/italy/x/740422/data+protection/Italian+Data+Protection+Code+Reformed+To+Enact+GDPR+What+Is+New.
430. *See* G. Olivi, Italy: Italian Data Protection Code Reformed To Enact GDPR. What Is New?, Dentons, 28 Sep. 2018, http://www.mondaq.com/italy/x/740422/data+protection/Italian+Data+Protection+Code+Reformed+To+Enact+GDPR+What+Is+New.
431. *See* G. Olivi, Italy: Italian Data Protection Code Reformed To Enact GDPR. What Is New?, Dentons, 28 Sep. 2018, http://www.mondaq.com/italy/x/740422/data+protection/Italian+Data+Protection+Code+Reformed+To+Enact+GDPR+What+Is+New.
432. *See* G. Olivi, Italy: Italian Data Protection Code Reformed To Enact GDPR. What Is New?, Dentons, 28 Sep. 2018, http://www.mondaq.com/italy/x/740422/data+protection/Italian+Data+Protection+Code+Reformed+To+Enact+GDPR+What+Is+New.

€10 million / up to 2 percent of the total worldwide annual turnover of the preceding financial year if higher) applies in case of violation of specific provisions of the DPC, such as: Article 2-*quinquies*(2) (Child's consent for information society services), namely in case the information notice does not meet the relevant requirement; Article 123(4) (Traffic Data), namely in case the information notice given by providers of a public communication network or publicly available electronic communications service does not comply with the relevant GDPR provisions (Articles 13-14); Article 110(1), namely in case of failure to carry out the data protection impact assessment in the context of medical, biomedical and epidemiological research. In addition, Article 83(5) of the GDPR (imposing administrative fines up to €20 million / up to 4 percent of the total worldwide annual turnover of the preceding financial year if higher) applies in case of most serious violations of the DPC, such as: Article 2-*ter* (Legal basis for personal data processing pursuant to a public interest); Article 2-*quinquies* (Child's consent for information society services), where the child's consent is not properly collected; Article 2-septies (Safeguards for the processing of biometric, genetic and health-related data); Article 2-octies (Unlawful processing of judicial data).[433]

1304. Criminal sanctions continue to play a fundamental role. The Decree confirms crimes already existing in the Privacy Code and introduces new ones.

To this regard, attention has been paid to avoid possible violations of 'ne bis in idem' principle, according to which no one shall be twice punished for the same offence.[434]

1305. A brand new offence is *Unlawful communication and dissemination of personal data*, where a large-scale processing takes place, with the aim of making profit or causing damage in violation of specific provisions of the same Privacy Code.

The sanction is the imprisonment from one to six years (it may be lowered in case administrative sanctions also apply).

This crime only refers to the communication or dissemination of a part of / an entire automated filing system (*'archivio automatizzato'*).

The expression *'automated filing system'* rises doubts of interpretation, as it is not defined either in the same Decree or in the GDPR.

Given the interpretation issue and all the elements expected to occur for this crime, in practice, the criminal sanction for this conduct is likely to apply in few cases.[435]

---

433. *See* G. Olivi, Italy: Italian Data Protection Code Reformed To Enact GDPR. What Is New?, Dentons, 28 Sep. 2018, http://www.mondaq.com/italy/x/740422/data+protection/Italian+Data+Protection+Code+Reformed+To+Enact+GDPR+What+Is+New.

434. *See* G. Olivi, Italy: Italian Data Protection Code Reformed To Enact GDPR. What Is New?, Dentons, 28 Sep. 2018, http://www.mondaq.com/italy/x/740422/data+protection/Italian+Data+Protection+Code+Reformed+To+Enact+GDPR+What+Is+New.

435. *See* G. Olivi, Italy: Italian Data Protection Code Reformed To Enact GDPR. What Is New?, Dentons, 28 Sep. 2018, http://www.mondaq.com/italy/x/740422/data+protection/Italian+Data+Protection+Code+Reformed+To+Enact+GDPR+What+Is+New.

1306. Fraudulent acquisition of personal data where a large-scale processing takes place (DPC, Article 167-*ter*) with the aim of making profit or causing a damage. The sanction is imprisonment from one to four years. This crime constitutes the other side of the wrongdoing under Article 167-*bis*: while the latter focus on the communication and dissemination of personal data, this one relates to the acquisition.[436]

1307. The Italian legislator has then made a few changes to existing criminal offences, specifically: *Misrepresentation / false declaration to the Garante* and intentional interruption of Garante's exercise of powers, for example the conduction of proceedings or investigations; *Non-compliance with Garante's decisions*; *Violation of provisions on employees' remote monitoring and the ban on surveys of opinions*, making reference to the sanctions established by the Italian Statute of Workers (Law no. 300/1970).[437]

1308. The Garante, by means of a general resolution, shall identify the provisions contained in the general authorizations currently in force, which are compliant with the GDPR and/or the new Italian Data Protection Code.

This will allow each stakeholder to take part in the legislative process.

Provisions which are not compliant with the GDPR and/or the new Privacy Code will cease to be effective starting from the publication, in the Official Journal, of the above-mentioned Garante's general resolution.[438]

1309. The Garante has been granted with the power of introducing simplified procedures/means for small- and medium-sized companies to comply with the data controller's obligations under the GDPR.[439]

---

436. *See* G. Olivi, Italy: Italian Data Protection Code Reformed To Enact GDPR. What Is New?, Dentons, 28 Sep. 2018, http://www.mondaq.com/italy/x/740422/data+protection/Italian+Data+Protection+Code+Reformed+To+Enact+GDPR+What+Is+New.
437. *See* G. Olivi, Italy: Italian Data Protection Code Reformed To Enact GDPR. What Is New?, Dentons, 28 Sep. 2018, http://www.mondaq.com/italy/x/740422/data+protection/Italian+Data+Protection+Code+Reformed+To+Enact+GDPR+What+Is+New.
438. *See* G. Olivi, Italy: Italian Data Protection Code Reformed To Enact GDPR. What Is New?, Dentons, 28 Sep. 2018, http://www.mondaq.com/italy/x/740422/data+protection/Italian+Data+Protection+Code+Reformed+To+Enact+GDPR+What+Is+New.
439. *See* G. Olivi, Italy: Italian Data Protection Code Reformed To Enact GDPR. What Is New?, Dentons, 28 Sep. 2018, http://www.mondaq.com/italy/x/740422/data+protection/Italian+Data+Protection+Code+Reformed+To+Enact+GDPR+What+Is+New.

Chapter 3. Protection of Telecommunication Privacy

§1. Regulation of Electronic Communication Services

1310. The scope of protecting users' privacy in telecommunications services and on platforms has undergone significant changes in recent years in Italy.

The main problem is that the Italian legislation, contained in the 'old' Privacy Code (remained in force, for some parts, even after the advent of the GDPR) must be harmonized and coordinated with the discipline issued by the European Union.

In the following lines, we will analyse the discipline remained in the Privacy Code after the implementation, also in Italy, of the GDPR.

In particular, the Title X ('Electronic Communications'), Chapter I ('Electronic Communication Services') of the Italian Privacy Code, as modified in 2018, explains, in Article 121, some preliminary definitions about the services concerned.

1311. The provisions of the Italian Privacy Code, first of all, apply to the processing of personal data connected to the provision of electronic communication services accessible to the public on public communications networks, including those that support data collection and identification devices.

1312. The term 'electronic communication', in this framework, means any information exchanged or transmitted between a finite number of subjects through an electronic communication service accessible to the public.

Information transmitted to the public via an electronic communication network, as part of a broadcasting service, is excluded, unless the same information is linked to a receiving, identified or identifiable contractor or user.

1313. With the term 'call' is intended as the connection established by an electronic communication service accessible to the public that allows two-way communication.

1314. The notion of 'electronic communications networks' includes transmission systems and, where appropriate, switching or routing equipment and other resources, including inactive network elements, which allow the transmission of signals via cable, radio, to fibre optic means or other electromagnetic means, including satellite networks, circuit-switched, packet-switched mobile and land-based terrestrial networks, including the Internet, networks used for the circular broadcasting of sound and television programmes, systems for transmission of electric current, to the extent that they are used to transmit signals, and the cable television networks, regardless of the type of information carried.

1315. The concept of 'public communications network' means an electronic communications network used wholly or mainly to provide electronic communication services accessible to the public, which supports the transfer of information between network termination points.

1316. The idea of 'electronic communication service' is connected to services consisting exclusively, or mainly, of transmitting signals on electronic communications networks, including telecommunications services and transmission services in networks used for broadcasting, within the limits laid down in Article 2, letter c) of Directive 2002/21 / EC of the European Parliament and of the Council of 7 March 2002.

1317. The term 'contractor' defines any natural person, legal person, entity or association party to a contract with a provider of publicly available electronic communication services for the provision of such services, or in any case recipient of such services via prepaid cards.

1318. The term 'user' means any natural person who uses an electronic communication service accessible to the public, for private or commercial reasons, without necessarily subscribing to it.

1319. 'Traffic data' means any data processed for the purpose of transmitting a communication over an electronic communications network or for billing it.

1320. 'Location data' involves any data processed in an electronic communication network or by an electronic communication service indicating the geographical location of the terminal equipment of the user of an electronic communication service accessible to the public.

1321. 'Value-added service' is, for the norm, the service that requires the processing of traffic data or location data other than traffic data, in addition to what is necessary for the transmission of a communication or related billing.

1322. Finally, with the definition 'Electronic Mail' are included messages containing texts, voices, sounds or images transmitted through a public communications network, which can be stored on the network or in the receiving terminal until the recipient has read them.

1323. Article 122 of the reformed Code of Privacy, regulating the information collected regarding the contractor or user, states that the storage of information in the terminal equipment of a contractor or a user or access to information already stored is permitted *only* on condition that the contractor or user has given his consent after being informed in a manner simplified.

This does not prohibit any technical archiving or access to information that has already been archived if it is solely aimed at transmitting a communication over an electronic communications network, or as strictly necessary for the provider of a service of the company of the information explicitly requested by the contractor or user to provide this service.

For the purpose of expressing the consent, specific configurations of computer programs or devices that are easy and clear to use for the contractor or the user may be used.

Except as provided for by the Code, the use of an electronic communication network to access information stored in the terminal device of a user or a contractor, or to store information or to monitor user operations, is *prohibited*.

1324. Concerning the core topic of data traffic, Article 123 of the Privacy Code states that data concerning contractors and users treated by the provider of a public communications network or an electronic communication service accessible to the public are *cancelled* or made *anonymous* when they are no longer necessary for the purpose of transmitting electronic communication.

The processing of traffic data strictly necessary for invoicing purposes for the contractor, or payments in case of interconnection, is allowed to the supplier, for documentation purposes in the event of disputing the invoice or for the claim of payment, for a period not exceeding *six months*, except for the further specific conservation necessary as a result of a dispute even in court.

The provider of an electronic communication service accessible to the public may process the data to the extent and for the duration necessary for the purpose of marketing electronic communication services or for the provision of value-added services, only if the contractor or the user to whom the data refer has first expressed his/her *consent*, which is revocable at any time.

In providing the information, the service provider shall inform the contractor or the user about the nature of the traffic data that are subject to processing and the duration of the same treatment.

On the other side, the processing of personal data relating to traffic is permitted only to persons who are authorized to process data and who operate under the direct authority of the provider of the electronic communication service accessible to the public or, to depending on the case, of the provider of the public communications network and who deal with billing or traffic management, analysis on behalf of clients, fraud detection or marketing of electronic communication services or provision of services to value added.

The processing must be limited to what is strictly necessary for the performance of these activities and must ensure the identification of the authorized person who accesses the data also through an automated interrogation operation.

The Communications Regulatory Authority may obtain the billing or traffic data necessary for the resolution of disputes relating, in particular, to interconnection or billing.

1325. Very interesting is also the norm regulating detailed invoicing (Article 124 of the Privacy Code): according to this norm, the contractor has the right to receive in detail, on request and without any additional cost, the demonstration of the elements making up the invoice, in particular, on the date and time of the beginning of the conversation, on the number selected, on the type numbering, location, duration and number of clicks charged for each conversation.

The provider of the electronic communication service accessible to the public is obliged to enable the user to make communications and request services from any terminal, free of charge and easily, making use of alternative methods for invoicing, including impersonal ones, such as credit cards or debit cards or prepaid cards.

In the documentation sent to the contractor concerning the communications made, the services and communications are not highlighted, nor the communications necessary to activate the alternative methods to invoicing.

In the invoicing to the contractor, the last three digits of the numbers called are not highlighted.

The contracting party may request the communication of the complete numbers of the communications in question for the exclusive purpose of specifically contesting the accuracy of charges determined or referring to limited periods.

1326. Concerning the problem of line identification, Article 125 of the Privacy Code states that if the presentation of the calling line identification is available, the provider of the electronic communication service accessible to the public shall ensure the calling user the possibility of preventing, free of charge and through a simple function, the presentation of the calling line identification, call by call.

The calling contractor must have this possibility line by line.

If the presentation of the calling line identification is available, the provider of the electronic communication service accessible to the public shall ensure that the called contractor has the possibility of preventing, free of charge and by means of a simple function, the presentation of the identification of incoming calls.

If the presentation of the calling line identification is available and this indication occurs before the communication is established, the provider of the electronic communication service accessible to the public shall ensure that the called contractor has the possibility, by means of a simple and free function, to *reject* incoming calls if the calling line identification presentation has been deleted by the calling user or contractor.

If the presentation of the connected line identification is available, the provider of the electronic communication service accessible to the public ensures to the called contractor the possibility of preventing, free of charge and through a simple function, the presentation of the identification of the line connected to the calling user.

The provision also applies to calls to countries outside the European Union.

If the presentation of the identification of the calling or connected line is available, the provider of the electronic communication service accessible to the public informs the contractors and users of the existence of this service and the possibilities provided in the Privacy Code.

1327. Article 126 of the Privacy Code deals with location data.

In particular, the location data other than traffic data, referring to users or contracting parties of public communication networks or electronic communication services accessible to the public, may be processed only if anonymous or if the user or contractor has previously expressed its consent, revocable at any time, and to the extent and for the duration necessary for the provision of the requested value-added service.

Before requesting consent, the service provider must inform users and contractors about the nature of the location data other than the traffic data that will be processed, the purpose and duration of the latter, as well as the possibility that the data will be transmitted to a third party for the provision of the value-added service.

The user and the contractor who express their consent to the processing of location data, other than traffic data, retain the right to request, free of charge and through a simple function, temporary interruption of the processing of such data for each connection to the network or for each transmission of communications.

The processing of location data other than traffic data is permitted only to persons authorized for processing who operate under the direct authority of the provider of the electronic communication service accessible to the public or, as the case may be, of the provider of the public communications network or of the third party providing the value-added service.

The processing is limited to what is strictly necessary for the provision of the value-added service and must ensure the identification of the authorized person who accesses the data also through an automated interrogation operation.

1328. Regarding disturbing and emergency calls, Article 127 of the Privacy Code states that the contractor who receives distress calls may request that the provider of the public communications network or electronic communication service accessible to the public temporarily renders the suppression of the presentation of the calling line identification ineffective and keeps the data relating to the origin of the call receipt.

The ineffectiveness of the suppression can be arranged only for the times during which disturbance calls occur for a period not exceeding fifteen days.

The request formulated in writing by the contracting party specifies the methods of receipt of the disturbance calls and, in the event that it is preceded by a telephone request, it is forwarded within forty-eight hours.

The data stored may be communicated to the contractor who declares to use them for exclusive protection purposes with respect to disturbance calls.

The supplier ensures transparent procedures towards the contracting parties and can request a contribution to costs not exceeding the costs actually incurred.

The provider of a public communications network or an electronic communication service accessible to the public shall set up transparent procedures to ensure, line by line, the ineffectiveness of the elimination of the calling line identification, as well as, where necessary, the processing of location-related data, despite the temporary refusal or non-consent of the contractor or user, by the services enabled by law to receive emergency calls.

1329. Article 128 of the Privacy Code states, about automatic call transfer, that the provider of an electronic communication service accessible to the public must take the necessary measures to allow each contractor, free of charge and by means of a simple function, to be able to block the automatic transfer of calls to its own terminal by third parties.

1330. Concerning lists of contractors, Article 129 states that the Authority identifies, by its own provision, in cooperation with the Communications Regulatory Authority and in accordance with European Union legislation, the methods of insertion and subsequent use of personal data relating to contractors in printed or electronic directories available to the public.

The provision identifies suitable methods for the expression of consent to the inclusion in the lists and, respectively, to the use of the data for the purpose of sending advertising materials or direct sales or for carrying out research of market or commercial communication, based on the principle of maximum simplification of the methods of inclusion in the lists for the sole purpose of searching for the contractor for interpersonal communications, and of the specific and express consent if the treatment goes beyond such purposes, as well as in terms of verification, rectification or cancellation of the data without charges.

1331. Article 130 regulates unsolicited communications. In this case, the norm states that the use of automated call or call communication systems without the intervention of an operator for sending advertising material or direct sales or for carrying out market research or commercial communication is permitted with the consent of the contractor or user.

The provision also applies to electronic communications, made for the purposes specified therein, by e-mail, fax, messages of the MMS (Multimedia Messaging Service) or SMS (Short Message Service) or other type.

The processing of data through the use of telephone and paper mail for the purposes of sending advertising materials or direct sales or for carrying out market research or commercial communication is allowed against those who have not exercised the right of opposition, with simplified procedures and also electronically, by registering the number of which is the holder and the other personal data referred to, in a register public of the oppositions.

If the data controller uses, for the purpose of direct sales of his own products or services, the e-mail coordinates provided by the interested party in the context of the sale of a product or service, he may not request the consent of the interested party, provided that they are services similar to those object of the sale and the interested party, adequately informed, does not refuse such use, initially or during subsequent communications. The interested party, at the time of collection and at the time of sending any communication, is informed of the possibility of objecting to processing at any time, easily and free of charge.

1332. Concerning information to contractors and users, Article 131 states that the provider of an electronic communication service accessible to the public must inform the contractor and, where possible, the user about the existence of situations that allow to unintentionally learn the contents of communications or conversations by subjects outside them.

The contractor also informs the user when the content of the communications or conversations can be learned by others due to the type of terminal equipment used or the connection made between them at the headquarters of the contractor himself.

3. The user must inform the other user when, during the conversation, devices are used that allow the listening of the same conversation by other subjects.

1333. Article 132 of the Privacy Code is the norm that regulates the storage of traffic data 'for other purposes'. In particular, it states that the data relating to telephone traffic are kept by the supplier for *twenty-four months* from the date of the communication, for the purpose of ascertaining and suppressing crimes, while, for the same purposes, the data relating to online traffic, excluding however the contents of the communications, are kept by the supplier for twelve months from the date of the communication.

Data related to unanswered calls, temporarily processed by providers of electronic communication services accessible to the public or a public communications network, are kept for *thirty days.*

By the deadline referred to in the article, the data are acquired from the supplier with a *motivated decree* of the public prosecutor also on the request of the defendant's attorney, the person under investigation, the injured party and other private parties.

The defendant of the accused or the person subject to the investigation may request, directly from the supplier, the data relating to the users registered in the person assisted in the manner indicated by Article 391-*quater* of the code of criminal procedure.

The request for direct access to incoming telephone communications can be made only when an effective and concrete prejudice may arise for the conduct of defensive investigations pursuant to the law of 7 December 2000, n. 397; otherwise, the rights referred to in Articles 12 to 22 of the Regulation can be exercised in the manner set out in Article 2-*undecies*, paragraph 3, third, fourth and fifth period.

The Minister of the Interior or, on his delegation, the heads of the specialized central offices in the field of information technology or telematics of the State Police, the Carabinieri Corps and the Financial Guard Corps, as well as the other subjects indicated in paragraph 1 of Article 226 of the implementation, coordination and transitional provisions of the Code of Criminal Procedure, pursuant to Legislative Decree 28 July 1989, n. 271, may order, also in relation to any requests made by foreign investigative authorities, to suppliers and operators of IT or telematic services to store and protect, in the manner indicated and for a period not exceeding ninety days, the data relating to the telematic traffic, excluding however the contents of the communications, for the purpose of carrying out the preventive investigations envisaged by the aforementioned Article 226 of the rules referred to in legislative decree n. 271 of 1989, or for purposes of ascertainment and repression of specific crimes.

The provision, which may be extended, for justified reasons, for a total duration not exceeding six months, may provide for particular methods of data storage and any unavailability of the data by suppliers and operators of IT or telematic services or third parties.

The supplier or operator of IT or telematic services for which the order set forth in the norm is addressed must comply without delay, immediately providing the authority requesting the insurance with compliance.

The supplier or operator of IT or telematic services is required to keep the *secret* concerning the order received and the activities consequently carried out for the period indicated by the authority.

1334. Concerning the activities of the suppliers of information, Article 132 states that suppliers must set up internal procedures to correspond to requests made in compliance with the provisions providing for forms of access to users' personal data.

1335. Article 132-*ter* deals with the security of processing. In particular, in compliance with the provisions of Article 32 of the Regulation, the provisions of this article apply to providers of electronic communications services accessible to the public.

The provider of an electronic communication service accessible to the public adopts, pursuant to Article 32 of the Regulation, also through other subjects entrusted with the provision of the service, technical and organizational measures appropriate to the existing risk.

The subjects that operate on the electronic communication networks guarantee that the personal data are accessible only to the authorized personnel for legally authorized purposes.

The measures referred to in paragraphs 2 and 3 guarantee the protection of data relating to traffic and location and other personal data stored or transmitted by accidental destruction, loss or alteration, even accidental, and by storage, processing, access or unauthorized or illegal disclosure, as well as guarantee the implementation of a security policy.

When the security of the service or personal data also requires the adoption of measures concerning the network, the provider of the electronic communication service accessible to the public shall adopt these measures jointly with the provider of the public communications network. In the event of failure to agree, at the request of one of the suppliers, the dispute is defined by the Authority for the guarantees in the communications according to the methods provided by the current legislation.

1336. The last Article on this topic, Article 132-*quater*, regulates information on risks and states that the provider of an electronic communication service accessible to the public must inform the subscribers and, where possible, the users, by means of clear language, appropriate and adequate with respect to the category and age group of the interested party to whom the aforementioned information is provided.

Particular attention must be held in the case of minors of age, if there is a particular risk of breaching the security of the network, indicating, when the risk is outside the scope of application of the measures that the supplier is required to adopt, all possible remedies and the related presumable costs.

Part VII. Computer-Related Crime

Chapter 1. General Legal Development of Computer Crimes in Italy

§1. Introduction: Computer Crimes in Italy

1337. The progressive emergence of forms of cybercrime during the early Seventies of the last century, placed the European and Italian Legislator in front of the awareness that the digital world cannot be regulated with the same tools elaborated for the analogical world, especially in a field such as the criminal law, connoted from a strong typicality of the cases.[440]

1338. Furthermore, in the case of the first electronic computer breaches, there was the need to distinguish between computer crimes in a strict sense, which we could define as 'computer crimes', and computer-related crimes in a broad sense, or crimes connected with the use of computer.[441]

1339. In the first category, it is possible to ascribe those crimes where the computers (or telecommunication systems) are, for all intents and purposes, the 'victims' of the criminal action, while in the second category fall those crimes committed through an IT device or, in any case, in which the computer system has an ancillary role with respect to the main conduct (think, for example, of the cases of sexual exploitation of minors with the digitalization of images and videos and subsequent diffusion through telematic channels).

1340. In Europe, a strong impulse to regulate these phenomena is offered by the Council of Europe, in particular with Recommendation 89 (9) of 13 September 1989 entitled, 'Sur la criminalité en relation avec lor ordinateur'.

1341. The Recommendation contains two lists of crimes that the States adhering to the Council of Europe can consider, and possibly include, in their penal system: a 'minimum' list containing the cases considered necessary given the

440. *See, generally*, A. Cadoppi, S. Canestrari, A. Manna (eds.), *Cybercrime*, UTET, Milan, 2019.
441. For an overview of computer crimes in the digital society *see* C. Frediani, *Cybercrime*, Hoepli, Milan, 2019.

progressive technological progress and an 'optional' list containing other cases for which, however, Member States had to carry out more coherent work with respect to their own penal system.

1342. The following cases were included in the 'minimum' list:

(a) computer fraud, meaning access, alteration or deletion of data or computer programs, or any other interference in computer processing which influences the result, and which for this reason determines an economic or material damage to another person, carried out with the intention of obtaining an illegitimate economic advantage for oneself, or for others;
(b) computer falsification: entry, alteration or deletion of data or computer programs or any other interference in computer processing, carried out with methods or conditions such as to constitute, according to national law, a crime of forgery if the facts themselves were committed in the regards of the traditional objects of this type of infringement;
(c) damage to data or computer programs: illegal damage, deterioration or cancellation of data or computer programs;
(d) cyber sabotage: entry, alteration or deletion of data or computer programs, or interference in computer systems, with the intention of hindering the functioning of an information system or a telecommunications system;
(e) unauthorized access: access without rights to a computer system or network by violating the security rules;
(f) unauthorized interception: interception without right and through technical means of communications sent, originating or existing within a computer system or network;
(g) unauthorized duplication of a protected computer program: reproduction, distribution or communication to the public, without right, of a computer program protected by the law;
(h) unauthorized reproduction of a topography: reproduction without right of a topography, protected by law, of a semiconductor product, or commercial exploitation or importation for this purpose, without having the right, of a topography or a semiconductor product manufactured with the help of this topography.

1343. The 'optional' list, however, included the following cases:

(a) alteration of data or computer programs by those who had no right to intervene on them;
(b) cyber espionage, indicated as the obtaining, through illegitimate means such as unauthorized disclosure, transfer or use without right or other legal justification, of a commercial or industrial secret, with the intention of causing an economic prejudice to the having the right to secrecy or to obtain, for himself or for others, an illegal economic advantage;
(c) unauthorized use of a computer, that is the use without right of a system or a computer network carried out stressing a significant risk of causing a prejudice to the person who has the right to use the system, or to harm the system or its

functioning, or in this way causing injury to the person who has the right to use the system or causing damage to the system or to its operation;

(d) unauthorized use of a protected computer program, i.e. the use without right of a program protected by law or reproduced without rights, with the intention of obtaining an illegal economic advantage for oneself or others, or to cause prejudice to the holder of this rights.

1344. The norms relating to the so-called computer crimes have been established, in Italy, after the need both to recover the pace compared to European Countries already with such legislation in force and to organize a defence against the growing phenomenon of cybercrime. The new legislation has followed the aforementioned directions of the Council of Europe and also benefited from the legislative experience gained in other Countries.

1345. These demands led the Minister of Justice of the time, the Hon Prof. Giuliano Vassalli, to appoint in January 1989 a commission composed of judges, academics and IT experts, to whom he entrusted the task to draw up a scheme to amend the relevant norms of the Criminal Code to fight cybercrime. The Law of 23 December 1993, n. 547, entitled 'Amendments and Additions to the Rules of the Criminal Code and the Code of Criminal Procedure on Cybercrime', is an outcome of the work of the Commission. This first computer crimes law of 1993 was emended in 2008 with Law n. 48 of 2008.

1346. The Italian legislator, by intervening on the Criminal Code and the Code of Criminal Procedure, had to make some considerations of legislative policy.

The choice was, on the one hand, to introduce new criminal offences or, on the other hand, to amend some criminal offences already in the codes which could be in some way related to cybercrimes, adapting them to the new cases.

1347. The following year the legislature's attention was devoted to traditional computer crime.

In the mid-years of this decade, there were reforms to regulate the sexual exploitation of minors and dissemination of child pornography on the net, while in more recent years the attention of the Italian legislature was dedicated to digital investigations and how best to manage the source of evidence in electronic form. Recent developments have occurred, also, with the Law on cyberbullying (Law 71/2017).

1348. Alongside legislative measures that were aimed at regulating precisely the phenomenon of computer crime, were also enacted laws which, although designed for other sectors, provided the offences are closely linked to the computer world.

The most striking example is the GDPR (EU) 2016/679 with implementing d.l. 101/2018, which replaced some parts of the Privacy Code of 2003.

GDPR provides the possibility of unlawful processing of data that can be done very effectively using the computer. Finally, certain crimes under Italian law that are considered in a sense, 'classic' or 'traditional' (as, for example, defamation or harassment) have become, now, cybercrime, since the cases in which involved computers or cell phones are higher than those made physically.

1349. The Law of 1993, n. 547, has to be considered the cornerstone of the Italian system with regards to the offences related to new technologies, on top of other legislative initiatives (such as, for example, d.lgs. no. 518/92 concerning protection of computer programs or d.lgs. no. 196/03 on privacy, recently amended according to the GDPR norms) in which additional cases of crime committed by computer and electronic instruments are identified.

The subject has suffered profound changes following the law of 18 March 2008 n. 48, which authorized the ratification of the Convention on Cybercrime of the Council of Europe that Italy signed among the first far back as of 2001.

1350. The aim of the Convention was essentially to harmonize the offences provided by internal laws and to provide the signatory states with a legislation for the effective conduct of investigations and the contrast of the cybercrimes.

Italian Law 48/2008 is composed of fourteen articles divided into four Chapters, of which the most relevant are Chapter II and Chapter III, which led on the one hand to the integration of the existing criminal code and the code of criminal procedure and on the other hand have even introduced new cases of offences.

1351. The Italian legislator, in intervening on cybercrimes topics, had to make legislative policy choices.

From a first point of view, in fact, he had to choose whether to create new incriminating cases or to modify, by adapting them, those pre-existing crime figures that were in any way attributable to computer crimes.

Law 547/1993 has followed both directions: it has introduced new types of crimes and integrated existing provisions.

1352. A second choice of criminal policy was to decide between a modification of the penal code, with the possible introduction of a new head or title, and the enactment of a law that would integrate existing items into our system.

The second solution was considered preferable.

1353. The new rules introduced by Law 547/1993 contain some important statements on the legal nature of various elements of the IT world.

Between these:

(a) the computer is also a new telecommunications medium;
(b) the most characteristic element of the computer is not so much its physical component (the so-called hardware), but the set of data recorded in its memories (the data) and the algorithms that allow its processing and use for specific tasks (the software);
(c) the computer represents in all respects an offshoot of the individual, which he uses to produce, receive and process information. To violate this personal 'space' is to violate the intimate of the person;
(d) computer crimes, due to the importance of the values they affect, constitute a very dangerous form of crime that would have been unreasonable to leave unpunished.

1354. Law 547/93, therefore, integrated the penal code, inserting new articles, such as the 615-*ter* and *quater* related to the abusive access to a computer or electronic system, the 615-*quinquies* relative to the c.d. virus, the 640-*ter* on computer fraud.

1355. However, the impact of the Law was not only supplementary but also extensive in existing articles, such as Article 392 of the penal code relating to violence against things or Article 420 of the criminal code concerning attacks on public utility plants.

1356. Although law 547/1993 is not the only one to provide for hypotheses of crime related to new technologies, it still remains one of the two cornerstones of our system in the field of cybercrime, despite other legislative interventions, such as the law of 6 February 2006 n. 38 (Provisions on the fight against the sexual exploitation of children and child pornography also through the Internet) and the law of 29 May 2017 n. 17 (Provisions for the protection of minors for the prevention and contrast of the phenomenon of cyberbullying), have contributed to identifying further hypotheses of illicit committed through IT and telematic tools.

§2. The Evolution of the Concept of Computer Crime

1357. It is hard to succeed in giving a precise and exhaustive definition of 'crimine informatico' (computer crime) or, more correctly according to the Italian penal taxonomy, 'delitto informatico' (informatic delict).[442]

1358. Many authors have failed in this operation that might apparently seem easy.

This difficulty is due to the many varied procedures through which it is possible to perform an action that can be considered a 'computer crime', the role that the information instrument can vest, and lastly, the technological evolution that renders outdated and inadequate every definition that refers to the instrument with which or on which the criminal conduct is performed.

1359. It could be possible to identify 'computer crime' in the simplistic way it usually happens, every behaviour defined and punished by the Italian Penal Code and by the related special legislation, namely every behaviour in which any computer or online (telematic) instrument is the object, subject or means of the crime, but this is incorrect.

442. Frequent use by the doctrine of the expression 'crimine informatico' comes from the translation of the expression 'computer crime' of clear Anglo-Saxon origin.

1360. The expression 'computer crime' has been borrowed in the Italian juridical taxonomy from Anglo-American law, to identify a range of unlawful phenomena related to computer sciences and activities, but this terminology has brought along the characteristics of Anglo-Saxon law that has the advantage of a practical approach to problems.

For this reason, the notion of 'computer crime' does not apply to delimit and frame the positive law provisions existing in the Italian juridical system.[443]

In substance, behaviours in abstraction qualifiable as 'computer crimes' and identifiable for the use, in particular forms, of the computer and/or online (telematic) instrument destined to perform actions that are qualified as unlawful by the juridical system can be classified if neither referred to the *genus* nor to the *species*; however, there are some elements that can help for a correct framing of the problem.

1361. First, the computer crime has to concern a computer; it is preferable to assume the widest notion possible of 'computer' in order to include both the variable program computers and the so-called dedicated, namely, both those in which the program is inserted by means of software and those in which such insertion is pre-established by means of firmware.

Moreover, four conditions are required:

(1) that it is an electronic instrument;
(2) that it functions 'by means of program';
(3) that the elaborated signals are digital and not analogue; and
(4) that such elaboration is performed on the basis of Boolean logic.

1362. Furthermore, in order to comprehend the concept of 'computer crime' in its entirety, it is necessary to consider the general notions of informatics and telematics:[444] by 'informatics' we mean 'the science that studies information and, more specifically, the elaboration of data and their automated processing through electronic processors'; by 'telematics', instead, 'the discipline that studies the technical and scientific aspects of the integration between telecommunication and electronic processing; the long-range managing of computer systems by means of

---

443. *See amplius* G. Amato-V.S. Destito-G. Dezzani-C. Santoriello, 'I reati informatici' (CEDAM, Padova, 2010; R. Borruso-G. Buonomo-G. Corasaniti-G. D'Aietti, 'Profili penali dell'informatica' (Giuffrè, Milano, 1994); L. Lupària (ed.), 'Sistema penale e criminalità informatica' (Giuffrè, Milano, 2009); P. Galdieri, 'Teoria e pratica nell'interpretazione del reato informatico' (Giuffrè, Milano, 1997); C. Pecorella, 'Diritto penale dell'informatica' (CEDAM, Padova, 2006); G. Pica, 'Diritto penale delle tecnologie informatiche' (UTET, Torino, 1999); L. Picotti, 'Il diritto penale dell'informatica nell'epoca di internet' (CEDAM, Padova, 2004); G. Ziccardi-P.Perri 'Tecnologia e Diritto' (Giuffré, Milano, 2017).

444. An eminent doctrine, indeed, observes that 'the interpretative problem is caused by the fact that the expression the legislator used, 'computer or telecommunication system', doesn't define a physically existing and identified good . . ., but expresses an abstract concept we have to fill with the notions that reality offers us' *see* G. Pica, *cit.*, pp. 22 ss.

employment of telecommunication networks; the entirety of services of computer nature or origin that can be supplied and used through a telecommunication network'.[445]

1363. It is therefore possible to distinguish two fundamental categories, now clearly identified by statute, into which computer crimes divide:

(1) those crimes perpetrated with the aid of computer instruments and programs; when, namely, the processor is the instrumental means through which the criminal behaviour is performed;
(2) those crimes perpetrated against computer instruments or programs, when, namely, the target of the crime is a computer or telecommunication system and the data, information or programs it contains.

1364. In an attempt to draw a first conclusion, it is possible to state that a 'magic formula' capable of including every possible meaning of the notion of 'computer crime' does not exist, but there are various definitions, all apt to define the concept of 'computer crime' but not individually exhaustive.

The main ones can be identified in the following:

- computer crimes are crimes perpetrated through the use of a computer;
- computer crime is every 'illegal, dishonest or unauthorized' behaviour 'that concerns the automated data processing or transmission';[446]
- computer crime is any act or fact against penal provisions, in which a computer has been involved as object of the fact, as mean or as symbol'.

1365. A sufficiently exhaustive definition, however, can be identified in the following formulation that identifies the computer crime in the wrongdoing in which a processing system or a part of it vests one of the next roles: object, namely including the distribution or manipulation of the processor, or of the data or the programs it contains and the related support instruments; subject, when what happens in relation to the processor is not illegal in itself but is needed to perform crimes of other kind (for example frauds or sabotages). Practically a processing system, and what is produced by the processor, is used as a mean to perform frauds, sabotages, falsifications.

Despite the apparent completeness, however, not even this definition is apt to include all the multiformity that is intrinsic in the notion of computer crime.

Up to the present day, therefore, we have a series of definitions that integrate and complete each other, but we lack a definition that succeeds in including in a single concept what we have to consider as computer crime in Italian penal law.

---

445. *See* entries 'Informatica' and 'Telematica' in VV.AA., 'Dizionario della lingua italiana' (Garzanti Linguistica, Milano, 2004).

446. This definition was formulated by the OECD Commission of experts, Paris, 1993.

§3. Characteristics of Computer Crimes According to Italian Law

1366. Computer crimes are characterized by an action aimed towards goods of relevant value. The action can be physical, when the object of the criminal behaviour is the hardware; or logic, when the crime focuses on data, information and programs.

It is sufficient to think, for an instant, of the computer managing of personal data carried out by professional firms or by the health service.

1367. Daily, moreover, the quality of telematic transactions grows exponentially, so that it is nowadays a widespread practice to buy goods and services from home, filling specific web forms with one's debit card data, with all the risks and possible problems that could come from this.

1368. The lack of proper security policies confronts the proverbial inventiveness of the authors who, able to rely also on a relevant degree of impunity caused by the difficulties related, for example, to the identification of the *locus commissi delicti*, the trans-frontier investigations and the assessment of facts, succeed in performing various potentially criminal actions without any consequence.

1369. A further aspect is represented by the victims' reluctance, in particular banks, to denounce the suffered damages.

This reluctance comes from the popular belief that the publicity of the crime will cause them more disadvantages than advantages, due to the customers' loss of esteem and trust towards them, with a further economic damage that overdoes the damage previously suffered; moreover, it is not easy at all to prove facts adequately, with the consequent risk for banks of being accused of defamation.

This produces an effect called dark-number, namely the uncertainty in the quantification of computer crimes, caused also by the belief that the trial might end with the discharge of the defendant or with a light punishment.

1370. In the *genus* of computer crimes identified beforehand, many *species* are identifiable. Usually, computer crimes are divided according to the discerning criteria of perpetration procedures and the criteria of the purpose of the criminal action.

For this purpose, three different categories can be identified:

(1) the first includes thoroughly heterogeneous cases: in some circumstances the profit of the author consisted in the accumulation of considerable sums; in others, the computer criminal acted with the only purpose, for example, of not paying phone bills, by deviating his charges on someone else's account;
(2) a second category includes those crimes in which the criminal action has the purpose of destroying or damaging totally or partially hardware and/or software. This includes those criminals who, by diffusing specific programs created ad hoc to damage systems, are able to destroy software and render the hardware unusable;
(3) the third category includes those crimes whose pursued aim is to cause physical damage to individuals, society or goods.

§4. Statute 23/12/1993 N. 547 and Law N. 48/2008: Inspiring Criteria

1371. The first penal statute in the computer field dates to about thirty years ago, and is the *Counterfeit Access Device and Computer Fraud and Abuse*, enforced in the United States in 1984, then integrated and replaced by the *Computer Fraud and Abuse Act*, published on 6 October 1986.[447]

The need to catch up with the European Countries that had already enforced penal legislation on informatics,[448] and to create a defence against the widespread phenomenon of computer criminality, on one side complying with the instructions issued by the European Council[449] and on the other to take advantage of the statutory experience acquired by other countries, brought the Minister of Justice, in those days Hon. Professor Giuliano Vassalli, to appoint a commission with an interministerial decree dated January 1989, countersigned in March of the same year by the Minister of the Treasury. This was presided by dott. Piero Callà, in those days General Secretary for Penal Affairs, and made up of magistrates, scholars and informatics experts. They had the task of creating a model to modify the Penal Code provisions in order to repress computer criminality.[450] The Commission met for the first time in May 1989 and concluded its work at the end of February 1991, issuing the Statute 547/1993.

1372. The national legislature, in its intervention, had to operate some choices in legislative policy.

First, it had to choose whether to create new criminal cases or modify the pre-existing crime profiles somehow assimilable to computer crimes by adapting them. Statute 547/1993 has followed both directions: it introduced new cases in point and integrated pre-existing provisions.

1373. A second choice of criminal policy regarded the alternatives of modifying the Penal Code, by introducing a new chapter or clause, or enforcing a new statute that would integrate pre-existing clauses of the Italian juridical system. The second solution was considered preferable.

The new provisions of Statute 547/1993 contain some highly important statements on the juridical nature of various elements of the computer field. Among them:

---

447. *See* S. Resta, 'I computer crimes tra informatica e telematica' (CEDAM, Padova, 2002); G. Ziccardi-P.Perri 'Tecnologia e Diritto' (Giuffré, Milano, 2017).

448. France in particular had already adopted statute n. 18-19, *relative à la fraude informatique*, on 15 Jan. 1998, while Great Britain had enacted the *Computer Misuse Act* on 29 Jun. 1990.

449. The European Council had identified two lists of crimes that should be taken into account and introduced in each Member State's juridical system: a so-called minimum list, that contained the cases on the point considered necessary premises of the legislative action, and a 'facultative' list. In the 'minimum' list the following categories were included: (a) computer fraud; (b) computer forgery; (c) damaging of data or computer programs; (d) computer sabotage; (e) unauthorized access; (f) unauthorized interceptions; (g) unauthorized reproduction of a protected computer program; (h) unauthorized topographic reproduction.

450. For an exhaustive view on European legislation regarding computer penal law, *see* C. Sarzana di S. Ippolito, 'Informatica, Internet e diritto penale' (Giuffrè, Milano, 2010); G. Ziccardi-P.Perri 'Tecnologia e Diritto' (Giuffré, Milano, 2017).

- the computer is also a new telecommunication instrument;
- the most characterizing element of a computer is not its physical structure (the so-called hardware) and not even the complex of data stored in its memories, but a sort of written last will (software or program);
- the computer represents an offspring that an individual uses only to obtain processed information or to make it interact in the outer world in his place. To violate its memories, its programs, its communications is to violate the intimate world of the individual;
- computer crimes, due to the importance of the values they affect, represent a very dangerous kind of criminality that would be unreasonable not to punish.

1374. Statute 547/93, therefore, integrated the Penal Code by inserting new provisions, such as 615-*ter* and *quater*, that relate to unauthorized access to a computer or telecommunication system, 615-*quinquies* that relates to so-called *viruses*, and 614-*ter* that relates to computer frauds.

1375. The Statute had not only an integrative impact but also an extensive one with reference to pre-existing provisions of the Penal Code, such as Article 392, related to offences to goods, or Article 420, concerning attacks to public-interest systems.

1376. Although Statute 547/93 is not the only statute that provides criminal provisions related to new technologies, it still remains the cornerstone on the matter in the Italian juridical system. Nevertheless, other interventions contributed to the identification of further crimes performed through computer or telematic instruments: for example, D.Lgs. 518/92, on the protection of computer programs, or Statute 675/96, repealed by D.Lgs. 196/03.

1377. In 2008 Italy ratified the Convention on Cybercrime, signed in Budapest (23 November 2001) with Law n. 48 of 18 March 2008.

This Law modified several parts of Statute 547/93. There is also the new crime of 'computer fraud' (Article 640-*ter* Penal Code) related to the entity providing electronic signature certification services (the person who provides services for the certification of electronic signature, which, in order to secure for himself or others an unfair advantage or to cause harm to others, violates the obligations required by law to issue a qualified certificate, shall be punished with imprisonment up to three years and a fine ranging from EUR 51 to EUR 1032).

1378. New is also the punishment of the provision of equipment, devices or software intended to damage or disrupt a computer system or computer (whoever, in order to unlawfully damage a computer system or electronic communication, information, data or programs contained in or relevant to it or to encourage disruption, total or partial alteration of its operation, obtains, produces, reproduces, imports, disseminates, communicates, delivers or otherwise makes available to other equipment, devices or computer programs, shall be punished with imprisonment up to two years and a fine of up to EUR 10,329).

1379. Important are also some modifications to Article 635-*bis*, concerning damage of information, data and computer programs (unless the act constitutes a serious crime, anyone who destroys, reduces, cancels, alters or deletes information, data or computer programs of another person shall be punished, on complaint of the victim, by imprisonment from six months to three years. If the act is committed violence to the person or with abuse of its role as operator of the system, the punishment shall be imprisonment from one to four years).

1380. The new Article 635-*quater*, concerning damage to computer or telecommunications, dispose that, unless the act constitutes a serious crime, anyone, by the conduct referred to in Article 635-*bis*, or through the introduction or transmission of data, information or programs, destroys, damages, makes, in whole or in part, useless telecommunications systems or seriously hinders the operation shall be punished with imprisonment from one to five years. If the act is committed violence to the person or with abuse of its role as operator of the system, the punishment shall be increased.

1381. Article 635-*ter*, concerning damage of information, data and programs used by governments or other public body or any public utility, dispose that, unless the act constitutes a serious crime, whoever commits a fact intended to destroy, damage, delete, alter or delete information, data or computer programs used by governments or other public body or relevant, or of public utility, shall be punished with imprisonment from one to four years.

If follows from the fact the destruction, damage, deletion, alteration or suppression of information, data or computer programs, the punishment shall be imprisonment from three to eight years.

If the act is committed violence to the person or with abuse of its role as operator of the system, the punishment shall be increased.

Similar discipline regulates also the damage to computer or telematic systems of public utility or the serious obstruction of their operation. Indeed, one of the main objectives of the Budapest Convention is to facilitate cooperation between the various Member States

1382. The Convention is, in fact, the first international treaty on criminal offences committed via the Internet and on other computer networks, and deals in particular with copyright infringement, computer fraud, child pornography and network security breaches.

It also contains a series of appropriate measures and procedures, such as the search of computer network systems and the interception of data.

1383. Its main objective, set out in the preamble, is to pursue a common penal policy for the protection of society against cybercrime, especially by adopting appropriate legislation and promoting international cooperation.

1384. In particular, what the Convention wants to achieve is a minimum target of protection of legal assets offended by cybercrimes and a common minimum essential level of strategies to combat these offences, especially due to their generally transnational nature, which involves clearly the need for the harmonization of the relative legislation of contrast in the ambit of the various legal systems.

1385. Increasing importance is also being acquired by the Additional Protocols to the Convention, which are intended to deal with specific areas of cybercrime where there is a need for ad hoc standardization.

The first protocol concerned xenophobia and racism conveyed through telematic channels and the second protocol, which at the time of writing is still being defined, aims to strengthen the cooperation tools between states, taking into account the growing dissemination of distributed technologies such as cloud computing, to be able to identify, collect and analyse the digital proof source also from a cross-border perspective.

It often happens, in fact, that telematic investigations should be interrupted when the trace crosses national borders, a circumstance that is fairly frequent if the nature of the Internet is taken into account, and it is therefore necessary to provide investigators with the appropriate procedural tools so that they can continue the investigation even outside of its competence, guaranteeing at the same time respect for fundamental rights.

1386. The Convention opens with some important definitions, which are used to outline the perimeter within which the subsequent rules will operate.

1387. First of all, it is necessary to define what is meant by an IT system, a concept that is apparently easy to identify but that, for example, in our system has often requested clarifications from the Italian Court of Cassation.

1388. The computer system is to be understood as any equipment or group of interconnected or connected devices, one or more of which, based on a program, perform automatic data processing. The necessary coexistence of a hardware component and a software component is then reiterated, which will be able to perform the most varied operations on the data, always falling within the definition of 'computer system'.

1389. The definition of computer data is also interesting, identified as any presentation of facts, information or concepts in a form likely to be used in a computerized system, including a program capable of allowing a computerized system to perform a function and that of service provider, which indicates: '1. any public or private entity that provides users of its services with the possibility of communicating through an IT system; 2. any other entity that processes or stores computer data on behalf of such communication service or for users of such service'.

1390. Finally, the last definition given is that of data transmission, which means 'any computerized information relating to a communication through an information system that forms a part in the communication chain, indicating the origin of the communication, the destination, the path, the time, date, size, duration or type of service'.

1391. With regard to the definitions referred to above, the Cassation reaffirmed that 'The art. 1 of the Budapest Convention of 23 November 2001, implemented in Italy with the law n. 48 of 2008, with the definition 'computer system' identifies any equipment or group of interconnected or connected devices, one or more of which, based on a program, perform automatic data processing; with the definition 'computer data' the same article identifies any presentation of facts, information or concepts in a form likely to be used in a computerized system, including a program capable of allowing a computerized system to perform a function; and with the definition 'data transmission' it identifies any computerized information relating to a communication through an information system that forms a part in the communication chain, indicating the origin of the communication, the destination, the path, the time, the date, the size, duration or type of service.

Precisely in consideration of the aforementioned characteristics, which according to the Treaty identify the essential elements of computer crimes, debit or credit cards, identified by a magnetic stripe or a chip, both elements suitable for storing and transmitting computer data, constitute a true and its own computer system, capable of processing data, making them operational, when they connect to the POS equipment, allowing authorized access to the Banks financial information system.'

1392. With regard to the substantive law measures, Chapter 2 of the Convention contains a series of crimes that can be divided into the following categories:

(1) crimes against confidentiality, integrity and availability of data and IT systems (offences of illegal access fall into this category to a computerized or telematic system, offences of abusive interception, crimes against the integrity of data, crimes against the integrity of computer systems and abuse of instruments aimed at committing the crimes listed up to this point or subtracting passwords and access codes for identification in computer systems);
(2) computer crimes in the strict sense (i.e., computer forgery and computer fraud);
(3) crimes related to content (essentially all crimes related to child pornography); and
(4) crimes against intellectual property and related rights, which recalls the need to provide for criminal sanctions in the event of copyright infringement, in accordance with the decision taken under the Paris Act of 24 July 1971, which revised the Berne Convention for the protection of literary and artistic works. According to the Convention, these crimes must be punished with penalties that are 'effective, proportionate and dissuasive, including the deprivation of personal freedom'.

1393. In compliance with both the principles and the detail of the cases contained in the Convention, law 48/2008 has profoundly modified some provisions of the Penal Code and the Code of Criminal Procedure.

In particular, as regards the criminal cases, Article 491-*bis* c.p. concerning the false computer and Article 495-*bis* c.p. relative to the false declaration or attestation to the certifier of electronic signature on the identity or personal qualities of oneself or others.

1394. Article 615 quinqies p.p., relating to the dissemination of equipment, devices or computer programs aimed at damaging or interrupting an IT or electronic system and the entire regulations relating to IT damage are profoundly modified.

In fact, in addition to the replacement of Article 635-*bis* c.p. that in its new version concerns the damage to information, data and computer programs, three new cases are added which are 635 *ter* c.p. (Damage to information, data and computer programs used by the State or by another public body or in any case of public utility), 635 *quater* cp. (Damage to computer or telecommunications systems) and 635 *quinquies* (Damage to computer or telematic systems of public utility).

1395. The catalogue of the cases relating to computer fraud is also expanded, where a new article is inserted, namely the 640 *quinquies* cp. concerning the computer fraud of the subject who provides electronic signature certification services.

Finally, paragraphs 2 and 3 of the article are repealed. 420 c.p.p., which in its new capacity states 'Anyone committing an act aimed at damaging or destroying public utility facilities is punished, unless the fact constitutes a more serious offense, with imprisonment from one to four years.'

Chapter 2. Application of Substantial Criminal Law in the Area of ICT

§1. 'Computer Violence' on Goods

1396. Article 1 of Statute 547/93 inserts after paragraph 2 of Article 392 of the Penal Code (titled 'arbitrary exert of one's reasons'), a paragraph with which the legal notion of 'violence on goods' is broadened, by its extension from traditional facts of offence, transformation or destination change to a series of behaviours that directly deal with computer programs or with the functioning of computer or telecommunication systems.

The newly formulated Article 392 allows conviction of any person who, in order to exert an alleged right and being able to apply to the Court, decides instead to take arbitrarily the law into his own hands.

Part of the doctrine, however, has already stressed the fact that, under the technical profile, it is not useful, but rather dangerous, to operate on the already controversial 'general' notion of 'violence on goods' by broadening it further to include alterations, modifications or partial deletions, or even the mere 'impediment or disturbance' of the functioning of a computer or telecommunication system.[451]

1397. A wide range of cases has imposed the broadening of the expression 'violence on goods', since often hardware and mostly software houses have performed unlawful manumissions of the computer systems (partial mutilations, alteration of the normal system functioning) they supplied to customers, claiming rights on the derived software and therefore exercising a form of self-protection that the penal law forbids. However, according to the doctrine,[452] it is necessary to distinguish further situations in which it would be possible to configure a concept of the crime defined by Article 392 of the Penal Code and the crime of damaging defined by Article 635 of the Penal Code: namely, when violence on goods aimed to exert an alleged right is accompanied by damaging, an extensive interpretation of the notion of 'goods or chattels' is performed and the hypothesis of concert of the cited crimes is considered.

Always according to the cited doctrine, it is possible to configure the concert of the crime of computer damaging and the crime of diffusion of virus-programs (or similar) defined by Article 615-*quinquies* of the Penal Code.

The crime defined by Article 392, violence on goods, does not apply to the case in which the alteration of the system is performed against the system user in order

451. *See*, L. Picotti, *Studi di diritto penale dell'informatica*, Verona, 1992, p. 106, where it is stated that 'this way, indeed, not only the typifying specificity of the material-corporeal notion of 'thing' is lost, but even the concept of 'violence' itself is radically altered, once we rarefy and idealize its naturalistic meaning, connected to a relevant material effect produced on the corporal object that the act we have to qualify affects'.

452. *See* G. Pica, *Diritto penale delle tecnologie informatiche*, UTET, Torino, 1999; G. Ziccardi-P.Perri 'Tecnologia e Diritto' (Giuffré, Milano, 2017).

to push him into a subordinate position, so that the user will have to do or not to do something to obtain the full restoration of the system.[453]

The modality of 'violence on goods' with reference to the configuration of the arbitrary exercise of one's reasons, therefore, can develop in many forms, and the crime can be performed, nevertheless, also through a conduct that dips into the functionality of a computer or telecommunication system even if it does not physically alter the program.

Article 5 of Law of 18 March 2008, n. 48, considerably extends the list of incriminating cases concerning data corruption, in addition to amending Article 635-*bis* of the Criminal Code with respect to the original wording introduced by Article 9 of the Law 23 December 1993, n. 547. In addition to updating the current crime-definition of 'corruption of data' (Article 635-*bis*, 'corruption of information, data and software': anyone who destroys, reduces, cancels, alters or deletes information, data or computer programs of another person shall be punished, on complaint of the victim, by imprisonment from six months to three years), there was the introduction of three new criminal cases. The first one, Article 635-*ter*, introduces the crime of 'corruption of information, data and programs used by governments or other public body': whoever commits a fact intended to destroy, damage, delete or alter information, data or computer programs used by governments or other public body, or of public utility, is punished with imprisonment from one to four years. The second one, Article 635-*quater*, introduces the crime of 'damage to computer or telematic systems': anyone who, by the conduct referred to in Article 635-*bis*, or through the introduction or transmission of data, information or programs, destroys, damages, makes, in whole or in part, useless a telecommunications systems or seriously hinders the operation, shall be punished with imprisonment from one to five years. The last one, Article 635-*quinquies*, introduces the crime of 'damage to public utility telecommunication systems': if the act referred to in Article 635-*quater* is intended to destroy, damage, render, in whole or in part, useless computer or telecommunications systems of public utility, the punishment shall be imprisonment from one to four years. In conclusion, with Law 48/2008, the standard is much changed and what was contained in a single case has been divided into four different scenarios with different rules, some of which also cover the possibility of damage to systems of public utilities actually included in the crime of attack on the facilities for public use.

§2. Attacks to Public-Interest Systems

1398. In consideration of the fundamental role played by public-interest systems in the social organization, the legislature has resolved to operate, by means of Article 2 of Statute 547/93, also on the case defined by Article 420 of the Penal Code, in order to extend the case to include those acts that are performed to damage 'public interest computer or telecommunication systems'.

453. *See* R. Borruso – G. Buonomo – G. Corasaniti – G. D'Aietti, *Profili penali dell'informatica*, Giuffrè, Milano, 1994, pp. 58 ss.

The material objects of the conduct are the 'technical systems'.[454] The main characteristic of this crime is represented by the 'public interest' of the systems that are the object of the crime, and consequentially of the data stored and the programs used in them.

Without any doubt, it is the great number of users served by the system that determines the 'publicity' of the interest: in the notion of public interest we cannot therefore include neither the system that serves an apartment block, due to the limited number of users, nor the computer system of a firm, which is covered instead by Article 635-*bis* of the Penal Code (damage of computer or telecommunication systems). The local road exchange is identifiable as public because even if it serves a limited number of wired users in the area, it does not restrict the possibility of use by anyone who wants to communicate with these users.

The indispensable aspect that allows a system to be regarded as a public-interest system is the indefinability of the number and type of potential users of the service. The systems that are instituted for the benefit of society, and are therefore of public interest, include, for example, all telecommunications systems, electronic control and monitoring systems for environmental protection, power production and switching plants and electronic and video-telematic systems for the control of moving vehicles.

§3. Computer Forgery

1399. Article 3 of Statute 547/93 has introduced the case of the so-called computer forgery by adding the specific provision of Article 491-*bis* of the Penal Code that concerns computer records: 'if any of the forgeries defined in this chapter regards a public or private computer record, the same provisions of this chapter that concern public or private records apply'.

In the same article there was the full definition, in the penal field, of what the legislature considered a 'computer record', that had to be read as 'any computer support that contains data or information that have probative value or programs that are specifically destined to process them'.

This definition, however, caused a wide debate about the perplexities it caused since it would have been much easier to identify the record with the data itself, unbundling it from its support, than with the physical support that contains it.[455] By hooking the computer record to a material entity (more specifically, with the support that contains it), the legislature had left unsolved all those problems that derive from the impossibility of distinguishing originals from copies in the digital world, leaving the statute to deal with the task of defining which computer supports have to be used in order to give probative value to the computer record. This definition is now removed since 2016.

---

454. 'System' is used to mean any complex of technical structures (mechanical, optical, electronic, etc.) assembled and connected between them to perform some specific technological functions (*see* Cass., Sez. II, 7 marzo 1983).

455. *See* P. Galdieri, *cit.*, Giuffrè, Milano, 1997, pp. 109 ss.

1400. The expression that has interested the doctrine the most, of course, is that of the 'probative value' that the article under analysis recognizes to the computer record: it has to be intersected with the various definitions and distinctions already existing on the traditional notion of 'record', in order to reach an exclusively penal settling of the concept contained in the provision under analysis. It is necessary to exclude a priori that a definition among the ones preceding the enforcement of Statute 547/93 could contain the elements needed to answer the difficulties of interpretation that the provision poses. It will then be necessary to proceed from other formulations, like those elaborated by jurisprudence about the telex and the telefax.

Therefore, having seen that the definition of the record cited by the provision is quite complex, the legislature has, at last, assigned a penal protection to those records to which a probative value is recognized according to other statutory provisions. Among them, there are:

– acts recorded on an optical support;
– Public Administration acts;
– administrative acts performed by means of a computer and regulated by special provisions; and
– public acts or private records apparently subscribed by the author, even if through a computer reproduction.

§4. Unauthorized Access to a Computer or Telecommunication System

1401. Article 4 of Statute 547/93 inserted, in the Italian Penal Code, Article 615-*ter*, regarding unauthorized access to a computer or telecommunication system.

This provision is placed in Title XII of Chapter I of the Penal Code that regards all acts that damage or endanger fundamental rights of the individual, namely life, physical integrity, honour and both moral and personal freedoms. It is placed, as highlighted in the report of the Ministerial Commission on the bill, among the crimes against domicile inviolability, because the computer or telecommunication systems, the violation of which is punished, are an expansion of the area of respect related to the interested subject, guaranteed by Article 14 of the Constitution and, in its more essential and traditional aspects, by the penal protection of Articles 614 and 615 of the Italian Penal Code.

The report justifies the placement of the provision among the crimes against domicile inviolability by stating the existence of a new concept of domicile, namely the computer domicile.

Article 615-*ter* provides two well-distinguished criminal scenarios:

(a) the act of 'the subject that abusively breaks in a computer or telecommunication system protected by security measures';
(b) the act of 'the subject that remains in a computer or telecommunication system protected by security measures against the expressed or tacit will of the subject that has the right to exclude him'.

1402. The conduct of 'breaking in' the computer system consists in the access to the system performed by using its same technology. Part of the doctrine has highlighted how the expression is excessively generalist and could therefore include any kind of conduct through which the agent enters the system. But it is clear that, even if the agent performs physical acts to approach the system (for example by forcing the entrances to the place where it is kept), nevertheless the final act of 'introduction' required by the case in point in Article 615-*ter* can only be performed by means of the same computer technologies. This is, therefore, a 'computer break-in' that will occur through the use of hardware and software components.

1403. The problem of what the legislation means when referring to 'a computer or telecommunication system' is tightly connected with the qualification of the conduct required by the provision. It is questionable whether this expression 'has to be interpreted as equipment fitted with structuring and complexity levels superior to those of a personal computer'.[456]

In the computer science field, 'system' has always been considered as the complex whole of hardware and software elements. In the juridical field, therefore, 'system' will be considered as a whole of interconnected elements (for example, an electronic processor, some input and output units connected to it and the software represented by the applicative programs used on that specific processor) that interact between them in a coordinated way, in order to obtain certain results for which the system has been created.

'Telecommunication system', instead, is considered as a defined term to mean systems that apply the telecommunication principles and technologies and allow users to perform any kind of long-distance communication.

1404. The conduct of 'breaking in' cited by the provision under analysis appears to be, on the logical side, always and necessarily distinct from the conduct of 'remaining inside', since it appears obvious that it is impossible to 'remain inside' the system if one has not got in. Anyway, the double law provision is not at all useless, since there are frequent cases of lawful introduction in a system (allowed by its proprietor), followed by a permanence that is unlawful because it is operated out of line and in contrast with the agreements concluded with the proprietor of the system or because it exceeds the borders of the access authorization. The conduct of 'remaining' in the computer system appears therefore to be provided precisely to punish those cases in which the introduction is lawful, as it is performed with the consent or the authorization of the proprietor, but the access to the system becomes unlawful during its duration (for example, due to the end of the time-course of allowed access).

Pica observes, on the point, that 'the hypothesis of unauthorized permanence represents anyway a hypothesis of commissive and not omissive conduct, because the permanence in the system is an action that lasts deliberately. The structure of the

456. *See* R. Borruso–G. Buonomo–G. Corasaniti–G. D'Aietti, *cit.*, Giuffrè, Milano, 1994, p. 69.

provision is not, indeed, centred on the punishment of the omitted desertion of the system, but on the voluntary permanence despite the expressed or tacit prohibition of the proprietor'.[457]

1405. The text of Article 615-*ter* of the Penal Code contains jointly both the adverbs 'abusively' and the parenthesis 'against the expressed or tacit will of the subject that has the right to exclude him'.

At the first reading of the provision the adverb 'abusively' appears related to the conduct of 'breaking in', while the parenthesis concerning the will of the proprietor appears related to the second conduct, the so-called permanence, in the computer or telecommunication system.

However, neither of the expressions refers with certainty to a conduct, with the automatic exclusion of the other. The repetition is due, presumably, to the desire to explicitly connote both the crime conducts with the requirement of the lack of the proprietor's authorization. It is more adequate, therefore, to use the adverb 'abusively' to qualify the introduction as an act unauthorized and therefore unlawful since the beginning, while to use the parenthesis 'against the expressed or tacit will of the subject that has the right to exclude him' to refer to the intervened unlawfulness of the 'permanence' conduct, which is autonomously defined to include in the provision the unlawful fact of unauthorized 'permanence' of the agent in the system after his lawful introduction.

1406. The penal case in point here under analysis restricts its scope only to cases of access to a computer or telecommunication system 'protected by security measures'.

Through this formulation, the legislature has intentionally subordinated the effectiveness of the penal provision to the circumstance that the proprietor of the computer or telecommunication system has provided some means of protection in order to make clear that the access and the permanence in the system are reserved only to subjects he himself authorizes. These means of protection, in the legislature's intention, can be represented by more or less effective means, so that it is the requirement of the expression of the proprietor's will that prevails, rather than that of the real effectiveness of the rejection of unauthorized subjects. The provision cites 'security measures' (plural form), and a simple keyword or an access code cannot be considered as 'security measures'; these have to be something more complex than a simple 'password'. The existence of a means of protection (even if, in substance, it is scarcely effective) has the mere function of rendering explicit and unequivocal the presence of a prohibition to the access to the computer system.

1407. Another question of interpretation that the provision poses regards the specification of the moment in which the access can be considered as performed, that is, the introduction into the system. For this purpose, we have to clarify the boundary beyond which the unauthorized access can be considered as performed, namely when the subject has effectively accessed to the system, and before which there is only an 'access attempt'. With reference to this matter, the provision on

457. *See* G. Pica, *cit.*, UTET, Torino, 1999, pp. 41-42.

'security measures' as characteristics of the material object of the conduct allows us to suppose that, in the case in point, the 'introduction' the legislation refers to is identifiable with the moment in which the subject has abusively (that is, without the authorization of the system's proprietor) and therefore unlawfully exceeded the hardware and/or software data protection barriers. This is the moment in which the subject effectively enters the system without authorization, intentionally bypassing the protections and therefore clearly showing his intention to unlawfully access the system.

The crime will occur only when the agent manages to elude the protection and access the data contained in the system. The effective knowledge on behalf of the subject of a part or of the whole data stored in the system he breaks into is not necessary since the provision does not require it.

1408. However, to commit the crime, it is required that the subject bypasses or cheats the protection measures and penetrates protected areas of the system. In every case in which the subject tries to bypass protections (for example, by attempting to type the required password many times) but does not succeed, it is instead possible to assess the 'attempt' (provided there is the dissent of the system's proprietor, as the word 'abusively' points out).

There is not even an 'attempt' in those cases in which the subject connects on long-distance or accesses from nearby a computer system belonging to another subject, but does not attempt to bypass the existing security measures: these cases are not acts aimed to the violation of the protection, and therefore the privacy, of the system, as the subject may have connected to the system still ignoring that the access to data is protected. The mere connection action is not included in the hypothesis of effective abusive intrusion.

1409. In case of 'physical' protection measures external to the computer system (for example, security doors that preclude the entrance to the room the system is in), or even placed in the hardware (for example, the security key of nearly every table computer, which does not allow to turn it on, use the keyboard or use other hardware components), a different approach applies. The mere bypassing of external barriers (doors, alarms that protect where the computer is kept) cannot be qualified as 'unequivocally aimed' to violate the computer system, so that even the possibility to assess the crime of 'attempted unauthorized access' is ruled out: general provisions on damaging, domicile violation or others will still be applicable.

1410. Article 615-*ter* of the Penal Code provides from one to five years of imprisonment, and the unauthorized access is not any more a crime indictable as a result of personal prosecution but an indictable offence, if it is performed:

- by a public officer or by a subject responsible for a public service, by abuse of his powers or infringement of the duties related to the function or service; by anyone who exercises even abusively the profession of private investigator; through the abuse of the quality of system operator (paragraph 2, n. 2).
- by performing violence on goods or persons; or if the culprit is evidently carrying weapons;

– if the destruction or damage of the system or the total or partial interruption of its functioning derive from the fact; or if the destruction or damage of data, information or programs the system contains derive from the fact.

These are cases that can all be qualified as 'special effect' cases: three distinct and aggravated hypotheses that relate to the subjective profile (qualities of the subject who performs the crime), to the modalities of the action and to the deriving consequences.

§5. Unauthorized Possession of Access Codes

1411. The activity described and punished by Article 615-*quater* of the Penal Code, consisting of the possession and diffusion of computer systems' access codes, according to some scholars,[458] is one of the behaviours that are prodromal to the crime defined by Article 615-*ter* of the Penal Code, namely the unauthorized access to computer systems.

It is not infrequent for an 'attacker' to acquire access codes before performing the computer intrusion, in order to penetrate the system in the least time possible and, as well, to arouse the least suspects possible. The qualifying element of the case in point consists of specific malice that, in the formulation of the provision, is contained in the expression 'to gain a profit for oneself or for others, or to cause a damage to others'. This excludes someone who lawfully communicates an access password to a third party. Due to this reason, many scholars consider this provision indissolubly tied to the provision contained in Article 615-*ter* (unauthorized access), since it aims to prevent those unauthorized accesses that occur not by means of software modifications, but through an unauthorized 'impersonation' of a subject that has the adequate credentials to access to the system.

The unlawful conducts that the provision prohibits are:

– to abusively acquire access codes or other means adequate (including biometrical credentials) to access a computer or telecommunication system protected by security measures;
– to diffuse, communicate or deliver to third parties, by any mean, access credentials unlawfully detained;
– to 'supply information or instructions adequate' to violate a computer or telecommunication system protected by security measures.

§6. Diffusion of Computer Viruses

1412. Article 4 of Statute 547/93 has introduced a new crime, defined by Article 615-*quinquies* and titled as 'Diffusion of Programs Aimed to Damage or Block a Computer System'.

458. *See* G. Pica, *cit.*, UTET, Torino, 1999, p. 79.

This provision was not present in the text written by the Commission, but it was added later by the legislative office. The authors of the definitive text considered necessary to repress specifically the behaviour of the subject that diffuses the so-called computer viruses.

The conduct of the crime consists in 'diffusing, communicating or delivering' to anyone, regardless of the reasons, a software self-made or made by others that has the characteristic, as an effect or an aim, of damaging a computer or telecommunication system or part of it (data, programs, information, etc.).

1413. The legislature has used three words that from an etymological point of view appear in partial superposition between them, in order to completely include every form of distribution and circulation of noxious programs. The concept of 'diffusion' has to be interpreted and considered according to the computer technologies through which noxious programs circulate. Therefore, it appears mostly related to the diffusion modalities of noxious programs through online (telecommunication) networks that allow the communication between different and distant computers and therefore allow the transfer between them not only of data and information but also of viruses. These, as stated, are created to diffuse themselves automatically, with the consequence of a progressive broadening of the infection, as in an epidemic. On this point, Pica stated that 'the concept of diffusion includes also the actions of material introduction of copies of virus-programs into computer systems, regardless of the fact that the action is performed surreptitiously, fraudulently or with violence or otherwise openly'.[459]

1414. The current text of Article 615-*quinquies* c.p., however, is profoundly renewed as a result of Law 18 March 2008 No. 48, since the Legislator has made a broad expansion of the categories of the relevant conducts, this way including in the offence all the activities that may endanger the integrity and security of a system.

The new wording of the norm, however, does not solve some problems of interpretation and application nature, already reported about the letter of the old art 615-*quinquies*, nor fully reflects the provisions of the European Convention on Cybercrime to which it should be inspired.

Article 6 of the Convention, entitled «Misuse of devices» provided the rule for national legislators by which:

> Each Party shall adopt such legislative and other measures as may be necessary to establish as criminal offences under its domestic law, when committed intentionally and without right:
>
> (a) the production, sale, procurement for use, import, distribution or otherwise making available of:

459. *See* G. Pica, *cit.*, UTET, Torino, 1999, p. 100. *See also See* P. Perri, 'La diffusione di programmi diretti a danneggiare', in L. Lupària (ed.), 'Sistema penale e criminalità informatica' (Giuffrè, Milano, 2009); G. Ziccardi-P.Perri 'Tecnologia e Diritto' (Giuffré, Milano, 2017).

i a device, including a computer program, designed or adapted primarily for the purpose of committing any of the offences established in accordance with the above Articles 2 through 5;

ii a computer password, access code, or similar data by which the whole or any part of a computer system is capable of being accessed, with intent that it be used for the purpose of committing any of the offences established in Articles 2 through 5; and

(b) the possession of an item referred to in paragraphs a.i or ii above, with intent that it be used for the purpose of committing any of the offences established in Articles 2 through 5. A Party may require by law that a number of such items be possessed before criminal liability attaches.

2 This article shall not be interpreted as imposing criminal liability where the production, sale, procurement for use, import, distribution or otherwise making available or possession referred to in paragraph 1 of this article is not for the purpose of committing an offence established in accordance with Articles 2 through 5 of this Convention, such as for the authorised testing or protection of a computer system.

3 Each Party may reserve the right not to apply paragraph 1 of this article, provided that the reservation does not concern the sale, distribution or otherwise making available of the items referred to in paragraph 1 a.ii of this article».

Considering that the provision was already present, to some extent, in our system, the present norm consists in an expansion of the offence, especially in relation to the provision of new conducts related to the production, sale, supply for use, distribution or usability of equipment that can allow illegal access to a computer system, an illegal interception, an attack to the integrity of data or of a system, given that the previous wording was limited only to 'programs', to be intended as software.

It is mainly the paragraph sub a.1. of Article 6 of the Convention concerning the issue under consideration, since the sub a.2. is better referred to the case contemplated in Article 615-*quater* c.p., related to the illegal detention or dissemination of access codes to computer or telecommunication systems, whose discipline has been already briefly explained above.

The second paragraph of Article 6 of the Convention helps to find an answer to the interpretational doubts always at the centre of the scholars' discussions, as it leaves the option to the signatory Member States not to consider as criminal conducts the activities which, even following the criminal pattern, are not made in order to accomplish a crime. The doubts concerning the lawful use of programs or devices which could be identified as harmful are finally over, since the new wording of Article 615-*quinquies* detects only the specific intent to cause damage or disrupt a computer or telecommunication system, a concept also clearly explained in the letter of Article 6, paragraph 2, mentioned above. This article expressly provides among the lawful hypothesis, *inter alia*, the 'authorized test' or 'the protection of a computer system', thereby recalling just

the assumptions the scholars feared to be conducted to the crime, on the basis of which a technician in his duties could have been found punishable under the old wording of Article 615-*quinquies*.
From a crime of generic intent, therefore, the Italian legislator switches to a crime of specific intent, being no longer sufficient the awareness and willingness of the dissemination, communication or delivery of the program, together with the knowledge of the technical characteristics and its harming potential.

§7. Electronic Mail

1415. Article 5 of Statute 547/93 intervenes also on Article 616 of the Penal Code (correspondence violation, subtraction and suppression), including in the general notion of 'correspondence' that which occurs through telecommunication or computer means (for example, e-mail or instant messaging programs such as Skype), or the one that occurs through any form of distant-range communication.[460]
The general case in point provided by Article 616 of the Penal Code is therefore unvaried: the article provides various hypotheses of crimes that damage other subjects' correspondence, all indictable as a result of personal prosecution and consisting of:

- acquiring knowledge of the content of closed correspondence not addressed to the agent;
- the subtraction or diversion of a closed or open correspondence not addressed to the agent, in order to acquire knowledge or let others acquire knowledge of the content;
- the destruction or suppression, total or partial, of other subjects' correspondence.

The second paragraph of the article examined, instead, regards the hypothesis of an agent that reveals the content of correspondence, totally or partly, without good cause.

1416. The only innovation brought by Statute 547/93, therefore, consists of an extension of the case in point that however has been severely criticized due to its total indeterminateness, that causes many problems on its interpretation and on the adaptation to new technologies (like, for example, the reference to 'any other form of distant-range communication').
Another problematic aspect, besides the terminological indeterminateness, concerns the effective operability of Article 616 of the Penal Code, with reference to

460. On this point Pica observes that 'we have to intend as correspondence the exchange of information and messages between determined persons, while the messaging destined to an undetermined public, for which no confidentiality is presumable, cannot be included and cannot therefore be object of penal protection in this place', *see* G. Pica, *cit.*, UTET, Torino, 1999, p. 173.

online (telematic) correspondence that occurs directly, namely through a self-owned mail server, or is mediated, namely by using a mail server generally supplied by providers. According to the commentators' opinions, indeed, it would be more adequate to the computer science reality to provide correspondence violations in the case in point in Article 617-*quarter*, rather than in Article 616 of the Penal Code.[461]

1417. Lastly, further problems have been posed on the hypothesis of concert of crimes, since the extension of Article 616 applies to every 'provision in this section' and therefore also for the cases in point provided by Article 618 (Revelation of the content of correspondence), 619 (Correspondence violation, subtraction and suppression performed by a subject in charge of mail, telegraph and telephone services) and 620 (Revelation of the content of correspondence performed by a subject in charge of mail, telegraph and telephone services) of the Penal Code.

With reference to the cases in point contained in Articles 619 and 620 of the Penal Code, in particular, to the extension is considered 'merely theoretical', since 'the particular subjective quality of the agent seems, in concrete, to render them less easily applicable, provided an exception for further developments that the public postal service will undergo under the profile of telematic communications'.[462] Further, since 2018 those articles can be activated by the injured person's complaint.

1418. In conclusion, therefore, the interpretative problems related to Article 616 of the Penal Code derive from the uncertain borders that belong to the computer and telecommunication technologies, so that clear distinctions, for example between 'open' and 'closed' correspondence, as well as between 'written' correspondence and 'oral phone communication', have lost their right to exist, since they are now incorporated and merged in the various communication modalities that new technologies allow.

§8. Communication Interceptions

1419. Some articles inserted by Statute 547/93 specifically refer to telematic communications such as Article 617-*quater* (interception, prevention or unlawful interruption of computer or telematic communications) and Article 617-*quinquies* (installation of devices apt to intercept, prevent or interrupt computer or telematic communications) of the Italian Penal Code.

It is necessary to immediately stress the terminological inadequacy of the legislation that indifferently refers to 'computer and telematic' communications, as communication performed by means of computer technologies can only be telematic.

461. *See* G. Pica, *cit.*, UTET, Torino, 1999, p. 173.
462. *See* G. Pica, *cit.*, UTET, Torino, 1999, p. 174.

The main characteristic of the conduct necessary to substantiate the crime is fraudulence.[463]

1420. With reference to the object of the protection, instead, doctrine has highlighted how the structure of the cases in point introduced by Articles 617-*quater*, 617-*quinquies* and 617-*sexies* of the Penal Code exceeds the scope of the protection of personal confidentiality and identifies a new kind of juridical good: 'the security of the computer or telematic system',[464] which consists of the genuineness (authenticity of the content) and confidentiality (knowledge or possible knowledge of information only by authorized subjects) of communications.

The crime requires personal prosecution, while the following aggravated circumstances are indictable offences:

- if the act is performed against a computer or telecommunication system used by the State or other public organizations or by enterprises that exercise public services or public-interest services;
- if the act is performed by a public officer or by a subject responsible for a public service, by abuse of his powers or infringement of the duties related to the function or service, or through the abuse of the quality of system operator;
- if the act is performed by anyone who exercises even abusively the profession of private investigator.

1421. Article 617-*quinquies* of the Penal Code, instead, punishes the installation of devices apt to intercept, prevent or interrupt computer or telematic communications, therefore recalling *in toto* the structure of Article 617-*bis* (installation of devices apt to intercept or prevent telegraphic or telephonic communications or conversations) leading to the observation that:

> the absolute structural identity of the case provided by Article 617-*quinquies* in comparison with the case that Article 617-*bis* already provides for the interception of telegraphic or telephonic communications or conversations, with a mere distinction of the forms of communication intercepted or to intercept, allows to deduce the unusefulness of the insertion of this new provision, that could have well been included in a new paragraph of the pre-existing Article 617-*bis* of the Penal Code, therefore avoiding the further proliferation of cases in point.[465]

463. Part of the doctrine has remarked how 'this fraudulence has to be intended in its objective meaning, namely as occult modality of interception performance, unbeknown to the subject that transmits the communication' (*See* G. Pica, *cit.*, UTET, Torino, 1999, p. 177). In other words, if instead there is, on behalf of the intercepted subject, a knowledge or consciousness of the action before this is carried out, the action will lack the requirement of fraudulence and the criminal case in point will not be substantiated.
464. *See* G. Pica, *cit*, UTET, Torino, 1999, p. 178.
465. *See* G. Pica, *cit.*, UTET, Torino, 1999, p. 181.

§9. Falsification

1422. Article 617-*sexies* introduces the crime of falsification, alteration or suppression of the content of telematic communications, therefore accomplishing, as with reference to Article 617-*quinquies*, a duplication of the case in point provided by Article 617-*ter* of the Penal Code (falsification, alteration or suppression of the content of telegraphic or telephonic communications or conversations).

The provision considers various forms of communication damaging, represented by falsity, alteration and suppression of the content and, since 2018, required the injured person's complaint.

The concept of 'falsity' includes all those activities aimed to undermine the authenticity of the communication; the word 'alteration', instead, refers to those activities aimed to modify the content of the communication, therefore rendering it non-conforming to the original; lastly, the word 'suppression' designates those activities that have an impact on the existence of the communication itself.

1423. Some categories of communication have to be ruled out from the provision examined: among these, correspondence (protected by Article 616 of the Penal Code), generic data or information and communications or conversations intervened between persons (already protected by Article 617-*ter*).

These distinctions, however, risk coming to nothing, as it is not easy to exclude 'generic data and information', since every telematic communication consists of data or information; likewise, interpretative problems are aroused with reference both to communications between persons (for example, chat or instant messaging services) or to correspondence (since, in absence of specific provisions, telematic correspondence can well be assimilated into the traditional one).

§10. Damaging

1424. Article 9 of Statute 547/93 has introduced a new crime by inserting Article 635-*bis*, titled 'Damaging of Computer or Telecommunication Systems', in the Penal Code.

The crime is included among the crimes against property, where 'property' has to be considered as the complex of active and passive judicial relationships, susceptible of economic evaluation, that belong to a person.

Damaging is a classic case of a crime against property, so that the legislature decided, in 1993, to insert the specific provision of damaging against computer structures immediately after Article 635 of the Penal Code and with the same conditions as the traditional case of damaging.

1425. The unlawful conduct provided by the new case in point is centred on the actions of destroying, deteriorating or rendering partially or totally unusable a computer or telecommunication system or programs, information and data there recorded and existing. 'The provision's expressions 'destroying', 'deteriorating', etc. have a precise meaning, that is 'to cause the destruction, the deterioration' of the good that is object of the action.'[466] Therefore the damage can be performed through both an omission and act.

1426. Moreover, the plurality of words used by the legislation to describe damaging conducts is not intended to render strictly the specific modality of the action but to point out every type of damage that can be caused to the good. Due to this reason, the provision contains words that are almost identical:

- 'to destroy' means to undo the thing, causing, namely, its total annihilation so that it is absolutely unusable for the function it had been destined to;
- 'to deteriorate' means to wreck something so that its instrumental function is impaired or, anyway, its value is considerably diminished (for example, to deteriorate a keyboard by breaking some keys);
- 'to render unusable' means to modify the thing so that it is not any more, temporarily or definitively, adequate for its intended use (for example, to remove the monitor of a computer).

1427. Therefore, with reference to hardware, namely the physical computer considered in its totality (complex of electric, electronic, optical, magnetic and mechanic components), 'destruction' will be any action that causes the loss of the original functional identity of the good, while 'deterioration' will be every kind of wear that renders its functioning unreliable, but the restoration of which is possible with the substitution of the single damaged component. This hypothetical possibility to repair the damage is exactly the distinctive characteristic of 'deterioration' in comparison with 'destruction'.

The conduct of 'rendering unusable' appears to be added to the conduct of total destruction or deterioration of the whole, while it maintains its own autonomy with reference to the cases of damaging single system components, that do not endanger its reuse, upon substitution of the damaged component.

1428. The subjective element required to assess the crime is specific malice, namely the conscience and will to destroy, deteriorate, dissipate or render totally or partially unusable computer or telecommunication systems that belong to others, besides programs, information and data belonging to others as well. The specific purpose of causing damage to others or to obtain a profit from the damaging is not required.

1429. Lastly, the psychological element of the damaging crime is identified in the conscience and will to damage, and motives or purposes due to which the crime is performed are not relevant. Even if the act takes place without the direct purpose of causing damage, but as a means to achieve a different purpose, there can be liability. The psychological moment of malice includes the awareness of the act and that the damaged thing belongs to someone else.

466. *See* G. Pica, *cit.*, UTET, Torino, 1999, p. 88.

But now, damage is probably the offence who has suffered the greatest distortion following the entry into force of Law no. 48/08. From a single offence brought by Article 9 of the Law no. 547/93, by which Article 635-*bis* of the Criminal Code was introduced with the title of 'Damage to Computer or Telecommunication Systems', there are now a variety of offences and, consequently, of articles of the Criminal Code.

Articles ranging from 635-*bis* to 635-*quinquies* can be defined as the regulatory set of rules on the crime of damage. These articles identify different types of damage, also according to the provisions of the Convention on Cybercrime, which in Articles 4 and 5 differentiates the conducts of 'damaging, deletion, deterioration, alteration or suppression of computer data without right' from those of 'serious hindering without right of the functioning of a computer system by inputting, transmitting, damaging, deleting, deteriorating, altering or suppressing computer data'.

The aggravating circumstances as well have been completely rearranged, first removing the reference to the aggravating circumstances of the general crime of damage and also providing two more aggravating circumstances for all crimes consisting in damage with violence to the person or threat and in performing the fact abusing the quality of the operator of the system.[467]

1430. 'System operator' is at least vague, since it does not identify any technical qualification of normative origin.

In the world of computer jobs, there are four 'typical' ranges of qualifications, divided in growing order of importance (under the profile of both technical and professional background and of responsibility): operators, programmers, system analysts, analysts.

– Operator: the subject who is appointed to input, output, computer start (bootstrap) or halt operations and to operate the console in order to check the regularity of its functioning, by manually performing, in case of need, operations of disk, tape, printout, upload or download.
– Programmer: the subject who has the task of writing in sequence the instructions (instructions that have to be written in a specific language that the computer can understand and that are organized in the most compact and rational way possible) necessary to accomplish the algorithm on which the program is based; – Systems analyst: the subject who has the task of studying and improving computers' operative systems (the so-called base software).
– Analyst: the subject who has the task of discovering and/or inventing and adjusting algorithms.

1431. Since all these four computer technicians operate on a computer and therefore, if they wanted to, they could more easily sabotage its software and hardware, they all seem to be included in the category of 'system operators' provided by the legislation with reference to computer crimes' aggravating circumstances.

467. *See* S. Aterno, 'Le fattispecie di danneggiamento informatico', in L. Lupària (ed.), 'Sistema penale e criminalità informatica' (Giuffrè, Milano, 2009).

Therefore, the function of the aggravating circumstance is exclusively to punish more severely those subjects who infringe the ban on the conduct by abusing their own personal and particular knowledge: the provision, however, does not refer to a general and abstract technical knowledge that the subjects has, even if highly sophisticated, but rather to the effective possibility to operate, in their capacity as persons for any reason in charge, on the specific violated system, about which the operator has a series of information that privileges him in performing the damaging (for example, he knows the access password, the structure of the various and possible access sills and the organization of stored data).

Article 635-*bis* now concerns only to information, data and software, and not also computer or telecommunication systems, which are included in a specific norm. Compared to the old formulation, in addition, the Legislator has better specified the conducts, providing for destruction, damage, deletion and alteration.

The non-aggravated offence can be proceeded by a complaint of the offended, while in the old formulation to the entire offence was punishable ex officio.

The two aggravating circumstances under which the crime can be prosecuted ex officio concern: (i) the conducts committed with violence to person or threat and (ii) the abuse of the quality of system operator.

It is evident that the Legislator has entrusted the protection of interests of private character to Article 635-*bis* which, not surprisingly, can be prosecuted after the complaint of the offended, except in the case of aggravating circumstances, while the protection of public data is entrusted to Article 635-*ter*, which, given the greater sensitivity of the data of public utility, can be prosecuted ex officio. It is to be noted, finally, that the Legislator punishes the 'fact directed to destroy, damage, delete, [...]' and not the 'destruction', 'deterioration', 'cancellation', etc., with a patent widening of the punishable conducts. They can be found, in fact, also in the case of no actual damage or deletion of data, even only for having performed an action that was likely to produce this effect.

The last issue concerns the identification of a system of 'public utility' included in Article 635-*quater*. These systems can be identified in all systems and equipment designed to meet the needs of public interest, irrespectively of their public or private property.

§11. Computer Fraud

1432. The criminal hypothesis contained in Article 640-*ter* of the Penal Code (computer fraud) has always aroused discussions in doctrine, since the enforcement of the statute, because the ambiguity of the word 'fraud' has caused many problems to interpreters, who would have probably preferred the more appropriate denomination of 'computer guile'. However, this does not mean that, in trying to identify a lowest common denominator of the various fraud hypotheses, this can be recognized only in the objective deceptive adequateness of the action, while the agent's subjective purposes, the psychological situation of the passive subject and the effective modality of action represent occasional variables that the legislature introduced online with the type of crimes to indict.

Likewise for the 'computer fraud', even in absence of any reference to leading someone astray, to artifices and to swindles, 'an objective deceptive adequateness of the action can be verified, since this is performed through the manipulation of computer systems, by altering and guiding their functioning according to logics that are consistent with the agent's intentions of unlawful profit but different from those wanted by the lawful proprietor and/or user of the system, and unbeknown to them'.[468]

By coordinating the character highlighted with reference to the interpretation of the word 'fraud' with the other basic requisite of the case in point, namely by coordinating the unjust profit with the damage to others (where, according to the most consolidated rulings, 'profit' has to be considered as any kind of advantage, also of a non-economic nature, and therefore even any kind of impoverishment of the victim's property, while 'unjust' refers to an achieved profit that consists of an advantage that does not belong to the agent), it is possible to include all the activities for which these stand as cause in the case in point of Article 640-*ter*. The doctrine states, indeed, that 'if the operation [of the agent of the fraud, *ndA*] is performed by altering the managing software of someone else's system, or the data contained in it, the subsisting crime will be of arbitrary exert of one's reasons by violence on goods, that, according to Article 392, paragraph 3 of the Penal Code, is integrated by any manipulation of data software'. Clearly, if this activity is aimed to voluntarily cause an impoverishment of the victim's property with consequent further pressure to accept conditions imposed by the producer, a violation of Article 640-*ter* also occurs.

§12. CYBERSTALKING

1433. Stalking crime was introduced in Italy by Law n. 38/2009 and is governed by Article 612-*bis* of the Criminal Code.

Cyberstalking is a harassment of a persecutory nature carried out mainly, or exclusively, with the aid of computer or telematic means and connected to electronic communication systems.

This particular case derives from the more general category of the crime of stalking, governed by Article 612-*bis* of the penal code, introduced in 2009 and titled 'Persecutory Acts'.

1434. The legislative decree 14 August 2013, n. 93 then added in the second Paragraph the aggravating circumstance of the 'fact committed through computer or telematic tools', flanking it with that of the crime committed against a subject linked to the perpetrator of the crime by a previous affective relationship.

1435. In spite of its name, the typical behaviour of the cyberstalker does not, however, realize a 'computer crime' properly so called but, as also happens for other crimes with free conduct, a criminal activity through the use of computer systems.

468. *See* G. Pica, *cit.*, UTET, Torino, 1999, p. 143.

1436. This offence can be counted among the crimes against *individual freedom* of people and against the particular aspect of their mental freedom; it has a residual nature because it does not apply in cases where the conduct assumes the features of a more serious crime.

It is not, therefore, a criminal hypothesis in its own right, but only a way in which a typical type of crime can come into being.

In order to have cyberstalking, a harassment by sending a simple e-mail or the use of common messaging services will not be enough, but it will be necessary to realize a real 'cyberstalking', meaning amplification of the harmful message and the annoying communication through the computer tool.

1437. It should not – in short – be criminalized the means by which one acts, confusing it with the purpose since, indeed, the casuistry does not report cases of stalkers who do not also use the electronic means to carry out their criminal conduct.

1438. According to the case provided for by the second Paragraph of Article 612-*bis* of the Italian Criminal Code, therefore, there is an amplification of the method of attack, using 'the IT or telematic tool' for the purpose of aggravating the harmful event.

1439. The reason for this, which is also at the origin of the expectation of the aggravating by the Legislator, is inherent in the nature of the attack and in the greater extent of its consequences.

1440. In recent years, in fact, there has been an exponential growth of the phenomenon, partly due to the increasing use and familiarity of electronic instruments and, in part, to the extreme ease, economy and speed of the medium, which make it a particularly weapon palatable and pernicious, if used for criminal purposes.

1441. As a consequence and corollary, this type of computer and telematic aggression can cause the victim far greater damage and extended to its sphere of relations than any other traditional means, precisely because of the diffusion and widespread use of the Web and its platforms in the public, by now certainly for the individual the 'social formations where his personality takes place' (*see* Article 2 of the Italian Constitution) of greater diffusivity and visibility, albeit digital.

1442. Consider, for example, the theft of credentials of the offended person, unauthorized access to his web pages, the possibility of introducing, in hypothesis, offensive or threatening phrases or images, such as to create damage that goes far beyond mere embarrassment, to get even the control of an entire computer system owned by the persecuted.

1443. Add to this the frequent anonymity of the cyberstalker, which can be hidden behind the computer screen (for example, by creating false profiles in a chat room, a newsgroup, a social network, etc.), which makes it difficult to identify the offender and secure the sources of evidence to reach his sentence.[469]

1444. According to the article, anyone who repeatedly, by any means, threatening or harassing someone in such a way to inflict serious psychological problems or to determine a justifiable fear for personal safety of self or someone close or however, to affect significantly its way of life, is punished, on complaint of the victim, by imprisonment from six months to four years.

1445. The text of the article literally states that 'Unless the act constitutes a more serious crime, is punished with imprisonment from six months to four years anyone who, with repeated conduct, threatens or harasses someone in such a way to cause a serious and continuing state of anxiety or fear, or to give rise to a justifiable fear for the safety of self or a close relative or person bound by the same loving relationship, and force himself to alter their habits of life'.

The deadline for applying for the lawsuit is six months. It is possible, however, to proceed ex officio if the offence is committed against a minor or a disabled person and when the fact is connected with another offence for which it is possible to proceed ex officio.

1446. The penalty is increased if the crime is committed by a spouse legally separated or divorced, or by a person who has been linked to emotional relationship to the victim.

The penalty is increased by up to half if the offence is committed against a minor, a pregnant woman or a disabled person, or by an armed person or a person who claims to be someone else.

The crime is punishable on a complaint of the victim.

1447. This crime includes not only the simple phone calls but also the use of SMS, MMS and e-mail.

The legal interests protected by this Law are, first of all, the moral freedom and the freedom of individual self-determination.

Furthermore, that criminal conduct could affect the constitutionally guaranteed human good health.

This Law represents a concrete response to the growing and worrying phenomenon linked to the commission of crimes of sexual violence perpetrated primarily against women.

This thorny issue of prevention and repression of crimes against the person has been previously, and in more than one occasion, discussed in the Italian Parliament.

1448. Until a lawsuit is brought for the offence referred to in Article 612-*bis* of the Penal Code, the victim may present the facts to a public security authority asking a formal *warning* against the author of the conduct.

---

469. *See* C. Parodi, 'Stalking e tutela penale: le novità introdotte nel sistema giuridico dalla l. 38/2009' (Giuffrè, Milano, 2009); G. Ziccardi-P.Perri 'Tecnologia e Diritto' (Giuffré, Milano, 2017).

1449. Moreover, in line with these provisions, Law n. 38/2009 has introduced a new coercive measure which consists in banning the possibility to stay close to the places frequented by the victim.

With the provision of the 'prohibition of approaching', the Court requires the offender not to approach certain places usually frequented by the victim, or to maintain a certain distance from such sites or the victim.

1450. If there are additional requirements for protection, the Court may order the offender not to approach certain places usually frequented by close relatives of the victim or by persons living with or otherwise related to this affective relationship or to maintain a certain distance from such places or by such persons.

1451. The Court may also prohibit the offender from communicating by any means (electronic means included) with the person.

As already anticipated, Article 612-*bis* of the Criminal Code is aimed at repressing those behaviours that, in the most varied forms, are characterized by their persecutory character.

These include, by way of example, not only simple phone calls and stalking, but also the 'distorted' use of SMS, MMS and e-mail, and also associated behaviours such as, sending and subscribing services not requested in favour of the victim, or even the termination of utilities, and even voice calls, with or without a reply.

1452. The typical nature of the conduct punished by the law, in the light of the now numerous, prevalent interpretative guidelines, is well defined.

1453. There is certainly a pluralistic offence, since the legal right immediately protected is, first and foremost, psychic freedom, as can be deduced from the systematic placement of the norm and, second, the physical safety and life of the passive subject, given the plurality of behaviours described and obtainable from the literal scope of Article 612-*bis* Italian Criminal Code.

1454. Physical violence is only a posthumous eventuality and is not necessary for the completion of the crime, which is characterized instead by:

(i) an atypical behaviour (i.e., not typed, in the sense that the offensive conduct can consist in any behaviour suitable to carry out the case), carried out with threatening or harassing acts;
(ii) frequent and repeated;
(iii) such as to cause 'a lasting and serious state of anxiety or fear' in the attacked party, or from 'generating a well-founded fear' for his safety or that of a next relative or other person who is emotionally connected;
(iv) or likely to cause an alteration of the victim's lifestyle.

1455. Therefore, it is a habitual crime and an event, characterized by reiteration, for which the identification of its most precise contours may be referred to the consolidated jurisprudence on mistreatment.

The action is, therefore, unique, although composed of several pipelines linked by a link of habituality and permanence and that is its protraction appreciably over time.

1456. Therefore, there must be more homogeneous and continuous, repeated and frequent behaviours, aimed at the realization of the harmful event.

Therefore, for example, a telephone call per year will not be sufficient, although repeated every year, in this case lacking the connotation of the frequency such as to integrate a 'habitual vexatious conduct' (*see* Cass. Pen., Section VI, 166250/1984), although not necessarily continuous, but also interspersed with moments of calm (*see* Cass. Pen., section VI, n. 183553/1989).

1457. The existence of the homogeneity, repetitiveness and frequency of the persecutory acts is, however, subject to the discretionary evaluation of the judge, with reference to the concrete case.

And this is how, in a recent past, there are more contradictory judgments, which make the jurisprudence of merit (even of legitimacy) particularly wavering.

1458. Article. 612-*bis* of the Criminal Code, in the second paragraph, states:

> The punishment is increased if the offense is committed by the spouse, even separated or divorced, or by a person who is or has been linked by an affective relationship to the injured party or if the offense is committed through computer or electronic means.

1459. As already mentioned above, a few years after the creation of the incriminating rule (Article 612-*bis*, introduced in 2009), the Legislator in 2013 decided to intervene to modify the original text, introducing a specific aggravating circumstance, which well it can be called 'cyberstalking'.

1460. As already mentioned if, on the one hand, even the use of SMS, as well as the pounding sending of e-mails, may fall within the *latu sensu* channel of this possible form of externalization, on the other hand, these modes are more properly referable to those 'classic' of perfection of the crime, well known since an age before the introduction of the Law 11/2009.

1461. In fact, only the medium with which the typical conduct is expressed changes, but in reality it always remains the same (for example, threat carried out with Skype or with voice MMS, rather than with the traditional landline connected to the common telephone line).

1462. The 'cyberstalking' and the related harassment, so that they can be said to be implemented by a real cyberstalker, will rather be those realized through the theft of digital identity, the activity of antiforensics, or the distorted use of social networks, or – in general – through the 'creative' use of IT means (in the most rigorous technical sense) to cause damage, embarrassment and, hence, anxiety and fear in the victim.

1463. There is now a case history both in the public prosecutor's offices and in the prefectures and police headquarters, of real cases of 'cyberstalking'; commons are, for example, cases of victims who, due to targeted attacks, were forced to cancel their profile on social networks.

1464. In the eyes of the operators, the 'fact committed through computer or telematic tools' is not represented by the simple e-mail or by the use of various messaging services, such as WhatsApp, or other.

As mentioned above, the *ratio* is not to criminalize the computer-telematic means (neutral in itself) but to verify the existence or not of the aggravating circumstance, verifying if the conduct was perpetrated by computer or telematic amplification of the harmful message.

Not the simple e-mail, therefore, if directed *ad personam*, so to speak but, for example, a massive, periodic and automatic sending of numerous e-mails can configure the aggravating circumstance here under consideration.

1465. What matters is, therefore, the use of the medium for the purpose, in order to realize an amplification of the attack, as such capable of causing more offence and damage to the target of the cyberstalker.

§13. CYBERBULLYING

1466. The procedure of formal *warning* against the author of the conduct is now applied also against the crime of cyberbullying, introduced in 2017 by the Law 29 may 2017 n. 71.

This law contains also the definition of cyberbullying as 'any form of pressure, aggression, harassment, blackmail, injury, denigration, defamation, identity theft, alteration, illicit acquisition, manipulation, unlawful processing of personal data to the detriment of minors, carried out electronically, and the dissemination of content online also concerning one or more members of the minor's family, whose intentional and predominant purpose is that of isolating a minor or a group of minors by carrying out a serious abuse, a harmful attack, or their ridicule'.[470]

1467. The victim of cyberbullying, who is at least 14 years of age, and the parents or those responsible for the minor, can present an application for the obscuration, removal or block to the data controller or operator of the website or social media of any other personal data of the child, disseminated in the Internet.

---

470. *See, generally*, M. Orofino, F. G. Pizzetti (eds.), *Privacy, minori e cyberbullismo*, Giappichelli, Turin, 2018.

If it is not provided within 48 hours, the interested party can contact the Privacy Authority that intervenes directly within the following 48 hours.

It is possible to activate all the measures provided by the Criminal Law, for example in the case of insults (Article 594 of the Criminal Law), defamation (Article 595), threat (Article 612).

1468. On 27 January 2014, the Democratic Party MP Elena Ferrara presented in the Senate the bill 'Provisions for the protection of minors for the prevention and contrast of the phenomenon of cyberbullying', designed to guarantee young and very young people a more secure and responsible digital experience.

The draft law S. 1261 was approved by unanimous vote on 20 May 2015 and was then transmitted to the Chamber for the continuation of the parliamentary procedure.

1469. Senator Ferrara herself had directly experienced the tragedy of one of her students, Carolina Picchio, who committed suicide at the age of fourteen on the night between 4 and 5 January 2013, after a video showing her drunk at a party was published on the Facebook platform.

1470. In the movie some boys, taking advantage of the state of unconsciousness due to the alcohol in which Carolina found herself, abused her by simulating sexual acts and humiliating her with obscene proposals.

1471. The images, besides being widespread among the girl's acquaintances, had also been published online, giving way to a series of insults and derisions that had caused a state of profound shame and prostration in the 14-year-old, so much so as to push her to take her own life.

1472. Precisely this episode represented the starting point for the start of the procedure for the approval of the Italian ad hoc law for the repression of the phenomenon of electronic bullying.

Thus, after a very troubled parliamentary process, which lasted three years, the law of 29 May 2017 was enacted n. 71, published in the Official Gazette on 3 June and entered into force on 18 June 2017.

1473. The first paragraph of Article 1 states that 'The objective is to counter the phenomenon of cyberbullying in all its manifestations, with preventive actions and with a strategy of attention, protection and education towards the children involved, both in the position of victims, and in that of responsible of illegal activities, ensuring the implementation of the interventions without distinction of age within the educational institutions.'

1474. It therefore appears evident that the intent of the law is strongly linked to awareness raising and explicitly aimed at protecting minors.

1475. Moreover, for the first time, with the law in question, we had in the Italian Code a legislative definition of cyberbullying, qualified as 'Any form of pressure, aggression, harassment, blackmail, insult, denigration, defamation, identity theft, alteration, illegal acquisition, manipulation, unlawful processing of personal data to the detriment of minors, carried out electronically, as well as the dissemination of content online also concerning one or more components of the child's family whose intentional and predominant purpose is to isolate a minor or a group of minors by implementing a serious abuse, a malicious attack, or their ridicule.'

1476. However, this definition is not homogeneous, as it combines de facto conducts (pressures, assaults, blackmail, identity theft) with legislative conducts (harassment, defamation, unlawful processing of personal data), some of which have been the subject of a decriminalization package in 2016, with the consequence that the law contains current crimes and decriminalized conducts.

1477. It is also interesting to note that the object of the discipline has been limited to cyberbullying, and no longer extended to bullying *tout court*: a small contradiction that sooner or later will have to be resolved, as it would seem inappropriate to leave all those unlawful acts excluded from the law performed daily by minors vis-à-vis other minors within the school walls or in places where children meet without the help of technology.

1478. Another aspect to be emphasized is the fact that the listing of the conducts carried out by the Legislator, far from being exhaustive, runs the risk of limiting the scope of the provision: it is indeed a shared opinion in doctrine the opportunity to introduce a final clause for the opening of the type 'unless the fact constitutes a more serious crime'.

1479. In Article 2, the provision in question provides that each victim of cyberbullying at the age of fourteen, as well as the parents and the responsibility of the child, may present to the data controller or website operator an application to obscure, remove or block the personal data of the child spread on the Web and perceived as harmful.

1480. When it is not possible to identify the data controller or the operator of the site or the social network, or when the latter, contacted by the interested party, has not taken steps to adopt the injunctive and prescriptive measures within 48 hours, it is possible to contact, via notification or complaint, the Privacy Authority, which intervenes directly within the next 48 hours.

1481. For the purposes of the law, any provider of information society services is included in the definition of website operator, with the exception of the provider of simple transport services (mere conduit), temporary storage (caching) and storage of information (hosting).

1482. Article 3 also provides for the establishment of a technical table for the prevention and contrast of cyberbullying, without burdens for public finance, since no type of emolument is given to the subjects participating in the work.

1483. The coordination of the technical table is entrusted to the Ministry of Education, University and Research, which must draw up an integrated action plan, in compliance with European directives on the subject, and set up a data collection system aimed at monitoring the evolution of the phenomenon.

1484. Information and prevention initiatives aimed at citizens must also be established, with the primary involvement of the socio-educational structures present in the area in synergy with the schools.

The Prime Minister, in collaboration with the Ministry of Education and the Communications Regulatory Authority, is entrusted with the task of activating periodic prevention and awareness campaigns on the main media.

1485. Article 4 sets guidelines for prevention and contrast in the school environment, also through the collaboration of the Postal Police and local associations.

1486. In particular, it is envisaged that in each institution a *referent* will be identified among the teachers with the task of coordinating the initiatives against cyberbullying, promoting an active role of students and former students in peer education activities, guaranteeing adequate training of the personnel education and providing support and rehabilitation measures for the children involved.

1487. Article 5 entrusts to the head teacher the task of promptly informing, unless the fact constitutes a crime, the families of the children involved and, if necessary, summon all the interested parties to adopt assistance measures in favour of the victim and sanctions and rehabilitation courses for the author.

1488. Article 6 is dedicated to the support measures provided for the activities of the Postal and Communications Police, which are also assigned annual reporting obligations to the technical table on the results of the law enforcement activity.

1489. Finally, Article 7 extends the warning procedure provided for by Article 612-*bis* of the Criminal Code for the crime of stalking: through this measure, as long as the victim has not made a complaint or presented a complaint for the crimes of insult, defamation, threat or unlawful processing of personal data committed through the Internet, the Questore, assuming if necessary information from the investigative bodies and hearing the informed persons on the facts, in the presence of at least one parent or other subject exercising parental authority, can summon the over-14-year-old minor responsible for cyberbullying acts, admonishing him orally about his conduct and urging him to restore a behaviour in accordance with the law.

The warning request can be presented at any police office and must contain a detailed description of the facts, of the persons in any way involved and any attachments proving the above.

1490. In this way, the Legislator wanted to make the children responsible while keeping them outside the penal circuit, with a provision that is fully consistent with the basic approach of the law, which aims to counter the phenomenon of cyberbullying with more educational than repressive actions.

§14. IDENTITY THEFT

1491. The 'identity theft', in the Italian criminal law system, is not regulated with a separate Article.

In the Italian legal framework, there are numerous predictions of crime that can be applied to the conduct at issue.

1492. First, the offence of *impersonation*, foreseen and punished by Article 494 of the Criminal Code.

1493. If the attack to the identity of others is, then, combined with an unauthorized access to a computer system or computer, to the possession of access codes or to the act of sending a virus, it includes the offences provided for and punished by 615-*ter*, 615-*quater* and 615-*quinquies*.

1494. There are, also, often two elements of traditional crime: fraud and computer frauds, according to Article 640 and Article 640-*ter*.

1495. On several occasions, the conduct also violates the provisions of Article 648-*bis* (illegal circulation of money) when financial managers are used; the unlawful processing of personal data, finally, is punished by Legislative Decree n. 196 of 2003 regarding privacy and Regulation (UE) n. 2016/679.

1496. The increasing use of the Internet has led to the creation of millions of digital identities, both as a representation of a natural or legal person within cyberspace and as a set of electronic codes that identify a physical subject in the virtual world.

1497. The concept of *identity* on the Web is related to the notion of IP (Internet Protocol), a numerical identifier that establishes the place of connection and that, being assigned when it connects to the network, can be easily combined with a telephone user and, therefore, to a natural person or to a specific place.

1498. Still on the subject of identity theft, Article 30-*bis* of Legislative Decree 11 April 2011, n. 64 establishes that identity theft means:

(i) total impersonation. Total concealment of one's identity through the appropriation of data relating to the identity and income of another person, whether alive or deceased;
(ii) partial impersonation. Partial concealment of one's identity through the combined use of data relating to one's own person and the improper use of data relating to another person.

1499. Obviously, this is a definition circumscribed by the legislative decree, but which directs the application of criminal cases and civil disputes concerning the appropriation of identification data of other people.

1500. In the digital world, identity can be an account, an e-mail address, a profile on social networks or in a role-playing game or all these elements together.

The creation of a false identity on the net, therefore, is an operation within the reach of anyone with basic computer skills, and this is considered one of the main reasons why, in recent years, the so-called identity theft has become one of the criminal phenomena most widespread in Italy.

1501. In fact, among users of the Internet and new technologies, the concept of changing and / or acquiring a new or others' identity for illicit purposes has become extremely simple.

1502. From a Legal Informatics point of view, identity theft is characterized by the presence of typical elements and, at the same time, of changing elements.

With regard to the typical elements, it should be noted first of all that, although the term *theft* has been coined, reference should not in any way be made to Article 624 of the Criminal Code: in this case, in fact, the term 'Theft' is used in order to indicate the conduct of a subject who appropriates someone else's digital identity, causing him harm.

1503. In the same way, the term 'identity' must be understood in a much broader way: indeed, in the present case, the theft can take place against the global identity of the subject or some parts of the identity itself, such as in the theft of sensitive data of the victim or, again, of medical, banking or social network account information to which the subject is registered.

Nevertheless, ad hoc legislation has not yet been dedicated to this offence within the penal code, although there have been numerous jurisprudential interpretations regarding identity theft.

1504. The crime of Article 494 c.p. it is a criminal phenomenon prodromal to the commission of further crimes, not necessarily against the heritage but also, by way of example only, through threats or defamation.

1505. The legal asset injured in the case of the creation of a false virtual profile on a social network or, more generally, on the net, is first of all that of the personal identity of the person impersonated, as protected by Article 2 of the Italian Constitution as well as by Article 9, legislative decree 14 August 2013, n. 93, subsequently converted into law 15 October 2013, n. 119.

1506. This decree inserts to Article 640-*ter* c.p. a penalty for the hypothesis in which the crime is committed 'with theft or undue use of the digital identity', providing for a penalty of imprisonment from two to six years and a fine from 600.00 euros to 3,000.00 euros if the action is committed using theft, or improper use, of the digital identity to the detriment of one or more parties.

1507. With this regulatory tool, however, the Legislator has not provided a precise definition of the concept of 'digital identity', nor has it clarified how theft should occur.

1508. As mentioned above, numerous crime cases are accumulated in the area of identity theft. As we will see, in our system, there have been numerous predictions of crime that the jurisprudence has deemed applicable to the conduct in question.

1509. Taking advantage of the instrument of extensive interpretation, the Supreme Court has, first of all, brought the case under Article. 494 c.p. ('Replacement of Person'), the new forms of aggression of digital identity.

1510. This crime is in fact easily achievable on the net, and the increasing use of social networks has become fertile ground for those who intend to take possession, unduly, of another person's personal data (name, surname, address, card number of credit, passwords, etc.) for unlawful purposes such as the execution of scams to the detriment of the victims.

1511. By way of example, Facebook does not carry out particularly strict controls on the veracity of a private profile.

It therefore appears very simple, for those who wish to use the Facebook tool for illicit purposes, to create false profiles, 'pass themselves off' for another subject by sharing personal data, communicating with other people or, in any case, compromising the victim's digital identity.

1512. According to the Italian Supreme Court, the conduct of the person who, through the creation of a profile that reproduces the effigy of a subject, uses his data to communicate or share the contents would complement the crime of substitution of person.

1513. In the same way, the use of the other person's Facebook profile image would integrate the crime referred to in Article 494 c.p.

1514. On this point, the Court ruled that even the creation of an e-mail account with a different name with respect to one's own could constitute the crime referred to in Article 494 c.p. provided that the users or site manager concerned are misled.

It is therefore necessary for the interlocutors to believe that they are communicating with a certain subject while they are dealing with a different person.

1515. In the present case, the Supreme Court found all the elements of the crime or the deception, the induction in error and the danger to the public faith configured.

1516. Still in the area of social networks, according to the Criminal Court of Cassation, the crime of replacing the person would be added to the creation of a Facebook profile illegally using the image of another person's profile, 'since it is a behavior suitable for the representation of a digital identity that does not correspond to the subject that uses it'.

1517. The techniques with which the personal information of the victims is taken are multiple and, over time, have become increasingly sophisticated.

1518. The implementation methods are changeable; it is a crime that takes shape and adapts to current technologies.

Identity theft was in fact born using electronic mail; the widespread use of mobile phones led to the theft of identity via SMS.

In recent years, the growing use (and abuse) of social networks has led the person who intends to carry out identity theft to act in that particular area.

1519. In addition to the so-called traditional techniques, such as the theft of an identity card, the most widely used and known technique is certainly phishing, a technique that aims to hit as many victims as possible, with the intent to steal passwords of access to home banking sites, e-mail accounts or infecting victims' computers so they can take control.

1520. Again with reference to the phenomenon of phishing, the Court of Milan recognized the competition between the various cases of personal substitution, fraud and unauthorized access to an IT or telematic system sanctioned by Article 615-*ter* of the civil code which provides, as a typical requirement of the criminal act, the presence of system protection measures.

1521. Moreover, having established that the digital identity theft conduct has its fulcrum in the subtraction of users' confidential data, further cases that could be relevant are those described in Article 615-*quater* p.p. and 615-*quinquies*.

1522. There are, in the Italian criminal code, two types of 'fraud', one pursuant to Article 640 c.p. and the second, a 'computer fraud', pursuant to Article 640-*ter* c.p.

On this point, even the doctrine questioned the possibility that the 'theft or undue use of digital identity' may appear conceived by the new c. 3, Article 640-*ter* c.p. only as an aggravation of computer fraud.

1523. According to part of the doctrine, the protection of the third paragraph, Article 640-*ter* c.p., will not be able to operate in the case of theft or undue use of the digital identity of others if they do not result in a decrease in assets.

1524. One of the characteristics of identity theft is the necessary, involuntary cooperation of the victim.

Generally, the agent aims at hitting a plurality of subjects, including those who, due to computer skills or culture on the subject, would hardly fall into a trap. In this way a sort of 'natural skimming' is carried out, in which the subject who intends to carry out an identity theft takes the following weaknesses of the victim as a target:

(i) computer incompetence. The victim does not realize that text messages or e-mail messages asking him to instal a software or to fill out forms are aimed at causing him harm;

(ii) deception brought about with tricks and deceptions and with accurate falsifications. In this case, the trap is so well designed that the victim will believe in the truthfulness of the message.

The perpetrator of the crime, masking the connections, providing the victim with telephone numbers to contact in case of need, will acquire the trust of the victim convincing her to keep certain behaviours; (iii) deception led to very high profits in a short time and in absolute safety. In this case, the offender will convince the victim to perform apparently legitimate financial transactions, ensuring that he has very high profits.

§15. Grooming Online

1525. The introduction of the crime of soliciting minors responds to the need to fulfil the obligations that Italy has assumed by signing the Lanzarote Convention of 2007, ratified and implemented with Law n. 172 of 2012.

1526. The Convention, in fact, required the signatory States to adopt the necessary measures to prevent any form of sexual exploitation and abuse against children and, to this end, required the introduction of new crimes, including the one of soliciting minors.

1527. In particular, Article 23 of the Lanzarote Convention has provided to States the obligation to adopt specific legislative measures to render the conduct of those who, in order to perform sexual acts with minors or to produce child pornography material, propose to a minor a meeting through the use of communication and information technologies, on condition that the proposal is followed by material documents referable to the said meeting.

1528. The purpose of this case is to anticipate the threshold of punishment before the actual meeting between the victim and the groomer, in order to protect the child but, at the same time, aims to ensure compliance with the principle of offensiveness by ensuring that repression criminal intervene only when the agent's criminal intentions have assumed a concrete dimension through the actual organization of the encounter with the victim.

1529. The objective pursued by Article 23 is to contain the phenomenon of the so-called child grooming, that is, the solicitation of the child on the Internet by means of psychological manipulation techniques such as to vitiate the will of the victim and create a relationship of trust for the purposes of abuse.

1530. In Italy, the ratification and implementation of Article 23 of the Convention took place with the approval of Law 172/2012 with which Article 609-*undecies* p.p. which punishes anyone, for the purpose of committing one or more crimes related to the exploitation or sexual abuse of minors, acquiring a minor of the sixteen years, unless the fact constitutes a more serious crime.

1531. The legislative provision, in order to eliminate the risk of indeterminacy of the case, was completed with an explicit definition of solicitation, understood as any act aimed at gaining the trust of the child through artifices, flattery or threats put in place also through the use of technologies.

1532. Comparing Article 609-*undecies* and Article 23 of the Convention, it is immediately evident the fact that the Italian Legislator has disregarded the guidelines, elaborating a case of autonomous solicitation different from that traced in the European offices.

1533. In terms of the objective element, Article 23 of the Convention places the threshold of punishment of child grooming at an advanced stage and, that is, at the moment in which the groomer has already performed executive acts aimed at meeting with the minor.

1534. On the contrary, in Article 609-*undecies* disappears any reference to the 'meeting proposal' and to the presence of 'material acts attributable to it', expressions replaced by a generic reference to the 'soliciting' conduct that goes beyond any appointment proposed to the minor.

1535. Consequently, the Italian legislator has provided for a drastic retreat of the punishment threshold, as it punishes the facts of solicitation not only when there are no executive acts aimed at organizing the meeting with the minor but also when there has been no proposal for meeting: in essence, child grooming is punished already in the construction phase of the relationship of trust with the child, provided that the person acting for the purpose of committing one of the sexual crimes indicated by the law.

1536. Under a second profile, the Italian Legislator has included in the field of application of Article 609-*undecies* also facts committed against infants and children, despite the Lanzarote Convention refers to minors who are unable to express a valid consent in sexual matters and, therefore, in our system, to children under 14.

The extension of the punishment to the case of subjects between the ages of 14 and 16 creates misunderstandings, above all in the cases in which the adherent, even if resorting to artifices and flattery, pursues the purpose of carrying out consensual sexual acts with the 15-year-old minor and therefore pursues legitimate and extraneous aims to the specific intent described by Article 609-*undecies*.

1537. Finally, unlike the provisions of the Lanzarote Convention, which described solicitation as a conduct committed essentially via the Internet or other means of communication, Article 609-*undecies* punishes any form of child grooming by merely identifying the use of technologies as one of the possible typical methods of conduct.

1538. In this way, the scope of application of the standard has been further extended based on the consideration that an enticement behaviour that occurs offline has the same offensive scope as an online conduct and is equally detrimental to the freedom of self-determination and the psychophysical integrity of the minor.

1539. The case in point envisaged by the Italian Legislator is configured, therefore, as a crime of so-called indirect danger, since the criminal repression is anticipated for preparatory conduct of crimes that remain confined to the subjective sphere of the offender and in relation to which have not yet been realized deeds suitable and unambiguously directed to their commission, so that a punishable attempt of the offences pursued by the agent, capable of absorbing the negative value of the facts of enticement, cannot be configured.

1540. The repression of crimes of indirect danger has raised wide debates in doctrine about the compatibility with the constitutional principles of offensiveness and proportion. Therefore, in order to recover a minimum threshold of offensiveness, it is essential to carry out a punctual screening of the concrete suitability of the conduct to achieve the aim pursued by the agent and a rigorous assessment of the specific intent, in relation to which it is necessary for the criminal purpose that soul and the mind of the offender is reflected in the concrete acts put in place.

1541. Article. 609-*undecies*, in fact, configures the solicitation of minors as a specific crime.

The Italian Legislator has chosen to include in the subject of specific intent all the cases put in place to protect the individual personality of the children.

Consequently, for there to be a criminally relevant enticement, it is necessary that the offender acts in order to commit the crimes of reduction or maintenance in slavery, child prostitution, child pornography, sexual violence, sexual acts with a minor, corruption of a minor or group sexual violence.

1542. The harmful value configured by the incriminating rule does focus not only on the basic ground of enticement but also on the teleological relationship between the latter and the illicit aim pursued.

The enticement conduct, therefore, constitutes the means for the attainment of the crime object of the specific intent, and, only where this instrumental connection exists, the basic fact of solicitation can be said to be typical and criminally relevant.

1543. These considerations require the judge to carry out a rigorous assessment of the suitability of the conduct to achieve the specific purpose pursued by the agent through the examination of objective elements capable of revealing to an external observer the purpose pursued by the giver, not being able to apply the case in point when the real intent of the groomer remains completely uncertain.

1544. As regards the methods of execution of the crime, Article 609-*undecies* p.p. requires that the perpetrator performs any act aimed at gaining the child's trust through artifices, flattery or threats.

1545. These methods constitute an essential element of the typical fact and must necessarily exist for the purposes of the integration of the criminal offence which is therefore configured as a restricted offence and, therefore, in the event that the conduct does not include the modus described in the rule, it will not be sufficient to supplement the details of the crime.

1546. The artifices, the enticements and the threats have in common the fact of being three mechanisms to which the recruiter can resort to exert a strong psychological leverage on the victim and to obtain his artificial cooperation, annulling the defence capacity and the freedom of self-determination of the minor.

1547. In particular, the artifice can be defined as a simulation, dissimulation, a deceitful and lying device capable of deceiving the victim and attracting her into the criminal plot devised by the offender.

1548. The concept of flattery, however, evokes conduct consisting in adulating, falsely gratifying, turning fake and excessive attention in order to win the sympathy and benevolence of someone to induce him to a certain behaviour.

1549. Finally, the Legislator has foreseen that solicitation can take place through threats and, that is, through the prospect of a future and unjust evil, whose verification depends on the will of the agent, and which presents itself suitable to generate a fear in the passive subject.

Chapter 3. Application of Criminal Procedure Law in the Area of ICT

§1. Modifications to the Penal Procedure Code Enacted by Law N. 547/93 and Law N. 48/2008

1550. The Italian *Criminal Procedure Code* was amended during the last 25 years, in order to facilitate the work of investigators and procedural mechanisms in case of events related to computer crime.

In particular, the topics that were covered during the year were that of telecommunication interception, that of acquiring the correct source of digital evidence and that of law enforcement, or covert, in telecommunication environments (with particular reference to cases of child pornography).

The changes, however, have not been many. Traditional institutions in the Code are often adapted without difficulty to the new technological framework.

1551. The first changes date back to 1993.

The Commission appointed to modify the Criminal Code in order to include those crimes that have as their object or means, an electronic processor, has also dealt with some provisions of the Criminal Procedure Code, in particular, for what concerns the interception of information or telematic communications: it has proposed, through Articles 11, 12 and 13 of Law n. 547/93, the insertion of Article 266-*bis* in the Criminal Procedure Code ('Interception of Computer and Telematic Communications') and the modification of Article 268 (relating to the execution of interception operations).

This choice was justified, by the bill's accompanying report, with the 'exigency to prepare more adequate forms of penal protection against the so-called computer criminality … jointly with the proposal to reassess the substantial cases in point of the Criminal Code'.

1552. It is useful to immediately observe that the provision contained in Article 266-*bis* allows the interception of the flow of communication between computer and telecommunication systems in all those cases in which the proceeding's object is the assessment of crimes performed by employing computer or telematic technologies.

On the object of the examined provision, that is 'telematic flows', doctrine and jurisprudence agree that this expression has to be identified with the collection, by means of computer or telematic instruments, of restricted communications or correspondences.

The strict hypothesis in which the interception of conversations or communications is allowed is the same provided by Article 266 of the Criminal Procedure Code and refer in particular to proceedings that regard: unintentional crimes for which the punishment provided is life imprisonment or imprisonment five years over the maximum, determined according to Article 4 include: (i) crimes against Public Administration for which the punishment provided is imprisonment not less than a maximum of five years, determined according to Article 4; (ii) crimes concerning drugs or psychotropic substances; (iii) crimes concerning weapons or explosive substances; (iv) crimes of contraband; (v) crimes of insult, threat, usury, abusive financial activity, harassment or disturbance of persons through a telephone; (vi) crimes provided by Article 600-*ter* (child pornography); (vii) ordinances relating to crimes performed through the use of computer or telematic technologies.

1553. The interception of flows, even if regards a computer or telematics communication, is subject to the general regulation provided by Article 266 of the Criminal Procedure Code with reference to its admissibility; therefore, the public prosecutor has to request the judge for preparatory investigations to authorize the disposition of interception operations, except in urgent cases in which the public prosecutor can dispose of the interception through a motivated ordinance that has to be validated within 48 hours from its issuance.

The length of interception operations cannot exceed 15 days, renewable by the judge for another 15 days.

1554. Regarding Article 268 c.p.p. that concerns the instruments the interception of computer or telematic communications can be performed with, Statute 547/93 has provided the inclusion of the possibility to perform interceptions through systems belonging to private parties that cannot deny their disposability. The implementation of the 2001 Council of Europe Convention on Cybercrime (Budapest Convention on Cybercrime) is done with Law of 18 March 2008 n. 48. Changes also affected the Code of Criminal Procedure. From the words used, it is clear that, for the first time, there is a legislator's attention to the techniques of computer forensic to search for digital evidence. Where the inspections cover digital traces, under Article 244 as amended, any technical operation in relation to computer systems or telecommunications must adopt technical measures aimed at ensuring the preservation of the original data and prevent the alteration. During the search, as amended by Article 247, where there are grounds to believe that data, information, software or other evidence relevant to the offence are in a computer system or computer, even if protected by security measures, the investigator must adopt technical measures aimed at ensuring the preservation of the original data and prevent tampering. The amended Article 352 authorizes law enforcement officers, adopting technical measures for the conservation and to prevent the alteration, to search the computer systems or computer, even if protected when there is reason to believe that there are hidden data, information, computer programs or traces still relevant to the offence that might be deleted or missing. The judicial police officers shall, also, adopt technical measures or provide prescriptions necessary to ensure preservation and prevent tampering and access, and provide, where possible, the bit-stream image copy to appropriate supports, through a procedure that ensures compliance of the original copy and its immutability.

Law n. 48 of the 18 March 2008 introduced in the Italian Code of Criminal Procedure some important rules on inspection and searching activities of computers or telecommunication networks.

The extreme volatility of the electronic data, in fact, has forced the Legislator of the Budapest Convention and, consequently, the Italian one, to indicate specific modalities to ensure a proper preservation of the data integrity, thereby fully incorporating the computer forensics in the Italian Criminal Procedure Code.

§2. The Role of Computer Forensics in Criminal Procedure Law

1555. The widespread diffusion of computers in every productive area, as well as in any private house, connected with the escalation of the so-called computer crimes, effectively represents a new challenge for investigators, who are forced to search for proof among the data contained in electronic processors, with all the possible consequent problems related to the adoption of investigative protocols, methods and procedures that are not yet fully standardized and accepted both by courts and by the defence.

For this reason, many foreign government bodies have produced, in these last years, investigative handbooks (*see, for example*, the handbook edited by the United States Department of Justice titled *Searching and Seizing Computers and Obtaining Electronic Evidence in Criminal Investigations*) that summarize the main points that have to be considered when investigating a computer crime (performed on or through a computer) or an electronic processor that could contain important data for the assessment of a certain crime.

1556. The regulation of computer forensics dates back to 1984, to the occasion of the development, by FBI and other American investigative agencies, of programs to employ in the extraction and analysis of data contained in a computer.

A very recent definition describes *computer forensics* as 'the discipline that combines elements of law and computer science to collect and analyse data from computer systems, networks, wireless communications, and storage devices, in a way that is admissible as evidence in a court of law'.

1557. The creation of CART (*Computer Analysis and Response Team*), that had the specific aim of helping investigators in the search of so-called digital evidence, dates back to the first half of the 1980s and inside the FBI as well. The whole regulation is focused on this principle and on its consequences with reference to identification, storage, analysis and production in court.

The expression 'digital evidence', coined in the US, flows into the general discipline concerning the research and analysis of evidence typical of common-law juridical systems: it is defined as information stored or transmitted in digital form that has a probative value. In particular, the use of the word 'evidence' implies, in the Anglo-Saxon world, the judicial nature of the digital data that is therefore collected for a trial. The merely judicial relevance of the matter is equally underlined by the use of the adjective 'forensics' that precisely means 'to be produced in court'. The acquisition of digital data, therefore, will start when the information and/or the hardware are collected or stored with the purpose of examining them to form proof in a trial.

1558. The first step of the forensics procedure of digital data collection has to be recognized in the identification of digital data. Once the kind of existing evidence and its location are known, it is in the first place necessary to determine the procedures to perform for its recovery. One of the most frequent errors, on this point, is to assume that only computers can be the object of computer forensics, while effectively the concept can be extended to any electronic device able to store information, like mobile phones, electronic diaries and smartphones. Furthermore, the forensics examiner has to be able to identify the kind of information stored in a device and its format, in order to choose the most appropriate technology for the extraction.

1559. A particularly crucial aspect is represented by the storage of digital evidence since it is necessary to guarantee the integrity and non-rejectability of the collected element. These should be assured, first of all, through a correct procedure of collection and storage of the supports that contain the data and, second, through the employment of instruments of analysis that produce repeatable results without altering the original contents. It is by accident that the traditional regulation of American computer forensics refers to the 'chain of custody' that designates the procedure or complex of procedures necessary to guarantee the integrity and authenticity of the evidence from the moment of its identification, through its collection, to its production in court.

To allow the establishment of proof in a real cross-examination with all the guarantees of the case, as provided by the Italian Penal Procedure Code, evidence has to be stored in order to be preserved against any possible alteration, to let the prosecution and the defence carry out the necessary investigations, obtain expert testimonies and valuations.

1560. There are, however, some circumstances in which a modification of the data is practically inevitable, but it is still important for this alteration to influence the digital evidence as little as possible: it will therefore be necessary to record and motivate any intervention particularly invasive and apt to corrupt the correct seizure of evidence, by adopting the procedure determined by Article 360 c.p.p. that provides proper guarantees for the unrepeatable technical ascertainments (advance notice to the enquired person, the offended person and the defence attorneys, as well as to the respective technical experts).

1561. Once the collection activity is completed, the activity of analysis of the digital evidence has to be carried out, and in this delicate operation the technical expert will have to identify the best means with which to handle the digital evidence in order to exclude every possible contamination that could falsify the result of the activity of the experts. The results of the scientific test, indeed, can be accomplished:

> sometimes through the employment of new and not yet undisputed methodological and operative options . . . pertinent to the present cultural heritage of science and technology, with reference to the highly specialized content of

which the judiciary actions of control on consultancy and of application of probative inference criteria and the conclusive decision of the judge on the confirmation or falsification of the hypothesis of reconstruction of the event prospected by the parts are both problematic.[471]

On this point, the scientific world has doubted the juridical validity of forensic analysis systems based on closed-source software, since the impossibility to access the source codes of the program, and therefore to effectively understand its functioning, would constitute an undue denial of the right of defence, while open-source software should be preferred due to its 'transparency'.

1562. The last step of the forensics procedure regards the exhibition of the digital evidence, matter into which flow the formalities of the exhibitions, the competences and qualifications of the expert, as well as the scientific nature of the procedures adopted to identify, extract and analyse the evidence. The peculiar characteristic of computer forensics that distinguishes it from every other area of the ICT sector is the requirement that the final result has to come from a procedure scientifically acceptable and compliant with the principles of the juridical system and Procedure Codes and its inadmissibility into the trial as the punishment for its deficiency. For these reasons, recently, also universities are dedicating proper attention to this emerging discipline.

§3. The Scope of Computer Forensics

1563. A widely known and exhaustively studied discipline in the US, computer forensics has recently reached Italian courts, with all the evident problems caused by the different probative systems of common law and private law, and, even before, by the definition of the questions computer forensics is based on. Computer forensics can be divided into network forensics if its object consists of computers connected in a network; computer forensics, if its object is only one electronic processor; electronic forensics, if its object consists of electronic components; and the recently emerging mobile forensics, aimed at the seizure of evidence on mobile phones.

1564. Computer forensics is a complex of activities involving 'the storage, identification, acquisition, documentation and interpretation of data contained in a computer'.[472]

It is likewise very important to identify the moment at which, in the presence of a probative need, forensics start having a determinant role. Scholars agree nowadays that it is an activity that has to be carried out *post mortem*, namely after a

---

471. *See* G. Canzio, *Prova scientifica nel processo penale*, in *Decisione giudiziaria e verità scientifica*, Quaderni della Rivista Trimestrale di Diritto e Procedura Civile, n. 8, Giuffrè, Milano, 2005, pp. 55 ss.

472. *See* C. Maioli, Dar voce alle prove: elementi di informatica forense, in P. Pozzi and others, Crimine virtuale, minaccia reale, Franco Angeli, Milano, 2004, p. 67.

so-called computer accident has occurred, in order to extract and analyse the data present in the system, reconstruct the event and evaluate its possible relevance in trial.

Objectives of this discipline are, therefore, the various types of analyses that can be carried out on devices, data or even on telematic communications.

In the scope of computer forensics we can, for example, include the analysis of hard disks, and removable supports (for example CD-ROM, DVD, etc.), analysis that will require that the expert possesses all the skills necessary for the full comprehension of the physical structure of the support that is being examined, as well as of its functioning, of the logical structure employed to store data, etc.

1565. These technically complex activities (the most complex operations of recovering and analysis are carried out in so-called white rooms, namely structures supplied with particularly sophisticated systems of analysis, apt to recover data even from ruined supports or from supports treated with expedients) have been progressively simplified, thanks to the development of specific tools that allow the automation of various steps of the acquisition procedure (among the best known are, for example, *EnCase*, *Autopsy*, *Addrescue* and *The Sleuth Kit*). This does not, however, impact in a significant way on the competences of the expert, who has to be able to interpret the output of the software in order to render it comprehensible to the parties in a trial.

1566. Besides software and hardware data, as previously stated, the communication of data can also be the object of the computer forensics. This will focus, according to the specific probative needs, on a part of or on all the information generated by a user and transferred through the most varied modalities (Wi-Fi, analogical, ISDN, optical fibre, etc.), in compliance with the procedures provided for computer or telematic interceptions.

§4. Best Practices to Follow for a Correct Acquisition of Digital Evidence

1567. Law n. 48/2008 points out the requirements that a best practice must accomplish to be accepted in courts. In particular, a paragraph 1-*bis* is added to Article 352 of the Code of Criminal Procedure:

> 1-*bis*. In the act of the offence, or in the cases referred to in paragraph 2 when occurring the assumption and other conditions set out therein, the judicial police officers, adopting the technical measures directed to ensure the preservation of the original data and to prevent their alteration, shall also proceed to the search of computer or telecommunication systems, even protected by security measures, when they have a reasonable motive to believe that in these there might be hidden data, information, software or traces anyway relevant to the offence that can be deleted or be lost.

This norm describes the hypothesis where the search initiated by the judicial officers is always done in an appropriate way, to preserve the integrity and the non-alteration of the source of digital evidence, even if that source of evidence is on systems protected by security measures. In this sense, the first commentators to the law found very difficult, if not impossible, to violate a security measure of a computer system without compromising its integrity.

Other changes included the second paragraph of Article 354 of the Code of Criminal Procedure:

> 2. If there is danger that things, tracks and places mentioned in paragraph 1 may be altered or lost or otherwise modified and the public prosecutor cannot act in good time, or he did not have yet taken the direction of the investigations, the officers of judicial police shall perform the necessary verifications and assessments on the state of the places and things. In relation to data, information and computer programs or computer or telecommunication systems, the officers of the judicial police shall, also, adopt the technical measures or provide for the needed requirements to ensure the conservation and to prevent the alteration and access and they provide, where possible, to their immediate duplication on the appropriate media, using a procedure that may ensure the conformity of the copy to the original and that it is not modifiable. If necessary, they seize the material evidence of the crime and the things relevant to this.

Where it is prescribed that in case of possible alteration, dispersion or modification of things, tracks and places there shall be adopted systems of duplication of the data under investigation, adopting technical procedures that ensure the conformity with the original and that they are not modifiable, being always possible to proceed to the seizure.

As Maioli rightly stated, 'as in other forensic ambits, also in computer forensics it is and useful to prepare a list of actions that have to be carried out and to punctually report the activities and tasks carried out in relation to each of them'.[473] The scholar, therefore, by adapting some guidelines to the national system, sets a possible checklist and supplies one of the first examples of a correct protocol to follow in case of investigations concerning a computer instrument.

In particular, the procedure consists of the following steps:

- accurate verification of the state of every magnetic support;
- inspection of spaces under the keyboard and the monitor in order to find a valid access;
- reconstruction, if required by the case, of the way the unauthorized access to the network occurred, perhaps by employing Intrusion Detection Systems (IDS) that prove to be very useful to trace the path of data inside the network and the source of origin of malicious data;
- individuation of the presence of viruses, rootkits or other malicious software;
- reconstruction of the succession of tasks and actions;

473. *See* C. Maioli, *cit.*, p. 70.

- confrontation of clues;
- individuation of the role vested in the whole dynamic of the event by the system that is the object of the investigation (if it is, for example, a target or only used to launch an attack to another system);
- redaction of a list of all the subjects who had access to that particular information system, in order to identify possible subjects acknowledged on the event, or simply to be able to supply information on the configuration of a certain network or system;
- redaction of an accurate inventory of the inspected instruments; and
- double repetition of the analysis, in order to verify the meticulousness of the performed operations.

This list is obviously adaptable and configurable according to the different situations and can reasonably be considered as a best practice of digital data recovery for trial purposes.

1568. But not only the Academy supplies guidelines but also various public order forces are developing evidence-acquisition protocols. However, the lack of a common protocol that would create uniform procedures with a consequent optimization of investigation activities is still felt.

The State Police, having a department assigned to the persecution of computer crimes, has set some principles of correct digital evidence acquisition that deserve closer examination.

For the police, the operation of computer acquisition is equal to any other forensic activity that is performed in order to find clues useful to the investigation of the *scena criminis* (taking pictures, detecting fingerprints and/or blood traces). In digital investigations, as in traditional ones, it is not possible, indeed, to know, already during technical operations, which data will be used as proof; therefore, the purpose of this phase is to save all the digital information available, in order to select the relevant ones in a further phase.

On this point it is adequate to note that:

- the object of the acquisition procedure is the copy of bit;
- the operation has to be carried out with modalities apt to guarantee that every single bit contained in the support is effectively copied, even if hiding, deleted and/or overwritten (so-called bit-stream copy).

1569. In order to let everything be carried out in the most genuine way possible, therefore, it will be necessary to perform a priori an accurate initialization of the supports where the digital evidence will be collected, by using wiping procedures adequate to assure that the support where the copy is being saved does not contain any remains of previous data; equally, another necessary operation is the verification of the connections of the system examined, as well as of the connected devices and of their state (for example, to establish if an Internet or intranet connection is active, if there are external memorization units or even devices containing memories or hard disks apt to store data, such as printers).

1570. Once the described preliminary operations have been accomplished, the acquisition technique will have to be calibrated according to various factors, with reference to which it is possible to identify, roughly, four different modalities of intervention:

(1) If the system is not in function and the data acquisition is not urgent, the acquisition can be carried out in a laboratory.
(2) If the system is not in function but it is necessary to immediately accomplish the acquisition of data, due to investigative exigencies or to proceed with inspections, the state of the connections and the various devices has to be verified; it will then be possible to turn on the system, while avoiding the modification of existing data. Indeed, if the system is started with the ordinary procedure (namely, the procedure performed daily by every user), of the operating system and of the other programs installed to automatically run during each could modify important elements, and in particular the data contained in the various chronological registers in which the system records events, besides the data contained in the so-called virtual memory (a portion of fixed disk used to store data destined to the processing in order to destine the most performing part of the RAM memory only to those operations that require speed in their execution).

To avoid such inconveniences, after having disconnected the supports that have to be analysed, the next step will be to start the system and access the basic input-output software (BIOS). After writing down the system time and date, one should modify the BIOS layout, so that the next start of the system will be carried out through external devices (for example, floppy disk or CD-ROM drive, USB door, flash memory and network connections) that are assuredly intact and clear of viruses (this happens through a procedure called 'cold boot').

Afterwards, the supports that have to be examined can be reconnected and the system can be restored in function, providing, however, that, through the external device, an adequate program is run to start the bit-stream copy of what is contained in the supports.

There are different types of software able to perform these copying operations, among which, besides those already cited (*EnCase*, *Autopsy*, etc.), there is the open-source program POLCAT, developed by mail and communications police operators.

Besides these appropriate types of software, the acquisition can be performed also by employing dedicated hardware, so-called write blockers, namely devices that allow the bit-by-bit copy of the content of a support while inhibiting any writing operation on the original support, and therefore guaranteeing the inalterability of the evidence.

The integrity of the acquired data can be guaranteed and verified through the employment of a hash algorithm. This is a particular kind of unidirectional mathematical function – in theory invertible, but not so in practice – through which the digests are obtained: these are 'summaries' of predefined and limited dimension, derived from bit sequences of variable length, that obviously have to be identical when the hash is applied to both the original and the copy. The most used algorithms in computer forensics are the *Message Digest* 5 (MD5) that however has recently been the object of successful cryptanalytical attacks that have therefore proved the vulnerability of this algorithm and its probable unusability in forensics, and the *secure hash algorithm* 1 (SHA1).

The verification through hash on two supports, one of which is original and one copied, is sufficient to state with reasonable certainty, provided no inconsequences appear (namely, the production of two different *digests*) with reference to the application of the hash, the authenticity of the support on which the operations of extraction and analysis of digital evidences take place.

Once the phase of data acquisition is completed, the next step is the filing-storage of the digital evidence, so the copy of the whole content of the disk (the so-called image copy) to analyse will be divided, if necessary, into a series of *files* that will be copied on non-rewritable supports, with the precaution of closing the burning session to prevent the possibility of further data additions. Obviously, also the physical integrity of the original support, the object of the seizure, has to be taken care of, by protecting it from bumps, excessive humidity or heat and most of all from magnetic fields.

(3) In case the system is in function and it is necessary to proceed to data acquisition, *in primis* the system has to be isolated (so-called *green circle*). These operations can, of course, be influenced by various factors such as the type of system to examine, the operating systems used in that certain system, the importance of the data the system contains, the eventual connections to a LAN or to the Internet, the necessity not to endanger, as far as possible, the licit activities running (in case, for example, one is working on a server).

All these elements will lead to the choice of the actions that will allow the following analysis of the data contained in the system, always in the attempt of balancing the needs of continuity of the system and of genuineness (veracity) of the evidence with the exigencies of rapidity in the execution.

Except in particular cases, the isolation consists, first of all, in circumscribing the area in which the devices are contained and excluding unauthorized use, in order to protect the integrity of the magnetic supports and of the data they contain. It will therefore be convenient to carry out a sort of 'freezing' of the system and acquisition of the data.

At this point, a precise order in the collection of the so-called volatile data has to be followed.

The first step will be to proceed to a meticulous observation of what is represented on the screens of the various computers, documenting it with photographs and, if necessary, through the print of the various visual displays.

The second step will be the saving of eventual open documents, on a floppy disk or on another support the use of which does not cause significant modifications of the system. By doing this it will also be possible to identify the programs running at the moment.

Successive steps, performed through the use of proper software, are the access to the system in secure mode (so-called trusted console), the memorization of the system's date and time, the identification of the users connected to the system, the recovery of the data contained in the RAM memory and in the virtual memory, the verification and memorization of all the processes that are active in the system (programs run for the automatic performance of certain operations on the system called 'demons', automatic execution programs, etc.), as well as of the connections to the net or to other eventual devices. Once this procedure is concluded, the analysis phase is next, with modalities that allow the repeatability of the analysis itself.

In case it becomes necessary to shut down the system for the purposes of its examination, the repeatability of acts can be guaranteed only if all the precautions described at point (2) are carried out. In case it is not possible to shut down the system without causing serious damage (let us think of computer systems that superintend critical structures), the activities of immediate analysis cannot have the feature of absolute repeatability. The police recognize that this case can be allowed only in a procedure of urgent inspection, ex Article 364, 5 and 6 paragraph c.p.p. (4). In case the computer system in function can be deactivated and seized to be analysed successively, the non-repeatable acts still have to be performed, as provided in point (3), but not the immediate analysis.

1571. One of the most controversial subjects regards the modalities of shutting down the system, in order to guarantee that the integrity of data is not compromised. In the majority of cases, the operative system influences the choice on this issue. With some operating systems, the preferable method is to push the button that turns off the whole machine; with other systems, this operation could irreparably compromise the system, damaging also data that are placed in particular areas of the memory or of the hard disks (*slack file*, Windows *swap file*, data contained in non-allocated space).

For this reason, the guidelines set by the State Police contain a list of operations to perform when shutting down a system, for the most common operating systems.

1572. With the reform implemented by Law 23 June 2017 n. 103 (Orlando reform) 'Modifications to the Penal Code, to the Code of Criminal Procedure and to the Penitentiary System' the case concerning the 'interception of communications or conversations between present by placing informers in electronic devices into portable devices' has been regulated.

The implementation of the aforementioned point has been included in Article 4 of Legislative Decree 216 of 29 December 2017. The use of the so-called trojan – or, in fact, an IT sensor – although widely practised in the investigative reality, had never previously been subject to any regulatory regulation.

As is known, it is a malware occultly installed by the user on an electronic device with an active internet connection, which allows the attacker to capture all data traffic (both incoming and outgoing) at any time, to activate from remote the microphone and the camera recording the activities, to 'search' the hard disk and to make a full copy of their content, to intercept everything entered on the keyboard, to photograph the images and documents displayed.

1573. The focus of the legislator is focused, first of all, on the place where the interceptions by means of sensors can be carried out. Article. 266 c.p.p. provides that the activation of the device is always permitted in the case of proceeding for the crimes pursuant to Article 51, paragraphs 3-*bis* and 3-*quater* c.p. while, outside these cases, in the places referred to in Article 614 c.p. only if there is a well-founded reason to believe that criminal activity is taking place there.

§5. Activities Contrasting Crimes of Sexual Exploitation of Minors

1574. The Legislator, having recognized the specificity and sensitivity of the investigations regarding crimes of paedophilia[474] performed through the employment of the Internet, has dedicated to the activities aimed to the contrast of the diffusion of these crimes the provisions of Article 14 of Law n. 269/98.

The first comma of the cited Article regards the investigation activities carried out at the initiative of the criminal police and provides that it is possible, 'for the sole purpose of acquiring elements of proof on the crimes contained in Articles 600-*bis*, first paragraph, 600-*ter*, first, second and third paragraph, and 600-*quinquies* of the Penal Code, introduced by the present statute, to proceed to the simulated purchase of pornographic material and to the related intermediation activities, as well as to take part to the touristic initiatives identified in Article 5 of the present statute. Of the purchase, immediate communication is given to the judiciary authority that, with a grounded ordinance, can differ the seizure to the conclusion of the investigations . . .'.

1575. In order to render licit these operations that in abstract are all framed as crimes it is necessary that: (i) the investigative activity is performed in the scope of operations ordered by the chief of the police or at least by the provincial police superintendent; (ii) that the activity is performed by criminal police officers (and not by simple agents); (iii) that the mentioned criminal police officers belong to the specialized structures indicated; that there is authorization of the judiciary authority to proceed to the simulated purchase of pornographic material, to the related intermediation activities and to participation in the touristic initiatives; (iv) that, precisely, the activity has the sole purpose of acquiring elements of proof on the crimes provided by Articles 600-*bis*, first paragraph, 600-*ter*, first, second and third paragraph, and 600-*quinquies* c.p.

1576. The second paragraph of Article 14, instead, regulated a different type of contrast activity. This provision sets out that, in the scope of the tasks of the Telecommunication Police, the unit of the Ministero dell'Interno ('Home Office', or 'Minister of Interior') for the security and the regularity of telecommunications services has to carry out, on request of the judiciary authority (grounded or otherwise void), the activities for the contrast of the crimes contained in the first paragraph of

474. For an overview *see* S. Lorusso, A. Manna (ed.), 'L'abuso sessuale sui minori: prassi giudiziarie e novità normative introdotte dalla legge 38/2006 sulla pedopornografia' (Giuffrè, Milano, 2007).

Article 14 itself, when such crimes are 'performed through the employment of computer systems or means of telematic communication or by using the telecommunication networks available to the public'.

For the accomplishment of these goals, the appointed staff 'can use marks of cover, also to activate sites on the networks, to create or manage areas of communication or exchange on telematic networks or systems, or to take part in them'. The same staff is furthermore allowed to perform, 'also through telematic means' the activities already provided for in the first paragraph.

1577. The two paragraphs under examination introduce a distinction between the subjects belonging to the police authority, by assigning to a specialist unit, as the Post and Communications Police seems to be, the task of performing particular types of investigations that presuppose high computer skills and the availability of technologically advanced instruments, yet never acting on its own initiative, but only on grounded ordinance of the judiciary authority.

The first paragraph of Article 14, instead, includes, in the categories of the subjects legitimated to the performance of the activities it regulates, different units that can operate only 'in the scope of operations ordered by the chief of the police or at least by the provincial police superintendent of the structure they belong to'.

In addition to this, exclusively the criminal police officers inserted in the mentioned structures, and not simple agents, can take part in the activities by way of contrast with paedophilia.

This limitation does not extend itself to the investigative activities carried out according to the first paragraph of the provision. Rather, due to the provision in point, such activities do not have to be ordered, but only authorized by the same judiciary authority.

This allows to presume the admissibility of spontaneous investigative initiatives by the provincial police superintendents of the indicated specialist structures; initiatives that, in any way, before becoming effective, have to be authorized.

It cannot be avoided to note that, at this point, the Legislator has provided nothing for the case in which the investigative activities allowed by the first paragraph are carried out without the prescribed authorization, as it has instead done for the operations provided for in the second paragraph.

1578. Another aspect of divergence between the provisions of the first and the second paragraph of Article 14 regards the range of operations that can be carried out by the staff appointed to the activities by way of contrast with paedophilia.

The second paragraph outlines a list that included each activity allowed according to the first paragraph; furthermore, the staff of the Postal Police appointed to the operations has the faculty to use marks of cover, even to activate so-called decoy sites, to create and manage areas of communication or exchange on telematic networks or systems, in other words to take part in illicit actions.

On the contrary, criminal police officers who operate in full respect of the conditions set by the first paragraph of Article 14 do not see their range of actions limited to the crimes performed through the modalities described in the second paragraph, and instead maintain their general competence on every paedophilia crime listed, regardless of the way it is performed.

1579. The two distinct hypotheses of contrasting activities regulated by the first and second paragraph of Article 14 find their point of contact in the fact that they both recognize the legitimacy of the provocation to perform the crimes they identify.

The figure of the 'provoker agent' can be considered as a particular form of *instigation* through which an agent, that under cover and pretending to agree with other people, provokes them to perform the criminal action in order to make them fall in the trap purpose-built by the police.

The Italian doctrine is controversial on the eventual penal liability of the agent: the majority of academic opinion opposes such liability due to both the absence of the subjective element of wilfulness and the justifying cause of the execution of duty, *ex* Article 51 of the Italian Criminal Code, and also due to the provision of Article 55 of the Italian Criminal Procedure Code, that requires the criminal police to search for the authors of crimes and to exploit every act necessary to ensure the sources of proof.

According to a more rigorous doctrinal stance, the purpose of prosecuting the guilty cannot justify in any way a behaviour that contributes to the endangering or the damaging of a juridical right (of the children): this, in particular, if the behaviour of the agent causes in someone else a criminal behaviour that otherwise would not have taken place.

1580. It is not casual that the Supreme Court of Cassation (Sent. 39706/03), with a stance strongly respectful of civil rights, has stressed the fact that any analogical application of this special regulation to cases that are different from those strictly provided by the mentioned Article 14 has to be considered absolutely forbidden according to Article 14 of the Preleggi ('Pre-Laws') to the Italian Civil Code.

1581. With regard to the types of contrast activities considered by Article 14 in the first and second paragraph, various behaviours, that correspond to as many criminal conducts that can be framed in the crime of paedo-pornography, are listed.

The 'simulated purchase of pornographic material' immediately recalls, indeed, the conduct described in Article 600-*quater* c.p., consisting of obtaining intentionally pornographic material 'produced through the exploitation of minors'.

1582. With regard to the intermediation activity for pornographic material, instead, this is meant as the behaviour of a subject that puts in contact, or anyway facilitates a contact already existing between them, subjects determined to exchange pornographic material that has minors as its object.

Among the provocation activities, there is also the activation of sites on networks that presupposes therefore the activity of installation of a server that allows the access to paedo-pornographic material by an undetermined public, in order to trace and identify eventual users (this is the mechanism of the so-called *honeypots*, namely decoy sites that are purpose-built to trace all the transactions that occur on them).

1583. Another specific investigative activity consists of creating or managing areas of communication or exchange on telematic networks or systems, or in taking part in them. Among these activities, for example, the management of a *newsgroup* or a *mailing list* can be included.

§6. Contrast Activities in The Reform Statute Approved on 23 January 2006

1584. Chapter II of the reform statute 'Provisions on the Matter of the Fight Against the Sexual Exploitation of Children and Paedo-pornography Performed also Through Internet', approved on 23 January 2006, in Article 19 inserts some statutory provisions after Article 14 of Law n. 269/98.[475]

More specifically, very important are Article 14-*bis*, concerning the creation of a *National Centre* for the contrast of paedo-pornography in the Internet; Article 14-*ter*, on the duties of the suppliers of services of the information society carried out through electronic communication networks; Article 14-*quarter*, on the use of technical instruments to prevent the access to sites that diffuse paedo-pornographic material; Article 14-*quinquies*, concerning the financial measures to contrast the commercialization of paedo-pornographic material.

1585. Article 19, therefore, opens first of all by providing, through the insertion of Article 14-*bis*, the creation of a unit purpose-built to receive 'all the reports, also those coming from foreign Police structures and from public and private subjects committed to the fight against minors pornography, regarding sites that diffuse material concerning the sexual exploitation of minors by means of the Internet and of other communication networks, as well as those regarding the managers and eventual beneficiary of the related payments'.

The purpose of this Centre is to write, through a previous verification of the exactness and veracity of the reports, a constantly updated *list* of the managers of sites and beneficiaries of payments eventually sent to exploit paedo-pornographic material.

1586. Article 14-*ter* of the Law, instead, provides precise duties of *report*, for the provider, of the enterprises or subjects that diffuse, distribute and trade paedo-pornographic material.

This duty, as it was frequently stated by the various trading associations during the debate over the bill, risks excessively burdening the provider, considering also the heavy punishments provided, and is lightened only by the parenthesis 'in case they acquire knowledge of it', therefore implying that the suppliers of services carried out through electronic communication networks do not have to perform an active research activity that would compromise the privacy of users.

---

475. *See, generally*, M. Crisafi, E. Trunfio, L. Bellissimo, 'Pedofilia: disciplina, tutele e strategie di contrasto' (Milano, Giuffrè, 2010); D. De Natale, 'Attività di contrasto alla pedopornografia on line: aspetti problematici della responsabilità delle persone fisiche e degli enti, in Rivista trimestrale di diritto penale dell'economia, 2009, fasc. 4 pp. 793–824'.

Among the other duties contained in the provision in exams, one stands out: that of communicating to the *National Centre for the Contrast of Pedo-pornography on the Internet* all information related to subjects or enterprises that diffuse, distribute or trade paedo-pornographic material, as well as the duty of storing for at least forty-five days the material that is the object of the report.

1587. Article 14-*quater* of the Law provides specific duties for the suppliers of connectivity to the Internet network, so that they predispose proper *instruments of filtration* aimed to prevent access to sites of paedo-pornographic content.

Such filtration systems must be identified by a Ministerial Decree, having listened to the most representative associations of connectivity suppliers, and always by means of the mentioned decree, the deadline within which all the providers have to implement the filtration systems. This decree was planned to be adopted within three months from the enforcement of the statute.

1588. Article 14-*quinquies* of the Law, finally, provides proper *financial measures* aimed to counteract the trade of paedo-pornographic material, most of all providing duties of report and rescission of contracts for banks, electronic currency companies, Italian Post Offices and financial intermediaries.

1589. This provision has given rise, already during the discussion on the bill, to a heated debate since it is considered, on one side, *inefficient* in preventing crimes related to the sexual exploitation of minors, and on the other side, excessively invasive of the *confidentiality* of citizens.

1590. While, indeed, it is highly unlikely that those who exercise the trade of paedo-pornographic material by selling it or buying it use a credit card, electronic currency or other payment methods that trace the transactions and render easily identifiable the person that makes or receives a payment, there is the risk of making the unaware citizen the object of the report, and even of the rescission of the contract, every time a *suspect* transaction takes place.

§7. The Use of Hacking Tools and Trojan Horses by Law Enforcement in Italy

1591. There is a very lively debate going on in Italy on the topic of trojan horses ('captatori informatici') used by the police during certain investigations.

The debate originated between 2016 and 2017, following an important decision by the Court of Cassation, United Sections ('Scurato' decision, 26889/2016) and a legislative reform ('Orlando Reform', Law 23/06/2017 n. 103) that placed this investigative tool in the attention of scholars.

In 2019, the Law n. 3 of 31 January 2019 returned to the subject further, extending the possibility of using Trojan horses to corruption cases.

The framework is, to date, very confused.

On the one hand, the Legislator has formally recognized the possibility of using trojan horses during certain types of investigations, but on the other it has not yet been issued a technical regulation that governs the computerized precautions to be taken while using tools that may be harmful for the rights of the suspect.

One of the parts of the Italian Criminal Procedure Code which was significantly amended by the Law of 23 June 2017, n. 103, which started the implementation of the so-called Orlando Reform, is the one that deals with the regulation of interceptions, a change that was further detailed in the expected legislative decree 216/2017.

The novel concerned both the 'traditional' wiretapping and those made through the most recent technological tools, already commonly referred to as 'trojan horses' or 'data collectors'.

1592. The more general debate on the use of hacking tools by law enforcement agencies, which also include the trojan horses, has recently exploded.

In the last ten years, both at European level and in our national framework, the most attentive scholars have enucleated all the critical aspects of the entry of such an invasive investigation tool alongside tools designed for the 'analogical era' and, above all, much more easily controllable and 'containable' (not only for the long jurisprudential tradition – and of rights protection – but, also, for the evident lower power of information acquisition that is manifested in the concrete investigative activities).

1593. At the same time, the jurisprudence had begun to 'dissect', with several pronunciations, all those elements that an investigative 'sensor' could present as problematic for the architecture of the code and, above all, for the interpreter. They are all knots, we'll see, which, in large part, still need to be solved.

1594. The importance of the 'Orlando Reform' manifests itself, in this attempt to clarify the picture, from a double aspect.

1595. On the one hand, the use of trojan horses is about to enter in the Italian legal system – and, indeed, has already entered! – as an investigative tool usable and admitted (within certain limits).

1596. On the other hand, the substantial equivalence between a software absolutely sui generis for the capturing of any type of data, and a 'simple' instrument for interceptions, despite the intrinsic complexity of trojans, is difficult to admit.

The explicit provision of an obligation, for the Government, to regulate the interception of communications or conversations between present persons by placing trojan horses in portable electronic devices has immediately focused the attention of the interpreters and operators towards the two aspects that most have been criticized in the text of the sentence of the United Sections: the possibility of using the trojan also in private places, and the possibility of using it even in the absence of the assumption of the commission of the crime.

1597. It was decided, then, to specify that the activation of the microphone can only take place as a result of a specific command sent remotely, and not only with the insertion of the computer sensor, in compliance with the limits established by the judge's authorization decree, and that the registration audio must be initiated by the Judicial Police or by the appointed personnel, on the indication of the operating Judicial Police, who will be required to indicate the start and end time of the recordings, according to circumstances to be attested in the report describing the procedures for carrying out the operations.

1598. The parameters that seem to us, then, to design the new framework are connected to a constant control by the Judicial Police, to the fact that it will not be possible to have an indiscriminate collection of information in places of private dwelling, limiting the use to cases only in the which in those places a criminal activity is taking place, and to an increase in motivation imposed on the GIP in the drafting of the authorization decree: for the first time it is envisaged that such a decree must indicate the reasons for which this specific method of interception is necessary for the carrying out the investigations.

1599. The 'transfer' of the registrations is then regulated, providing that the same must be carried out only to the server of the Prosecutor's Office, so as to guarantee the originality and integrity of the registrations.

1600. A further innovation is that, at the end of the registration, the trojan will have to be deactivated and made permanently unusable on the indication of the Judicial Police personnel operating in the specific context.

Only specific computer programs can be used that comply with technical requirements established by (a future) ministerial decree.

1601. At the same time, the power of the Public Prosecutor to use such an instrument in cases of urgency is limited, and the results of the information collected by the collector can be used for trial purposes only of the crimes covered by the authorization provision and may be used in different procedures provided that they are indispensable for ascertaining the crimes referred to in Article 380 of the Criminal Procedure Code.

1602. Protection against the invasive capacity of the sensor would then be guaranteed by the fact that the results of interceptions that have occasionally involved subjects unrelated to the facts for which they are proceeding cannot be known in any way.

If this framework is analysed with a Legal Informatics approach, the principle that most seems to worry the Legislator, and that clearly transpires, is the desire to achieve a good balance between the use of innovative tools and the limitation of circulation of data which, inevitably, are acquired without directly involving the suspects and are detrimental to the privacy of the people.

There is almost a sort of 'awareness' that the sensor is 'genetically' designed to intercept any type of information in any context and with reference to all the people in the vicinity of the device or who come into contact and communicate with that computer tool. Without any possibility of distinction.

1603. It should be noted that, despite technical doubts (and awaiting a technical specification), Articles 4, 6 and 7 of legislative decree n. 216, however, try to draw an organic picture, addressing the main problems.

1604. Article 266 c. 2 the first part of the Code of Criminal Procedure, for example, has been modified indicating that 'in the same cases the interception of communications between present individuals is allowed, which can also be performed through the insertion of a computer sensor on a portable electronic device'.

1605. Therefore, only the interceptions seem to be governed by means of a computer sensor of conversations 'between present' on 'mobile' devices, which are, however, as was said above, only one of the many possible uses of the sensor.

1606. The sensors are inserted in the genus of interceptions between present persons, so they are always allowed in places other than a private residence, while if they are to be carried out in places of private residence they can be authorized by the Judge for crimes other than those indicated by the Code only if they exist justified reason to believe that criminal activity is taking place there (for organized crime offences such interception is always allowed, and therefore even if it takes place in domiciliary places regardless of whether criminal activity is taking place there, and for the crimes of public officials against the Public Administration punished with imprisonment of no less than a maximum of five years, when there is reason to believe that criminal activity is taking place there).

1607. A series of conditions connected to the authorization decrees is, instead, inserted in Article 267 of the Code of Criminal Procedure, requiring that in the case of use of an IT trojan for interceptions on portable devices the authorization decree must indicate the reasons that make this method necessary for the conduct of the investigations and, if there are crimes other than those referred to in Article 51, paragraphs 3-*bis* and 3-*quater*, the places and time, even indirectly determined, in relation to which the activation of the microphone is allowed.

In summary, a further motivational effort is required to justify the use of such an instrument.

Article 268 then modified the methods of conducting interceptions, for which it is possible to make use of suitable persons for the start-up and termination of registrations (therefore: technicians of private companies who manage services interception).

1608. The intercepted communications are transferred exclusively to the plants of the Public Prosecutor's Office, and the data acquired during the operations preliminary to the insertion of the computer sensor on the portable electronic device and the data acquired outside the time and place limits indicated cannot be used in the authorization decree (this last aspect is not easy to understand, and will certainly be better clarified by the Legislator or by the Ministry later on).

1609. As can be seen from this brief review, the legislative decree did not 'insist' very much on the technical side, limiting itself to a nod to the 'targeted' use of the sensor ('place' and 'time', and a sort of 'switch') for activation and deactivation), on the security that must have the flow of data generated by the sensor (which should reach directly the servers of the Prosecutor) and on the possibility of using 'external' specialized technicians to perform such delicate operations.

1610. The framework will be completed (we hope) by a technical specification, but it was useful to highlight the most debated Legal Informatics aspects in Italy on this point.

Index

The numbers here refer to paragraph numbers.

Index